Healthcare Big Data Analytics

Intelligent Biomedical Data Analysis (IBDA)

Edited by
Deepak Gupta, Nhu Gia Nguyen,
Ashish Khanna and Siddhartha Bhattacharyya

Volume 10

Healthcare Big Data Analytics

Computational Optimization and Cohesive Approaches

Edited by
Akash Kumar Bhoi, Ranjit Panigrahi,
Victor Hugo C. de Albuquerque and Rutvij H. Jhaveri

DE GRUYTER

Editors
Dr. Akash Kumar Bhoi
Directorate of Research,
Sikkim Manipal University,
Gangtok 737102,
Sikkim,
India
akashkrbhoi@gmail.com

Dr. Ranjit Panigrahi
Department of Computer Applications,
Sikkim Manipal Institute of Technology,
Sikkim Manipal University,
Majitar 737136 Sikkim,
India
ranjit.panigrahi@gmail.com

Prof. Victor Hugo C. de Albuquerque
Department of Teleinformatics Engineering (DETI)
Federal University of Ceará,
Brazil
victor.albuquerque@ieee.org

Dr. Rutvij H. Jhaveri
Pandit Deendayal Petroleum University,
Gandhinagar 382426,
Gujarat,
India
rutvij.jhaveri@gmail.com

ISBN 978-3-11-075073-7
e-ISBN (PDF) 978-3-11-075094-2
e-ISBN (EPUB) 978-3-11-075098-0
ISSN 2629-7140

Library of Congress Control Number: 2023944011

Bibliographic information published by the Deutsche Nationalbibliothek
The Deutsche Nationalbibliothek lists this publication in the Deutsche Nationalbibliografie;
detailed bibliographic data are available on the Internet at http://dnb.dnb.de.

© 2024 Walter de Gruyter GmbH, Berlin/Boston
Cover image: gettyimages/thinkstockphotos, Abalone Shell
Typesetting: Integra Software Services Pvt. Ltd.
Printing and binding: CPI books GmbH, Leck

www.degruyter.com

Preface

In the fast-paced and ever-evolving landscape of healthcare, one of the most transformative developments in recent times has been the explosion of big data and analytics. The digitization of patient records, the widespread adoption of electronic health records and the proliferation of connected medical devices have generated an unprecedented wealth of healthcare data. This influx of information holds the potential to revolutionize the way we approach medical research, diagnosis, treatment and overall healthcare management.

Welcome to *Healthcare Big Data Analytics: Computational Optimization and Cohesive Approaches*. In this book, the authors embark on a journey through the exciting world of leveraging big data and advanced analytics to unlock the hidden insights within healthcare data. They explore the intersection of computational optimization techniques and cohesive approaches, empowering healthcare professionals, researchers, data scientists and policymakers to harness the power of big data effectively and efficiently. As the volume of healthcare data continues to grow exponentially, traditional methods of analysis and decision-making prove insufficient to handle the complexity and magnitude of information. This book serves as a comprehensive guide to the state-of-the-art computational tools and techniques that address these challenges head-on. From optimizing patient care pathways to improving operational efficiency in healthcare institutions, the applications of big data analytics are wide-ranging and deeply impactful.

The book is divided into several sections, each delving into crucial aspects of healthcare big data analytics:

In Chapter 1, the authors explore the growing popularity of artificial intelligence (AI) and machine learning (ML) algorithms, their adoption in various industries, including healthcare. They shed light on the pressing need to accelerate AI adoption in healthcare to improve patient outcomes, with a focus on using machine learning to advance cancer research and treatment. Chapter 2 delves into the critical aspect of securing medical images through watermarking. The application of optimization techniques, such as particle swarm optimization (PSO) and genetic algorithm (GA), is explored to enhance the robustness of watermarking techniques, ensuring secure exchange of sensitive medical information. Machine learning algorithms particularly deep learning has been explored in Chapter 3, to aid mental health providers in making more informed decisions based on patients' historical data, electronic media use and other behavioral indicators.

The COVID-19 pandemic has challenged healthcare systems globally, which is the theme of Chapter 4. This chapter focuses on utilizing regression models to predict COVID-19 death rates, aiding in effective healthcare management. Various regression algorithms, such as Extra Tree Regression and Random Forest Regression, are compared to identify the most accurate prediction method. Similarly, in Chapter 5 the authors explore the applications of computer vision, artificial intelligence and machine learning algorithms in medical imaging, including computed tomography and X-rays, to improve diagnosis and patient care. Chapter 6, on the other hand, deals with detection of COVID-19 in IoMT cloud-based system using ensemble machine learning algorithms. The Internet of Medical Things (IoMT) has transformed healthcare with wireless devices and sensors. This chapter presents an IoMT cloud-based diagnostics framework leveraging machine learning algorithms, such as XGBoost, Extra Tree, Random Forest and LGBM, for COVID-19 detection, offering insights into efficient patient management. Similarly, machine learning has been explored in Chapter 7 to predict and classify big medical data for disease prevention and early detection. In Chapter 7, the authors delve into the intersection of data analytics and big medical data, exploring how machine learning and deep learning algorithms contribute to accurate patient prediction, diagnosis and monitoring. In a similar node, Chapter 8 highlights how hyperspectral imaging is a vital domain in medical research. This chapter focuses on how deep learning techniques enhance hyperspectral image analysis for disease diagnosis, detection and segmentation, revolutionizing surgical procedures and disease diagnosis.

Big data analytics plays a critical role in healthcare diagnostics, disease prediction and patient management. Managing the healthcare sector is challenging, and the influx of big data requires advanced analytics for efficient decision-making. In Chapter 9, the authors elaborate the application of big data analytics, its characteristics and workflow, offering insights into how it can revolutionize healthcare management. Application of Big Data Analytic Techniques for Healthcare Systems is also discussed in brief in Chapter 10, where the emphasis is given on application of various machine learning and deep learning algorithms in healthcare systems to uncover patterns and knowledge for better patient care.

The security and privacy aspects of big data have been explained in Chapter 11. As big data becomes integral to healthcare, ensuring security and privacy is paramount. In this context, Chapter 11 discusses state-of-the-art methods and techniques to tackle security and privacy issues, along with the challenges that arise in the healthcare industry. Likewise, augmented intelligence, coupled with machine learning and neural networks, plays a vital role in securing medical data and enhancing brain tumor detection. In Chapter 12, the authors explore the use of encryption algorithms for secure healthcare systems. Extending security of medical big data a Layered Security Framework has been proposed in Chapter 13 to protect medical big data, addressing privacy and security concerns in healthcare.

Our goal with *Healthcare Big Data Analytics: Computational Optimization and Cohesive Approaches* is to equip readers with the knowledge and tools necessary to navigate the vast sea of healthcare data, extract meaningful insights and transform these insights into tangible improvements in patient outcomes and healthcare management. Whether you are a healthcare professional, researcher, data scientist or policymaker, we believe that the content within these pages will empower you to harness the full potential of big data and analytics for the betterment of healthcare worldwide.

As the authors and editors of this volume, we extend our gratitude to all contributors who have shared their knowledge, expertise and research findings, making *Healthcare Big Data Analytics: Computational Optimization and Cohesive Approaches* a comprehensive resource for all those engaged in the transformative field of healthcare analytics. We hope that this book will pave the way for a data-driven healthcare future, where computational optimization and cohesive approaches lead to improved patient outcomes and revolutionized healthcare management.

Dr. Akash Kumar Bhoi
Directorate of Research, Sikkim Manipal University, Gangtok 737102, Sikkim, India
Institute of Information Science and Technologies, National Research Council, 56124 Pisa, Italy

Dr. Ranjit Panigrahi
Assistant Professor, Department of Computer Applications, Sikkim Manipal Institute of Technology, Sikkim Manipal University, Majitar 737136, Sikkim, India

Prof. Victor Hugo C. de Albuquerque
Department of Teleinformatics Engineering (DETI), Federal University of Ceará, Brazil

Dr. Rutvij H. Jhaveri
Assistant Professor, Department of Computer Science and Engineering, School of Technology, Pandit Deendayal Energy University, Gandhinagar 382007, Gujarat, India

Contents

Preface —— V

Sitikantha Mallik, Suneeta Mohanty, Bhabani Shankar Mishra
1 Integration of neutrosophic logic for faster effective treatment of cancer patients —— 1

Ganga Holi, Madhu B
2 Comparison of optimization techniques particle swarm optimization with genetic algorithm for medical image watermarking —— 25

Subandhu Agravanshi, Muskaan Walia, Sushruta Mishra
3 An analytical study of AI in overcoming mental illness —— 55

S. Visalakshi
4 COVID-19 case analysis and prediction using regression models —— 85

Asit Kumar Lenka, Hrudaya Kumar Tripathy
5 Computer vision for medical diagnosis and surgery —— 101

Joseph Bamidele Awotunde, Akash Kumar Bhoi, Ranjit Panigrahi
6 Detection of COVID-19 in IoMT cloud-based system using ensemble machine learning algorithms —— 125

Idowu Dauda Oladipo, Joseph Bamidele Awotunde, Emmanuel Abidemi Adeniyi, Agbotiname Lucky Imoize, Muyideen Abdulraheem, Ige Oluwasegun Osemudiame
7 Prediction of big medical data using data analytics and deep learning —— 149

Niyati Mishra, Sushruta Mishra
8 Impact of deep learning applications in medical hyper spectral imaging —— 179

M. Ganeshkumar, V. Sowmya, E. A. Gopalakrishnan, K. P. Soman
9 Disease prediction mechanisms on large-scale big data with explainable deep learning models for multi-label classification problems in healthcare —— 207

Idowu Dauda Oladipo, Muyideen Abdulraheem, Joseph Bamidele Awotunde,
Sulaimon Olayinka Dauda, Roseline Oluwasenu Ogundokun,
Muiz Olalekan Raheem, Ige Oluwasegun Osemudiame
10 Application of big data analytic techniques for healthcare systems —— 225

Jay Patel
11 Big data security and privacy in healthcare —— 245

Arpan Maity, Sushruta Mishra
12 Healthcare encryption using augmented intelligence —— 261

Navod Neranjan Thilakarathne, Rohan Samarasinghe, Rakesh Kumar Mahendran
13 Security system design for medical big data: layered security framework for protecting medical big data —— 287

Jay Gohil
14 Big data analytics in effective implementation of healthcare management —— 311

Brief biographies —— 329

Index —— 331

Sitikantha Mallik, Suneeta Mohanty*, Bhabani Shankar Mishra*

1 Integration of neutrosophic logic for faster effective treatment of cancer patients

Abstract: Artificial intelligence (AI) and machine learning algorithms are becoming more popular as people are adopting these technologies in daily life activities. People are starting to see them in self-driving cars, robots, user interfaces, smart devices, retail, and healthcare products, albeit the latter is lagging in adopting these new technologies. The world spends almost many trillions per year on healthcare, making it the world's important sector. Healthcare accounts for over a quarter of all government spending in the world. As a result, there's a pressing need to accelerate AI adoption in healthcare so that healthcare practitioners can harness the technology's potential to improve patient outcomes. With the rapid rise in new technologies especially machine learning, deep learning, and big data analytics, the role of these technologies in the healthcare sector has increased to a large extent. So, there is a need to integrate these new advanced technologies into health infrastructure that can improve the quality of healthcare service a lot and analyze the patients suffering from different diseases at a time. Machine learning allows smart machines to extend capabilities by allowing people to achieve better clinical services. Cancer research has emerged as one of the unexplored sectors in which machine learning has yet to find steps. Cancer is the deadliest disease in human history. It is a condition that occurs when biological alterations result in unregulated cell growth and division. Some cancers cause cells to grow and divide quickly, while others cause them to grow and divide slowly. There is no effective cure or treatment for it. So, there is a need for research into the effective treatment of cancer using new advanced technologies.

    Neutrosophic logic is a new branch of computer science that deals with AI, machine learning, and smart machines that are capable of mimicking tasks that require human intelligence. Some of the main applications of this technique are the use of virtual healthcare assistants to monitor conditions and vital signs of patients at home so that the patients do not need to visit the hospital regularly and robots assisting surgeons in operation theater procedures. Sensor-embedded wearable devices connected through the web enable better healthcare with remote monitoring of patients' conditions. Hospitals and healthcare centers use machine learning to optimize the flow of patients' data and health history and deliver better optimized efficient healthcare.

***Corresponding author: Suneeta Mohanty,** KIIT Deemed to be University, Bhubaneswar, Odisha, India, e-mail: smohantyfcs@kiit.ac.in
***Corresponding author: Bhabani Shankar Mishra,** KIIT Deemed to be University, Bhubaneswar, Odisha, India, e-mail: bsmishrafcs@kiit.ac.in
Sitikantha Mallik, KIIT Deemed to be University, Bhubaneswar, Odisha, India,
e-mail: sitikanthamallik@gmail.com

The machine learning approach provides a unique radiation dose for each patient based on the patient's electronic patient record data and medical health conditions. Patients will experience fewer negative side effects as a result of this method as well as fewer cancer therapy failures. AI allows users to analyze different scenarios and find out the optimal solution for the patients. This technology allows much more efficient, faster, and less risk-free computation and analysis.

Keywords: Neutrosophic logic, healthcare, smart machines, sensor, cancer, data analysis

1.1 Introduction

Artificial intelligence (AI) is a conglomeration of many technologies like machine learning, pattern recognition, natural learning processing (NLP), fuzzy logic, and neutrosophic logic. The industry has been transformed by technology, and technology has sparked advancement and innovation in the healthcare sector. In the last few years, with the advent of AI and the continuous use of new emerging technologies in healthcare, medical care has experienced a rapid rise in improvements in patient healthcare and treatment. Hospitals throughout the world will be impacted by quickly expanding technologies, according to healthcare service companies. The acquisition, analysis, and storage of large amounts of unprocessed data from various clinics, hospitals, and research labs have been made possible by social networking, sensor networks, wearables, mobile computing, cloud computing, and virtualization as well as data mining methods and machine learning techniques. Health prescriptions, emails, and online financial transactions, multimedia content like video, music, and images, X-rays, CT scans, and other sources can all be used to gather this data. With the rapid development of computational intelligence, there is a rise in the application of machine learning techniques for modeling data in various domains. Healthcare IT solutions are revolutionizing the world of patient care and the overall healthcare framework. There has been a major improvement in the operations of the entire health ecosystem. Electronic patient records in the healthcare sector improve medical data access for faster treatment. Healthcare practitioners can now quickly identify improved health treatment strategies with the help of neutrosophic logic. New technologies are also lowering the cost of medical education and providing more cost-effective diagnostic technologies that can be repeated on a big scale. But there are many deadliest diseases like cancer for which the earliest detection and treatment are the utmost priority. There are over a hundred different varieties of cancer that are attacking different cells or organs in the body. Cancer is categorized in general based on the organ in which aberrant cell proliferation originates. Breast cancer, one of the types of cancers that are found in women, starts in the breast. Cancerous cells can occur in the skin or tissues that cover internal organs (carcinoma), connective tissues (sarcoma), blood-forming tissue (leukemia), the immune system (lymphoma and multiple myeloma), and the brain or spinal cord (brain or spinal cord cancer) (central nervous system). Some malignancies encourage rapid cell division and development, whereas others induce cells to divide and develop more slowly. Some malignancies develop visible tumors, such as leukemia, while others, such as breast cancer, do not. Since earlier technologies were not able to detect cancer for earlier diagnosis and quick treatment, there is a need for effective and quick treatment that leads to the integration of machine learning, AI, and big data analytics into the healthcare system. Adoption of AI and machine learning in cancer treatment was one of the unexplored research areas recently, but recent research work in this area has led to companies, institutions, and governments investing a lot of resources [1]. A team of doctors and scientists from MIT and Massachusetts General Hospital recently discovered a deep learning model that can predict if a patient will develop breast cancer five years from now using a mammogram. The algorithm learnt the hidden patterns in breast tissue that are precursors to cancerous tumors based on mammograms and known outcomes from over 60,000 patients. Machine learning is already being used and applied in healthcare. AI and machine learning empower, educate, and entertain patients and doctors about cancer treatment through edge-to-edge technology. Diseases will be promptly and accurately diagnosed, and medicine will be highly personalized. Patients will recognize if they are sick before they experience even a single symptom, thanks to wearable technology with built-in machine learning capabilities. Meanwhile, new drugs will reach the market at a faster rate as clinical studies become faster and more accurate [9].

1.2 Background

1.2.1 Artificial intelligence

AI is a broad field of computer science concerned with creating intelligent machines that can accomplish activities that would normally need human intelligence.

1.2.2 Fuzzy logic

Fuzzy logic is a type of many-valued logic with membership degrees ranging from 1 to 0. Fuzzy logic proposed a fuzzy set theory which states that a fuzzy set is a collection of ordered pairs which is represented by

$$A = \{(y, \mu_A(y)) | y \in U\},$$

where $\mu_A(y)$ is the membership function in fuzzy set A and U the universe of discourse.

In the case of fuzzy sets, partial membership exists. The membership function, whose value ranges from 0 to 1, is used to determine the degree of uncertainty of the items of the fuzzy set. The truth value of variables in fuzzy logic can be any real number between 0 and 1, both inclusive [3].

1.2.3 Neutrosophic logic

Neutrosophic logic refers to a logic in which the following parameters of the proposition are defined:
1. Truth (T), percentage of truth
2. Falsehood (F), percentage of falsity
3. Indeterminacy (I), the condition or percentage of being indeterminate

where Truth, Indeterminacy, and Falsehood are standard or non-standard real subsets of [0,1+], that isn't inherently connected.

For single-valued neutrosophic logic, the total value of the elements is
1. $0 \le t + i + f \le 3$, when each of the elements is self-contained.
2. $0 \le t + i + f \le 2$, when dual elements are interdependent, but the final part is unaffected.
3. $0 \le t + i + f \le 1$, when all elements are interconnected.

When three or two of the t, i, f components are independent, there is room for inadequate information (total < 1), paraconsistent and contradictory information (total > 1), or complete information (total = 1). If all three elements, Truth, Indeterminacy, and Falsity, are interdependent, one can provide provision for partial information (total < 1) or complete information (total = 1) in the same way.

1.2.4 Different techniques under computational intelligence

1.2.4.1 Machine learning

Machine learning is a subdomain of A.I. that aims on simulating human learning processes using sophisticated algorithms to improve accuracy over time.

Gathering data is the initial step in the machine learning process. Cleaning and preprocessing data entails reducing noise if necessary, gathering the information needed to model or account for noise, and deciding on strategies for dealing with missing data fields. The given data set is split into training and test sets, with the former being used to develop the model and the latter being used to validate it. The standard split between training and test sets is 70/30. The data set is linked to an algorithm, which learns and develops predictions using advanced mathematical modeling. The whole process is explained in Figure 1.1.

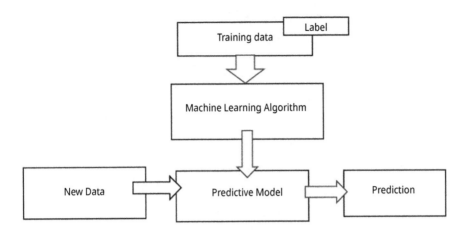

Figure 1.1: Machine learning algorithm.

Unsupervised learning, supervised learning, and reinforcement learning are examples of machine learning algorithms explained in Figure 1.2.
i.   Unsupervised learning: It is a type of machine learning algorithm used to draw inferences from datasets consisting of input data without labeled responses.
ii. Supervised learning: It uses the training data to derive a function. Each record has a set of attributes, with the class being one of them.
iii. Reinforcement learning: It's a controlled environment in which records are categorized using grades. Machines typically use it to perform relevant actions in order to enhance the reward in order to acquire the best feasible answer through trial and error and feedback [3].

a. **Supervised learning**
    i.   **Classification**: Supervised learning problem that involves predicting a class label.
    ii. **Regression**: A set of statistical procedures for estimating relationships between a dependent variable and one or more independent variables is referred to as regression analysis.
    iii. **Naïve Bayes:** The Naive Bayes classifier uses Bayes' theorem to classify all values as independent of each other. It allows us to use probability to predict a class/category based on a set of features.
    iv. **Nearest neighbor:** It's the problem of determining which point in a set is the nearest to a specified point.
b. **Reinforcement learning**
    i.   **Q-learning:** It is a value-based learning algorithm. Value-based algorithms update the value function based on an equation. The "Q" in Q-learning stands for quality.
    ii. **Temporal difference learning**: It is a method that is used to compute the long-term utility of a pattern of behavior from a series of intermediate rewards.

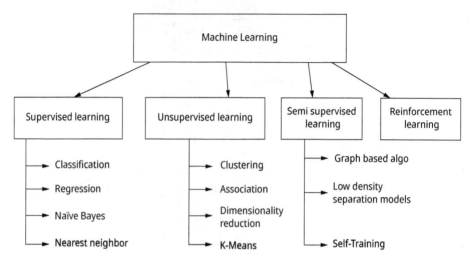

Figure 1.2: Techniques under machine learning.

 c. **Unsupervised learning**
  i. **Clustering**: The process of organizing objects into groups whose members are similar in some way.
  ii. **Dimensionality reduction**: It identifies and removes the features that are hurting the machine learning model's performance or aren't contributing to its accuracy.
  iii. **K-means algorithm:** The algorithm works by identifying groups within the data, with the parameter K representing the number of groups.
  iv. **Association**: Finding frequent patterns, correlations, or causal structures among sets of items or objects in transaction databases, relational databases, and other information repositories.

1.2.4.2 Natural language processing (NLP)

It is the interaction between computers and human language in which the computers have been programmed to process natural languages. In NLP, machine learning is a reliable method of extracting meaning from human languages. NLP is a computational representation and analysis of human language. NLP is a branch of linguistics, computer science, information engineering, and AI that studies how computers interact with human languages. NLP allows computers to understand natural language in the same manner that humans do. NLP, whether spoken or written, uses AI to absorb real-world data, interpret it, and make sense of it in a form that a computer can understand. Computers, like people, have many senses such as ears to hear and eyes to see as well as programs to read and microphones to gather audio. Similar to how people's brains absorb information, computers have software that does the same. At some point during the processing, the input is converted to code that the computer can understand [6].

NLP is divided into two stages: data pretreatment and algorithm development. This new technology has been extremely beneficial to the healthcare industry. NLP in healthcare is growing as analytic tools and deep learning are used to analyses medical data and improve treatment decisions. The unstructured clinical record contains a wealth of information about patients that the structured record does not [2].

Natural language processing techniques and approaches
Syntax: The syntax of a sentence refers to how words are arranged in a sentence to make grammatical meaning. NLP analyzes a language's meaning using syntax and grammatical rules.
Syntax techniques include the following:
a. Parsing: This is a sentence's grammatical analysis.
b. Word segmentation: This is the process of deriving word formations from a string of text.
c. Sentence breaking: This places sentence boundaries in large texts.
d. Morphological segmentation: This divides words into smaller parts called morphemes.
e. Stemming: This divides words with inflection in them to root forms, its conjugations.

Semantics: It involves the use of and meaning behind words. NLP applies algorithms to understand the meaning and structure of sentences. Semantics techniques include:
a. Word sense disambiguation: This derives the meaning of a word based on context.
b. Named entity recognition: This determines words that can be categorized into groups.
c. Natural language generation: This uses a database to determine semantics behind words and generate new text.

1.2.4.3 Automation and robotics

Automation means using computer software, machines, or other technology to carry out a task that would otherwise be done by a human worker. There are many types of automation, ranging from the fully mechanical to the fully virtual and from the very simple to the mind-blowingly complex.

The goal of automation is to have machines perform monotonous and repetitive work, resulting in increased production and more cost-effective and efficient results. Several organizations use machine learning, neural networks, and graphs in automation. Such automation, when combined with CAPTCHA technology, can help to prevent fraud in online financial transactions. Robotics is a branch of engineering which

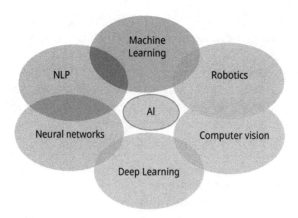

Figure 1.3: Techniques under artificial intelligence.

incorporates multiple disciplines to design, build, program, and use robotic machines. Robotic process automation is intended to carry out high-volume, repetitive tasks while adjusting to changing circumstances.

1.2.4.4 Computer vision

Analog-to-digital conversion and digital signal processing are employed with one or more video cameras. A computer receives the image data. The ability of a computer to see is usually associated with machine vision. The term "computer vision" refers to the process of a computer digitizing an image, processing the data, and taking some sort of action. These techniques are subdomains of computational intelligence, explained in Figure 1.3.

Machines are capable of capturing and analyzing visual data. Visual data is captured using cameras, and the image is converted to digital data using analogue to digital conversion, which is then analyzed using digital signal processing. The information is then entered into a computer. Sensitivity, or the system's ability to identify weak signals, and resolution, or the range across which the machine can distinguish objects, are two crucial properties of machine vision. Machine vision is utilized in a variety of applications, including signature identification, pattern recognition, and medical image analysis.

1.2.5 Cancer

Cancer refers to the dreadful disease in which abnormal cells divide severely and affect body tissue. These abnormal cells are described as cancer cells. These cells are malignant or tumor cells. These cells can penetrate and damage normal body tissues, shown in Figure 1.4.

Detecting cancer at its earliest stages often provides the best chance for a cure. Before going for cancer treatment, discussion with the doctor regarding specific cancer screening. [18]

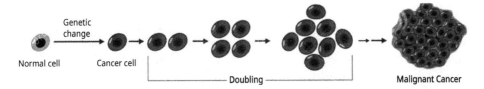

Figure 1.4: Cancer cells development.

Screening tests can save lives by finding cancer early in certain cancers, according to studies. Once you've been diagnosed with cancer, your doctor will try to figure out what stage it is. The doctor uses the cancer stage to assess the treatment options and chances of a cure.

To see if cancer has spread to other parts of the body, imaging tests like bone scans or X-rays may be done as part of the staging process. The cancer stages are indicated by the numbers 0 through 4, which are usually written as Roman numerals 0 through IV. Cancer has advanced if the numbers are higher. In various kinds of cancer, the stage is indicated by letters or phrases.

1.2.6 Most common types of cancer

1.2.6.1 Breast cancer

Breast cancer is the cancer commonly occurs in women's breasts. Breast cancer is the most common invasive cancer in females. It is also a leading cause of cancer deaths among females. A lump or a mass in the breast is often one of the first signs of breast cancer. Symptoms of breast cancer include:
- lumps in the breast
- lymph nodes swelling under the arms or in the neck
- inexplicable changes in breast size, shape, or symmetry

1.2.6.2 Prostate cancer

One of the most common types of cancer is prostate cancer. It is discovered in a man's prostate gland. The prostate is a tiny gland that generates seminal fluid in the body. Many prostate tumors are slow-growing and only affect the prostate gland. The prostate gland, some surrounding tissue, and a few lymph nodes are all removed during prostate cancer surgery (radical prostatectomy).

1.2.6.3 Basal cell cancer

Basal cell cancer is a form of skin cancer that starts in the cells of the basal layer of the skin. Basal cells are a type of skin cell that produces new skin cells in response to the death of existing ones. Basal cell carcinoma most commonly develops on sun-exposed parts of the skin, such as the head and neck.

Long-term exposure to ultraviolet (UV) radiation from sunshine is assumed to be the origin of most basal cell carcinomas. Basal cell carcinoma can be prevented by avoiding the sun and using sunscreen. The most frequent therapy for basal cell carcinoma is surgery, which involves removing all of the cancerous cells as well as some healthy tissue around them [12]. Treatment methods might include:

i. **Surgical excision:** In this treatment, the doctor removes the malignant lesion as well as a healthy skin margin around it. To ensure that there are no cancer cells present, the margin is checked under a microscope. For basal cell carcinomas that are less prone to recur, such as those on the chest, back, hands, and feet, excision may be indicated.
ii. **Mohs surgery:** The surgeon eliminates the cancer layer after layer during Mohs surgery, inspecting each layer under a microscope until no malignant cells remain.

1.2.6.4 Pancreatic cancer

Some of the symptoms are abdominal pain which can spread to the back, unexplained weight loss and loss of appetite, indigestion. More than half of pancreatic cancer patients die within 3 months. The pancreas secretes digestive enzymes as well as hormones that assist regulate sugar metabolism. This cancer is frequently discovered late, spreads quickly, and has a bad prognosis. In the early stages, there are no symptoms.

Pancreatic cancer comes in a variety of forms. The critical difference is whether the exocrine or endocrine glands are affected [13].

i. Exocrine pancreatic cancer
Exocrine glands create enzymes that aid fat, protein, and carbohydrate digestion in the intestines. Exocrine glands make up the majority of the pancreas.

ii. **Endocrine pancreatic cancer**
The islets of Langerhans are microscopic clusters of cells that make up the endocrine glands. Insulin and glucagon are released into the bloodstream by them. They assist in the control of blood sugar levels there. Diabetes can be caused by problems with these glands [14].

1.2.6.5 Ovarian cancer

It is a cell proliferation that occurs in the ovaries. The cells reproduce rapidly and have the ability to infiltrate and kill healthy body tissue. Two ovaries, one on each side of the uterus, make up the female reproductive system. Ovarian cancer, according to doctors, begins at the ends of the fallopian tubes and progresses to the ovaries as it grows. The carcinoma of the ovary is a type of gynecological cancer. It is the world's fifth most common cause of death among women [11].

1.2.6.6 Skin cancer (melanoma)

Melanoma refers to the most dangerous cancer found in skin of body. It grows in the melanocytes, the cells that generate melanin, the pigment that provides the skin its colour. The region of the skin that has been exposed to the sun is where skin cancer, or abnormal skin cell proliferation, most frequently occurs. However, this prevalent type of cancer can also develop on parts of your skin that are not often exposed to sunlight. By reducing or eliminating your access to UV radiation, we can lower our chances of developing skin cancer. Skin cancer can be found in its earlier stages by checking for unusual changes in our skin [5].

1.2.6.7 Colon cancer

Colon cancer is a type of cancer that starts in your colon (large intestine) or rectum. The colon or rectum, which is located at the lower end of the digestive tract. The colon is the last section of the digestive system.

Older adults are more likely to develop colon cancer, while it can affect anyone at any time. The earliest symptoms of colon cancer are typically polyps, which are microscopic noncancerous (benign) clumps of cells that develop on the interior of the colon. Some of these polyps may eventually develop into colon cancer. We have the potential to beat colon cancer if we are diagnosed early. Since colon cancer often has no symptoms during the early stages, it is often caught during routine screenings.

1.2.6.8 Lung cancer

Cancer that begins in the lungs and most often occurs in people who smoke. The risk of lung cancer increases with the length of time and number of cigarettes you've smoked. Lung cancer occurs when cells divide in the lungs uncontrollably. This causes tumors to grow. These can reduce a person's ability to breathe and spread to other parts of the body [4]. People who are at a high risk of lung cancer should consider being screened on a regular basis. This can help detect early signs of cancer and allow for therapy before it spreads. Some possible symptoms of lung cancer are:

i. Hoarseness, for example, is a shift in a person's voice.
ii. Chest infections, such as bronchitis or pneumonia, that are common
iii. The lymph nodes in the center of the chest are swollen.
iv. a persistent cough that may become worse
v. chest pain

1.2.6.9 Leukemia

Leukemia is a type of blood cancer that starts in the bone marrow and results in a large number of abnormal blood cells. These blood cells, often known as blasts or leukemia cells, are not fully matured, shown in Figure 1.5. Bruising and bleeding, as well as bone discomfort and weariness, are all possible symptoms. This cancer began in blood-forming tissues, compromising the human body's ability to combat infection.

1.2.6.10 Cervical cancer

It is a type of cancer that occurs in the cells of the cervix – the lower part of the uterus that connects to the vagina. Cervical cancer is another type of gynecological cancer. The most common symptoms of cervical cancer are:
- bleeding between periods
- bleeding after sexual intercourse
- bleeding in post-menopausal women
- discomfort during sexual intercourse
- vaginal discharge with a strong odor
- vaginal discharge tinged with blood
- pelvic pain

Cervical cancer can be treated with surgery, radiation, chemotherapy, or a combination of these treatments. Surgery is a common therapeutic option when cancer has not spread beyond the cervix. Radiation therapy may be advantageous if a doctor suspects that cancer cells are present inside the body following surgery [19].

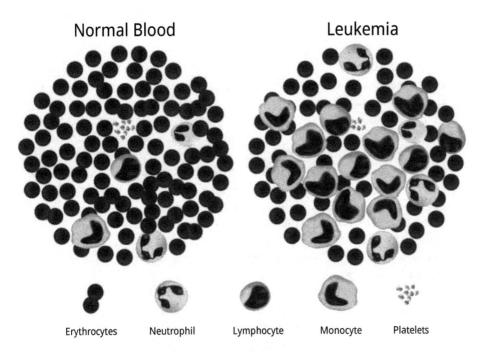

Figure 1.5: The difference between normal blood cells and leukemia blood cells.

1.2.6.11 Lymphoma

Cancer generally occurs in the lymphatic system of the body, which is part of the body's germ-fighting network. Lymphoma is a cancer of lymphocytes. These white blood cells originate in the bone marrow and are present in blood and lymph tissue. Symptoms of lymphoma include the presence of a lump under the skin, itchy skin, fatigue, loss of appetite, coughing, and chest pain.

1.2.7 Major causes of cancer

The following are major causes of cancer:
a. **Exposure to chemicals or toxic compounds**: Toxic substances such as benzene, asbestos, nickel, cadmium, vinyl chloride, benzidine, *N*-nitrosamines, tobacco or cigarette smoke, asbestos, and aflatoxin can cause cancer when exposed to them. Radon is a radioactive gas that is colorless and odorless. Lung cancer can be caused by long-term radon exposure. Children who have been exposed to these substances may acquire a second cancer in the future in some situations. These potent anticancer drugs can change cells and/or the immune system. Cancer that

develops as a result of the treatment of many cancers and other illnesses, and those who are exposed to high quantities of radiation at work, such as uranium miners, are a second malignancy.

b. **Ionizing radiation**: Uranium, radon, UV rays from sunlight, radiation from alpha, beta, gamma, and X-ray-emitting sources. X-rays and gamma rays are known human carcinogens (cancer-causing agents). The evidence for this comes from many different sources, including studies of atomic bomb survivors in Japan, people exposed during the Chernobyl nuclear accident, people treated with high doses of radiation for cancer.

c. **Pathogens**: Other possible agents are human papillomavirus, EBV or Epstein-Barr virus, hepatitis viruses B and C, other bacteria. People with HIV infection or AIDS can get cancer, just like anyone else. They are more likely to get some types of cancer than people who are not infected.

d. **Genetics**: Genetics played an important role in specific cancers like ovarian, colorectal, breast, prostate, skin, and melanoma. These types of cancer have been linked to human genes.

e. **Tobacco**: Tobacco smoke contains thousands of compounds, including at least 50 cancer-causing agents. The chemicals that cause cancer are known as carcinogens. Nicotine and carbon monoxide are two substances found in tobacco smoke.

f. **Unhealthy lifestyle habits**: Obesity raises the risk of cancer in a variety of ways. One of the most common ways is that being overweight leads the body to produce and circulate more estrogen and insulin, hormones that promote cancer growth. It's critical to achieve and maintain a healthy weight to minimize the risk of cancer and other chronic diseases like heart disease and diabetes. Breast cancer (in women past menopause), colon and rectum cancers, endometrium (the lining of the uterus), esophagus, pancreas, liver, and kidney cancers, among others, are all increased by being overweight or obese.

1.2.8 Applications of neutrosophic logic

i. Neutrosophic algorithms are utilized in the business, stock, and finance industry to provide financial advice, predict the future value of stocks, and monitor assets. Chatbots can serve as brokers, providing real-time quotes to their users. By engaging with the trading and stock market environment, bots powered by deep learning can learn from it.

ii. In the education industry, neutrosophic algorithms can be used to evaluate students' overall performance and to automate the grading system. This is true in the education industry all across the world. Various schools across the country are utilizing AI in the classroom. Teachers, students, parents, and, of course, educational institutions have all gained a fresh perspective on education as a result of the application of AI in education.

iii. In the domain of healthcare, neutrosophic algorithms are utilized to provide a more accurate diagnosis, with the technology that has been used to detect and diagnose diseases such as breast cancer earlier. Additionally, computer programs such as bots are utilized to assist doctors in organizing patient appointments and maintaining patient health information, among other things. This cutting-edge technology allows elderly patients to track and monitor their health status. There is an alarm mechanism in place to notify or transmit signals to family members and healthcare providers in the event of any deviation or change in routine activities.
iv. With the use of robotic process automation, neutrosophic algorithms are utilized in industry to automate the repetitive operations performed by humans. Machine learning algorithms are combined with analytics to acquire information that aids in understanding client needs to boost customer satisfaction. For the fusion of information received from various sensors, information that can be conflicting to a certain degree, the robot uses the fuzzy and neutrosophic logic or set. In real time it is used as a neutrosophic dynamic fusion, so an autonomous robot can decide at any moment.
v. Smartphones, smart TVs, surveillance systems, guidance and travel, audio and entertainment streaming, and computer games are all using AI approaches like neutrosophic algorithms. Smart Homes collect and analyze data using AI and Internet of things (IoT) devices such as connected sensors, lighting, and meters. This information is utilized to make better use of house infrastructure, utilities, and other services to make daily life easier and more efficient. In the instance of Smart Homes, IoT frameworks provide the data, and AI uses that data to execute specific tasks that reduce human stress.
vi. Neutrosophic logic is also used in the field of robotics and sensing devices, expert systems.

1.3 Role of neutrosophic logic in medical sector

Computational intelligence techniques like fuzzy logic and neutrosophic logic are changing the way patients communicate with others. They also help to close the information gap between patients and doctors. Neutrosophic logic will improve the accuracy and efficiency of practitioners' practices. They can use robotic process automation in the ICU to better schedule patients, assist with surgery and medical image interpretation, and make better judgments. The main useful benefits of neutrosophic logic in the health sector are given as follows.

1.3.1 Guiding treatment choice

Based on conventional electronic health data and existing test findings, the company is creating several algorithms to detect subtle, early indicators of disease in high-risk patients. Lower GI diseases, prediabetic development to diabetes, chronic renal disease, and coronary artery disease are among the conditions that the company is pursuing. Neutrosophic logic is being used by many essential healthcare operations to evaluate potential diagnoses and select the optimal treatment plan for a specific patient. Furthermore, neutrosophic logic can assist in predicting which patients are more likely to experience post-operative difficulties, allowing healthcare systems to intervene earlier if necessary. In today's environment, being able to properly and precisely use data allows for more efficient decision-making in almost every industry. There is no exception in the healthcare industry. Large amounts of data will become available for analysis as healthcare providers move toward a uniform framework for recording patient outcomes using neutrosophic algorithms-enabled systems that can track outcome patterns following treatment and identify optimal treatments based on patients' profiles. As a result, neutrosophic algorithms facilitate clinical decision-making and ensure that the most relevant interventions and therapies are adjusted to each patient, resulting in a more personalized approach to care. The immediate effect will be a huge improvement in outcomes, resulting in the elimination of post-treatment difficulties as a primary cost factor in most healthcare ecosystems around the world [15].

1.3.2 Fast response in emergency health situations

Every patient's record is stored in an electronic storage repository that can be accessed anywhere which can be easily accessed by doctors to know the health status of the patient. These neutrosophic-based systems can accurately analyze CT scans and specific tests, decreasing physician error and allowing for early diagnosis and management before diseases worsen. An Israeli start-up, for example, has developed these neutrosophic algorithms that are as good as or better than people at detecting illnesses including breast cancer [7].

These algorithms have shown to be more accurate and faster than people in reviewing and translating mammograms, allowing for considerably earlier diagnosis of breast cancer. Early detection of oncoming breast cancer – which is frequently missed by human diagnosis – can significantly minimize the expense of this condition to healthcare.

1.3.3 Clinical trials optimization and drug development

Neutrosophic algorithms have the potential to reduce the time it takes to develop life-saving drugs, allowing billions of dollars to be reallocated to healthcare systems. A start-up supported by the University of Toronto recently installed an algorithm on a supercomputer that simulates and analyses millions of potential medicines to predict their efficacy against Ebola, saving money and, most importantly, patients' lives by repurposing the existing treatments [8]. Given the increased volume and speed of published research, clinical trial enrollment, medication development, and biomarker discovery in oncology in recent years, AI has a better chance than ever to assist in data analysis and decision-making. To this end, some commercial apps in development use neutrosophic logic and NLP. Neutrosophic algorithms can help improve the development of medications in clinical trials.

1.3.4 Empowering the patient

Neutrosophic algorithms have the potential to empower us to make better health decisions on an individual basis. A vast number of people all around the world are already using wearable technology to capture common data such as sleep habits and heart rate. Patients now have more convenient methods to receive medical treatment thanks to recent advancements in telehealth. Remote consultations through live stream and telephone are a cost-effective way to get medical advice without having to travel to a hospital or a doctor's office.

1.3.5 Reduction in costs and time saving

Using AI to automate these interactions can substantially reduce costs and provide barrier-free healthcare by providing health consultations without patients needing to visit clinics occasionally. Recent advancements in NLP have paved the way for a new contact-proof patient interface that can automatically communicate with patients. The interface enables the patients to communicate their symptoms, send questions directly to concerned doctors. Similarly, AIs can be programmed to contact patients frequently to ensure that they remain engaged and follow their treatment plan.

1.3.6 Remote support for patients in real-time

An AI-connected emergency vehicle is a machine coupled with smart multi-technology and communication services that generate high connectivity and specialized communication to receive specialized remote access in real time via high-definition video while caring for a patient inside an ambulance. It will soon be able to connect the health and medical emergency unit with other cars or infrastructures, allowing it to bypass traffic and get to the hospital faster.

1.4 Neutrosophic logic in cancer treatment

Smartphones, connected devices, machine learning, informatics, and cryptography would help the health and healthcare sector collect, access, and utilize scattered data sources more effectively. Patients' clinical information was also recorded, such as blood test results showing any abnormalities in white blood cell counts or lymphocyte counts as well as their age, sex, and symptoms. These concentrated on CT scans and blood tests since they are used by doctors all around the world to diagnose cancer patients.

According to recent research, 500,000 people are diagnosed with cancer each year. It is crucial to discover this condition early to provide patients the best chance of recovery and survival. Many countries are increasing their investments in cancer research and development with the hopes of achieving a decade's worth of progress in cancer prevention, diagnosis, and treatment in a short period [10].

Neutrosophic algorithms-based cancer diagnosis therapy also emphasizes the use of AI and machine learning to assist pathologists in making more precise diagnostic judgments which would ultimately lead to earlier detection and better cancer treatment. These techniques combine tumor genomic sequencing with AI-powered tools for structuring varied information such as oncology notes and pathology reports. Machine-learning algorithms are used for analyzing radiology and pathology images. The outcome, according to the business, is a data-driven treatment that is personalized for each patient. Medication discovery and clinical validation, as well as how these treatments are provided at the point of care, are all part of cancer treatment. In recent years, these operations have become both costly and time-consuming. Furthermore, medications can have a wide range of therapeutic results for patients. The convergence of neutrosophic algorithms and cancer therapy has yielded several solutions to these problems. Patients can be accurately matched to clinical trials using biomarkers, and approaches ranging from machine learning to neural networks and neutrosophic algorithms can speed up drug discovery and truly customized cancer therapy using only a patient's data. These advancements are significant. Researchers develop algorithms that properly predict when lesions in the lungs are malignant using a data set of thousands of high-resolution CT scans provided by the repository containing health records of patients. This will significantly reduce the present detection technology's false-positive rate, provide patients quicker access to life-saving interventions, and give radiologists more time to spend with their patients [16].

The researchers then combined the data from the CT scans with the clinical data to create a neutrosophic algorithm. The program simulates a physician's workflow for diagnosing cancer-related disorders and provides a final diagnosis prediction of positive or negative. Based on CT scans, clinical data, or both, the model generates independent probabilities of being cancer-affected. Various healthcare centers and clinics use the neutrosophic logic technique, which uses machine learning to combine and filter out medical scans and electronic health records (EHR) to provide personalized radiation treatment doses for cancer patients. When it comes to cancer diagnosis, there is a lack of accuracy among practicing medical experts; therefore this computer-based automated technique holds a lot of promise. Using tissue fingerprinting, researchers can instruct a machine to scan through millions of tumor photographs and discriminate visual features to identify a single tumor. Through training, we have essentially evolved a computer eye that's optimized to look at cancer patterns. Because no two patients' tumors are alike, the initial phase in the procedure introduces the concept of tissue fingerprints or distinguishing architectural features in tumor tissue that an algorithm can use to discern between samples. The findings demonstrated that AI algorithms discovered structural differences in pathology slides with more precision and reliability than the human eye and that these variations could be recognized without the need for human intervention. The researchers broke digital pathology images in half for the study and then used a deep learning algorithm to reassemble them based on their chemical fingerprints. Breast cancer is the most frequent type of cancer in women all over the world. The only method to treat it is to get regular health checkups and early detection. The neutrosophic system may assist in the early detection of disease and thereby lower the chance of getting breast cancer.

Although the advantages of implementing computers to improve cancer diagnosis have been around for decades, and computer-aided detection (CAD) systems are widely used in mammography clinics, CAD programs have not improved clinical performance. The problem is that existing CAD programs are programmed to discover features that only human radiologists can perceive, whereas neutrosophic algorithms train computers to detect malignancies based on thousands of mammograms [17].

1.5 Advantages of neutrosophic logic in healthcare

Healthcare firms are looking for innovative solutions that can seamlessly integrate everything from connectivity to the cloud to IoT endpoints in a secure tech ecosystem. Healthcare institutions may use sophisticated technology to fully harness the connection provided by smart devices to assist improve clinical outcomes, control costs, and provide a better patient experience. The neutrosophic logic algorithm is one of the best solutions for healthcare productivity. It assists hospitals and health systems to enhance efficiency by reducing long lines of patients waiting in clinics and hospitals.

The neutrosophic logic-powered healthcare frameworks are assisting in the reduction of wait times, the improvement of staff workflows, and the alleviation of the ever-increasing administrative burden.

This network can reduce system constraints and ensure that patients and healthcare professionals are deployed to regions where they can provide the best treatment or are most required as well as using a neutrosophic logic algorithm to detect patients in danger of deterioration. The researchers reasoned the neutrosophic logic algorithms could provide more precise readings regularly. It makes use of a large dataset that allows the machine learning system to detect cancer-related trends that doctors may miss.

Based on medical imaging data and clinical risk factors, an AI-based technique generates a tailored radiation dose for each patient. As a result of this strategy, patients will experience fewer negative side effects, and treatment failures will be rare. An algorithm trained on hundreds of images regularly outperformed the commonly used risk model, even when the tool had no additional patient data and simply had access to the image itself. With over a million new breast cancer diagnoses each year, enhancing the health system's ability to identify at-risk persons and give early treatment to those who have cancer might have a significant impact on the outcomes for hundreds of thousands of women. Similarly, another example is glaucoma. If not treated early enough, glaucoma can cause blindness, and it accounts for nearly all direct cash medical expenses each year. It usually remains unreported by doctors until it is rather advanced due to its slow progression. Nearly half of all glaucoma cases go unnoticed. This is partly owing to the absence of a genuine risk category other than the elderly. AI, fuzzy logic, neutrosophic logic, and other computational intelligence approaches can begin to fill in the gaps where an efficient and effective screening tool is necessary to make testing more accessible. Using neutrosophic algorithms to help health systems conduct successful screenings, decrease pain points in the treatment process, and supplement the clinical decision-making process can save the industry billions of dollars each year and perhaps save an untold number of lives.

1.6 Drawbacks

Outside of hospitals, a healthcare system based on neutrosophic logic is assisting in the identification of specific at-risk groups to lessen the need for hospital admissions through proactive primary or community care. However, it is a lengthy and difficult path that no single company or organization can undertake on its own. To ensure that neutrosophic algorithm-based systems are completely interoperable and transparent, and to minimize prejudice and inequity, there is a need for close collaboration between health organizations, health departments and governments, health systems, and commercial firms. As healthcare becomes more global, international regulations to protect how neutrosophic algorithms utilize personal data will become increasingly important.

One of the major roadblocks to a more effective healthcare system is the fragmented data environment. Strict regulatory restrictions, out-of-date software designs, and mismatched stakeholder incentives all conspire to prevent meaningful data sharing and collaboration. It is now prohibitively difficult to put together a complete picture of a single patient's health, the efficacy of a novel treatment, or the health patterns of a population. The gathering, sharing, and utilization of data – both between countries and inside single governments or organizations – is complicated by the complex and shifting landscape of data privacy and localization regulations. Healthcare data barriers are more than simply an administrative nuisance. They obstruct medical progress and make it difficult to provide the proper care to the correct patient at the correct time, leading to the loss of precious life.

Diagnostic errors are a major source of harm to patients, resulting in gaps in treatment, needless procedures, and patient injury. These errors can also be attributed to healthcare systems missing information. By identifying ordered tests that haven't been completed or reporting incidental discoveries that need to be followed up on, healthcare interventions can aid in the prevention of diagnostic inaccuracies. When you have a medical imaging procedure, you will have a scanning procedure followed by a visit from a radiologist who will analyze the medical images. They could be kept for any amount of time, which comes at a cost. Along with the image, there is a report that outlines the conclusion made by the medical specialist who assessed the image – usually a radiologist.

Data security is a significant concern for healthcare organizations, especially in the wake of a slew of high-profile data breaches, hackings, and ransomware attacks. Healthcare data is exposed to a wide range of dangers, including phishing attacks, viruses, etc. Healthcare data isn't static; therefore, most elements will need to be updated regularly to be current and useful. For some datasets, such as patient vital signs, these updates may occur every few seconds. Other information, such as a person's home address or contact information, may only change a few times throughout their lifetime. Understanding the volatility of big data, or how often and to what degree it changes, can be challenging for organizations that do not regularly monitor their data assets.

1.7 Conclusion and future work

Since the 1990s, when the earlier breast-cancer risk model was considered, human knowledge and intuition about what key risk variables leading to cancer could be, such as age, family history of breast and ovarian cancer, hormonal and reproductive factors, and breast density, are primary factors that doctors verify in cancer patients.

However, the majority of these markers have just a questionable link to breast cancer. As a result, the current situation of the healthcare system is quite concerning. Since such models still aren't very accurate at the individual level, and many organizations continue to feel risk-based screening programs are not possible, given those limitations. Rather than manually identifying the patterns in a mammogram that drive future cancer, the MIT/MGH team trained a deep-learning model to deduce the patterns directly from the data. In healthcare, AI techniques like neutrosophic logic support, enhance, and assist medical professionals in evaluating patient data more quickly and effectively, increasing decision-making, allowing them to spend more quality time with their patients by freeing up time from monotonous administrative activities. Deep learning and other machine learning capabilities are poised to play a key role in the healthcare system's resurrection. Health monitoring, disease detection and diagnosis, drug research, treatment pathway design, and precision medicine are all being transformed by the neutrosophic algorithm. This algorithm has the potential to personalize a variety of cancer therapy which would be a breakthrough forward in radiation precision medicine. Too much focus is spent on the data collection; instead, data analysis should be given more preference. So, a lot of time is wasted valiantly through this process on finding the cure. The neutrosophic system helps in data analysis. By 2050, neutrosophic algorithms will be able to access different data sources to show disease patterns and improve therapy and care. The impact of neutrosophic algorithms on our activities is significant. Organizations are also adapting to neutrosophic algorithm-based technology, which can give them new methods of doing things and analyzing data patterns, helping them to be more productive. Neutrosophic algorithms are also effective in streamlining cancer screening and detection.

Smart devices and algorithms based on neutrosophic algorithms can aid to prevent diseases, enabling the early treatment, and reducing the country's dependency on a large number of hospitals in major cities. Patients, on the other hand, must be able to trust neutrosophic algorithms and comprehend the meaning of the results. Many healthcare institutions are using AI in medical imaging and data analysis to get better results and early diagnosis of diseases for each specific patient. The researchers are currently working on improving the system's ability to detect different types of cancer.

When building such healthcare gadgets for cancer patients, accessibility of use and data connectivity are two crucial elements to be considered. Some entrepreneurs are rushing to establish smart clinics with remote consultation services in rural areas. AI-powered diagnostic systems are useful in remote places where data access, transportation, and a lack of advanced medical equipment are the main factors contributing to a poorer standard of healthcare. Other tech giants are also investing in neutrosophic algorithms based on medical diagnostics research. In the future, many hospitals will launch their first AI healthcare centers based on neutrosophic algorithms to assist clinical decisions. These programs are aimed toward detecting cancer at an early stage. Many health-tech businesses are now heavily investing in AI, machine learning, and neuroscientific algorithms, which will power systems that can converse with patients and give doctors diagnosis suggestions.

Improved healthcare value through offering better medical care to patients at reduced costs is a fundamental demand in a world marked by an aging society, an increasing number of individuals suffering from long-term serious conditions and ever-increasing healthcare expenses. Stakeholders in the healthcare organization must define and promote industry standards, create global multipliers for value-based healthcare, and build innovative platforms for increased collaboration. Machine learning and AI are becoming popular for their role in the healthcare system. AI has a lot of potentials to change the healthcare business by cutting costs and enhancing access to and quality of care. We're still finding out how to best implement AI in healthcare, but it's increasingly playing a role in enhancing patient care and arming clinicians with data so they can make more informed diagnoses and design individualized care plans. Over the next few years, AI applications in healthcare will only become more prevalent. According to a recent survey, more than half of healthcare specialists anticipate that AI will be widely adopted in the next five years. We have a long way to go in terms of creating global health systems that put people first, and we feel it is our joint responsibility to do so. We are at a critical juncture in the global healthcare value chain.

References

[1] Lo, C. M., Iqbal, U. & Li, Y. J. (2017). Cancer quantification from data mining to artificial intelligence. Computer Methods and Programs in Biomedicine, 145, A1.

[2] Bresnick, J. (2019). neutrosophic algorithms, Deep Learning Start to Tackle Common Problems in Healthcare, https://healthitanalytics.com/.

[3] Bi, W. L., Hosny, A., Schabath, M. B., Giger, M. L., Birkbak, N. J., Mehrtash, A., Allison, T., Arnaout, O., Abbosh, C., Dunn, I. F., Mak, R. H., Tamimi, R. M., Tempany, C. M., Swanton, C., Hoffmann, U., Schwartz, L. H., Gillies, R. J., Huang, R. Y. & Aerts, H. (2019). Artificial intelligence in cancer imaging: clinical challenges and applications, CA: Cancer Journal for Clinicians, 69(2), 127–157.

[4] Tartar, A., Akan, A. & Kilic, N. (2014). A novel approach to malignant-benign classification of pulmonary nodules by using ensemble learning classifiers, Conference proceedings: Annual International Conference of the IEEE engineering in medicine and biology society, IEEE Engineering in Medicine and Biology Society. Annual Conference, 2014, 4651–4654.

[5] Van der waal, I., Skin cancer diagnosed using artificial intelligence on clinical images. Oral Diseases, 24.

[6] Kent, J. (2020). Deep Learning Technique Could Improve Cancer Diagnostics. https://healthitanalytics.com/.

[7] Houssami, N., Kirkpatrick-Jones, G., Noguchi, N. & Lee, C. I. (2019). Artificial Intelligence (neutrosophic algorithms) for the early detection of breast cancer: a scoping review to assess neutrosophic algorithms's potential in breast screening practice. Expert Review of Medical Devices, 16(5), 351–362.

[8] Sherbet, G. V., Woo, W. L. & Dlay, S. (2018). Application of artificial intelligence-based technology in Cancer management: a commentary on the deployment of artificial neural networks. Anticancer Research, 38(12), 6607–6613.

[9] Lind, A. P. & Anderson, P. C. (2019). Predicting drug activity against cancer cells by random forest models based on minimal genomic information and chemical properties. PLoS One, 14(7), e0219774.

[10] Wang, Y., Wang, Z., Xu, J., Li, J., Li, S., Zhang, M. & Yang, D. (2018). Systematic identification of non-coding pharmacogenomic landscape in cancer. Nature Communications, 9(1), 3192.

[11] Hossain, M. A., Saiful Islam, S. M., Quinn, J. M. W., Huq, F. & Moni, M. A. (2019). Machine learning and bioinformatics models to identify gene expression patterns of ovarian cancer associated with disease progression and mortality. Journal of Biomedical Informatics, 100, 103313.

[12] McDezhong Bi, Dongxia Zhu, Fatima Rashid Sheykhahmad, Mingqi Qiao,. (2021). Computer-aided skin cancer diagnosis based on a New meta-heuristic algorithm combined with support vector method, Biomedical Signal Processing and Control, 68, Article 102631.

[13] Li, Q., Qi, L., Feng, Q. X., Liu, C., Sun, S. W., Zhang, J., Yang, G., Ge, Y. Q., Zhang, Y. D., & Liu, X. S. (2019). Machine learning-based computational models derived from large-scale radiographic-radiomic images can help predict adverse histopathological status of gastric Cancer. Clinical and Translational Gastroenterology, 10(10), e00079.

[14] Taninaga, J., Nishiyama, Y., Fujibayashi, K., Gunji, T., Sasabe, N., Iijima, K., & Naito, T. (2019). Prediction of future gastric cancer risk using a machine learning algorithm and comprehensive medical check-up data: a case-control study. Scientific Reports, 9(1), 12384.

[15] Sahoo, A. K., Mallik, S., Pradhan, C., Prasad Mishra, B. S., Barik, R. K. & Das, H., Chapter 9 – Intelligence-Based Health Recommendation System Using Big Data Analytics. In Big Data Analytics for Intelligent Healthcare Management (pp. 227–246). Academic Press, 2019.

[16] Skaane, P., Bandos, A. I., Gullien, R., et al. (2013). Comparison of digital mammography alone and digital mammography plus tomosynthesis in a population-based screening program. Radiology, 267 (1), 47–56.

[17] Ganesan, K., Acharya, U. R., Chua, C. K., Min, L. C., Abraham, K. T. & Ng, K.-H. (2013). Computer-aided breast Cancer detection using mammograms: a review, IEEE Reviews in Biomedical Engineering, 6, 77–98.

[18] Ruddon, R. W. (2003). What Makes a Cancer Cell a Cancer Cell? In Kufe, D. W., Pollock, R. E., Weichselbaum, R. R., et al., editors. Holland-Frei Cancer Medicine (6th edition). BC Decker, Hamilton (ON). Available from: https://www.ncbi.nlm.nih.gov/books/NBK12516/.

[19] Dillner, J.; Elfström, K.M.; Baussano, I. Prospects for Accelerated Elimination of Cervical Cancer. Prev. Med. 2021, 153, 106827. doi: 10.1016/j.ypmed.2021.106827.

[20] Smarandache, F., & Vlădăreanu, L. (2011). Applications of neutrosophic logic to robotics: An introduction. In 2011 IEEE International Conference on Granular Computing (pp. 607–612). DOI: 10.1109/GRC.2011.6122666.

Ganga Holi, Madhu B

2 Comparison of optimization techniques particle swarm optimization with genetic algorithm for medical image watermarking

Abstract: The rapid growth of digital imaging and information technology has led to the adoption of telemedicine applications. For tele-health services, the exchange of patient records via the network necessitated a method to ensure confidentiality and privacy. For diagnosis and treatment, medical information including digital medical images and patient information is exchanged through insecure networks. Image watermarking is one of the most common methods for securing medical images. With performance statistics, this paper provides a comparison of particle swarm optimization (PSO) and genetic algorithm (GA) optimization methodologies. With assaults like pepper, Gaussian, speckle, JPEG compression and equalization, the proposed technique shows good results in terms of robustness.

Keywords: Optimization technique, Particle Swarm Optimization, Genetic Algorithm, PSNR

2.1 Introduction

Emerging networks [1] of health professionals, medical communities, patients, organizations and other stakeholders are currently reshaping regional radiology practices. The technologies used in medical image processing allow for the integration of common radiology principles as well as global radiology reconciliation. In this industry, new opportunities also offer new hazards. Abduldaim et al. [2] suggested watermarking scheme on Hessenberg matrix and discrete wavelets. Hessenberg factor is used to each block of the cover image by DWT. Aljuaid and Parah [3] reported health 4.0 patient data transfer using information using hyperchaos. Health 4.0 is a tool of Industry 4.0 with an aim of virtualization in healthcare systems. Double-layer security is provided to the electronic health record (EHR) using hyperchaos to encrypt the EHR. Alshanbari et al. [4] suggested ROI-based multiple watermarking for tamper detection to medical images. Lempel–Ziv–Welch (LZW) compression and principal components-based insertion make the method to be secured toward ownership attack. Amiri and Mirzakuchaki [5] suggested non-subsampled contourlet transform (NSCT) and singu-

Ganga Holi, Geektrust Bengaluru 560102, Karnataka, India
Madhu B, Department of CSE, Dr. Ambedkar Institute of Technology, Bengaluru 560056, Karnataka, India

https://doi.org/10.1515/9783110750942-002

lar value decomposition watermark scheme with neural networks. The algorithm provides greater stability using larger scaling factors (SFs) with PSO-GA and artificial intelligence. The NSCT transform is used to deconstruct the cover image into images below the coefficients of low frequency. These coefficients are given to SVD after a single application of the stationary wavelet transform (SWT). After that, the watermark picture is SWT-transformed, and the transform from the HL coefficients once more and the LL-frequencies are passed to the SVD conversion. For medical information security, Anand and Singh [6] proposed an improved SVD domain watermarking. The hamming code was used to text watermark and watermarked image was encrypted and compressed. Anand et al. [7, 8] suggested RDWT-SVD and firefly-based watermarking algorithms. The text watermark was encoded using Turbo code, and the final watermark was created by combining the text watermark with DWT in a medical watermark image. Ariatmanto and Ernawan [9] reported a copyright protection method with different embedding factors. The method divides the image as 8 × 8 blocks using discrete cosine transformation and the image block with the highest variance value was chosen as embedding regions. The binary watermark was scrambled using Arnold transform. Swaraja [10] described a blind medical image watermarking system that was optimized. The method concentrates on tamper recognition and authenticity parameter. Dual watermarks are embedded into the region of non-interest blocks using DWT, Schur transforms and bacterial foraging optimization algorithm. LZW was used as a compression algorithm to compress the watermark. Kazemi et al. [11] mentioned an optimized CT-NSCT-neural network model based on Kurtosis coefficients. Embedding and extraction were implemented with the help of a neural network learning algorithm. Khare et al. [12] reported hybrid homomorphic transform RDWT-SVD method for medical image watermarking. The reflectance component of the medical image was obtained with transform and the 2D Arnold transform was used to provide extra security to the watermark. Luo et al. [13] reported a multi-scale image watermarking system based on the integer wavelet transform and the SVD. The ideal scaling variables for the embedding process were found using a 3D optimal mapping technique. Shen et al. [14] suggested Grey Wolf Optimization-PSO technique with DWT. Hybrid optimization methods were used to find optimal embedding regions and strength factors for color image watermarking. Soni et al. [15] reported spatial domain LSB pixel-based watermarking technique with the GA optimization algorithm. A two-dimensional (2D) barcode was used to encrypt information about the patient. Tayachi et al. [16] suggested a clone-resistant cryptographic technique based on secret keys with secret unknown ciphers for medical images. Thakur et al. [17] reported NSCT-RDWT-SVD with a chaotic watermarking approach for medical images. The cover image was initially splitted into coefficients and NSCT was used to find maximum entropy. Thanki and Kothari [18] suggested ridgelet transform (RT) and SVD-based multi-level security of medical images. Arnold scrambling was used to provide additional encryption.

Optimization is a problem-solving technique that involves fine-tuning a set of variables in order to arrive at the optimum answer for a certain goal. It might be interesting to find the maximum or least value of a function, for example. The function might be related to a real-world problem, and the options are endless. The function could, for example, reflect a company's profit, which should be maximized, or expenses, which should be reduced. The purpose of using optimization techniques is to fine-tune certain parameters that affect earnings and expenses in order to maximize or minimize the function. For our application, we choose to optimize an image processing algorithm, specifically object matching. Image processing is a vast topic that includes a number of different academic subfields. Popular image processing subfields include pattern recognition, object-matching, picture-blurring, image compression, edge detection and image restoration. The processing of partially damaged and/or missing information images collected from satellites is an example of an image processing application. In general, images can be analogue or digital. In the most recent uses, digital images are utilized. Digital images are rectangular arrays with many values, with each pixel referring to a position in the array.

2.2 Proposed method

The proposed heuristic-driven watermarking model is applied SWT/RDWT with SVD. The embedding efficiency and allied imperceptibility are improved by applying the PSO algorithm. The PSO has been applied to identify the optimal coefficients in the HH-sub-plane. Thus, once identifying the optimal HH-plane coefficients, the proposed model embeds the watermark, which is taken as the hospital's logo. A detailed discussion of the overall proposed model is given in the subsequent sections.

2.2.1 Redundant Discrete Wavelet Transformation

Redundant discrete wavelet transformation (RDWT) has been known as aa-trous method, the over complete DWT (ODWT), the undecimated DWT (UDWT), the discrete wavelet frames (DWF) and the shift-invariant DWT. The initial implementation used a variant of the aa-trous method, which removes the down-sampling operator from the standard DWT implementation. Essential textures in the original image will be at the same spatial location in each sub-band if each sub-band maintains the same size as the original image. The sizes of each sub-band will be reduced with DWT decomposition. Thus RDWT is invariance in nature. In the proposed method SWT-SVD [19] model was applied to extract the features and embedding purpose. In the proposed model, SWT or RDWT algorithm was applied to both the cover image and the watermark, which obtained the first-layer frequency/coefficients comprising low and high frequency coefficients. However, in the proposed model, the HH sub-plane was taken into consideration for further SVD processing.

2.2.2 Singular Value Decomposition

SVD is applied as a matrix with three matrices in linear algebra. It possesses algebraic properties and conveys key geometrical and theoretical insights into linear transformations. With a small distortion to an image, the singular values are very stable, and larger variation does not occur in the singular value. An image can be seen as a matrix with non-negative scalar elements from the standpoint of image processing. SVD [23] takes a rectangular matrix of input image A as n × p matrix in which the n rows and p columns. The SVD theorem states:

$$A_{nxp} = U_{nxn} S_{nxp} V^T_{pxp} \qquad (2.1)$$

where

$$U^T U = I_{nxn} \text{ and } V^T V = I_{pxp} (U \text{ and } V \text{ are orthogonal matrices}) \qquad (2.2)$$

where U has left singular vectors in its columns, S has singular values and is diagonal and V^T has right singular vectors in its rows. The SVD is a diagonal covariance matrix that represents an expansion of the original data in a coordinate system. A new method for picture watermarking is proposed based on the fact that the SVD subspace can preserve a large amount of information in an image. In the proposed model, SVD algorithm has been applied onto the HH-plane coefficients obtained from the SWT or RDWT method. Noticeably, unlike previous works, where processing SVD onto the pre-extracted HH-sub-plane coefficients, the embedding was performed; in this method, PSO is applied to identify the optimal position across the HH sub-plane to perform embedding. A snippet of the heuristic model, PSO is given in the subsequent section.

2.2.3 Particle swarm optimization

PSO is an artificial intelligence approach focused on the self-organized, decentralized natural systems like bird flocks, fish schools and ant colonies, among others. Kennedy and Elberhart were the first to incorporate PSO. Because of its ability to adapt to changes, it has become a more relevant biologically influenced process. PSO is a well-known methodology for stochastic global optimization. In the watermarking process, the coefficient selection is extremely significant. In watermarking, the PSO method is used to select the best location in the required band to encode the watermark into the host image. Each problem's solution is referred to as a "particle" in PSO. Similar to the other heuristic models, each participating candidate or particle has a "mean" and "standard deviation" (SD). Initially, these parameters of a particle are chosen at random. The variable named *pbest* states the best "mean" of a particle in search for the solution. The best mean *gbest* of all the considered particles during the quest for a solution. Functionally, PSO intends to direct the particle mean toward a specific *pbest* and *gbest* solution. The *quest* for a solution to the problem ends if all of the particles have reached mean values. A snippet of the optimization mechanism involved in PSO [20] is given as follows:

Consider that the *i*th particle with *D*-dimensional space is (2.3).

$$X_i = (X_{i1}, X_{i2}, \ldots, X_{iD}) \qquad (2.3)$$

The *i*th particle in the swarm has its personal best mean given as (2.4).

$$P_i = (P_{i1}, P_{i2}, \ldots, P_{iD}) \qquad (2.4)$$

Similarly, the global best means be (2.5):

$$P_g = (P_{g1}, P_{g2}, \ldots, P_{gD}) \qquad (2.5)$$

Thus, the current SD can be defined as per equation (2.6):

$$V_g = (V_{i1}, V_{i2}, \ldots, V_{iD}) \qquad (2.6)$$

The particle modifies its SD as per the function defined in equations (2.7) and (2.8):

$$V_{id} = w * V_{id} + C1 * rand1 * (P_{id} - X_{id}) + C2 * rand2 * (P_{gd} - X_{id}) \qquad (2.7)$$

$$X_{id} = X_{id} + V_{id} \qquad (2.8)$$

In the above equation, *w* represents the user-defined parameter for inertia weight. The weights of acceleration C1 are a cognitive component, and C2 is a social parameter that influences the particle velocities' previous values on the current one. The random number generated by the function *rand* () is uniformly distributed in the range [0–1].

PSO simulation takes approximately 35 s on a Pentium IV computer for swarm size of 50 particles with 100 iterations. Where *w* is the inertia weight, *rand1* and *rand2* are the two random functions for *i*th particle within a range of [0–1], the constants C1 and C2 are equal to 2, SD is 50 and maximum of 100 iterations are used in the beginning. In the proposed PSO model, the fitness function used is defined in eq. (2.9). Noticeably, the fitness function from 0.2 to 0.9.

$$\text{Fitness} = \text{abs}(\text{mean}) + \text{abs}(\text{SD}) \qquad (2.9)$$

The steps of the PSO algorithm have been given in Figure 2.1.

An encoding and decoding process based on redundant wavelet transformed PSO was developed for watermarking. Functionally, at first, the input image is split into several pixel size blocks. Subsequently, the image is converted into blocks where it generates coefficients in different sub-planes or bands. More specifically, SWT transformed input image as well as watermark into LL, LH and HH, HL sub-planes; however, the proposed model considered HH sub-plane or allied coefficient for watermark embedding. In this process, the HH coefficients were further processed for SVD; The PSO method was applied in sync with SVD to perform watermark embedding.

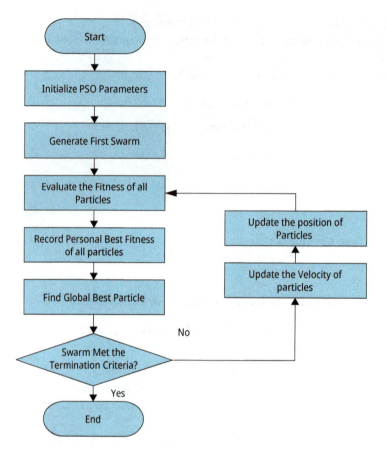

Figure 2.1: Steps of PSO algorithm.

As in Figure 2.2 once embedding the watermark coefficient inside the cover, inverse SVD is performed followed by inverse-SWT, and thus the final reconstructed image is preserved for further communication. Noticeably the receiver side the same process is used to extract the watermark.

Similar to the PSO-based embedding, other heuristics such as GA is used to approximate optimal position for watermark embedding. GA evolution starts from randomly generated individual of a population, where the population generation takes place iteratively, also called (over) generations. Each generation evaluates the fitness of each person in the population; fitness is often the value of the objective function in the optimization problem to be addressed.

From the current population, the fittest individuals are chosen at random and their genomes are edited (recombined and sometimes randomly altered) to create a new generation. Then, in the following iteration of the algorithm, use a new generation of potential solutions. Typically, the process stops when the population reaches a

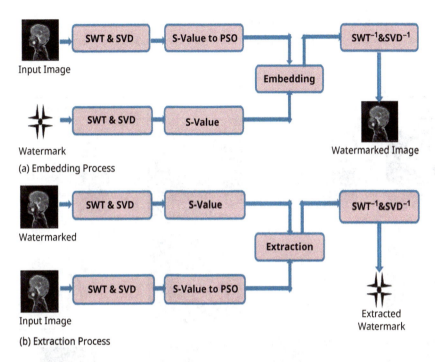

Figure 2.2: Implementation schematic for the proposed PSO algorithm.

sufficient fitness level or when the maximum number of generations is reached. A genetic algorithm along with SWT and SVD watermarking is used in this section. The methodology of embedding and extraction is very similar to the above PSO method. The algorithm has been implemented with a population size of 50 and 100 iterations with a mutation rate of 0.1. Thus, implementing these heuristic-driven watermarking models, the respective performance was examined with the different input images.

2.3 Experimentation and results

This section mainly discusses the simulation results and allied inferences. It begins with experimental results of the PSO optimization and concludes with the comparison of PSO and GA optimization techniques. To substantiate the efficiency of the proposed methodology experiments have been conducted on medical images of 2,500 images of size 512×512 with 10 watermark images. The following five distinct images with size same as the watermark (i.e., 512×512) were taken into consideration. Table 2.1 shows the different watermarks used for the implementation. Before discussing the statistical results and allied inferences, the visual inspection has been done for both the original image as well as the watermarked images. Figure 2.3 presents the histogram analysis of the original (i.e., host or cover image) and the watermarked images.

Table 2.1: Example of different watermarks used for the experimentation.

Input image	Watermark	Watermarked	Extracted watermark

2 Comparision of Optimization Techniques PSO and GA — 33

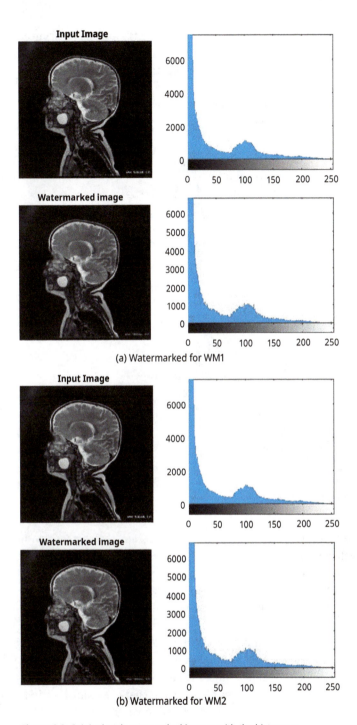

Figure 2.3: Original and watermarked images with the histogram.

Observing each outcome, it can easily be visualized that there is a negligible or near-zero change in histogram projection for both the original image as well as the watermarked image. It exhibits the structural similarity or the higher correlation between the input and the watermarked images. In other words, the above-stated results indicate optimal embedding efficiency by the proposed PSO-based model with both Lena (WM1) and hospital logo (WM2) watermarks.

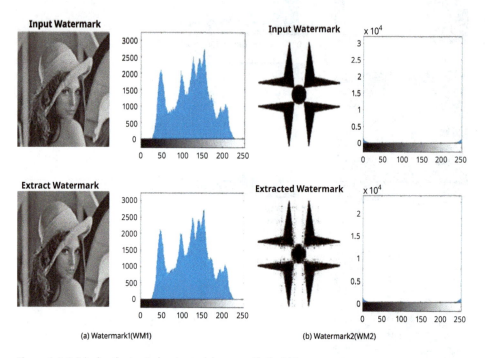

Figure 2.4: Original and extracted watermark images with the histogram.

The above-presented results (Figure 2.4) represent the histogram performance with WM1 and WM2 as a watermark. The results shows the similarity between the input and extracted watermark. To assess attack-resiliency, the proposed model was examined under the different attacks like Gaussian, salt and pepper, rotation, compression, intensity adjustment and histogram. The results obtained for the different attack conditions are given in Table 2.2.

Table 2.3 represents the extracted watermarks with different attacks.

To assess whether the watermark information has been completely extracted and error is near zero signifying optimal embedding efficiency, the structural difference between the host and watermarked images was obtained. To check the imperceptibility original image and watermarked images are subtracted to get the absolute difference as in Table 2.4 with two watermarks (WM1 and WM2). Observing the results, it can easily be found that the difference between the host and the watermarked images

Table 2.2: Watermarked images for WM1 and WM2 under different attack conditions.

Sl. No	Attacks	Watermarked image (WM1)	Watermarked image (WM2)
1	Salt–pepper	Salt and Pepper Noise Attacked Image	Salt and Pepper Noise Attacked Image
2	Gaussian	Gaussian Noise Attacked Image	Gaussian Noise Attacked Image
3	Speckle	Speckle Noise Attacked Image	Speckle Noise Attacked Image
4	JPEG2000 Comp	JPEG2000 Compression Attacked Image	JPEG2000 Compression Attacked Image
5	Rotation	Rotation Attacked Image	Rotation Attacked Image

Table 2.2 (continued)

Sl. No	Attacks	Watermarked image (WM1)	Watermarked image (WM2)
6	Gaussian filter	Gaussian Noise Attacked Image	Gaussian Noise Attacked Image
7	Gaussian blur	Gaussian Noise Attacked Image	Gaussian filter Attacked Image
8	Intensity adjustment	Intensity Adjustment Attacked Image	Intensity Adjustment Attacked Image
9	Histogram adj	Histogram Adjustment Attacked Image	Histogram Adjustment Attacked Image
10	Motion blur	Motion Blur Attacked Image	Motion Blur Attacked Image

Table 2.2 (continued)

Sl. No	Attacks	Watermarked image (WM1)	Watermarked image (WM2)
11	Average filter	Average filter Attacked Image	Average filter Attacked Image
12	Sharpening	Shapened Image	Shapened Image
13	Scaling	Resize Attacked Image	Resize Attacked Image
14	Gamma correction	Gamma Correction Attacked Image	Gamma Correction Attacked Image
15	JPEG compression	JPEG Compression Attacked Image	JPEG Compression Attacked Image

Table 2.3: Extracted watermark images with different attacks.

Sl. no	Attack type	Extracted watermark (WM1)	Extracted watermark (WM2)
1	Pepper	Extracted Watermark Image	Extracted Watermark Image
2	Gaussian	Extracted Watermark Image	Extracted Watermark Image
3	Speckle	Extracted Watermark Image	Extracted Watermark Image
4	JPEG2000 compression	Extracted Watermark Image	Extracted Watermark Image
5	Rotation	Extracted Watermark Image	Extracted Watermark Image

Table 2.3 (continued)

Sl. no	Attack type	Extracted watermark (WM1)	Extracted watermark (WM2)
6	Gaussian filter	Extracted Watermark Image	Extracted Watermark Image
7	Gaussian blur	Extracted Watermark Image	Extracted Watermark Image
8	Intensity adjustment	Extracted Watermark Image	Extracted Watermark Image
9	Histogram adj	Extracted Watermark Image	Extracted Watermark Image
10	Motion blur	Extracted Watermark Image	Extracted Watermark Image

Table 2.3 (continued)

Sl. no	Attack type	Extracted watermark (WM1)	Extracted watermark (WM2)
11	Average filter	Extracted Watermark Image	Extracted Watermark Image
12	Sharpening	Extracted Watermark Image	Extracted Watermark Image
13	Scaling	Extracted Watermark Image	Extracted Watermark Image
14	Gamma correction	Extracted Watermark Image	Extracted Watermark Image
15	JPEG compression	Extracted Watermark Image	Extracted Watermark Image

is almost zero, signifying optimal embedding efficacy by the proposed PSO-driven SWT-SVD watermarking model.

Table 2.4: Difference of input and watermarked images with WM1 and WM2.

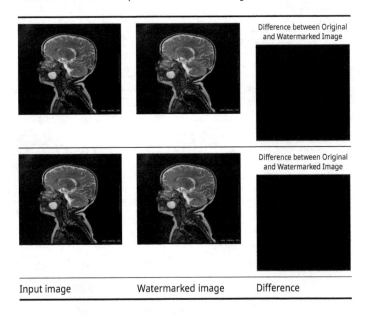

Input image	Watermarked image	Difference

To test the imperceptibility of proposed algorithm, the watermarked image is subjected to the following attacks with the image dataset. Figure 2.5 represents some of the sample images used for the implementation. Table 2.5 represents PSNR and NC for the sample image dataset with WM1 as a watermark, the same has been shown in Figure 2.6 to 2.11.

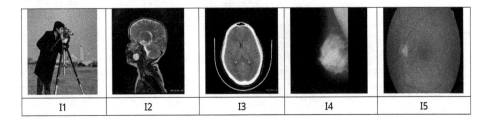

Figure 2.5: Sample images used for the implementation.

The different attacks like SP (Pepper), GN (Gaussian) and speckle with 0.001 density, JPEG2000 compression ($Q = 65$), 50° rotation, and Gaussian filter 3 × 3 are used. All the images perform well with all the aforesaid attacks with PSNR of more than 65 dB for the sample images.

Table 2.5: PSO performance with different sample images.

Sl. no	Attack type	Parameters	I1	I2	I3	I4	I5
1	SP	PSNR	68.6241	71.3497	70.7148	78.1778	71.2029
		NC	1.0000	1.0000	1.0000	1.0000	1.0000
2	GN	PSNR	68.4207	70.8023	70.4887	78.5099	71.1973
		NC	1.0000	1.0000	1.0000	1.0000	1.0000
3	Speckle noise	PSNR	68.7718	70.6727	70.7383	78.395	71.6938
		NC	1.0000	1.0000	1.0000	1.0000	1.0000
4	JPEG2000	PSNR	68.8269	71.0678	70.5995	70.2732	71.4202
		NC	1.0000	1.0000	0.9998	1.0000	1.0000
5	Rotation (50)	PSNR	68.9246	71.3376	70.5491	80.8142	71.0431
		NC	0.6748	0.6829	0.5976	0.8067	0.7035
6	Gaussian Filter	PSNR	76.0293	78.6701	73.9567	86.7037	82.9204
		NC	0.9766	0.9648	0.8715	0.9999	0.9954
7	Gaussian blur	PSNR	72.0964	72.7519	71.9962	81.6336	79.9003
		NC	0.9750	0.9463	0.8531	0.9998	0.9998
8	Int. adj	PSNR	65.9927	65.0125	69.0796	69.091	62.6631
		NC	0.5788	0.6283	0.5702	0.7829	0.6314
9	Hist. adj	PSNR	66.519	87.7622	79.5141	79.5141	70.2862
		NC	0.5926	0.5775	0.6069	0.6230	0.5800
10	Motion blur	PSNR	71.2592	72.1501	71.1834	81.0007	78.0863
		NC	0.8821	0.9424	0.8511	0.9832	0.9278
11	Avg. filter	PSNR	75.1272	77.5479	73.6155	86.0584	82.0829
		NC	0.9644	0.9683	0.8672	0.9994	0.9889
12	Sharp	PSNR	65.2554	65.2247	67.6555	71.4202	66.6884
		NC	0.5331	0.6416	0.6595	0.8049	0.7351
13	Resize	PSNR	68.8268	71.2824	70.3738	80.5492	71.6354
		NC	0.8831	0.9097	0.8244	0.9751	0.9120
14	Gamma correction	PSNR	77.8092	76.6593	76.1654	92.3445	90.8939
		NC	0.8611	0.8284	0.7805	0.9259	0.9036
15	JPEG comp	PSNR	68.9009	72.947	70.0458	84.562	75.217
		NC	0.8604	0.9133	0.8030	0.9929	0.9409

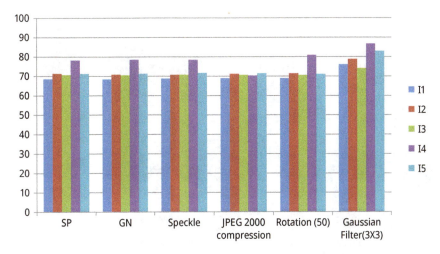

Figure 2.6: PSNR values for SP, GN, speckle, JPEG2000, rotation and Gaussian filter attacks.

The Gaussian blur is used with a standard deviation of 2. The intensity is adjusted from a minimum of 0.3 to a maximum of 0.7-pixel values. The watermarked image is transformed into 64 bins using a histogram equalization attack. The motion blur is applied with a length of 10 pixels and 45° in a counter-clockwise direction. The filter size of 3 × 3 is used for the average filter. All five images perform well with the said attacks. MRI image performs better with histogram equalization because the attack increases the contrast range of the refereed image with an average brightness which leads to the highest PSNR with localized adaptive effect. The PSNR performance for the aforementioned attacks is more than 60 dB for I1 to I5 images depicts the PSNR values under the different attack conditions including sharpening, resize, gamma correction and compression attacks. Sharpening returns a 3 × 3 contrast enhancement filter on the Laplacian filter negative with parameter with $\alpha = 0.2$. Noticeably, in the proposed model, for simulation, the high alpha value was taken into consideration. In such a case, the PSNR values observed were in the range of 64–70 dB. Resize attack was done by introducing or converting 512 × 512 to 256 × 256 image and vice versa. The gamma correction was tested with a value of 0.6 and compression ($Q = 65$) and got good results for all images. The method performs well with the said attacks with PSNR of more than 60 dB.

Figure 2.9 presents the robustness of the method with NC. NC values are good in all the attacks with almost equal to 1 except rotation of 50°. In rotation, I4 performs better compared to the other four images.

Figure 2.10 depicts NC values for blurring, adjustment, filter and cropping attacks. NC values of intensity and histogram adjustment for all the images are poor and it is above 0.5. NC values for Gaussian blur and the average filter are high for all the images.

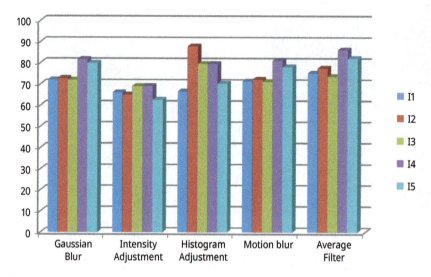

Figure 2.7: PSNR values for blurring, adjustment and filter attacks.

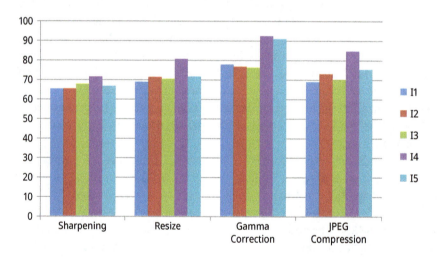

Figure 2.8: PSNR values for sharpening, resize, gamma correction and compression attacks.

NC values are good for resizing, gamma correction and compression attacks. NC values are less in sharpening attack I1 image for the other images. NC value is above 0.65 (Figure 2.11).

The proposed method is extended to implement with five different watermarks as in Tables 2.6 and 2.7 Results show that different watermarks have a high PSNR of 60 DB with evident imperceptibility.

Table 2.7 extends table 2.6 results in terms of NC. Except for intensity adjustment and histogram equalization watermark (WM1), the NC value is 0.7. For all the other

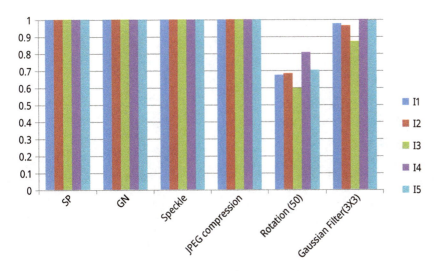

Figure 2.9: NC values for SP, GN, speckle, JPEG, rotation and Gaussian filter attacks.

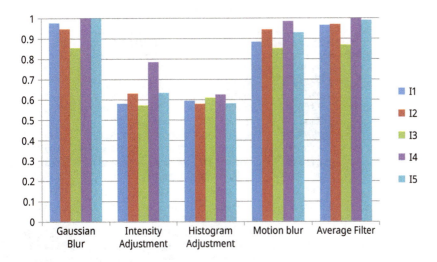

Figure 2.10: NC values for blurring, adjustment, filter and cropping attacks.

attack scenarios NC value is above 0.8. Figure 2.12 and 2.13 illustrate the analysis of PSNR and NC under different attacks.

The implementation of the proposed method is extended with a genetic algorithm. Table 2.8 presents the relative performance of the different heuristic-driven SWT-SVD watermarking models. The performance characterization is done with I2 image data.

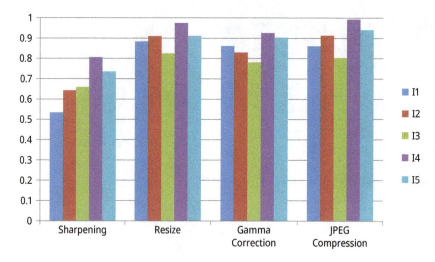

Figure 2.11: NC values for sharpening, resize, gamma correction and compression attacks.

Table 2.6: PSNR performance of PSO method with different watermark images.

PSNR/attacks	PSNR (WM1)	PSNR (WM2)	PSNR (WM3)	PSNR (WM4)	PSNR (WM5)
Salt and pepper (0.001)	64.1659	64.1662	61.8839	64.1751	64.175
Gaussian noise (0.001)	68.4207	65.1658	64.1751	63.4259	64.1972
Speckle noise (0.001)	64.1675	64.1668	64.1751	64.6881	64.8102
JPEG2000 Compression (65)	73.6618	73.6094	73.9631	73.6196	73.9933
Rotation (45)	75.4459	75.7652	75.5054	75.4872	75.3476
Gaussian filter(3 × 3)	75.7528	75.3332	76.6618	76.6662	78.6693
Gaussian blur	72.3174	72.7474	72.63	72.3458	72.63
Intensity adj	64.8415	65.0265	64.8501	64.9841	64.8501
Histogram adj	75.2313	74.5802	75.2819	75.9913	76.6574
Motion blur (45)	71.9771	72.1469	72.2146	72.2144	72.2153
Average filter(3 × 3)	74.9195	77.5521	77.5291	77.5283	77.5287
Sharpening	70.3246	67.7521	72.4816	72.4689	72.4774
Scaling	71.4994	71.103	71.4871	71.0123	71.4054
Gamma correction	75.7646	76.8189	75.7865	75.9346	75.9669
JPEG compression (75)	76.5524	71.3107	74.4537	71.5632	74.4814

The overall results affirm sound stating that retaining higher PSNR and NC makes PSO-driven watermarking more efficient. In other words, the simulation with the different attack conditions reveals that under the different attack conditions PSO-driven watermarking model (say, PSO-driven SWT-SVD) retains PSNR of more than 70 dB, characterizing superior image quality. On the other hand, GA-based model could achieve the highest PSNR of 24 dB with salt and pepper attack, whereas for the same data and attack conditions, PSO-based SWT-SVD watermarking achieved 64 dB of PSNR. Except for compression and attack-free scenarios the NC value of the PSO

Table 2.7: NC for PSO method with different watermark images.

NC/attacks	NC (WM1)	NC (WM2)	NC (WM3)	NC (WM4)	NC (WM5)
Pepper (0.001)	0.9624	0.9979	0.9827	0.9533	0.9733
Gaussian (0.001)	0.9246	0.9979	0.9861	0.9532	0.9734
Speckle (0.001)	0.9621	0.9945	0.9532	0.9532	0.9732
JPEG2000 compression (65)	0.9660	0.9957	0.9903	0.9732	0.9909
Rotation (45)	0.9448	1.0000	0.9929	0.9794	0.9938
Gaussian (3 × 3)	0.8185	0.9980	0.9866	0.9585	0.9782
Blur	0.8816	0.9980	0.9867	0.9793	0.9761
Intensity adj	**0.6986**	0.9923	0.9764	0.9364	0.9486
Histogram adj	**0.7071**	0.9923	0.9684	0.8955	0.8775
Motion blur (45)	0.9697	1.0000	0.9871	0.9599	0.9794
Average (3 × 3)	0.8914	0.9981	0.9866	0.9579	0.9776
Sharpening	0.8570	0.9725	0.9745	0.9156	0.9149
Scaling	0.9463	1.0000	0.9935	0.9800	0.9939
Gamma correction	0.9319	0.9975	0.9428	0.8479	0.7903
JPEG compression (75)	0.9823	0.9993	0.9950	0.9821	0.9962

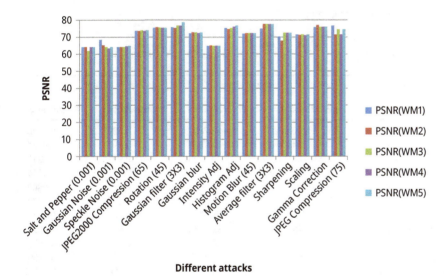

Figure 2.12: Statistical analysis of in terms of PSNR.

method is superior to the GA method. Similar to the PSNR performance, the NC performance too confirmed that the proposed PSO-driven SWT-SVD model performs superior toward medical image watermarking.

Now, considering the superiority of the proposed PSO-driven SWT-SVD watermarking model, to further examine the efficacy, a state-of-art existing method using ant colony optimization (ACO) was taken into consideration. To enable equi-experimental conditions, Lena and cameraman images were considered for performance analysis.

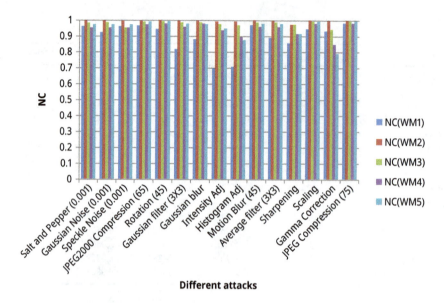

Figure 2.13: Statistical analyses in terms of NC.

Table 2.8: PSO and GA-driven SWT-SVD watermarking models (with scaling factor 0.01).

Attack methods	PSNR		NC	
	Proposed PSO	Proposed GA	Proposed PSO	Proposed GA
Attack free	70.8025	58.7890	0.9800	**0.9990**
Salt and pepper noise (0.01)	64.1349	24.9033	0.9978	0.9594
Gaussian noise (0.01)	64.1331	20.2796	0.9978	0.8042
Speckle noise (0.01)	64.1346	25.5330	0.9977	0.9064
JPEG2000 compression (95)	72.5814	73.2895	0.9986	**1.0000**
Average filter 3 × 3	77.5449	32.31	0.9982	0.7870
Rotation (45)	71.3236	6.8395	0.9827	0.15332
Gaussian filter (3 × 3)	78.6703	32.0688	0.9981	0.5750
Gaussian blur	72.756	26.1465	0.9977	0.7529
Sharpening	67.6813	39.4262	0.9079	0.7166
Scaling	70.9488	29.2567	0.9840	0.59122
Intensity adj	65.0111	15.3524	0.9732	0.9594
Histogram adj	75.9871	24.6114	0.9487	0.9994
Gamma correction	75.8655	19.9069	0.9715	0.9594

Noticeably, in this experiment, the input images were considered of 256 × 256 size, while WM2 (hospital logo) was considered as the watermark.

According to the findings, the suggested PSO-driven SWT-SVD watermarking method outperforms the ACO method. The reference author has given PSNR of 50 DB for Lena and Cameraman as 48 DB. In the proposed PSO-driven SWT-SVD watermarking model,

PSNR for Lena is 75 DB and 74 DB for cameraman images without applying attacks. From Table 2.9, it can easily be found that the proposed PSO-driven SWT-SVD model outperforms the existing approach, that is, the Khaled algorithm [21]. ACO approach applies pheromone update and hence merely locally pheromone update can't yield estimation of the optimal set of (multiple) positions for watermark embedding.

Table 2.9: Performance comparison with PSO and ACO watermarking under the different attack conditions.

Image/attacks	ACO-Lena	PSO-Lena	ACO-Cameraman	PSO-Cameraman
Pepper (0.05)	0.968	0.9980	0.968	0.9985
Gaussian filter (3 × 3)	0.993	0.9975	0.970	0.9995
Cropping (image center)	0.946	1.0000	0.941	1.0000
Compression ($Q = 5$)	0.976	1.0000	0.963	1.0000
Sharpening	0.986	0.9861	0.982	0.9863
Scaling (256 ≥ 512 ≥ 256)	1.0000	1.0000	1.0000	1.0000
Histogram equation	0.991	0.9975	0.981	0.9984
Gamma correction ($y = 0.2$)	0.982	1.0000	0.964	1.0000
Rotation (25)	**0.396**	1.0000	**0.783**	**1.0000**
Motion blur (45)	0.975	1.0000	0.964	1.0000
Median filter (3 × 3)	**0.418**	0.9992	0.870	0.9995

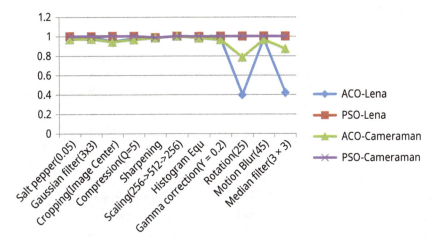

Figure 2.14: Comparison of ACO with PSO.

To compare the performance (i.e., PSO-driven SWT-SVD watermarking), a state-of-art method using Bat Algorithm (BA) was considered in Ali's [22] method. The relative performance analysis was done with PSNR and NC.

The performance comparison of PSO and BA algorithm [22] with scaling factor 4 is shown in Table 2.10. The proposed PSO-driven SWT-SVD watermarking model results are better with state-of-art work in all noises except sharpening, histogram equalization attacks. The proposed PSO-driven method concentrates both on PSNR and NC performs well with all the possible attacks. The analysis chart of both methods has been shown in Figure 2.15.

Table 2.10: Relative performance characterization with the BA [22].

Reference method/attacks	Ali [22]	Proposed PSO-driven watermarking
Attack free	0.999	**0.9707**
Pepper (0.01)	1	**0.9920**
Pepper (0.02)	0.982	0.9919
Pepper (0.03)	0.894	0.9910
Speckle (0.001)	1.0000	1.0000
Speckle (0.005)	0.998	0.9985
Speckle (0.009)	0.961	0.9983
Gaussian (0.001)	0.991	0.9920
Gaussian (0.005)	0.852	**0.9921**
Gaussian (0.009)	0.724	**0.9916**
Scaling (2)	1	0.9427
Scaling(0.9)	0.803	**0.9423**
Scaling(0.7)	0.479	**0.9443**
Gamma (0.9)	1	0.9420
Gamma (0.6)	1	0.9407
Compression (Q = 95)	1	0.9408
Compression (Q = 90)	0.968	0.9382
JPEG compression (Q = 85)	0.821	0.9384
Gaussian (3 × 3)	1	0.9929
Average filter (3 × 3)	0.283	0.9921
Hist. equalization	1	**0.9309**
Sharpening filter	1	**0.8294**
Weiner filter (3 × 3)	0.390	0.9633
Rotation (10)	0.986	**0.9446**
Rotation (45)	0.982	**0.9414**

Considering real-time medical data security and allied communication, maintaining minimum processing time is equally important as the quality constraints. Considering this fact, the proposed model was examined for allied processing time.

Table 2.11 represents the time optimization in the proposed PSO-driven watermarking model. Here, the key emphasis was made on phases that include running the algorithm with and without PSO and attack and attack-free scenarios. The images I1 to I10 are some of the sample images used to represent the execution time of the algorithm. With PSO and with attack phase takes an average of 37.4426 s. With PSO and without attack phase takes an average of 33.676 s. Without PSO and attack phase takes an average of 27.1003 s. Without PSO and with attack phase takes an average of

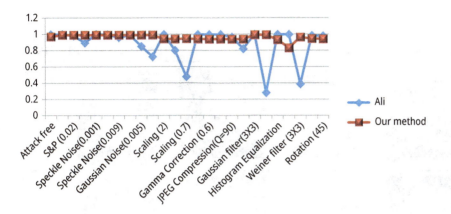

Figure 2.15: Comparison of BA [22] with the proposed PSO-driven SWT-SVD model.

Table 2.11: Processing time analysis for PSO-driven SWT-SVD watermarking.

Images/modality	PSO-attack	PSO–without attack	Without PSO–attack	Without PSO with attack
I1	34.427	30.761	24.061	25.345
I2	33.898	31.310	31.273	26.016
I3	36.273	36.937	25.646	34.656
I4	39.322	33.633	21.203	42.933
I5	39.071	37.663	27.436	45.282
I6	39.282	26.161	26.908	37.726
I7	37.601	38.578	28.415	27.562
I8	39.567	34.335	36.951	35.292
I9	35.198	33.118	21.403	35.266
I10	39.787	34.264	27.707	45.915

35.5993 s. Based on the findings, it appears reasonable to conclude that the significant improvement is due to a decrease in processing time.

The obtained results are given in Table 2.12. A false-positive test is carried out by considering a copyright as a forgery image as shown in the above figure. Here is a part of reconstruction if the unauthenticated person has changed the coefficients of the watermark by using a false watermark, the result will lead to extract a false watermark itself. The extraction will never be similar to the original watermark image as shown with the NC value. In the proposed simulation both watermarks WM1 and WM2 were taken into consideration. The NC value is 0.6190 and 0.5960 relates to not a correlation with the original watermark image.

Table 2.12: Relative performance comparison for false-positive.

Input image	Watermark	False watermark	Extracted watermark	NC
			Extracted watermark Image	0.6190
			Extracted watermark Image	0.5960

2.4 Conclusion

PSO-driven SWT-SVD watermarking concept was developed with a key emphasis to improve image quality, minimum error, higher correlation and attack resilience. In this reference, the proposed PSO model was mainly applied to optimize the embedding processing by identifying the optimal position for watermark embedding in the cover of the host image. To assess relative performance in comparison to the other heuristic models, two other approaches, the GA-driven SWT-SVD watermarking model was developed and allied performance was examined. The overall results confirm that the proposed PSO-driven SWT-SVD model performs superior in terms of PSNR, NC and other visual performance outputs, even under the different attack conditions. Undeniably, the use of PSO as an embedding optimization tool has resulted in such affirmative results. Thus, the proposed PSO-driven SWT-SVD watermarking model can be applied for real-time watermarking purposes. Moreover, the higher image quality, minimum quality destruction, higher imperceptibility, lower computational or processing time make the proposed PSO-driven SWT–SVD model suitable for the medical healthcare data security and allied communication. Further we can extend our algorithm with elephant herding optimization.

References

[1] Roček, A., Javorník, M., Slavíček, K. & Dostál, O. Zero watermarking: Critical analysis of its role in current medical imaging. Journal of Digital Imaging, 1–8.

[2] Abduldaim, A. M., Waleed, J. & Mazher, A. N. (2020). An efficient scheme of digital image watermarking based on Hessenberg factorization and DWT, Proc. 2020 International Conference of Computer Science Software Engineering CSASE 2020, pp. 180–185.

[3] Aljuaid, H. & Parah, S. A. (2021). Secure patient data transfer using information embedding and hyperchaos. Sensors, 21(1), 282.

[4] Alshanbari, H. S. (2020). Medical image watermarking for ownership & tamper detection. Multimedia Tools and Applications.

[5] Amiri, A. & Mirzakuchaki, S. (2020). A digital watermarking method based on NSCT transform and hybrid evolutionary algorithms with neural networks. SN Applied Sciences, 2(10).

[6] Anand, A. & Singh, A. K. (2020). RDWT-SVD-firefly based dual watermarking technique for medical images (workshop paper), Proc. – 2020 IEEE 6th Int. Conf. Multimed. Big Data, BigMM 2020, pp. 366–372.

[7] Anand, A. & Singh, A. K. (2020). An improved DWT-SVD domain watermarking for medical information security. Computing Communication, 152(November 2019), 72–80.

[8] Anand, A., Singh, A. K., Lv, Z. & Bhatnagar, G. (2020). Compression-then-encryption–based secure watermarking technique for smart healthcare system. IEEE Multimedia, 27(4), 133–143.

[9] Ariatmanto, D. & Ernawan, F. (2020). An improved robust image watermarking by using different embedding strengths. Multimedia Tools and Applications, 79(17–18), 12041–12067.

[10] Swaraja, K., Meenakshi, K. & Kora, P. (2020). An optimized blind dual medical image watermarking framework for tamper localization and content authentication in secured telemedicine. Biomedical Signal Processing and Control, 55, 1–15.

[11] Kazemi, M. F., Pourmina, M. A. & Mazinan, A. H. (2020). Analysis of watermarking framework for a color image through a neural network-based approach. Complex & Intelligent Systems, 6(1), 213–220.

[12] Khare, P. & Srivastava, V. K. (2020). A secured and robust medical image watermarking approach for protecting integrity of medical images. Transactions on Emerging Telecommunications Technologies, November 2019, 1–17.

[13] Luo, Y., et al. (2020). A multi-scale image watermarking based on integer wavelet transform and singular value decomposition. Expert Systems with Applications, November, 114–272.

[14] Shen, Y., Tang, C., Xu, M., Chen, M. & Lei, Z. (2021). A DWT-SVD based adaptive color multi-watermarking scheme for copyright protection using AMEF and PSO-GWO. Expert Systems with Applications, 168(July 2019), 114–414.

[15] Soni, G. K., Rawat, A., Jain, S. & Sharma, S. K. (2020). A Pixel-Based Digital Medical Images Protection Using Genetic Algorithm with LSB Watermark Technique, Vol. 141. Springer Singapore.

[16] Tayachi, M., Mulhem, S., Adi, W., Nana, L., Pascu, A. & Benzarti, F. (2020). Tamper and clone-resistant authentication scheme for medical image systems. Cryptography, 4(3), 19.

[17] Thakur, S., Singh, A. K., Ghrera, S. P. & Mohan, A. (2020). Chaotic based secure watermarking approach for medical images. Multimedia Tools Applications, 79(7–8), 4263–4276.

[18] Thanki, R. & Kothari, A. (2020). Multi-level security of medical images based on encryption and watermarking for telemedicine applications. Multimedia Tools Applications.

[19] Holi, G. U., An imperceptible secure transfer of medical, images for telemedicine applications, International Conference on Recent Trends in Image Processing and Pattern Recognition, Springer, Singapore.

[20] Holi, G. U. An optimal and secure watermarking system using SWT-SVD and PSO. Indonesian Journal of Electrical Engineering and Computer Science, 18(2), 917–926.

[21] Loukhaoukha, K., Chouinard, J. Y. & Taieb, M. H. (2011). Optimal image watermarking algorithm based on LWT-SVD via multi-objective ant colony optimization. International Journal of Information Hiding Multimedia Signal Processing, 2(4), 303–319.

[22] Pourhadi, A. & Mahdavi-Nasab, H. (2020). A robust digital image watermarking scheme based on Bat algorithm optimization and SURF detector in SWT domain. Multimedia Tools and Applications, 79(29–30), 21653–21677.

[23] Run, R.-S., Horng, S.-J., Lai, J.-L., Kao, T.-W. & Chen, R.-J. (2012). An improved SVD-based watermarking technique for copyright protection. Expert Systems with Applications, 39, 673–689.

Subandhu Agravanshi, Muskaan Walia, Sushruta Mishra

3 An analytical study of AI in overcoming mental illness

Abstract: Psychological instabilities like depression, attention-deficit hyperactivity disorder and schizophrenia (SZ) are astoundingly normal and have been shown to influence an individual's genuine prosperity. Lately, artificial intelligence (AI) strategies have been familiar with assistance passionate health providers, including subject matter experts and clinicians, for dynamic ward on patients' chronicled data (e.g., clinical records, direct data and electronic media use) Deep learning (DL), as may be the most recent period of AI headways, has displayed predominant execution in some certified applications going from PC vision to clinical benefits. An investigation on recently bombed models is acted to get information that sets up patterns that start to clarify why specific methodologies in the past flopped and how they can be hyper tuned to more readily serve our current requirements. The target of this examination is to review existing assessments on usages of profound learning computations in mental prosperity result research. A careful assessment and inside and out investigation of how a few sicknesses contrast across the globe and how broadened their patients just as their analysis and manifestations are directed to a smaller quest for models and structures that can be effortlessly applied to patients dependent on their particular side effects. The utilization of various philosophies is inspected, their outcomes arranged and a result is focused on that helps the objective of use of cutting-edge DL in working on the state of psychological wellness afflictions and patients. Specifically, we first immediately diagram the state-of-the-art DL strategies. Then we review the composing appropriate to DL applications in enthusiastic prosperity results.

Keywords: Deep learning, recurrent neural network, schizophrenia, convolutional neural network, mental health, depression

---

Subandhu Agravanshi, School of Computer Engineering, Kalinga Institute of Industrial Technology, Bhubaneswar, Odisha, India, e-mail: subandhu333@gmail.com
Muskaan Walia, School of Computer Engineering, Kalinga Institute of Industrial Technology, Bhubaneswar, Odisha, India, e-mail: walia.muskaan007@gmail.com
Sushruta Mishra, School of Computer Engineering, Kalinga Institute of Industrial Technology, Bhubaneswar, Odisha, India, e-mail: sushruta.mishrafcs@kiit.ac.in

https://doi.org/10.1515/9783110750942-003

3.1 Introduction to schizophrenia and mental illness

Mental illnesses are a burgeoning concern in the present day. Research and development in the fields of mental health are yet to find absolutely successful outcomes that would assist patients and be a broad approach to their ailments.

Mental health is thought to impair the individual's cognitive ability, reasoning, peace and state of mind. Recent studies show that about 450 million individuals in the USA alone suffer from mental health disorders of some form. However, developments have betrayed the impact of mental health issues on the physical health of those suffering. These may involve physical harm, tendencies to take one's life, be a threat to their caregivers all while suffering that which they cannot control. It is thus imperative to find solutions to mental health problems, the four major issues include

1. Depression
2. Attention-deficit hyperactivity disorder (ADHD)
3. Schizophrenia
4. Autism spectrum disorder (ASD)

So as to better analyze ways to detect, solve, aid and/or prevent these conditions we need a detailed analysis of the availability of data pertaining to individuals under the above-stated disorders primarily. Chronic disorders can be analyzed in laboratories and a generalized suggestion for them can be derived. However, mental illnesses are almost always unique to an individual because of their nature and reaction based on the individual's conditions, surroundings and previous history starting from reasons that might have first triggered signs of ailment. Currently, most of the data regarding adolescents, adults and senior citizens suffering from mental health issues is gathered via surveys and public health forums. Artificial intelligence (AI) plays a pivotal role in assisting us to find patterns that are common among patients which might escape the human eye.

Deep learning (DL) systems can also work with data gathered from a unique individual through sensors and work on each dataset separately. This allows us room for researching daily activities, routines and schedules of healthy individuals as well as those who are concerned to predict those who might be or show early signs. Data availability has made it possible to actively work on solutions in cancer, heart conditions and similar serious ailments. While data on what causes mental issues, schizophrenia (SZ) in particular is bleak, DL allows us to prepare synthetic data based on hypotheticals which we can work with and curb this problem.

The following is a detailed 2017 research on data collected from 792 million individuals, which gives us a detailed understanding of the prevalence of mental health concerns globally. With an understanding of the causes of specific disorders, their global spread and the sex which is most likely to be affected we can comprehend an idea about the urgency of finding solutions in the domain [1].

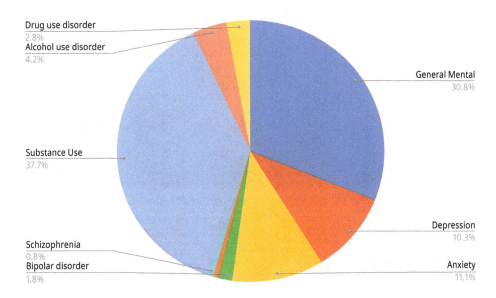

Figure 3.1: Prevalence of mental illness [1].

3.2 AI and deep learning in healthcare

While a few noticeable areas of society are prepared to accept the capability of AI, alert remaining parts common in medication, including psychiatry, proven by late features in the news media like "A.I. Can Be a Boon to Medicine That Could Easily Go, Rogue." Notwithstanding evident concerns, AI applications in medication are consistently expanding. As psychological well-being specialists, we need to acclimate ourselves with AI, comprehend its current and future uses and be ready to proficiently work with AI as it enters the clinical standard.

Machine learning targets create computational calculations or measurable models that can consequently construct stowed examples from data. Ongoing years have seen an expanding number of ML models being created to break down medical care data. In any case, regular ML approaches require a lot of highlight designing for ideal execution – a stage that is vital for most application situations to get great execution, which is normally asset and tedious.

As the freshest flood of ML and AI innovations, DL approaches focus on the advancement of a start to finish component that maps the information crude highlights straightforwardly into the yields through a multi-facet network structure that can catch the secret examples inside the information. In this part, we will survey a few mainstream DL model structures, including profound feedforward neural organization (DFNN), repetitive neural organization (RNN), convolutional neural organization (CNN) and autoencoder.

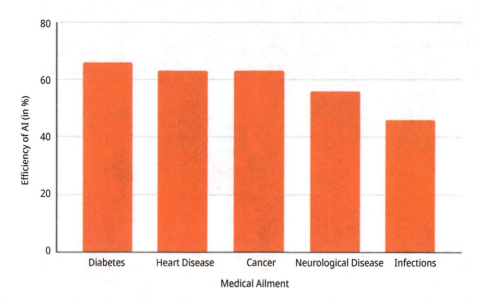

Figure 3.2: Efficiency of AI in chronic health diseases.

DL is an advanced method of ML which relies on the use of artificial neural networks that train and learn overtime through data provided and reach a prediction based on the model type used, such systems are different from traditionally equipped software designs since they learn on their own and aid problem-solving and classification-related projects [2].

The essential component of artificial neural networks is a single artificial neuron which is a mathematical model that works by non-linear and/or linear activation functions. In general, an artificial neuron comprises a given number of weighted inputs from the training data on which a nonlinear activation function is applied that is differentiable and results in the output from that particular neuron and collectively from the neural network. The inputs are the trainable parameters of a DL model, their product is taken with associated weights in order to remove biases; in this sense one may say that artificial neurons are inspired by biological neurons. Like biological neurons have an output associated with their function, for example, the activity potential that are yielded once the neuron's membrane potential exceeds its threshold potential, similarly artificial neurons also yield once their activation function begins to exceed their minimum value which is in most cases near or equal to 0 [3].

3.3 Work on mental health leading up to the use of AI

Disorders like SZ are enfeebling mental diseases that affect the reasoning and feeling capacities in the suffering patients. Although a cure for such disorders is yet to be found, AI and machine learning might help in the early detection in predicting the behavior and show the decline of functioning.

3.4 Application of traditional ML models to ailments

Several machine learning models and procedures can now be applied to day-to-day tasks, they can be employed for project work, research and development: for example, previously it was almost impossible for regular software to assist in the detailed task of understanding and elaborating patterns in detailed and complex data sets, this prevented application of results to meaningful work and studies; however, machine learning models assist expanding the scope of our progress by analyzing patterns which might escape the human eye and yield these outputs in a form interpretable for humans. With advancements in machine learning, models and approaches can be segregated into four categories:
1. Supervised
2. Un-supervised
3. Semi-supervised
4. State-of-the-art (new) approaches

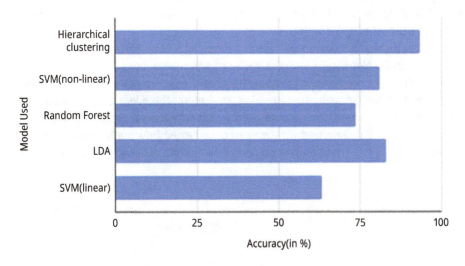

Figure 3.3: Accuracy of traditional models in predicting mental illness [52].

Supervised learning models are primarily used in several applications today, and they dominate a major aspect of classification and recognition problem-solving softwares. Some commonly used techniques of supervised learning include
1. Support vector machines
2. Random forests
3. Logistic regression among other approaches constantly being hyper-tuned and advanced for progress

In supervised learning the training data on which a certain model is applied contains both values as well as target classes to be classified into, the data is trained with the final outcome already predefined, this is one of the reasons why supervised learning models are common place in applications today. Some examples where supervised learning models can be applied are predicting the class of cancer as benign or malignant based on provided data which trains our system to learn the categorical division and accordingly segregate.

The other process of machine learning, unsupervised learning employs the model's ability to be able to comprehend patterns in provided data, string these bits together and collectively group them thereby performing classification since datasets used in unsupervised learning do not have predefined classes associated with them.

Among a number of researches works and models, only one paper incorporated the use of semi-supervised learning [4] the dataset for such models provides both labeled and unlabeled data to their algorithm. State-of-the-art models are new models made by fine-tuning previously available approaches to enhance and improve their application [5–7].

At last, the examination of natural language processing, analyzing audio and textual inputs, presents a specific space of machine learning that for the most part uses unsupervised procedures. Different works applied vocabulary and other content mining draws near [8] to assist with removing keywords (i.e., discouragement), themes or etymological highlights from text to take in top-notch highlights from manual input or textual data to develop classification model's or analyze semantics [7].

Accordingly, in keeping with most of the papers' emphasis on psychological wellbeing appraisal, the works basically used supervised machine learning procedures to research if, and how well, certain emotional wellness practices, mental conditions or illnesses could be characterized through recently created information models. Unsupervised learning has been applied on several occasions to assist classification into categories [7].

3.5 Probable reasons for the failure of traditional models

For medical classification tasks, predicting the correct category is of utmost importance as it allows a better, detail-oriented diagnosis of the illness of the patients whose data is provided to the model. For this reason, data sets where categories are already previously known analyze the accuracy of their models by comparing the predicted classes of their algorithm against the previously known class, a number of prediction metrics are employed to assure the validity of a model. However, if the model is trained with the classes already known, this would cause over-fitting, a serious issue that hampers model performance on unknown datasets; for this reason, therefore, most models tend to hide or keep out a segment of the dataset from training and then test the model's predictions against this unknown data category. This helps in really understanding the model's accuracy.

Commonly used metrics for classification model performance are accuracy, F1-scores [7], recall and precision metrics. In certain studies, another metric of classification called log loss is also used, and this checks the correctness of a prediction based on its shift from a given threshold point. [9]. Precision metric checks the low false-positive rate and recall checks the completeness of the low false-negative rate of classification. Accuracy of the model is simply an analysis of correct outcomes against all outputs combined. F1-score is applied to the precision and recall metrics, and it is their weighted harmonic mean. For imbalanced datasets with inconsistent blunder costs, the region under the ROC bend (AUC) metric was frequently utilized (cf. [10]) and portrayed as a more proper assessment procedure [7]. These were the most commonly used accuracy and prediction metrics for classification models.

In rundown, created ML models were regularly assessed utilizing total measurements like mean square error, area under the curve and accuracy metric [7]. The works portrayed various normal information modeling difficulties. Fundamentally, these incorporated the following: (I) troubles to vigorously gauge and name people groups' psychological well-being as a detailed, multi-layered and different idea from regularly loud or equivocal information, (ii) specialized difficulties in creating low-dimensional highlights that diminish (at first maybe more extravagant, various) information sources into few quantifiable classes appropriate for models, (iii) decisions in choosing models and subsequent training using algorithms, (iv) acknowledgment of requirements for "additional information" to expand model predictions and allow wider application and (v) to lessen risks of blunders, biases and inclinations.

3.6 Advent of deep learning in countering mental illness

Previous assessments and research have found proofs of psychiatric problems associated with neurology from the neuroimages obtained [11, 12]. Two normal kinds of neuroimage information broken down into emotional well-being are utilitarian attractive reverberation imaging (fMRI) and underlying MRI (sMRI) information. In the fMRI information, the cerebrum action is estimated by distinguishing proof of the progressions related to the bloodstream, in light of the way that blood flow from the cerebrum and neural initiation is grouped collectively [13]. In sMRI information, the neurological part of a mind is depicted dependent on the underlying surfaces, which present data as far as the spatial plans of voxel forces in 3D. As of late, DL innovations have been exhibited in investigating both fMRI and sMRI information [14]. Artificial neural networks are the basic building elements of a DL model. They work on a system based on gradient descent. Recurrent neural networks and CNNs all of which are improved and advanced forms of an artificial neural network, the basic structure of which is presented in Figure 3.4.

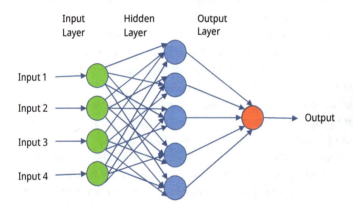

Figure 3.4: Structure of an artificial neural network.

Contingent upon the kinds of layers utilized, most neural networks can be extensively delegated convolutional neural networks (CNNs), multi-layer perceptron (MLPs) or RNNs. MLPs are forward propagating neural organizations comprising completely associated layers of perceptron. The term totally related shows that all neurons of a specific layer are related with all neurons in the subsequent following layers. Then again, the engineering of CNNs is rooted in the visual arrangement of well evolved creatures, following crafts by Hubel and Wiesel (1968) which has been custom-fitted to incorporate invariability in scaling, interpretation and twisting. CNNs are made out of multiple convolutional layers that draw attention on open fields, similar to image recognition neurons in the retina of human eye [3].

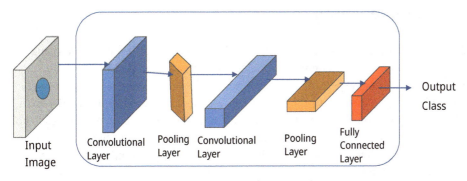

Figure 3.5: Architecture of a convolutional neural network [53].

The convolutional layers separate a chain of importance of highlights. To solve a classification or recognition task end to end, a couple of layers of a completely associated ANN (an MLP) or repetitive ANN are usually applied chained to multiple convolutional layers. At last, RNNs have intermittent associations that permit ANNs to use past yields notwithstanding current data sources. Current RNNs, like long short-term memory (LSTM), incorporate neurons that are shielded from immaterial bothers through entryways. Generally, these doors direct the peruse and compose admittance to a memory cell when another info shows up and permit a memory item to be reverted to original value when its substance becomes outdated. Along these lines, present-day RNNs can learn long haul conditions all the more without any problem [3].

One use of deep learning in sMRI and fMRI information is the ID of ADHD [14, 15]. To take in significant data from the obtained neural images, CNN and profound conviction organization (DBN) models were utilized. Specifically, the CNN-based models predominantly were used to recognize neighborhood dimensional examples and DBN models were used to acquire a profound progressive portrayal of the neuroimages. Various examples found among controls in the prefrontal cortex and ADHDs and cingulate cortex. Likewise, a few examinations dissected sMRIs to explore SZ [16], where autoencoder, DFNN and DBN were the applied practices.

These examinations revealed unusual examples of cortical areas and cortical–striatal–cerebellar circuit in the mind of those afflicted with SZ, particularly in separate cortices, parietal, transient and front facing, and in some subcortical districts, which includes the parts of brain, corpus callosum, the putamen and cerebellum. The utilization of deep learning in neuroimages is additionally designated at tending to other emotional wellness problems [17] put forward to utilize CNN and autoencoder to get significant highlights from the first run through series of fMRI information for foreseeing sorrow. Two investigations [18, 19] incorporated the sMRI and fMRI information modalities to foster prescient models for ASDs. Critical connections among sMRI and fMRI information were seen concerning ASD expectation [14].

3.7 Deep learning in depression

As an insignificant cost, smaller size and high transient objective sign comprising up to 200 or 300 channels, examination of electroencephalogram (EEG) information/data has gained gigantic respect for research on frontal cortex issues [20]. The one sort of streaming information that presents a high thickness and persistent qualities is the EEG signal, and it questions conventional component designing built techniques to acquire adequate data from crude EEG information to make precise expectations. To address this, as of late the DL models have been utilized to examine the crude EEG signal information [14].

Four articles evaluated and put forth to use DL in understanding mental health conditions reliant upon the assessment of EEG signals. The paper [21] utilized CNN to remove highlights from the EEG data signals. They tracked down that the EEG signals from the right half of the globe of human mind are more particular as far as the location of sorrow than those from the left side of the equator. The discoveries gave proof that downturn is related to a hyperactive right side of the equator. Paper [22] displayed the crude EEG flags by the DFNN to acquire data about human mind waves. They tracked down that the signs gathered from the focal (C3 and C4) districts are hardly higher contrasted and other mind areas that can be utilized to recognize the typical and discouraged subjects from the cerebrum wave signals. Paper [23] proposed a connected design of profound intermittent and 3D CNN to acquire EEG highlights across various errands [14].

They detailed that the DL model can catch the ghastly changes of EEG hemispheric lopsidedness to separate diverse mental responsibility viably [24] introduced a PC-supported recognition framework by extricating numerous kinds of data (e.g., ghastly, spatial and transient data) to perceive gentle discouragement dependent on CNN design. The creators tracked down that both ghostly and transient data of EEG are urgent for the forecast of despondency [14].

Presently we are analyzing an investigation of a suggested DL model. In this examination, two remarkable DL frameworks were exhibited. The essential model relied upon a "CNN" with one-dimensional input (1DCNN) while the resulting model utilized a blend of 1DCNN with "LSTM" model. The models expected that they got both the spatial and transient credits of the sign from the "EEG" data. In this assessment, the proposed DL structures relied upon fascinating mixes of several networks and were assessed on EEG data obtained during research and analysis. The 1DCNN can isolate transient parts viably. The suggested model blends structures outfit enormous execution as differentiated and the current deep models [25].

Figure 3.6 presents an outline of the suggested machine learning algorithm along with the calculation of the mathematical elaboration and execution metrics. According to the suggested algorithm, EEG data were divided with a window length of one second (256 samples). As the examining rate was 256 samples each second, every EEG portion contains 19 segments and 256 input variables (window length). It was

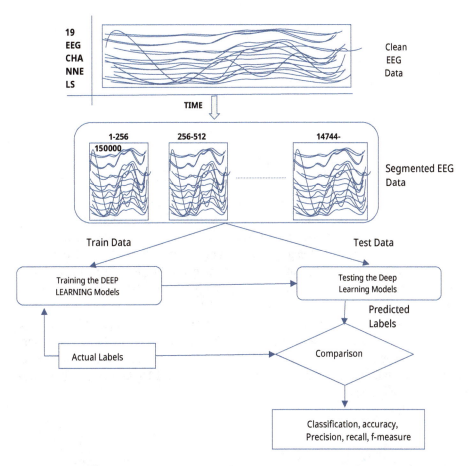

Figure 3.6: Deep learning model working to output.

seen that a gap of one second time gave the best outcomes. According to the classification perspective, the information data measurement was 256 × 19 for every moment of class for two EEG datasets (EO and EC). In addition, the information data were isolated into training and testing sets with an 80% and 20% proportion. The training data passed to the DL algorithms of depression and healthy state. The testing set was utilized to evaluate the presentation of the classifier utilizing different execution metrics (accuracy, exactness, F1-score and recall) [25].

DL engineering algorithm, Figure 3.7 depicts square stage portrayal of the proposed model. The model depended on a CNN with a single dimensional input. The model used an alternate number of convolutional and pooling layers with various channel sizes. During training, the suggested models both chose training cluster size and the combined total of ages were 50 for all batches. The proposed model has four convolutional layers utilizing 50 element maps with a similar channel size as the first

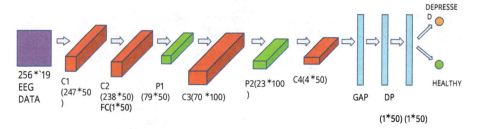

Figure 3.7: Proposed deep learning model for prediction.

convolutional layer. The lone third convolutional layer used 100 that includes maps with 10 × 1 channel sizes. Two sequential convolutional layers toward the beginning of the network and the following a different convolution and pooling layer have been proposed in this model. The global normal pooling that used to level the "neurons and dropout layer" has been utilized to stay away from overfitting and for better variation of the network at running data tests. This proposed model delivered fantastic outcomes for the classification of the EEG datasets [25].

Figure 3.8 shows the block portrayal of the suggested framework. This is a single dimension convolution neural network-LSTM because of the cascaded arrangement of different layers of 1D CNN and LSTM. The model has used an alternate number of "1D convolutional and pooling layers" with two embedded LSTM layers at the lower part of the model [25].

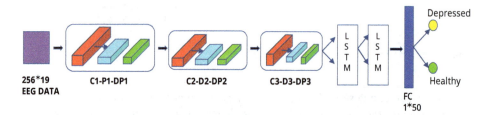

Figure 3.8: Applying long short-term memory to the proposed model.

3.8 Deep learning in schizophrenia

Our fundamental objective is to investigate the capability of DNN calculations for conveying elite models, and consequently we center around articles that utilize these models instead of conventional ML procedures to tackle SZ-related issues. By the way, we incorporate some unique uses of customary ML methods that could spur future examination [3].

Now we are analyzing a study of a proposed Going Deep into SZ with AI as experimented in [3]. To make it simpler for the user to find out about the expected universalizability of the outcomes detailed in the content, the model testing methods of the investigations were grouped into two general classifications, the in-conveyance testing and the out-of-circulation testing where each testing has two subcategories each, the autonomous testing and the non-free testing [26]. These classifications depend on the measurable connection the testing have between them (execution appraisal) and both the preparation (boundary change) and approval datasets (model determination) [3].

The "grouping of schizophrenias" is a profoundly convoluted issue at various levels. In any case, proof proposes that there isn't one entrancing causal way to SZ yet numerous, each one containing a few risk factors teaming up together. Next, SZ signs are not uniform between subjects hence incorporate basically all aspects of the brain, like communication (e.g., mental excursions and needing discourse), volition (e.g., avolition), discernment (e.g., working memory shortfalls), sentiments (e.g., dulled effect) and movement (e.g., control over nerves). At last, SZ being a mental problem that stresses the psyche, which is a multi-scale inconsistent framework at various stages (e.g., neighborhoods circuits, single neurons, huge scope utilitarian organizations, centers like the striatum and so on). Conventional statistical and ML techniques have failed to show and seat the information contained in this intricacy. During research significant learning approaches are now deficient to thoroughly show arrangements that provide an exceptional method to expect while improved understanding of SZ [3].

In fields like healthcare, in which choices include the prosperity of people, medical researchers and scientists might be hesitant to endow choices to applied algorithms without an unmistakable understanding of the measures or factors engaged with settling on those choices [27]. There is no simple method to make a deep neural network (DNN) straightforward without working on it in a manner that might think twice about execution (e.g., by utilizing fewer information factors and neurons). Nonetheless, there are numerous retrospectives applications pointed toward clarifying a DNN's yield after the yield has been created (for a survey, see [28]).

In the wake of preparing information (e.g., an ailing person's neural scan), after finish strategies permit analysts to figure out what factors among information (e.g., examination of MRI voxel) impacted the DNN's yield (e.g., subject-delegated SZ) the most. While these structures don't give thinking, legitimization or robotized clarification for a DNN's yield, by exhibiting principal data factors, these strategies are furnishing clinicians and researchers with the key development squares to push novel illustrative models and testable hypotheses. For a case in point, imagine a DNN arranged to ponder sets of pictures of consequences of the soil whether the two regular things are of a comparative sort. In the event that the DNN discovers that similar colored fruits can be various sorts, an after event technique would in all likelihood uncover that pixels arranged at the normal things' forms were especially appropriate for the yield. Thus, it becomes possible to gather an informative algorithm exhibiting similar structure instead of eclipsing is the main quality isolating pictures of similar colored different fruits. Considering everything, if the DNN finds that two different fruits of same color are distinguishable, a structure would in all likelihood uncover that the most important pixels were distributed inside regions of the normal things. Moreover, we could conjecture that the dominating instead of structure is the essential brand name isolating pictures of such regular things. Also, DNNs arranged in SZ grouping tasks can be utilized as surprising "amplifying instruments" to investigate the frameworks of SZ. For instance, a DNN organized to orchestrate two psychological circumstances utilizing multimodal cortex improvement data (like continuous EEG) are grilled to explain critical every factor (biomarker) is for depicting (isolating) the conditions. For the current situation, while the level of a data's pertinence in a neural network is possible to be understood comparably to the meaning of a backslide coefficient (β) in straight backslide, the connection among information sources and yield tended to by the size is totally divergent in the two cases: inconsistent and detailed multi scale coordinated effort of a neural network (deep) and direct with focal small scale trades in a backslide [3].

Notable strategies in the past incorporate component pertinence, which appraises the impact that changing every data point has on the neural network's yield, with function representation, which pictures highlights at the various stages of an organization ([29]). Further clarifications of DNN assumptions are achieved through strategies clearly appropriate for almost all prepared DNNs without including design changes or by techniques that fuse unique compositional plans into DNNs prior to preparing. The union of thought modules into a DNN configuration is an all-around utilized procedure in the last choice that grants clients to see the parts in the information that "got" a neural network's thought maximum if made a specific yield (e.g., a particular determination) [28, 30, 31]. One more procedure in the second assembling that is turning out to be progressively well known is the execution of generator run algorithms (e.g., significant conviction organizations), an extraordinary quality of DNN that, other than realizing particular elements belonging to different classes (e.g., unmistakable commencement designs in the fMRIs of SZ ailing individuals), figures out how to create engineered instances of different groups [32]. The assessment between engineered instances of various classes can be used to uncover class-express provisions [3].

A few examinations separating among SZ and sound controls have endeavored to recognize the information sources (for the most part mind regions) that were by and large pertinent for to reach a conclusion utilizing illustrative methodologies. While post hoc clarifications are steadily beginning to give innovative experiences into the components of SZ, unquestionably the commonly employed post hoc clarifications in SZ studies have critical limitations that may have subverted the nature of the data acquired with them. Enormous quantities of these hurdles can however be outperformed utilizing elective after process executions made in different spaces of exploration, for instance, picture affirmation and NLP [3].

Supposedly, the potential presented by post hoc examination strategies in subtyping SZ stays ignored. In order endeavors, the people from a class may have huge alterability in their characterizing attributes (e.g., methodology of record maintaining contraptions thus incorporate pictures of several time keeping instruments). Likewise, better executing prepared DNNs can appoint the very name to parts which might contain near nothing or nothing in like the way (like time keeping watches or instruments). While there might be no parts ordinary to all individuals from a class, subgroups of individuals from the class might be more homogeneous and propose numerous components (e.g., eight-formed shape shared by hourglass and circle-formed structure shared by pocket watches). For this situation, present hoc strategies applied on prepared DNN classifiers could uncover that the arrangement of elements that were by and large applicable to characterize a couple of people from a class (e.g., eight-formed form for hourglasses), is one of a kind comparable to the arrangement of elements used to group others from a similar class (e.g., round-molded shape with hands for pocket watches). By sorting out some way to allocate encapsulating term imprints to non-similar parts, DNN classification models could sort out some way to eliminate the courses of action of data factors that depict the different subgroups of individuals having a place with a class [3].

In light of SZ research, the examination of unparalleled DNN classifiers arranged on gigantic, different data groups can give detailed analysis sceptic sets of data factors (e.g., f-mri receptiveness designs) that could be utilized for improved analysis of rich whim stowing away under the general term of SZ. Domain of logical AI systems is a functioning space of examination, testing the possibility that DNNs are principal "secret components" and new techniques are being presented every year. A few difficulties stay, as current clarifications are now confined to featuring the wellsprings of data related to a particular yield. Consequently, they are inadequate to comprehend the astonishing information/yield connections shown by DNNs [33].

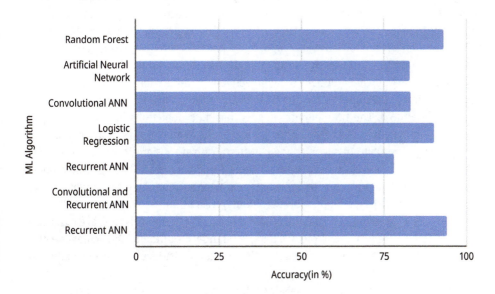

Figure 3.9: Accuracy in predicting schizophrenia using various models [54].

3.9 Assessing algorithms with validation and training data

To stay away from the overfitting issue [34], a 10-overlap cross-approval in preparing the profound learning calculation is applied [35]. The essential educational amendment was carelessly designated into 10 comparatively assessed data sets, and a solitary data subset was utilized as the endorsement set for testing the model prepared with different sub data sets. Similarly, cross endorsement to all of the five instructive assortments was applied autonomously; one of the five enlightening files was allotted as a test set, and the extra four were used for planning. The significant learning model was ready with four of five instructive lists in this endorsement, and for the test set, an overabundance enlightening file was used. For instance, the significant learning model organized ward on COBRE and NMorph illuminating records were evaluated for the ability to see SZ in the BrainGluSchi informational assortment. This framework empowered us to review whether the coordinated huge learning computation could portray crucial pictures got from SZ patients with various isolating cutoff points and scanner field qualities [36].

One anticipated that the approach to address this test is to diminish the scope of the data by including planning preceding dealing with information to the DL models. Feature extraction approaches can be used to get different kinds of features from the rough data. For instance, in this review, a couple of assessments have attempted to use preprocessing devices to isolate features from neuroimaging data. Of course, incorporate decision that is by and large used in customary machine learning models is similarly a choice to decrease data dimensionality. Regardless, the component assurance approaches are not oftentimes used in the DL application circumstance, as one of the regular credits of DL is the capacity to take in huge features from "each and every" open datum. The elective strategy to determine the issue of data inclination is to use move acknowledging where the objective is to additionally foster learning one more endeavor through the trading of data from an associated task that has viably been learned [37]. The fundamental idea is that data depictions learned in the past layers are more extensive, while those learned in the last layers are more unequivocal to the gauge task [38]. In specific, one can first pre-train a significant neural association in an enormous extension "source" dataset and then stack totally related layers on the most elevated place of the association and adjust it in the little "target" dataset in a standard backpropagation way. Commonly, tests in the "source" dataset are more extensive (e.g., general picture data), while those in the "target" dataset are expressed to the endeavor (e.g., clinical picture data). A standard outline of the achievement of move learning in the prosperity space is the dermatologist-level request of malignant skin cancer [39].

The creators presented Google's Inception v3 CNN engineering prepared beforehand more than 1.28 million general pictures and tweaked the medical picture dataset.

The model accomplished exceptionally elite consequences of skin malignancy grouping in epidermal (AUC = 0.96), melanocytic (AUC = 0.96) and melanocytic–thermoscopic pictures (AUC = 0.94). In look-based sorrow expectation [40], pre-prepared CNN on the public face acknowledgment dataset to display the static facial appearance, which defeats the issue that there is no look mark data. In Chao et al. [41], likewise pre-prepared CNN to encode look data. The exchange plan of both of the two examinations has been exhibited to have the option to further develop the expectation execution.

The DL estimation was instructed in regards to simply the name of every data video in this review ("schizophrenia" or "common"); furthermore, no other unequivocal bearings were given. In like manner, the significant learning computation perceived specific brain credits of SZ isolated during the readiness and used this information to arrange frontal cortex MR pictures. Regardless of the way that we utilized unique systems rather than careful cortical parcellation to isolate mind districts [42], these outcomes recommend that a huge learning assessment could be utilized to see explicit frontal cortex elements of SZ, upgrading the disclosures of past assessments [36].

Distinguishing SZ utilizing underlying MR pictures is unprecedented in the clinical settings. Analysis of SZ fundamentally relies upon the specialist's definite meeting with patients and his/her family and the utilization of precise demonstrative apparatuses [43]. The generally low execution of the clinicians in this investigation might have been on the grounds that they were not in the slightest degree acquainted with recognizing the infection through MR pictures. The clinical experts were well aware of many cortical elements of the frontal cortex in SZ, yet they were not correspondingly proficient contenders with the critical learning computation. The strategy of the records, in which pre-post cuts couldn't be straightforwardly examined which is conceivable in the "PACS framework"; moreover, it may have added to the trouble experienced by clinicians in certain characteristics of SZ. Thus, the frail building up the momentum of these seven clinical specialists would not be deciphered to recommend the normality of critical learning or AI computations to people in seeing "Schizophrenia" subject to fundamental MRI enlightening assortments. Late examinations in other clinical fields have taken a gander at individuals and AI computations [44] and proposed that for the best display of electronic thinking, extending human information is fundamental [36, 45].

There are a few hindrances to this assessment. All MRI information utilized in setting up the critical learning estimation had twofold names (SZ or conventional). This dichotomous social occasion is exhaustively utilized in assessments of electronic reasoning; anyhow, it may very well be a block in the application of this design in clinical practice. Well, most psychological instabilities makeover a consistent reach [46], and there are different diseases that can be used in comparison of patients. As our evaluation dismissed a clinical association group, further assessment including other psychological sicknesses, as bipolar reach and neurodegenerative issues, is required. Due to this deficit of clinical benchmark social affairs, it is hard to reason that the saw elements of SZ, that is, ordinary normal projection irregularities are explicit to SZ [36].

Besides, inside the instructive assortments, no specific information as for nuances of the infection was mentioned, which, for example, is the existence of positive and negative signs of SZ or the number of scenes. Consequently, it was dim whether the coordinated significant learning computation could detach reformist morphological changes in the patients suffering from SZ from the elements of sound commands [36].

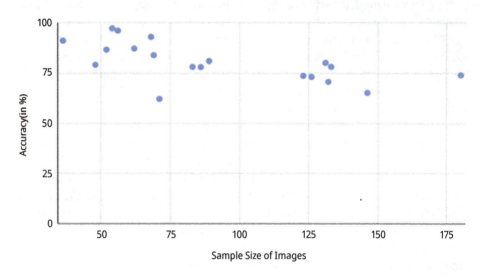

Figure 3.10: Trends in prediction accuracy with change in sample images [54].

Another important breakthrough is whether SZ can be dissected solely by essential highlights of the cerebrum. Not at all like different illnesses that can be precisely distinguished by photos [47], SZ is an infection joined by both primary and utilitarian irregularities. Late examinations have shown that practical MRI information and man-made consciousness procedures can likewise be utilized to dependably distinguish SZ [48]; consequently, consolidating underlying and useful highlights of cerebrum pictures would be relied upon to build the potential for clinical use [36].

There is another limitation which is that the space of interest was not shown in our regional assessment, wherein one of eight regions in get over portions was by and large impeded. A more point by point cortical parcellation which might be expected to exactly arrange with the regions that contributed the most to significant learning with locale recognized in past examinations using the voxel-based assessments. The clashing data quality inside the instructive assortment is another limitation [49]. For instance, "the NUSDAST and MCICShare educational files had MRI data accumulated using a 1.5T scanner, which has a lower signal-to-commotion extent and picture objective than data assembled using a 3T scanner." This mediocre quality educational assortment may have obfuscated the presentation of the computation. Finally, we observe that the results procured from seven clinicians don't propose that the limit of individuals to recognize SZ from MR pictures is lessened appeared differently in relation to that of significant learning computations. Careful interpretation of the results is needed considering the way that the clinical specialists in this examination were not experts in determining mental illnesses through MR pictures [36, 50].

3.10 Results of models

In the arrangement instructive record, the DL model was unrivaled in portraying the essential MRI data of SZ versus conventional subjects, having the AUC of 0.96. The general accuracy rate was 97%, deriving that among 866 pictures, 840 pictures were accumulated successfully. The likelihood of discretionarily picked pictures being assigned "Schizophrenia by chance was 51.2% (443 Schizophrenia and 423 standard pictures). The affectability of the calculation at the high-affectability working point was 96%, and the character at the high-expresses working point was 96%. The affectability and disposition at the ideal working point was 92% and 85%, freely. The mean picture power which has a range of 0 to 255, across all photos in the Schizophrenia pack was 52.52 (SD = 23.68), and that in the normal social occasion was 50.40 (SD = 22.57)." The determined backslide AI computation fail to organize SZ and customary subjects (chance level = 51.1%, accuracy rate = 51.2%) in these instructive assortments; thus, picture quality and power didn't impact the gathering execution [36, 51].

To test the presentation of the calculation across each preparation informational collection, we further assessed the characterization execution utilizing a different informational collection as the test set [52]. Profound learning accomplished the most noteworthy grouping execution when the MCICShare information collection was introduced as another information (AUC of 0.90) furthermore, showed the least exhibition in characterizing BrainGluSchi informational collection (AUC of 0.71). These outcomes recommend that the informational indexes gave inconsistent to characterizing the attributes of SZ; these BrainGluSchi informational collection may contain pivotal data for recognizing patients with SZ from ordinary subjects [36, 53].

The presentation of the critical learning estimation that perceived patients suffering with SZ was appropriately brought down in a totally new informational assortment (Uijeongbu St. Mary's) [54]. Right when the significant taking in estimation had one more commitment from the endorsement set comprising of 60 essential pictures that had hardly remarkable disease credits practically identical with the readiness sets, its insightful AUC regard dropped from 0.95 to 0.72. The precision speed of the huge learning estimation in the support illuminating rundown was 70.0%, which stood apart from a half possibility level. This revelation shows that the discerning force of the huge learning computation fundamentally diminished when it experienced MRI data by no means as old as data utilized for arranging [36, 55].

Table 3.1: Model approaches and applications [52].

Reference	Purpose	Machine learning application/approach	Mental health target
Chang [56]	Detecting symptoms/ condition	The progression of a programmed mental-health screen is subject to the human voice. Beginning development: making order of voice articulations for assessment of psychiatric prodrome.	Depression
Broek [57]	Detecting symptoms/ condition	A target comprehension of patients' emotional distress is required for the capable ministrations of PTSD.	PTSD
Salekin [58]	Detecting symptoms/ condition	To distinguish speakers high in depression symptoms or social phobia/anxiety that don't require broad gear or clinical preparing fairly and unassumingly.	Anxiety
Mitra [59]	Detecting symptoms/ condition	To help precise conclusion of depressive symptoms.	Depression
Frogner [60]	Detecting symptoms/ condition	To precisely recognize depression from exceptionally simple to acquire motor activity.	Depression
Mallol-Ragolta [61]	Detecting symptoms/ condition	To help unintrusive extents of PTSD symptom seriousness through the skin conductance responses, which reduces the prerequisite for self-report.	PTSD
Rabbi [62]	Detecting symptoms/ condition	To reliably screen a person's psychological health through mobile detecting that is negligible cost, straightforward, secure + guarantees protection.	Mental health (generic)
Gjoreski [63]	Detecting symptoms/ condition	To help condition and mental health self-administering by encouraging a stress-observation application as a component of a smartphone application.	Stress
DeMasi and Recht [64]	Detecting symptoms/ condition	To investigate if mental health can be interpreted from mobile phone social data and consequently followed over the long haul.	Depression
Zakaria [65]	Detecting symptoms/ condition	To non-intrusively and spontaneously identify indications of imprudent stress from smartphones without the prerequisite of the installation of an application.	Stress

Table 3.1 (continued)

Reference	Purpose	Machine learning application/approach	Mental health target
Zakaria [66]	Detecting symptoms/condition	To help with the early detection of stress and depression and rout the necessity for application use.	Multiple: stress + depression
Morshed [67]	Detecting symptoms/condition	To model states at scale so as to encourage a yielding strategy.	Mood
Wang [68]	Understanding mental health	To perform a detailed analysis of the effect of education systems in a student's mental health.	Mental health
Nosakhare and Picard [69]	Understanding mental health	Performing analysis based on in world metrics to develop tools to gauge general mental health.	Stress
Alam [70]	Understanding/predicting risks	Improving prediction accuracy of previously diagnosed mental health patients at risk of suicide	Suicide
Hirsch [71]	Improving treatment	Improving recommendations in order to develop as per the need of patients in recovery.	Substance abuse
Saha and De Choudhury [72]	Understanding mental health content	Analyze the effect of aftermaths of gun violence episodes in schools causing mental stress among students.	Stress
Park [73]	Understanding mental health content	Develop and improve far sighted online connectivity for patient treatment.	Multiple
Fatima [74]	Detecting symptoms/condition	Comprehending patient's test results to understand causes of depression and clustering it based on level of intensity.	Depression
Yazdavar [75]	Detecting symptoms/condition	To monitor clinical depressive manifestations in online media unobtrusively.	Depression
Chen [76]	Detecting symptoms/condition	To better monitor and distinguish between individuals with, or in danger of depression, from Twitter.	Depression
Pestian [77]	Understanding/predicting risks	To furnish emergency divisions with a proof-based danger appraisal apparatus for predicting rehashed suicide attempts.	Suicide

Table 3.1 (continued)

Reference	Purpose	Machine learning application/approach	Mental health target
Adamou [78]	Understanding/ predicting risks	To grow the accuracy of predictive model in ventures to give a gadget that could uphold clinical evaluation of self-destruction (suicide) risk.	Suicide
Wilbourne [79]	Improving treatment	To assess and improve on the quality of the reactions that Silby mentors give.	Mental health (generic)
Galiatsatos [80]	Understanding mental health	To more readily fathom such factors that impact emotional wellness and the mental health of the patients who have contemplations of death or self-destruction (suicide).	Depression
Feng [81]	Detecting symptoms/ condition	To more helpfully, productively and precisely recognize bipolar I and II assessment.	Bipolar
Patterson and Cloud [82]	Understanding/ predicting risks	To convey and develop systematic danger/risk evaluation decision support to coordinate intervention; costs of rehospitalization and diminishing rates.	Multiple
Tran [83]	Understanding/ predicting risks	To work on early detection of suicide and counteraction.	Suicide

The DNNs are prepared with multicenter essential MRI informational assortments showed high affectability and expresses in distinctive SZ. The DL computations separated SZ really well in one more MRI informational assortment got by a singular spot wherein the affliction credits of the patients were somewhat interesting. DL calculations prepared with huge enlightening assortments of various stages and severities of sicknesses could assist clinicians with isolating SZ from other dysfunctional behaviors and portray the particular fundamental and utilitarian credits of the brain in patients with SZ. The profound learning calculation relied mostly upon data from the right transient region in grouping SZ.

Ongoing years have seen the extending usage of DL estimations in clinical consideration, medical care and medication. In this examination, we investigated existing assessments on DL applications to consider psychological well-being results. All of the results open in the composing investigated in this work lay out the guarantee and materialism of DL in working on the treatment and conclusion of patients with psychological wellness conditions. Also, this study highlights different existing challenges in making DL computations clinically critical for routine thought, similarly as promising future headings in this field.

3.11 Challenges faced in application and prediction

Psychological medical problems like nervousness, misery and stress have become exceptionally normal among the majority. In this paper, forecasts of uneasiness, gloom and stress were made utilizing AI calculations. The recently referenced investigations have displayed that the use of DL systems in taking apart neuroimages can give evidence the extent that enthusiastic prosperity issues, which can be changed over into clinical practice and work with the finish of psychological prosperity sickness. Notwithstanding the way that an instinctual property of DL is the capacity to take in huge parts from crude pictures, highlight designing practices are required especially because of little dataset and high-dimensionality. DL models can profit from include designing methods and have been displayed to beat the customary ML models in the expectation of different conditions like melancholy, SZ and ADHD. In any case, such instruments extricate highlights depending on earlier information; thus, might preclude some data that is significant for mental result research however ever obscure yet.

3.12 Conclusions

Mental health has been a major concern for the medical domain researchers since it has been difficult to find patterns in patients which often escape the human eye. With rapid advancements in AI and image processing however, it seems that analyzing points of concern for a particular patient and using relevant algorithms to cluster such patients will enable better solutions and rapid results in assessing and treating mental health conditions. In this work we have reviewed methods implemented, work done previously and how with time it has been hyper tuned to meet the needs of ailing patients. Artificial neural networks play a major role not only in developing state of the art softwares but also providing us useful information about the data collected on these individuals which furthers research and thereby opens doors for problem-solving with medical research and technology in tandem. It is imperative to understand that with advancements in image and text recognition systems patterns will continue to emerge and with transfer learning and collaboration these works will go a long way in bringing solutions to mental illnesses. The research works reviewed in this chapter have at best reached improved accuracies and are not only a stepping stone toward a mentally fit and healthier future but also a ray of hope for research, analysis and development in coming times.

References

[1] Dattani, S., Ritchie, H. & Roser, M. (2021). Mental health. Published online at OurWorldInData.org. 1. https://ourworldindata.org/mental-health

[2] LeCun, Y., Bengio, Y. & Hinton, G. (2015). Deep learning. Nature, 521(7553), 436–444. https://doi.org/10.1038/nature14539.

[3] Cortes-Briones, J. A., Tapia-Rivas, N. I., Cyril D'Souza, D. & Estevez, P. A. (2021). Going deep into schizophrenia with artificial intelligence. Schizophrenia Research, 4–5, 9–11. https://www.sciencedirect.com/science/article/pii/S0920996421001791?via%3Dihub.

[4] Yazdavar, A. H., Al-Olimat, H. S., Ebrahimi, M., Bajaj, G., Banerjee, T., Thirunarayan, K., Pathak, J. & Sheth, A. (2017). Semi-supervised approach to monitoring clinical depressive symptoms in social media. Proceedings of the 2017 IEEE/ACM International Conference on Advances in Social Networks Analysis and Mining 2017 (ASONAM'17). Diesner J., Ferrari E. & Xu G. (Eds.), ACM, 1191–1198. https://doi.org/10.1145/3110025.3123028

[5] Ojeme, B. & Mbogho, A. (2016). Selecting learning algorithms for simultaneous identification of depression and comorbid disorders. Procedia Computer Science, 96, 1294–1303. https://doi.org/10.1016/j.procs.2016.08.174.

[6] Quisel, T., Lee, W.-N. & Foschini, L. (2017). Observation time vs. performance in digital phenotyping. Proceedings of the 1st Workshop on Digital Biomarkers (DigitalBiomarkers'17). ACM, 33–36. https://doi.org/10.1145/3089341.3089347]

[7] Thieme, A., Belgrave, D. & Doherty, G. (2020). Machine learning in mental health: A systematic review of the HCI literature to support the development of effective and implementable ML systems. ACM Transactions on Computer-Human Interaction, 27(5), 38–40. https://doi.org/10.1145/3398069.

[8] Griffiths, T. L. & Steyvers, M. (2004). Finding scientific topics. Proceedings of the National academy of Sciences, 101(1), 5228–5235. https://doi.org/10.1073/pnas.0307752101.

[9] Yang, H. & Bath, P. A. (2019). Automatic prediction of depression in older age. Proceedings of the 3rd International Conference on Medical and Health Informatics 2019 (ICMHI'19). ACM, 36–44. https://doi.org/10.1145/3340037.3340042

[10] Kiranmai Ernala, S., Birnbaum, M. L., Candan, K. A., Rizvi, A. F., Sterling, W. A., Kane, J. M. & De Choudhury, M. (2019). Methodological gaps in predicting mental health states from social media: Triangulating diagnostic signals. Proceedings of the 2019 CHI Conference on Human Factors in Computing Systems (CHI'19). ACM, Paper 134, 16. https://doi.org/10.1145/3290605.3300364

[11] Schnack, H. G., Nieuwenhuis, M., Van haren, N. E. M., Abramovic, L., Scheewe, T. W., Brouwer, R. M., Hulshoff Pol, H. E. & Kahn, R. S. (2014). Can structural MRI aid in clinical classification? A machine learning study in two independent samples of patients with schizophrenia, bipolar disorder and healthy subjects. NeuroImage, 84, 299–306. https://doi.org/10.1016/j.neuroimage.2013.08.053.

[12] O'Toole, A. J., Jiang, F., Abdi, H., Pénard, N., Dunlop, J. P. & Parent, M. A. (2007). Theoretical, statistical, and practical perspectives on pattern-based classification approaches to the analysis of functional neuroimaging data. Journal of Cognitive Neuroscience, 19, 1735–1752. https://doi.org/10.1162/jocn.2007.19.11.1735.

[13] Logothetis Nikos, K., Jon, P. & Mark, A. (2001). Trinath Torsten, Oeltermann Axel, Neurophysiological investigation of the basis of the fMRI signal. Nature, 412, 150. https://doi.org/10.1038/35084005.

[14] Chang, S., Zhenxing, X., Jyotishman, P. & Fei, W. (2020). Deep learning in mental health outcome research: A scoping review. Transl Psychiat, 4–5. https://doi.org/10.1038/s41398-020-0780-3.

[15] Kuang, D. & He, L. (2014). Classification on ADHD with Deep Learning International Conference on Cloud Computing and Big Data. 27–32. https://ieeexplore.ieee.org/abstract/document/7062868

[16] Zeng, L.-L., Wang, H., Hu, P., Yang, B., Pu, W., Shen, H., Chen, X., Liu, Z., Yin, H., Tan, Q., Wang, K. & Hu, D. (2018). Multi-site diagnostic classification of schizophrenia using discriminant deep learning with functional connectivity MRI. EBioMedicine, 30, 74–85. https://doi.org/10.1016/j.ebiom.2018.03.017.

[17] Xiang-Fei, G. E. N. G. & Jun-Hai, X. U. (2017). Application of autoencoder in depression diagnosis, DEStech Transactions on Computer Science and Engineering, https://www.dpi-proceedings.com/index.php/dtcse/article/view/17335/16839

[18] Bhaskar, S., Borle Neil, C., Russell, G. & Brown Matthew, R. G. (2018). A general prediction model for the detection of ADHD and Autism using structural and functional MRI. PLoS One, 13, e0194856. https://doi.org/10.1371/journal.pone.0194856.

[19] Aghdam, M. A., Sharifi, A. & Pedram, M. M. (2018). Combination of rs-fMRI and sMRI data to discriminate autism spectrum disorders in young children using deep belief networks. Journal of Digital Imaging, 31, 895–903. https://doi.org/10.1007/s10278-018-0093-8.

[20] Herrmann, C. S. & Demiralp, T. (2005). Human EEG gamma oscillations in neuropsychiatric disorders. Clinical Neurophysiology, 116, 2719–2733. https://doi.org/10.1016/j.clinph.2005.07.007.

[21] Rajendra Acharya, U., Oh, S. L., Hagiwara, Y., Hong Tan, J., Adeli, H. & Subha, D. P. (2018). Automated EEG-based screening of depression using deep convolutional neural network. Computer Methods and Programs in Biomedicine, 161, 103–113. https://doi.org/10.1016/j.cmpb.2018.04.012.

[22] Mohan, Y., Chee, S. S., Xin, D. K. P. & Foong, L. P. (2016). Artificial neural network for classification of depressive and normal. EEG Proc. 2016 IEEE EMBS Conference on Biomedical Engineering and Sciences 286–290.

[23] Zhang, P., Wang, X., Zhang, W. & Chen, J. (2019). Learning spatial–spectral–temporal EEG features with recurrent 3D convolutional neural networks for cross-task mental workload assessment. IEEE Transactions on Neural Systems and Rehabilitation Engineering, 27, 31–42. https://doi.org/10.1109/TNSRE.2018.2884641.

[24] Li, X., La, R., Wang, Y., Niu, J., Zeng, S., Sun, S. & Zhu, J. (2019). EEG-based mild depression recognition using convolutional neural networks. Medical & Biological Engineering & Computing, 47, 1341–1352.

[25] Mumtaz, W. & Qayyum, A. (2019). A deep learning framework for automatic diagnosis of unipolar depression. International Journal of Medical Informatics, 132, 2–3. https://doi.org/10.1016/j.ijmedinf.2019.103983.

[26] Damien, T., Kafle, K., Shrestha, R., Abbasnejad, E., Kanan, C. & Van den hengel, A. (2020). On the value of out-of-distribution testing: An example of goodhart's law. https://arxiv.org/abs/2005.09241v1

[27] Lipton, Z. C. (2018). The mythos of model interpretability: In machine learning, the concept of interpretability is both important and slippery. Queue, 16(3), 31–57. https://doi.org/10.1145/3236386.3241340.

[28] Arrieta, A. B. & D'iaz-rodr'iguez, N. (2020). Explainable Artificial Intelligence (XAI): Concepts, taxonomies, opportunities and challenges toward responsible AI. Information Fusion, 58, 82–115.

[29] Chris, O., Alexander, M. & Ludwig, S. (2017). Feature visualization: How neural networks build up their understanding of images. Distillation, 2(11). https://doi.org/10.23915/distill.00007.

[30] Bahdanau, D., Cho, K. & Bengio, Y. (2014). Neural Machine Translation by Jointly Learning to Align and Translate. https://arxiv.org/abs/1409.0473

[31] Xu, K., Ba, J., Kiros, R., Cho, K., Courville, A., Salakhudinov, R., Zemel, R. & Show, B. Y. (2015). Attend and tell: Neural image caption generation with visual attention. International Conference on Machine Learning, 2048–2057.

[32] Jungang, X., Hui, L. & Shilong, Z. (2015). An overview of deep generative models. IETE Technical Review, 32(2), 131–139. https://doi.org/10.1080/02564602.2014.987328.

[33] Darwiche, A. (2018). Human-level intelligence or animal-like abilities?, Commun. ACM, 61(10), 56–67. https://doi.org/10.1145/3271625.

[34] Srivastava, N., Hinton, G., Krizhevsky, A., Sutskever, I. & Salakhutdinov, R. (2014). Dropout: A simple way to prevent neural networks from overfitting. The Journal of Machine Learning Research, 15, 1929–1958.

[35] Kohavi, R. (1995). A study of cross-validation and bootstrap for accuracy estimation and model selection. InIjcai.

[36] Jihoon, O., Baek-Lok, O., Kyong-Uk, L., Jeong-Ho, C. & Kyongsi, Y. (2020). Identifying Schizophrenia using structural MRI With a Deep Learning algorithm. Frontiers in Psychiatry, 4, 6–8. https://www.frontiersin.org/article/10.3389/fpsyt.2020.00016.

[37] Torrey, L. & Shavlik, J. (2010). Handbook of Research on Machine Learning Applications and Trends: Algorithms, Methods, and Techniques.

[38] Yosinski, J., Clune, J., Bengio, Y. & Lipson, H. (2014). How transferable are features in deep neural networks? Proc. Advances in Neural Information Processing Systems, Montreal, Canada, 3320–3328. https://arxiv.org/abs/1411.1792

[39] Andre, E., Brett, K., Novoa Roberto, A., Justin, K., Swetter Susan, M., Blau Helen, M. & Sebastian, T. (2017). Dermatologist-level classification of skin cancer with deep neural networks. Nature, 542, 115. https://doi.org/10.1038/nature21056.

[40] Zhu, Y., Shang, Y., Shao, Z. & Guo, G. (2018). Automated depression diagnosis based on deep networks to encode facial appearance and dynamics. IEEE Transactions on Affective Computing, 9, 578–584. https://doi.org/10.1109/TAFFC.2017.2650899.

[41] Chao, L., Tao, J., Yang, M. & Li, Y. (2015). Multi task sequence learning for depression scale prediction from video. International Conference on Affective Computing and Intelligent Interaction (ACII). 526–531. https://doi.org/10.1109/ACII.2015.7344620

[42] Fischl, B., Van der kouwe, A., Destrieux, C., Halgren, E., Ségonne, F., Salat, D. H., Busa, E., Seidman, L. J., Goldstein, J., Kennedy, D., Caviness, V., Makris, N., Rosen, B. & Dale, A. M. (2004). Automatically parcellating the human cerebral cortex, cerebral cortex, 14, 11–22. https://doi.org/10.1093/cercor/bhg087.

[43] American Psychiatric Association (2000). Diagnostic and Statistical Manual of Mental Disorders, 4th Ed. Text Rev American Psychiatric Association, Washington, DC.

[44] Graham, B. (2015). Kaggle diabetic retinopathy detection competition report. University of Warwick. https://www.kaggle.com/c/diabetic%0A-retinopathy-detection

[45] Stead, W. W. (2018). Clinical implications and challenges of artificial intelligence and deep learning. JAMA, 320(11), 1107–1108. https://doi.org/10.1001/jama.2018.11029.

[46] Keshavan, M. S., Morris, D. W., Sweeney, J. A., Pearlson, G., Thaker, G., Seidman, L. J., Eack, S. M. & Tamminga, C. (2011). A dimensional approach to the psychosis spectrum between bipolar disorder and schizophrenia: The Schizo-Bipolar Scale. Schizophrenia Research, 133, 250–254. https://doi.org/10.1016/j.schres.2011.09.005.

[47] Varun, G., Lily, P., Marc, C., Stumpe Martin, C., Derek, W., Arunachalam, N., Subhashini, V., Kasumi, W., Tom, M., Jorge, C., Ramasamy, K., Rajiv, R., Nelson Philip, C., Mega Jessica, L. & Webster Dale, R. (2016). Development and validation of a deep learning algorithm for detection of diabetic retinopathy in retinal fundus photographs. JAMA, 316, 2402–2410. https://doi.org/10.1001/jama.2016.17216.

[48] Zeng, L.-L., Wang, H., Hu, P., Yang, B., Pu, W., Shen, H., Chen, X., Liu, Z., Yin, H., Tan, Q., Wang, K. & Hu, D. (2018). Multi-site diagnostic classification of Schizophrenia using discriminant deep learning with functional connectivity MRI. EBioMedicine, 30, 74–85. https://doi.org/10.1016/j.ebiom.2018.03.017.

[49] Mishra, S., Mishra, B. K. & Tripathy, H. K. (2015, December). A neuro-genetic model to predict hepatitis disease risk. In 2015 IEEE International Conference on Computational Intelligence and Computing Research (ICCIC) (pp. 1–3). IEEE.

[50] Tripathy, H. K., Mishra, S., Thakkar, H. K. & Rai, D. (2021). CARE: A collision-aware mobile robot navigation in grid environment using improved breadth first search. Computers and Electrical Engineering, 94, 107327.

[51] Mishra, S., Dash, A. & Mishra, B. K. (2020). An insight of Internet of Things applications in pharmaceutical domain. In Emergence of Pharmaceutical Industry Growth with Industrial IoT Approach. Academic Press, 245–273.

[52] Mishra, S., Thakkar, H., Mallick, P. K., Tiwari, P. & Alamri, A. (2021). A sustainable IoHT based computationally intelligent healthcare monitoring system for lung cancer risk detection. Sustainable Cities and Society, 103079.
[53] Ray, C., Tripathy, H. K. & Mishra, S. (2019). A review on facial expression based behavioral analysis using computational technique for autistic disorder patients. In Singh M., Gupta P., Tyagi V., Flusser J., Ören T. & Kashyap R. ((eds.)). Advances in Computing and Data Sciences. ICACDS 2019. Communications in Computer and Information Science, Vol. 1046. Springer, Singapore. https://doi.org/10.1007/978-981-13-9942-8_43.
[54] Mishra, S., Thakkar, H., Mallick, P. K., Tiwari, P. & Alamri, A. (2021). A sustainable IoHT based computationally intelligent healthcare monitoring system for lung cancer risk detection. Sustainable Cities and Society, 103079.
[55] Tripathy, H. K., Mallick, P. K. & Mishra, S. (2021). Application and evaluation of classification model to detect autistic spectrum disorders in children. International Journal of Computer Applications in Technology, 65(4), 368–377.
[56] Chang, K.-H., Chan, M. K. & Canny, J. (2011). Analyze This: Unobtrusive mental health monitoring by voice. In Proceedings of the CHI'11 Extended Abstracts on Human Factors in Computing Systems (CHI EA'11). ACM, 1951–1956. https://doi.org/10.1145/1979742.1979859
[57] Broek, E. L., Sluis, F. & Dijkstra, T. (2013). Cross-validation of bimodal health-related stress assessment. Personal Ubiquitous Computing, 17(2), 215–227. http://dx.doi.org/10.1007/s00779-011-0468-z.
[58] Salekin, A., Eberle, J. W., Glenn, J. J., Teachman, B. A. & Stankovic, J. A. (2018). A weakly supervised learning framework for detecting social anxiety and depression. Proceedings of the ACM on Interactive Mobile Wearable Ubiquitous Technology, 2(2), 26. https://doi.org/10.1145/3214284.
[59] Mitra, V., Shriberg, E., McLaren, M., Kathol, A., Richey, C., Vergyri, D. & Graciarena, M. (2014). The SRI AVEC-2014 evaluation system. Proceedings of the 4th International Workshop on Audio/Visual Emotion Challenge (AVEC'14). ACM, 93–101. https://doi.org/10.1145/2661806.2661818
[60] Ihle Frogner, J., Majeed Noori, F., Halvorsen, P., Alexander Hicks, S., Garcia-Ceja, E., Torresen, J. & Alexander Riegler, M. (2019). One-dimensional convolutional neural networks on motor activity measurements in detection of depression. Proceedings of the 4th International Workshop on Multimedia for Personal Health & Health Care (HealthMedia'19). ACM, 9–15. https://doi.org/10.1145/3347444.3356238
[61] Mallol-Ragolta, A., Dhamija, S. & Boult, T. E. (2018). A multimodal approach for predicting changes in PTSD symptom severity. Proceedings of the 20th ACM International Conference on Multimodal Interaction (ICMI'18). ACM, 324–333. https://doi.org/10.1145/3242969.3242981
[62] Rabbi, M., Ali, S., Choudhury, T. & Berke, E. (2011). Passive and in-situ assessment of mental and physical well-being using mobile sensors. Proceedings of the 13th international conference on Ubiquitous computing (UbiComp'11). ACM, 385–394. https://doi.org/10.1145/2030112.2030164
[63] Gjoreski, M., Gjoreski, H., Luštrek, M. & Gams, M. (2016). Continuous stress detection using a wrist device: In laboratory and real life. Proceedings of the 2016 ACM International Joint Conference on Pervasive and Ubiquitous Computing: AdjunctAdjunct (UbiComp'16). 1185–1193. https://doi.org/10.1145/2968219.2968306
[64] DeMasi, O. & Recht, B. (2017). A step towards quantifying when an algorithm can and cannot predict an individual's wellbeing. Proceedings of the 2017 ACM International Joint Conference on Pervasive and Ubiquitous Computing and Proceedings of the 2017 ACM International Symposium on Wearable Computers. 763–771. https://doi.org/10.1145/3123024.3125609
[65] Zakaria, C., Lee, Y. & Balan, R. (2019). Passive detection of perceived stress using location-driven sensing technologies at scale (demo). Proceedings of the 17th Annual International Conference on Mobile Systems, Applications, and Services (MobiSys'19). ACM, 667–668. https://doi.org/10.1145/3307334.3328574

[66] Zakaria, C., Balan, R. & Lee, Y. (November, 2019). StressMon: Scalable detection of perceived stress and depression using passive sensing of changes in work routines and group interactions. Proceedings of the ACM on Human-Computer Interaction 3, CSCW, Article 37, 29. https://doi.org/10.1145/3359139

[67] Bin Morshed, M., Saha, K., Li, R., D'Mello, S. K., De Choudhury, M., Abowd, G. D. & Plötz, T. (2019). Prediction of mood instability with passive sensing. Proceedings of the ACM on Interactive, Mobile, Wearable and Ubiquitous Technologies, 3(3), 21. https://doi.org/10.1145/3351233.

[68] Wang, R., Chen, F., Chen, Z., Li, T., Harari, G., Tignor, S., Zhou, X., Ben-Zeev, D. & Campbell, A. T. (2014). StudentLife: Assessing mental health, academic performance and behavioral trends of college students using smartphones. Proceedings of the 2014 ACM International Joint Conference on Pervasive and Ubiquitous Computing (UbiComp'14). ACM, 3–14. https://doi.org/10.1145/2632048.2632054

[69] Nosakhare, E. & Picard, R. (2019). Probabilistic latent variable modeling for assessing behavioral influences on well-being. Proceedings of the 25th ACM SIGKDD International Conference on Knowledge Discovery & Data Mining (KDD'19). ACM, 2718–2726. https://doi.org/10.1145/3292500.3330738

[70] Alam, M. G. R., Jun Cho, E., Huh, E.-N. & Seon Hong, C. (2014). Cloud based mental state monitoring system for suicide risk reconnaissance using wearable bio-sensors. Proceedings of the 8th International Conference on Ubiquitous Information Management and Communication (ICUIMC'14). ACM, Paper 56, 6. https://doi.org/10.1145/2557977.2558020

[71] Hirsch, T., Merced, K., Narayanan, S., Imel, Z. E. & Atkins, D. C. (2017). Designing contestability: Interaction design, machine learning, and mental health. Proceedings of the 2017 Conference on Designing Interactive Systems (DIS'17). ACM, 95–99. https://doi.org/10.1145/3064663.3064703

[72] Saha, K. & De Choudhury, M. (2017). Modeling stress with social media around incidents of gun violence on college campuses. Proceedings of the ACM on Human-Computer Interaction 1, CSCW, Article 92 27. https://doi.org/10.1145/3134727

[73] Park, A., Conway, M. & Chen, A. T. (2018). Examining thematic similarity, difference, and membership in three online mental health communities from Reddit: A text mining and visualization approach. Computers in Human Behavior, 78, 98–112. https://doi.org/10.1016/j.chb.2017.09.001.

[74] Fatima, I., Mukhtar, H., Farooq Ahmad, H. & Rajpoot, K. (2018). Analysis of user-generated content from online social communities to characterise and predict depression degree. Journal of Information Science, 44(5), 683–695. https://doi.org/10.1177/0165551517740835.

[75] Hossein Yazdavar, A., Al-Olimat, H. S., Ebrahimi, M., Bajaj, G., Banerjee, T., Thirunarayan, K., Pathak, J. & Sheth, A. (2017). Semi-supervised approach to monitoring clinical depressive symptoms in social media. Proceedings of the 2017 IEEE/ACM International Conference on Advances in Social Networks Analysis and Mining 2017 (ASONAM'17). Diesner J., Ferrari E. & Xu G. (Eds.), ACM, 1191–1198. https://doi.org/10.1145/3110025.3123028

[76] Chen, X., Sykora, M. D., Jackson, T. W. & Elayan, S. (2018). What about mood swings: Identifying depression on twitter with temporal measures of emotions. Proceedings of the Companion the Web Conference 2018 (WWW'18), 1653–1660. https://doi.org/10.1145/3184558.3191624

[77] Pestian, J. P., Matykiewicz, P. & Grupp-Phelan, J. (2008). Using natural language processing to classify suicide notes. Proceedings of the Workshop on Current Trends in Biomedical Natural Language Processing (BioNLP'08). ACM, Stroudsburg, PA, 96–97.

[78] Adamou, M., Antoniou, G., Greasidou, E., Lagani, V., Charonyktakis, P. & Tsamardinos, I. (2018). Mining free-text medical notes for suicide risk assessment. Proceedings of the 10th Hellenic Conference on Artificial Intelligence (SETN'18). ACM, Paper 47, 8. https://doi.org/10.1145/3200947.3201020

[79] Wilbourne, P., Dexter, G. & Shoup, D. (2018). Research driven: Sibly and the transformation of mental health and wellness. Proceedings of the 12th EAI International Conference on Pervasive

Computing Technologies for Healthcare (PervasiveHealth'18). ACM, 389–391. https://doi.org/10.1145/3240925.3240932]
[80] Galiatsatos, D., Konstantopoulou, G., Anastassopoulos, G., Nerantzaki, M., Assimakopoulos, K. & Lymberopoulos, D. (2015). Classification of the most significant psychological symptoms in mental patients with depression using bayesian network. Proceedings of the 16th International Conference on Engineering Applications of Neural Networks (INNS) (EANN'15). Iliadis L. & Jane C. (Eds.), ACM, Paper 15, 8. https://doi.org/10.1145/2797143.2797159
[81] Feng, C., Gao, H., Ling, X. B., Ji, J. & Ma, Y. (2018). Shorten bipolarity checklist for the differentiation of subtypes of bipolar disorder using machine learning. Proceedings of the 2018 6th International Conference on Bioinformatics and Computational Biology (ICBCB'18). ACM, 162–166. https://doi.org/10.1145/3194480.3194508
[82] Patterson, D. A. & Cloud, R. N. (2000). The application of artificial neural networks for outcome prediction in a cohort of severely mentally ill outpatients. Journal of Technology and Human Services, 16(2/3), 47–61. http://dx.doi.org/10.1300/J017v16n02_05.
[83] Tran, T., Phung, D., Luo, W., Harvey, R., Berk, M. & Venkatesh, S. (2013). An integrated framework for suicide risk prediction. Proceedings of the 19th ACM SIGKDD International Conference on Knowledge Discovery and Data Mining (KDD'13). Ghani R., Senator T. E., Bradley P., Parekh R. & He J. (Eds.), ACM, 1410–1418. https://doi.org/10.1145/2487575.2488196

S. Visalakshi
4 COVID-19 case analysis and prediction using regression models

Abstract: In both humans and animals, coronaviruses will be the source of sickness. There are seven main types of viruses that can be detected in humans, including the SARS, MERS and COVID-19 epidemics. In December 2019, the virus is transmitted for the first time in the Chinese city of Wuhan. The requirement for adequate screening of SARS-CoV2 allows for the fast and effective diagnosis of COVID-19 and, as a result, reduces the load on the healthcare system. For this study, the most recent COVID-19 India state-by-state data is used to examine the COVID condition that exists in India. The primary goal of this study is to use five different regression models to estimate the death rate owing to infection. The regression model contributes to the achievement of a high-accuracy prediction rate. This inquiry intends to apply regression models to the COVID-19 dataset to determine which model performs better when it comes to forecasting the number of patients that have died. Extra tree regression, decision tree regression, gradient boosting regression, random forest regression and AdaBoost regression are some of the models that were used in this investigation. For predicting the accurate death rate, these regression models are evaluated using a variety of error metrics, including mean absolute error (MAE), mean square error (MSE), R^2 score, root mean square error (RMSE), root mean squared logarithmic error (RMSLE) and mean absolute percentage error (MAPE). Whenever any one of the models produces the least value of RMSE, RMSLE, R^2 or MAE, that model outperforms the prediction. Experimentation has revealed that the extra tree regression resulting in the least significant differences in metrics such as RMSE is 7,392.12, RMSLE is 0.5952, R^2 is 0.5385 and MAE metric has a value of 4,568.58, which is the minimum value. As a result, the extra tree regressor improves the accuracy of the prediction of the death rate in the COVID-19 dataset.

Keywords: COVID-19, mortality, extra tree regressor, decision tree regressor gradient boosting regressor, random forest regressor, AdaBoost regressor

4.1 Introduction

China's Wuhan province has been infected with the COVID-19 virus, wh ich was spread by faunae and has been feasting everywhere since December 2019 [1]. This

---

S. Visalakshi, Department of Computer Applications, Sikkim Manipal Institute of Technology, Sikkim Manipal University, Majitar, Sikkim, India, e-mail: visaraji@gmail.com

https://doi.org/10.1515/9783110750942-004

virus can spread easily through the air and by direct contact with an infected individual [2]. When a virus enters a humanoid, it will target the lungs and respiratory system, where it will multiply [3]. COVID-19 is composed of ribonucleic acid (RNA), and because of its mutational properties, it is extremely difficult to identify and cure [4]. COVID-19 symptoms include infection, coughing, fast breathing, shakiness, discomfort and sinew pain (cold viral infection). The sickness is exceedingly deadly and has the ability to kill people in a short period of time [5]. Even now, studies are being carried out to discover the most effective treatment for corona. In numerous nations, including the United States, Spain, Italy, China, the United Kingdom, Iran and others, this syndrome is the leading cause of mortality. The most recent global number of people affected is depicted in Figure 4.1. This virus must be detected as soon as possible because it is particularly hazardous in its early stages. A collection of medical imaging, a complete blood count (CBC) and a polymerase chain reaction (PCR) have all been offered as ways to diagnose COVID-19 (PCR). Only the reverse-transcription polymerase chain reaction (RTPCR) [1] can be performed to confirm corona disease diagnosis, according to the World Health Organization. RTPCR testing, on the other hand, will take a long time and may be dangerous for COVID-19 patients. As a result, medical imaging is performed first for the initial detection of COVID-19, and then the RTPCR test is finished for the final and correct detection of the virus. For the diagnosis of COVID-19, two types of medical imaging are used: X-rays and computed tomography [4, 6]. Machine learning (ML) has been shown to be a superior field of research for handling complicated and difficult real-world application issues in areas such as healthcare, autonomous vehicles (AV), business applications, natural language processing (NLP), smart robotics, games and weather forecasting. Learning this algorithm is often accomplished through trial and error, in contrast to traditional algorithms, which follow software design commands based on decision instructions such as if-else [7] and other decision instructions. Prediction [8], in which a range of ML methods are used to regulate the path of a section, is one of the most essential components of ML and is required in various application fields like as weather forecasting, disease prediction and stock market forecasting [15].

Several neural network and regression models have been developed for broad application in projecting the future status of patients [9]. To forecast diseases such as breast cancer, coronary artery disease [10] and cardiovascular disease, many studies have been carried out utilizing ML approaches. This study [11] focuses on confirmed cases, whereas the previous study [12] focused on the prediction of the COVID-19 outbreak and the implementation of an early response. This approach is extremely useful in making judgments, understanding how to interact with the current situation, guiding early action and treating these terrible diseases in a highly effective manner [13].

According to the findings of the literature research, a variety of ML algorithms are used to produce predictions based on patterns or rules found in the input data. The linear regression technique facilitates the prediction of the output for a certain dataset. Regression analysis is frequently used in forecasting the price of the house,

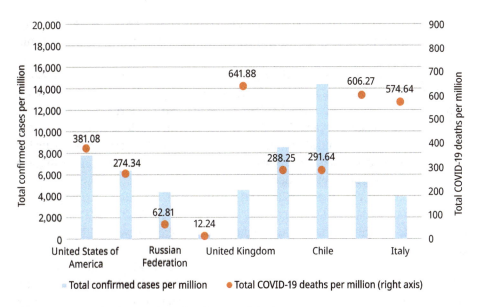

Figure 4.1: International comparison of total cases and death rate.
(*Source:* https://www.brookings.edu/blog/future-development/2020/07/02/how-well-is-india-responding-to-covid-19/) [24]

the stock market and even the compensation of an employee. This technique also attempts to uncover the link between a dependent on multiple independent variables by examining the data. As a result, various regression models are utilized for this study to see which one is the most accurate at predicting sickness development. The rest of the work is divided into five portions: Section 3.2 discusses about the literature review; Section 3.3 has labels describing the materials and construction procedures of the models; Section 3.4 of the research paper analyses the findings; and Section 3.5 of the research paper concludes the paper.

4.2 Literature reviews

The year 2020 has become a disastrous year for human. The coronavirus is found all around the world. Since January 2020, India has been experiencing an outbreak of COVID-19. From January 2020 to November 2020, we don't know how to handle this virus. WHO come out with few antibodies at the end of 2020. Many physicians and researchers have begun to construct a variety of frameworks for detecting and predicting using ML algorithms.

In [19], this study, predicting and forecasting the COVID-19 outbreak by using ML approach. Here they have taken dataset from March 12 to October 31, 2020 on a day-by-day basis. Uses linear regression, polynomial regression, ridge regression, polynomial ridge regression and support vector regression models are used. Based on the metric, the authors concluded that the performance of polynomial gives better result than linear regression.

For predicting the growth in the number of infected, recovered and death cases, this study recommends ML algorithms such as linear regression, polynomial regression, ridge regression, polynomial ridge regression and support vector regression model [20]. The model is evaluated using multiple metrics such as MSE, MAE, RMSE and R^2 score. They determined that polynomial ridge is the best model for predicting confirmed cases, linear model for recovered cases and SVM regression for death cases based on the results of the evaluation.

In [21], an overview of AI applications, as well as ML and deep learning (DL), is presented in the context of COVID-19. Using keywords like AI, COVID-19, ML, predicting, DL, X-ray and computed tomography 440 publications were reviewed. Different ML regression methods were used first to predict the number of confirmed and death cases, then a comprehensive survey was conducted to classify COVID-19 patients, and finally, different medical imaging datasets were compared in terms of total number of images, number of positive samples and number of classes available in datasets as part of their review. Pre-processing, segmentation and feature extraction are all steps in the diagnosis process. Generative adversial network (GAN), extreme learning machine (ELM), long/short-term memory (LSTM), support vector machine (SVM), linear and logistic regression, ensemble eXtreme gradient boosting (XGBoost) and other ML and DL techniques are used to detect and predict. According to the results of the experiment, the residual neural network (ResNet-18) and densely connected convolutional network (DenseNet 169) have great classification accuracy for X-ray images, while the DenseNet-201 has the highest classification accuracy for CT scan images. As a result of the review, ARIMA models such as PR, RIDGE, SVR, logistic models and hybrid wavelet ARIMA models are good at predicting the number of confirmed cases. Multilayer perceptron, SVM, random forest (RF) and XGBoost are better for classification.

Develop an ML model to detect whether the patient is suffering from COVID-19 in this study [22]. The major goal of this study is to find the best ML technique for prediction, build a ML model that reliably predicts COVID-19 and pinpoint the exact factors that influence COVID-19 prediction in patients. Dataset gathered from Yanyan Xu's figure share collection of open source data. SVM, RF and artificial neural networks (ANN) are used for prediction (ANN). Quantitative results are analyzed for the prediction of COVID-19, and SVM showed better result for smaller training data records when compared with other algorithms. RF gives reliable result for prediction. ANN gives lowest accuracy for small dataset, but the accuracy rate has consistent growth when the dataset increases. Among these algorithms the performance of RF was identified to be better in terms of accuracy for predicting the COVID-19.

ML was utilized in [23] to forecast the number of COVID-19 confirmed and dying cases. The author of this study uses a graph to illustrate the most relevant component of COVID-19 symptoms and predict future cases in New York. Decision tree, RF, linear regression, gradient boosting, LGBM and XGboosting are some of the approaches employed. The RMSE and MAE are used to evaluate these methods. The LGBM gives the highest value of RMSE and MAE; it means the prediction is worst compared with other algorithms. Boosting models and RF have the best accuracy metrics, but in the instance of COVID-19 prediction, the linear regression model has superior accuracy and a lower error rate.

4.3 Materials and methods

Regression analysis examines the relationship between a target or individual variable in a dataset. It is employed in a variety of domains, including statistical analysis, econometrics, computational science and is particularly useful in ML problems [14]. A few key factors should be considered when selecting an appropriate regression model, including determining the relationship and effect of variables, evaluating the model with various metrics such as R^2, regulated R^2, AIC, BIC and the error term. Evaluate and validate the trained data by using simple mean square error (MSE); and finally, selecting the best model based on the dataset. If the given dataset is large, various regular regression approaches will be able to handle the high dimensionality and multicollinearity among the variables contained in the dataset. Five different popular regression algorithms were used to predict the COVID-19 mortality scenario, namely extra tree regression, decision tree, AdaBoost regression, gradient boosting and finally RF regression.

4.3.1 Extra tree regressor

This method is an ensemble ML algorithm that uses ML techniques to combine the predictions from a decision tree into a single forecast [15]. Another name for this sort of tree is "very randomized trees," which can also be referred to as "extra trees." To put it simply, it works by creating an un-pruned decision tree using the training dataset that has been supplied. It is appropriate for each unique tree in the training data set. During the sampling operation, extra tree will informally sample the features for each split point in a tree to get the best fit. It makes use of a greedy method to identify an ideal point, and it makes use of a learning sample to grow the trees when expanding the trees. Excessive random tree regression (also known as extremely random trees) [16] is a type of regression in which overfitting and prediction precision are controlled by applying a series of random decision trees (also known as additional trees) to various sub-samples of a dataset and averaging the results.

4.3.2 Decision tree regressor

When dealing with data that has both numerical and category features, this approach can be used for any data set. Using a decision tree, you can capture non-linear interaction between the characteristics and the target variables quite effectively. Briefly stated, decision trees are trees in which each node represents a feature, each branch provides an option for deciding and each leaf indicates the result of making the decision. Regression or classification models [20] with a tree topology are generated using generalized decision trees [19]. The dataset is divided into smaller chunks, and an accompanying decision tree is built incrementally in the background. This approach can deal with both categorical and numerical information. J. R. Quinlan developed the ID3 method, which is the central technique for generating decision trees. To build the trees, it performs a greedy top-down search across the space of feasible branches with no backtracking. By replacing the information gain with a reduction in the standard deviation, the ID3 technique can be utilized to build a decision tree for regression.

4.3.3 AdaBoost regressor

This method, which is specific to the first boosting algorithm, allows you to merge many "weak classifiers" into a single "strong classifier." It enhances your ability to forecast reliably and increases the accuracy of your predictions. It makes use of a decision tree with a level of depth specific to everyone (it means decision trees with only one split). In some quarters, this tree is referred to as "decision stumps" because of its ability to make decisions. In the beginning, the model will assign equal weight to all points, and subsequently, it will assign higher weights to points that have been mistakenly classified by the user in the future. There are a couple of facts that must be always followed: AdaBoost's feeble learners are decision trees that have been split into two parts; these trees are referred to as decision stumps. It is primarily through the application of higher weights to situations that this method is successful in making it more difficult to categorize them. AdaBoost was utilized to get around issues in categorization and regression that were encountered.

In this situation, the judgment stumps are the most straightforward model to design by simply assuming the same label, regardless of how it appears to have been constructed in the first place. Although we may have to guess the answer, the model will be chosen as the most correct depending on how accurate it is (1 or 0). After determining how much data there is and what qualities the data possesses, the dataset is divided into two groups, each of which contains a subset of the other (i.e., each stump will choose a feature to say X1, threshold T and then splits the dataset into two groups on either side of the threshold). To determine the best possible match for the decision stump, each feature of the input, as well as every potential threshold, is examined to determine which one delivers the highest level of accuracy and precision.

As shown in Figure 4.1, the AdaBoost regressor starts by fitting a regression model to the original dataset and then fits additional copies of the regression model to the same dataset. The current forecast error, which is updated hourly, is used to alter occurrence weights. As a result, the posterior regressors concentrate their efforts on tough cases and deliver very accurate outputs [17].

4.3.4 Gradient boosting regressor

The gradient boosting regressor transforms weak students into strong students using a gradient increase in the number of points they receive. During tree construction, each new tree is checked against a modified version of the original dataset, which is called boosting. Models are trained in a progressive, additive and sequential way using the gradient boosting algorithm (GBA), which is a combination of progressive, additive and sequential training. If you're looking for decision tree prediction, gradient boosting and AdaBoost are two methods that are extremely similar in that they both rely on an ensemble of decision trees to predict the label of the target. Gradient boost trees, like AdaBoost trees, will have a depth of more than one; however AdaBoost trees will not. The AdaBoost model discovers the deficiency by utilizing high-weight data points, whereas the gradient boosting strategy detects the shortcoming by employing the loss function (or loss function-based approach) [18]. It will be possible to use the loss function to determine how well the coefficients of the model perform when it comes to fitting the underlying data. The big advantage of using gradient boosting is that it allows optimizing a cost function that has been provided by the user rather than a loss function, which normally affords less flexibility. Boosting is an ML strategy for regression, classification and other problems that generates an accurate predictive model from a collection of unsatisfactory predictive models, most commonly decision trees. Gradient boosting is another name for boosting.

4.3.5 Random forest regressor

Among the supervised learning algorithms, RF regression uses the ensemble learning method to predict the outcome of a regression problem. When you use the ensemble learning method, you can make more accurate predictions than you might if you used a single ML algorithm alone. In this scenario, the input data is passed through several decision trees. As a result, it generates a variable number of decision trees during the training phase and outputs the individual tree based on the mode of classes or the average forecast of the individual trees [17]. Predicting outcomes with a RF regression model is a powerful and accurate means of doing so. A wide range of situations, including those involving features with non-linear correlations, are frequently successfully addressed using this method.

4.3.6 Methodology

This section discusses different methods applied to India's dataset for COVID-19 (state-wise dataset from Kaggle, the size is approximately 300,000) for the analysis and prediction of different cases. This dataset contains confirmed COVID-19 instances as well as the overall number of mortality cases from 2020 to 2021, according to the CDC.

Figure 4.2: Flowchart for the implemented methodology.

According to Figure 4.2, the data is pre-processed to remove any missing values or values that are not acceptable. A time history of deaths from COVID-19 is contained within these data. A predictive attribute in this situation is death, and a response attribute or an independent attribute, in this case, is a confirmed case. The attributes available in the dataset include the following: state name, total cases, active, discharged, deaths, active ratio (percent), discharge ratio (percent) and death ratio (percent), among others (percent). Figure 4.3 shows the total number of COVID-19 cases recorded in India's various states. Figure 4.4 depicts COVID-19 instances that are currently active in various states, while Figure 4.5 depicts death cases.

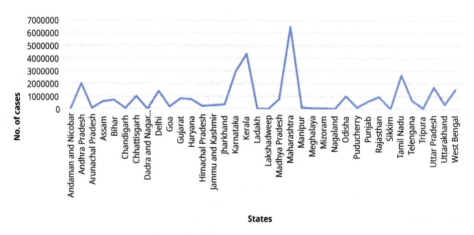

Figure 4.3: Total COVID-19 cases in all states of India.

To find missing and redundant data in a data set, data pre-processing is a crucial step to complete. For the sake of consistency, all missing data (NAN) should be eliminated from the dataset. This experiment only considers the total number of cases, active cases and deaths when forecasting the number of fatalities every year.

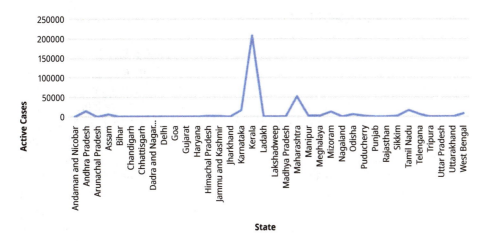

Figure 4.4: Active cases.

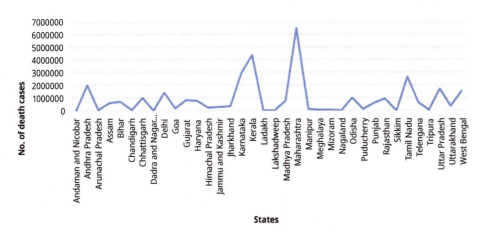

Figure 4.5: Death cases.

All these characteristics are combined into five models that are used to forecast the death rate for a particular dataset. All of these models are evaluated using a variety of metrics, including mean absolute error (MAE), mean square error (MSE), R^2 score, root mean square error (RMSE), RMSLE and MAPE. Table 4.1 shows the results of the performance analysis for the COVID-19 dataset. The models are evaluated and finally compared with one another using all these metrics; with that, the extra tree regressor gives robust results when contrasted with other models.

4.4 Results and discussions

It is a dangerous disease that is spreading over the world, and it has claimed the lives of many people while causing numerous health problems in others. The vaccine was developed by the government, the World Health Organization and medical professionals to guard against this disease. There are numerous vaccines available, including COVIDSHIELD, COVAXIN, Sputnik V and others. Even now, the globe is suffering from new viruses that are constantly changing, and we are living in the Omicron situation. As a result, a prediction system and a detection system are required. ML algorithms are important in prediction and detection, and this research focuses on this form of analysis. There are a variety of regression models available, and five of the most prominent models are taken into consideration in this study. The analysis of the regression model is depicted in Figure 4.6. Despite the fact that the dataset contains no missing values, the system checks for missing data in this system. After normalizing the dataset with robust, the data is divided into two groups with an 80:20 split between training and testing data. As previously stated, this dataset contains a range of features/attributes, with state and total case features being utilized to train and test the regression model. The model forecasts the number of deaths in India based on these two attributes. To examine the model, a variety of error measures are employed.

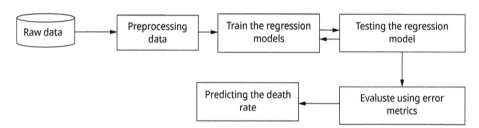

Figure 4.6: Flow of regression model for prediction.

Table 4.1 indicates that the selected regression algorithms outperform when it comes to estimating the mortality rate of the pandemic COVID-19 virus disease outbreak. When looking at R^2 values, expect the AdaBoost regression model to have the highest value; all other models have low values. This demonstrates that the chosen regression models are well-suited to our findings. The lower the MSE score, the more accurate the model is anticipated to be. All of the chosen regression models have a lower mean square error (MSE), indicating that the chosen model performs better than the others in terms of prediction.

4.4.1 Performance metrics

When evaluating ML models or ML algorithms, a variety of measures are utilized, such as accuracy, confusion matrix, precision and recall. Other metrics include the F1 score, the ROC curve, the AUC curve and the precision-recall curve. The accuracy of a regression problem is measured using mean squared error (MSE) and MAE. MAE, mean square error (MSE), R^2 score, root mean square error (RMSE), RMSLE and MAPE are all used to assess the accuracy of prediction models (MAPE).

Table 4.1: Performance comparisons of a regression model with a COVID-19 dataset.

Model	MAE	MSE	RMSE	R^2	RMSLE	MAPE
Extra trees regression	4,568.58	2.72e + 06	7,392.12	0.538	0.596	1.183
Decision tree regression	5,093.82	2.73e + 06	8,227.45	0.418	0.831	1.063
Gradient boosting regression	4,806.02	2.70e + 08	7,744.00	0.340	0.689	1.473
Random forest regression	5,209.97	2.99e + 08	8,579.39	0.244	0.867	4.263
Adaboost regression	5,194.22	2.71e + 08	8,102.52	0.096	1.132	12.741

Table 4.1 indicates that the selected regression algorithms outperform when it comes to estimating the mortality rate of the pandemic COVID-19 virus disease outbreak. When looking at R^2 values, expect the AdaBoost regression model to have the highest value; all other models have low values. This demonstrates that the chosen regression models are well-suited to our findings. The lower the MSE score, the more accurate the model is anticipated to be. All of the selected regression models have a lower MSE, indicating that the chosen model performs better than the others in terms of prediction.

4.4.2 Mean absolute error (MAE)

MAE is a statistic for measuring and summarizing the quality of ML models. First, we will calculate the prediction error for each record, and then we will change each error to a positive figure if it is now a negative figure. In other words, we calculate the absolute value of each inaccuracy. Finally, compute the mean value of all absolute errors and then, using the following eq. (4.1), evaluate the performance of the model:

$$MAE = \sum_{i=1}^{n} abs(y_i - \lambda(x_i)) \tag{4.1}$$

As shown in Table 4.1, the comparisons of MAE with five different regression models were performed. Extra tree regression and gradient boosting regression models had the lowest MAE rates of all the models tested, demonstrating that these two models beat the forecast mortality rate of the COVID-19 model.

4.4.3 Mean squared error (MSE)

In this metric, the average of the squared difference between a dataset's original value and projected value is used to calculate the outcome. The formula for calculating MSE is given in the section following eq. (4.2):

$$\text{MSE} = \frac{1}{n}\sum_{i=1}^{n}(\text{actual values} - \text{predicted values})^2 \tag{4.2}$$

Here, n equals the total number of observations divided by the number of rows, sigma equals the difference between actual and predicted values and I equals an integer between 1 and n. Using the previous eq. (4.2), all models are evaluated, and the result is shown in Table 4.1. The decision tree regression and extra tree regression models had the lowest mean-squared error rates of all the models tested, indicating that they outperform the forecast mortality rate of COVID-19.

4.4.4 R^2 score

It's also known as the R^2 score or coefficient of determination. This statistic is used to assess the performance of the linear regression model. Using this method, determine how observed outcomes are replicated by the model. The formulation to be evaluated is given in the following eq. (4.3):

$$R^2 = 1 - SS_{res}/SS_{tot} \tag{4.3}$$

wherein which SS_{res} denotes the sum of squares of residual errors and SS_{tot} total sum of the errors. The proportion of data points that fall within the line drawn by the regression equation is represented by the coefficient R^2. A greater number of R^2 is preferable because it shows that the experiment produced better results. The comparisons of the R^2 statistic score with five different regression models are shown in Table 4.1. Extra tree regression and decision tree regression models have the highest R^2 statistics score among them, indicating that these two models beat the prediction mortality rate of COVID-19 in terms of survival prediction.

4.4.5 Root mean square error (RMSE)

When a model is used to predict quantitative data, this metric is used to assess the level of error that occurs. The Euclidean distance is used to show how far predictions depart from measured true values. The formula for calculating the RMSE equation is as follows (4):

$$\text{RMSE} = \sqrt{\sum_{i=1}^{n} \frac{(\widehat{y_i} - y_i)^2}{n}} \qquad (4.4)$$

Each data point is subjected to RMSE computations, which include computing the difference between forecast and truth, the norm of residuals for each point, the mean of residuals and lastly the square root of that mean. The first column of Table 4.1 shows the comparisons of root mean-squared error with five different regression models. Extra tree regression and gradient boosting regression models have the lowest root MAE rates of any of the models tested, demonstrating that these two models beat the forecast mortality rate of COVID-19.

4.4.6 Root mean-squared log error (RMSLE)

This measure is mostly used to determine the logarithmic scale, as the name implies. Overall, the RMSE log-transformed for prediction and the log-transformed for actual values are used. RMSLE adds 1 to both the actual and forecasted values before calculating the natural log of possible values (0):

$$\text{RMSLE} = \sqrt{\frac{1}{n}\sum_{i=1}^{n} \left(\log(y_i + 1) - \widehat{(y+1)}^2\right)} \qquad (4.5)$$

The lowest RMSLE is determined by using eq. (4.5). RMSLE rates for five different regression models are shown in Table 4.1, with that, extra tree regression and gradient boosting regression models achieving the lowest root means squared logarithmic error rates. As a result, when compared to other models, the extra tree regression and gradient boosting regression models produce superior results.

4.4.7 Mean absolute percentage error (MAPE)

This metric is based on the basic evaluation of MAE, but with alterations to convert everything to a percentage of the original value. In eq. (4.6), the following formula is used:

$$\text{MAPE} = \frac{100}{n}\sum \left|\frac{y - \hat{y}}{y}\right| \qquad (4.6)$$

where y denotes the actual value, and $\hat{y}$ denotes the predicted value. The difference between the two numbers is divided by y. This ratio's absolute value is calculated by summing the absolute values of each predicted point in time and dividing the total by a number of fitting points, n. The comparisons of mean absolute percentage error with five different regression models are shown in Table 4.1. Extra tree regression and decision tree regression models have the lowest mean absolute percentage error rate of all of them, demonstrating that these two models exceed the predicted mortality rate of COVID-19 by a significant margin. To predict the death rate, the linear regression model is applied. The expected death rate for active cases is approximately 1,200 out of a total of 1,201 active cases. The results of the experiments show that the extra tress regression model surpasses all other models in terms of precision and accuracy.

4.5 Conclusion

In the context of the COVID-19 pandemic, the prediction of the mortality prognosis is an important idea that can help us minimize illness fatality rates by providing us with information on where and with whom to intervene. The severe acute respiratory syndrome coronavirus 2 (SARS-CoV-2) has emerged as the most serious national security worry for many countries throughout the world, as it is responsible for the SARS pandemic. To gain insight into the transmission and implications of this infectious disease, accurate outbreak prediction models must be developed and refined. Standard epidemiological models have demonstrated poor accuracy for long-term prediction, owing to a high level of uncertainty and a scarcity of critical data points. Using regression models to anticipate the COVID-19 outbreak, this research conducts a comparative examination of the models. The extra tree regression model demonstrated a significant degree of generalization ability for long-term prediction, as demonstrated by the results. COVID-19 datasets were gathered from online COVID-19 repositories, and multiple regression models were tested for COVID-19. Using the regression models they used, which comprised additional tree regression, decision trees regression, gradient boosting regression, RF and AdaBoost, the researchers were able to accurately estimate the mortality of the pandemic virus COVID-19. The MAE, MSE, R^2 score, root mean-squared error (RMSE), RMSLE and MAPE are all used to evaluate these models (MAPE). As a result, in this work, the initial step in the analysis is to look for missing numbers, only the state and active cases of various states are considered while estimating the death rate of various states. The extra tree regression model, among others, outperforms all other models in terms of performance in every aspect of analysis.

References

[1] Ghosh, K., Sengupta, N., Manna, D. & De, S. K. (2020). Inter-state transmission potential and vulnerability of COVID-19 in India. Progress in Disaster Science, 7, 100114.

[2] Darapaneni, N., Reddy, D., Paduri, A. R., Acharya, P. & Nithin, H. S. (2020). Forecasting of COVID-19 in India using ARIMA model, in 2020 11th IEEE Annual Ubiquitous Computing, Electronics & Mobile Communication Conference (UEMCON), pp. 0894–0899.

[3] Tomar, A. & Gupta, N. (2020). Prediction for the spread of COVID-19 in India and effectiveness of preventive measures. Science of the Total Environment, 728.

[4] Rustam, F., Reshi, A. A., Mehmood, A., Ullah, S., On, B.-W., Aslam, W. & Choi, G. S. (2020). COVID-19 future forecasting using supervised machine learning models. IEEE Access, 8, 101489–101499.

[5] Chowdhury, M. E. H., Rahman, T., Khandakar, A., AI-Madeed, S., Zughaier, S. M., Doi, S. A. R., Hassen, H. & Islam, M. T. (2021). An Early Warning Tool for Predicting Mortality Risk of COVID-19 Patients using Machine Learning. Cognitive Computation, PubMed, Springer.

[6] Rath, S., Tripathy, A. & Tripathy, A. R. (2020). Prediction of new active cases of coronavirus disease (COVID-19) pandemic using multiple linear regression model. Diabetes & Metabolic Syndrome: Clinical Research & Reviews, 14(5), 1467–1474.

[7] Shino, E. & Binder, M. (2020). Defying the rally during COVID-19 pandemic: A regression discontinuity approach. Social Science Quarterly, 101(5), 1979–1994.

[8] Hills, S. & Eraso, Y. (2021). Factors associated with non-adherence to social distancing rules during the COVID-19 pandemic: A logistic regression analysis. BMC Public Health, 21(1), 1–25.

[9] Gupta, A. K., Singh, V., Mathur, P. & Travieso-Gonzalez, C. M. (2021). Prediction of COVID-19 pandemic measuring criteria using support vector machine, prophet and linear regression models in Indian scenario. Journal of Interdisciplinary Mathematics, 24(1), 89–108.

[10] Velásquez, R. M. A. & Lara, J. V. M. (2020). Forecast and evaluation of COVID-19 spreading in USA with reduced-space Gaussian process regression. Chaos, Solitons & Fractals, 136, 109–924.

[11] Mandayam, A. U., Rakshith, A. C., Siddesha, S. & Niranjan, S. K. (November, 2020). Prediction of Covid-19 pandemic based on Regression, In 2020 Fifth International Conference on Research in Computational Intelligence and Communication Networks (ICRCICN) pp. 1–5. IEEE.

[12] Gunay, S., Can, G. & Ocak, M. (2020). Forecast of China's economic growth during the COVID-19 pandemic: A MIDAS regression analysis. Journal of Chinese Economic and Foreign Trade Studies.

[13] Albu, L. L., Preda, C. I., Lupu, R., Dobrotă, C. E., Călin, G. M. & Boghicevici, C. M. (2020). Estimates of dynamics of the covid-19 pandemic and of its impact on the economy. Romanian Journal of Economic Forecasting, 23(2), 5–17.

[14] Zhang, J. J., Lee, K. S., Ang, L. W., Leo, Y. S. & Young, B. E. (2020). Risk factors for severe disease and efficacy of treatment in patients infected with COVID-19: A systematic review, meta-analysis, and meta-regression analysis. Clinical Infectious Diseases, 71(16), 2199–2206.

[15] Kwame Ampomah, E., Qin, Z. & Nyame, G. (2020). Evaluation of tree-based ensemble machine learning models in predicting stock price direction of movement. Information, 11, 2–21.

[16] Majeed Hameed, M., Khalid Alomar, M., Lrahman Khaleel, F. & Al-Ansari, N. (2021). An extra tree regression model for discharge coefficient prediction: Novel, practical applications in the hydraulic sector and future research directions. Mathematical Problems in Engineering, 1–19.

[17] Iwendi, C., Bashir, A. K., Peshkar, A., Sujatha, R., Chatterjee, J. M., Pasupuleti, S., Mishra, R., Pillai, S. & Jo, O. (2020). COVID-19 patient health prediction using boosted random forest algorithm. Frontiers in Public Health, 8, 1–9.

[18] Gumaei, A., AI-Rakhami, M., AI Rahhal, M. M., Raddah, F., Albogamy, H., Maghayreh, E. A. I. & Salman, H. A. I. (2021). Prediction of COVID-19 confirmed cases using gradient boosting regression method. Computer, Materials & Continual (CMC), 6(1), 316–329.

[19] PRS legislative research. (March, 2020), [online] Available: https://prsindia.org/covid-19/cases.

[20] Ayoub Khan, M., Khan, R., Algarni, F., Kumar, I., Choundhary, A. & Srivastava, A. (2022). Performance evaluation of regression models for COVID-19: A statistical and predictive perspective. Ains Shams Engineering Journal, 12(2), 1–18.
[21] Rubaiyat Hossain Mondal, M., Bharati, S. & Podder, P. (2021). Diagnosis of COVID-19 using machine learning and deep learning: A review. arXiv, 1–17.
[22] Mahesh Matta, D. & Kumar Saraf, M. (May, 2020). Prediction of COVID-19 using machine learning techniques. Faculty of Computing, Blekinge Institute of Technology, 371, Karlskrona, Sweden, 79.
[23] Shinjae Kim, J. (2021). COVID-19 prediction and detection using machine learning algorithms: Catboost and linear regression. American Journal of Theoretical and Applied Statistics, 10(5), 208–215.
[24] https://www.brookings.edu/blog/future-development/2020/07/02/how-well-is-india-responding-to-covid-19/)

Asit Kumar Lenka, Hrudaya Kumar Tripathy

5 Computer vision for medical diagnosis and surgery

Abstract: In healthcare, diagnosis is very important which identify the diseases and track it. For this machine learning, artificial intelligence (AI) or computer vision (CV) algorithms has been used. CV has lot of applications in healthcare like it processes the image and extracts the data and analyzes it which is helpful in predicting various diseases. Due to very powerful image processing analysis, CV has a wide range of application in healthcare sector like diagnosis, tracking diseases, analysis, treatment and also in very complicated surgery. Here, various applications of CV and machine learning algorithms have been highlighted. CV application in medical gives highly precision disease diagnosis result which is helpful for better treatment. The major application of CV is in computed tomography and X-rays which are used to take image of various body parts for disease's diagnosis and treatment. Moreover, CV and AI are now an integral part of healthcare system which has been discussed here with some of its real-time application.

Keywords: Computer vision, machine learning, artificial intelligence, image processing, computed tomography, X-rays

5.1 Introduction

Medical diagnosis process is very complicated. A simple human being has limited power which can perform diagnosis in medical. So, it is necessary for automated computer system to be developed to tackle these challenges. Although there are some powerful systems already available still some advance feature is required. Machine learning (ML) and computer vision (CV) have powerful algorithms and are very much useful for the creation of automated system for diseases diagnosis, analysis, prediction and its treatment. CV has the capability of 3-D image processing and analysis which will help the identification and tracking of various diseases in real time. A lot of diseases and surgeries have been done by CV and artificial intelligence (AI). Due to the most precise result and analysis CV, AI, etc. are most popular in recent years. Since diagnosis is very essential part of medical field for treatment in correct way, manual diagnosis of a human arises a lot of diagnostic errors which causes wrong

---

Asit Kumar Lenka, Kalinga Institute of Industrial Technology (Deemed to be University), Bhubaneswar, Odisha, India, e-mail: asitlenka.kumar@gmail.com
Hrudaya Kumar Tripathy, Kalinga Institute of Industrial Technology (Deemed to be University), Bhubaneswar, Odisha, India, e-mail: hktripathyfcs@kiit.ac.in

treatment. The diagnosis error by human is due to various factor like limited visual capability of human being, sometimes more pressure on medical or hospital management creates some wrong treatment. So, to overcome these diagnostic errors ML, CV and AI applications should be used more and more which will also minimize time and cost. Also, CV has implementation in various devices which records data of patient called electronic health record (EHR) which is also analyzed and predicted by CV and ML for better treatment. Figure 5.1 represents the basic visual and working of CV.

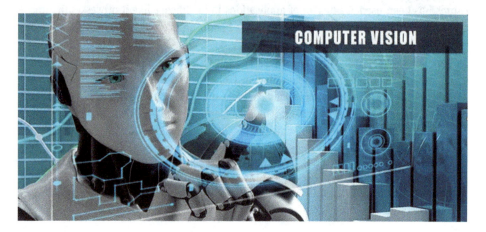

Figure 5.1: Basic representation of computer vision.

5.2 Computer vision in healthcare

5.2.1 What is computer vision?

It is a branch of computer science and machine learning which is used to understand the pattern and automate the tasks from digital images and videos. CV extracts data from digital images and videos to analyze it to achieve automatic visual understanding. It takes required action after analyzing and understanding the pattern. It works like human vision.

5.2.2 Computer vision in healthcare

CV in healthcare is very widely used and very important topic nowadays. Because it is very useful due to its advance feature in medical treatment which is not only cost-saving but also life-saving. It mostly used in X-rays and CT-scans as well as used in identification of patient, treatment monitoring, etc. CV is also a powerful technology which helps doctors to diagnose patient with better treatment and its monitoring. CV has been used in sensor-based technology which collects data from patient and sends it to analyze the involvement of specific disease. Unlike human vision, it is a powerful computer algorithm to analyze the visual data. Human perception is limited to diagnose the diseases but CV gives more clarity on diagnosis. CV helps reducing workload on doctors, nurses and medical staffs. Figure 5.2 is the basic representation or application of CV in healthcare which takes body images and analyses to diagnose various diseases.

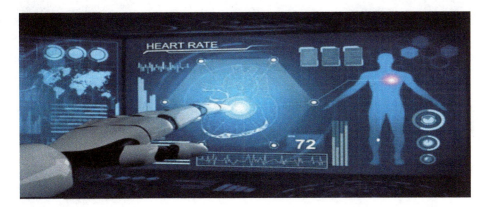

Figure 5.2: Basic representation of computer vision in healthcare.

5.3 Benefits of computer vision in healthcare

5.3.1 Faster with higher accuracy

The first benefit of CV in healthcare is it is faster and more accurate to diagnose diseases. As the algorithm is trained by a large number of data set with greater precision than doctors as doctors' eye may not able to identify patterns. Use of CV in X-rays, ultra sound, CT-scan or MRI are giving high accuracy. So, CV gives precise diagnosis by minimizing false positives. Since the algorithm is being trained using a large amount of training data, it can detect small presence of a condition. Due to high precision imaging capability of advance CV and AI, it saves the time of patient and healthcare worker.

5.3.2 Timely/early detection of illness

There are some diseases that can be cured or controlled by the medical treatment only in the early stages. So, CV allows to identify the early symptoms of that diseases and doctors can take decisions like to take drug or to go for surgery to prevent or cure the diseases early which is very useful nowadays. The main goal of this in CV is to speed up the diagnosis of any diseases as early as possible so that a life can be saved. Like deadly illness cancer can be cured in early stages. The powerful pattern recognition capability of CV gives the opportunity to identify the early symptoms of cancer so that doctors can take the decision for treatment as early.

5.3.3 Heightened medical process

Computer Vision in healthcare can save the time of doctors as it takes lot of time to diagnose and analyze the report for a doctor. Doctors can spend more time with patient so that doctor can understand patient's feelings and prescribed best solution of the diseases. CV and ML algorithm models facilitate the integration of testing lab with doctors' appointment chamber for which a doctor can access all the lab report directly from lab virtually and can advise a better prescription to the patient. This increase the efficiency of doctors and healthcare. Due to the wide range application of CNN, it is very easy to understand the language and symptoms which helps the healthcare worker and AI can predict and track the patient's health in very less time with very less effort.

5.3.4 Enhanced healthcare system

Computer Vision provides high accuracy diagnosis efficiently. So, it reduces the patient-doctor interaction. This will help when there is a shortage of physicians. CV gives potential to maintain workflow in healthcare which is cost-effective. Application of CV and AI in healthcare system minimizes the human error and consumes very less time. Nowadays the AI has been implemented for every work like from appointment of patient to screening, sample collection, testing, analysis, medication and so on with very smoothly and it is possible because of advanced CV and AI technology. CNN-based algorithms are used to take video consultation with doctors and NLP is being used to understand the language sentiment of patient through which it is easy for a doctor understand the patient. A wide range of applications of CV are able to collect and store the high quality images and data which are very much useful for analysis and also for simplification of healthcare system.

5.3.5 Medical imaging analysis

Nowadays, computer-generated imaging is very useful for doctors and widely used in healthcare as it diagnoses and analyzes from the image which is easier for a doctor to advice treatment. To make medical imaging more effective and accurate CV gives 3D visualization. So, now CV became most popular and important in machine learning as it has the capability to convert 2D scan images to 3D model which helps to get details about patient. As we know that CV has high efficiency which can detect very small object to save life. It also can compare the difference between images and most widely used in CT-scan, X-rays, MRIs, etc. CV uses training data to train the algorithm and all the objects are represented in visual data to detect various illness like fracture or condition after surgery.

5.3.6 Automatic generation of medical reports

CV is used to get complete medical information of patient by diagnosis and also prescribe medicine. Also, it helps to predict diseases and analyze report generation. CV extracts data from X-rays, CT-scans and prepares a detailed report which is easy to understand and diagnose. The prepared report consists of all the information of patient with 2D images and sometimes 3D images. By observing these report healthcare specialist or doctors can prescribe appropriate treatment with very less time. It also predicts the diseases from symptoms which is very helpful for treatment. Some CNN and DNN algorithm-based models are able to extract feature, analyze the 3D images of CT-scan, MRI, X-ray and generate a detailed report on that basis which reduces the work burden of healthcare workers. Natural language processing plays a crucial role in generating report. In manual report generation there might have human error, but in automatic generation it has been minimized.

5.3.7 Computer vision for health monitoring

CV played very crucial role by continuously monitoring the health and fitness of patient. CV and ML algorithm-based AI applications are now commonly used to track and monitor patient's health in real time. In the last decade, specially various types of wearable bands are used to monitor patient's health like BP, heart beat rate, pulse and others. These AI systems collect the data from patient and store in cloud which can be analyzed and sent to doctors who can check patient condition in very less time with better medical treatment. This monitoring is done sometimes by different types of sensors and images. Scientist has developed various CNN- and CV-based application which can measure blood loss during a surgery and also suggest emergency measures. Health monitoring is very crucial better treatment and that is why CV and AI are in high demand nowadays.

5.3.8 Nuclear medicine

Nuclear medicine mainly used radio-nuclide pharmaceuticals in diagnosis. But nowadays CV techniques are also used by using single-photon emission computed tomography and positron emission tomography. Basically, there are two types of nuclear medicine imaging like PET and SPECT which measures gamma radiations. Here application of ML and DL in PET attenuation correction (AC) has good performance. Both PET and SPECT have two aspects as attenuation and scatter correction which have been observed. In the past PET application was limited like for helmet PET. Sometimes AC can get only by X-ray or from barium and it was time-consuming. But now pCT nuclear image can be used for quick AC. Scientists have now proposed unsupervised learning called CAE (convolutional auto-encoder) and CED for the prediction of pCT from attenuation UN-corrected image. Both the CAE and CED have similar structures, but CED most likely used U-Net. GAN is the most popular attenuation process.

5.3.9 Blood cell counting

Louis-Charles Malassez invented the A chamber device named as hemocytometer which is invented by Louis-Charles Malassez to count all the red blood cells accurately. But nowadays CV has been used to detect and count cell nuclei very faster and accurately with the help of a trained CV model. Here CV model takes microscopic images as input and analyzes it to count how many number of cells are present. Microscopic images are sent to the CV model which calculated the number of cells. Researchers have also used faster region-based CNN which is used to count blood cells from which we can detect diseases.

5.3.10 AI surgical logs

The main objective is to make surgery efficiently. CV operating room is advance surgical room where all the electronic record facility is available. All the actions are being track by using CV. Widespread of AI now is very much popular in pathologist as it can help surgery without any error. All types of surgeries like bariatric surgery and heart surgery can be done and also can track the development after surgery as well as it helps patients physical real-time activity which can analyze and predict the next course of action. This helps speed treatment and recovery monitoring system. Scientist has built the application by using CV and ML algorithm which helps detecting all the surgical equipments at the time of requirement as application well trained before. Also AI system can store the video of surgery which can be analyzed for better performance.

5.3.11 Patient identification

In healthcare, CV played an important role in the identification of patient from face reorganization or by some other way of detection. It gives an integrated healthcare system by facial authentication. In the recent world, many patients died or suffer due to wrong treatment or some other's prescription given by healthcare workers due to wrong health record. So here CV played an important role in identifying patient specially by facial authentication. Healthcare workers can identify patient by bar-code with their medical records. But nowadays CV-based application available which can take photo or video of patient and analyze it before storing the data into cloud as patient identification information (PII) which is used to identify the patient specially by skin and face structure. All the data can be found or stored in medical information system (MIS). After analysis of image captured by camera ML and CV-based algorithm detects region of interest (ROI) through which patient can be identify and also can diagnose the diseases for timely treatment.

5.3.12 Accurate result with minimum cost

In the past decades, due to lack of technological advancement some healthcare organization provides very critical and important services with very high cost which was very difficult to bear by a poor or middle-class family. But now due to technological advancement specially in the field of CV and AI in healthcare sector which implies less human interference and error free. Due to the automation system, it is the labor-free and unbiased result that leads to a very low or affordable price for a patient in healthcare. Specially CV, ML in X-ray, MRI, ultrasound, etc. are in low cost with maximum efficiency and in very less time. Since it is automation system by CV and AI all the healthcare processes took care of technology with high accuracy.

5.4 Applications of computer vision in healthcare

AI is now the important part of healthcare and it gives a revolution in healthcare. Almost all the healthcare organizations are implementing machine learning, CV to know the details about drugs, diseases, etc. Also, they facilitate predictive analytics and real-time patient health condition to healthcare workers. Specially CV is mostly being used. Here some of the applications CV in healthcare. Some applications of CV in healthcare are discussed below.

5.4.1 Application of CV in radiology

CV is used to detect and monitoring tumor, any bone fracture, state of tissue and cancer cells. IBM Watson is the powerful imaging solution used to image analysis and interpret faster with high accuracy in radiology. It gives a better and reliable medical facility.

Radiologist frequently used CV and ML algorithm-based application to detect the damaged part in body with its depth which helps the radiologist to analyze the condition better. Due to technological advancement in the field of CNN, CV and others it is very easy to identify the exact location of the damaged part of body with the help of high-quality CT-scan, X-ray or MRI scans which gives detailed analysis and clarity for better treatment. Here image processing plays a significant role and since nowadays advancement of image processing, it has high success rate.

5.4.2 Application of CV in dermatology

Dermatology is the visual inspection of skin. CV has the powerful algorithm which can detect the patterns in images and any sign in skin may be crucial for diagnosis. AI gives advance feature which enables diagnosis with high accuracy having expert decision-making process for better treatment. CV is able to detect skin cancer. Also, nowadays CV is the regular part of dermatology department.

CV and ML are able to diagnose any type of skin-related diseases which is of great help to the dermatologist. Since ML models have very large datasets with very fast computing skills and high storage capability, these models have more importance in dermatology. Some CV and ML models take the 3D image of skin and analyze the lesion of skin to diagnose the skin-related diseases in very short time and also has capability to recommend treatment for those diseases. Since the availability of large datasets of skin, it has significant success in diagnosis. Initially CNN is used to pre-train feature extraction process and from which data are analyzed by ML algorithms like K-means, SVM and other which has very good success rate. Some scientists have developed application with CNN which has high accuracy in diagnose skin-related diseases.

5.4.3 Lab automation

CV takes the image of blood or take an input in the form of a picture. Then trained professionals take it to microscope. By the help of CV technology automatically detects any abnormality in blood. Basically, AI has a wider range of applications in lab testing in healthcare. From testing to result, all the steps can be done by AI.

Implementation of CV and AI in lab automation enhances the safety of patient in very less time with accurate result. By the help of CV and ML algorithm all the samples can be tested by automation which is very high accuracy than a normal healthcare professional. Due to the advancement of CNN it has lot of implementations in lab automation.

5.4.4 Cancer screening

Nowadays, cancer is the most dangerous disease which can be prevented by early detection and that can be done by machine learning algorithm as part of CV application.

CV is also used to compare mammogram images which can identify abnormality of patient. CV has great success in the field of detection of cancer cells and tumor from image. CV also now can analyze patient's skin more quickly with high accuracy which solve many problems of a dermatologist. Also, CT-scan images of lung used in CV algorithms have shown a high accuracy in identifying lung cancer.

As we know there are different types of cancers of which skin cancer is one of them which is sometime difficult to identify as it has some symptoms common to other skin-related diseases. But nowadays researchers have developed some applications which can easily detect the cancerous and non-cancerous lesions. Scientists have developed a neural network model which has been trained a lot of cancer images which can identify anomalies in cells. Some models give high accuracy result. CV models detect cancer cells by analyzing patterns in images. IBM Watson and NVIDIA also used CV for various cancer cell detections with high accuracy and success rate.

5.4.5 Application of computer vision in cardiology

Cardiovascular pathology is the most difficult cardiac diagnosis in which pattern reorganization and determination of severity are important. CV has some applications in cardiology like cardio-vascular imaging and its automatic pathology with anomaly detection, automatic analysis, diagnosis and prognosis in CT. By using the abovementioned pathology a report will be generated and sent to doctors for in-depth analysis and patient's consultation for treatment. CV algorithm is able to detect early sign of any cardio-vascular sign which can be treated.

In the past decade, imaging technique advancement reached new heights by the help of CV. In cardiology, non-invasive imaging process like single photon emission computed tomography (SPECT), CT scan, MRI scan, PET with others are used to diagnose and predict the any heart-related diseases by checking heart and artery condition. This also gives the treatment for the diseases and helps for training and education. Some CNN model for heart disease can track the blood, veins and others more precisely.

5.4.6 Musculoskeletal radiography abnormality identification

Many patients suffer bone diseases like fracture which can be a long-term disability. CV application like X-ray is able to detect any type of bone diseases or fractures and gives clear visual. By using X-ray, healthcare professionals can easily identify the severity of the bone problem and its risk in future and also prescribed appropriate treatment to the patient. It makes the radiologist job easier with more effective results.

Nowadays CV and ML applications are used to detect musculoskeletal radiology abnormality. DNN and CNN algorithms extract data and its characteristics of given input data. Some algorithms of generative adversarial networks which are able to create new data can combine with discriminative network and give a very good performance. For muscle tissue ultrasonography is used which is CNN or semi-automated CAD program; for bone X-ray it is used which is CNN or SVM program. In musculoskeletal radiology for knee and lumber spine MRI is used which is 3D CNN or GNNs program. Similarly, natural language processing (NLP) is now being used to detect fracture in bone in radiology such as severely damaged or partially damaged.

5.4.7 Blood vessel segmentation of retina

Very complicated is blood vessel segmentation as it has high scale. It takes some pixels with background which is very difficult to spot. But CV makes it possible. Neural network uses structured analysis of retina with STARE data set. Stare data set contains 999×960 annotated images. Below are the ways machine learning can improve blood vessel segmentation of retina:

A. Enhancement of image for quality images
B. Segmentation of substructure can detect blood vessels

Application of CV in this field minimizes the time span of the work flow so that healthcare worker can focus on other manual operation.

5.4.8 Track of tumor development

CV has the ability to extract important information from image and can compare and track the development. CV continuously monitors the tumor with its various stages, transition point and defects. Training for tumor tracking CNN requires small number of clinical trials. Image classification algorithm extracts various important features like location, shape, area and intensity of tumor. Also, tumor can be predicted by predictive analysis with a common method tumor probability heat map which classifies the state of the tumor on the basis of tissue patch overlap. Mask RCNN is used for the detection of brain tumor which is dangerous to human if not diagnosed early.

5.4.9 Application of computer vision in surgery

Surgery is very important and complicated in healthcare and CV plays an important role to make it risk-free and effective treatment of any diseases. CV also helps surgeons to train and take decision during surgery. CV increases its recognition capability; as a result CV algorithm can provide guidance, warning and can update in real time during surgery.

In last two decades rapid advancement of CV and AI is used to analyze intraoperative videos. This gives multi-dimensional application of DL and ANN in medical surgery which enables complex operations accurately. Due to the use of CV and deep neural network (DNN) these models which has been developed for automatic surgery can identify the target more precisely and can take required action in real time as well as it can detect the previous surgical events. All the models have the capability which can analyze surgical video and extract all the features and it helps in performance at the time of surgical task. Nowadays robotics machine which has CV and ML models inside are used in healthcare for better performance and safety. These models can detect anatomical regions and can take necessary action without damaging other important body parts like nervous system. In the surgical system due to the capability of capturing 3D measurement, stereo endoscope has more advantage.

5.4.10 Managing clinical trial retention

Clinical trial is one of the crucial stages for the development of any antidote for a disease. But it has been seen that some clinical trials failed due to mismanagement of proper trial process from both patient and healthcare side. There are a lot of problems during clinical trial. So researchers have developed and implemented some algorithm to manage all the process during trial of patient like whether patient has taken medicine in time or not by face detection technique or by recording video. Furthermore, Computer Vision technology has been incorporated into wearable devices, permitting for the thorough recording and ongoing monitoring of a variety of bodily responses and changes both during and after clinical trials. These advanced wearables collect and analyze an extensive array of physiological and behavioral data, presenting worthwhile insights into how our bodies respond and evolve over time. Also it can remind us to take medicine on time. AiCure, a software, is created to manage clinical trials.

5.4.11 Training

Training is an important work in healthcare domain. Each and every healthcare workers including doctors required to be trained specially for surgery. In manual training it will take a lot of time. Because of the unavailability of previous research data, it makes training difficult and time-consuming. Also it is very difficult to analyze manually. So nowadays scientists have developed algorithms which give immersive and smooth in surgery. All the 3D videos of surgery are stored in cloud so that surgeons can access the videos. Also all the stored videos are analyzed and given with some useful data like total time taken for surgery, procedure and success rate so that surgeons can learn the procedure quickly and safely with high efficiency.

5.4.12 Application of computer vision in predictive analytics

Earlier days it is very difficult to identify a disease. But now due to technology enhancement specially CV and machine learning we can not only detect the diseases but also predict the future diseases with high accuracy. There are some CV and machine learning algorithms that can track continuously the current body development like heartbeat, pulse, oxygen level and temperature stored in cloud, analyze and detect future diseases. CV has lot of application in predictive analytics. CV has 3D modeling medical image analysis which can help predict and analyze any diseases by CT-scan or X-ray. Some model used hybrid architecture with CV and machine learning algorithm for predictive analysis with high accuracy in a short period of time. Tumors, cancers and skin diseases can be predicted.

5.4.13 Diagnosis of COVID-19

As we all know world is still battling with COVID-19 virus although vaccination is already available in the market. Still all the healthcare systems couldn't able to handle such number of patients. But due to the application of CV, machine learning and image processing algorithm some part of the burden is sorted out. It is specially for X-ray, 3D MRI scan and other image scanner. COVID-19 virus can only be detected by taking X-ray image of chest or by high resolution of lung MRI scan. ML and image processing algorithm takes these images as input and analyzes it by using different methodologies and then gives output whether the patient is suffered from COVID-19 virus or not with its severity. Not only diagnosis but also management of COVID-19 like tracing, tracking and treatment CV and AI has a lot of contribution. Some CV and ML-based application can monitor health condition in real time like temperature and cough to detect COVID-19.

5.5 Comparative analysis of computer vision applications in healthcare

5.5.1 Diagnosis of COVID-19 using computer vision and artificial intelligence

5.5.1.1 Introduction

The COVID-19 pandemic outbreak has created lot of problems for whole world population. The name of corona virus due to elector-microscopic appearance to COVID-19 virus and also called SARS-COV-2. COVID-19 which has 14 types of bonded residues combines to angiotensin enzyme 2. Mainly it is the reason of respiratory infection with cold and fever.

During this pandemic, all the systems like industry, supply chain, transport and agriculture have been stopped and due to this global economy in recession. The economy for the year 2020 is lowest. The main symptoms are fever, dry cough, lung infiltrates, problem in breathing, etc. Due to COVID-19 severity, WHO declared it pandemic on March 11, 2020. Due to the rise of infected people, several countries declared nation-wide lockdown and curfew. The healthcare system is unable to tackle the burden due to the increase of the number of COVID-19 positive cases. So, CV and medical imaging have been started and widely used to find a solution. A lot of researchers have given a lot of solutions with different techniques. So, computer vision (CV) and AI are the most important topic nowadays.

5.5.1.2 Image processing

This is a different type of taking images for the analysis and to detect whether COVID-19 virus exists or not.

5.5.1.2.1 Computed tomography scan

It has the enhanced capacity to take image of chest in comparison to X-ray. It shows fats, bones, organs and muscles to diagnose accurately by doctors. In spiral chest CT-scan, spiral lane always lies in front of X-ray scanner which gives three-dimensional images of lungs. But in case of very good-quality(resolution) scan, it gives an image of single rotation by the X-ray scanner. Radiologist identifies the diseases which take a lot of time. So, the CV's role is important specially when the number of COVID-19 patients is increasing. From Figure 5.3, the working process of CT-scan has been clearly understood. Table 5.1 shows that some researchers have already found out the accuracy of the result by taking various methods on different COVID-19 data which was available. They have taken some CT-scan images and analyzed it to detect the COVID-19 and other major data.

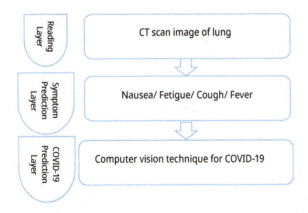

Figure 5.3: Steps to detect COVID-19 by medical imaging.

Table 5.1: Basic technology/process to diagnose COVID-19 using computer tomography scan.

Author name	CT images	Segmentation technology	Total patients	Accuracy (%)
Chen et al. [1]	46,096	UNet++	106 with 51 +ve	95.24
Wang et al. [2]	453	2D CNN	99	82.9
Xu et al. [3]	618	VNet	219 with 110 +ve	86.7
Song et al. [4]	777	2D CNN	88	86
Gozes et al. [5]	From COVID-19 dataset	U-Net	56	99.6
Shan [6]	249	VB-Net	249	91.6
Jin et al. [7]	970	2D CNN	496	94.98
Barstuga et al. [8]	150	3D CNN	53	99.68
Li [9]	4356	U-Net	3322	95
Zheng [10]	Some data from COVID-19 database	U-Net	540	95.9
Jin [11]	Some data from COVID-19 database	UNet++	1,136 with 723 +ve	92

From Figure 5.4 it has been observed that the COVID-19 virus damaged the lungs which has been detected by CT-scan image. In this figure, it clearly shows that COVID-19 virus affects the lungs more and more as days pass. These CT-scan images are very efficient to detect COVID-19 in the body.

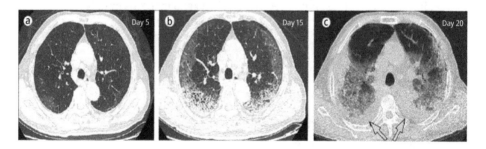

Figure 5.4: Lungs after COVID-19 symptoms: (a) after 5th day, (b) after 15th day and (c) after 20th day.

5.5.1.2.2 COVID-19 diagnosis using X-ray imaging

The chest X-ray is used in radiography for imaging as it is very clearly visible with lower price. It also has low contrast and hence pre-processing is done in X-ray. Specifically, it gives a 2D image of body-like bone from which doctors can identify bone-related diseases like bone fracture. Table 5.2 shows some experiment result. Some X-ray images have been taken and analyzed by using different methods to find out the accuracy.

Table 5.2: Basic process to detect COVID-19 by using an X-ray image.

Author name	X-ray images	Segmentation technology	Accuracy (%)
Guszt et al. [12]	662	U-Net+	97.5
Asmaa et al. [13]	80	CNN	95.12
Narin et al. [14]	Some image from COVID hospital	ResNet50	97
Wang et al. [15]	16,756	ResNet50	92.4
Ei et al. [16]	Some image from COVID hospital	DCNN	89
Khalid et al. [17]	5,856	ResNet50	96
Prabira et al. [18]	Some image from COVID hospital	ResNet50	95.38
Ioannis et al. [19]	1,427	VGG19	95.57
Ghoshal et al. [20]	68	BCNN	88.39
Farooq and Hafeez [21]	Some image from COVID hospital	ResNet50	96.23

Figure 5.5 is the sample X-ray image of a COVID-19 +ve patient. From the figure it is clearly visible that as days increase COVID-19 virus damages the human body and that's why image shows more white areas on chest as days increase.

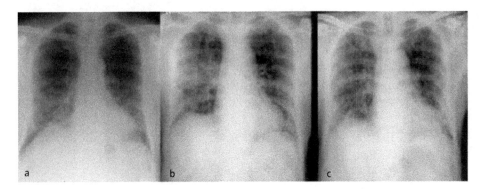

Figure 5.5: Chest X-ray images: (a) on the first day of COVID diagnosis, (b) on fifth day and (c) on eighth day.

5.5.1.3 Segmentation of images

This is the second step as image acquiring is first step. The second step is segmentation of images which will process for the analysis of COVID-19. The segmented portion describes that the ROI of lungs, lesions, etc. are in image and all the segments are used for the extraction of data, analysis and diagnosis. CT scan provides high-quality

3D image which is very much useful to detect COVID-19. By pretrained model convolutional neural network extracts data like texture and colors from X-ray image.

Figure 5.6 clearly shows the working principle of X-ray medical imaging for COVID-19 diagnosis. First, X-ray image has been taken and then the process is followed by training the model which is an important phase to diagnose the COVID-19 virus.

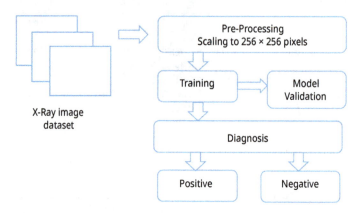

Figure 5.6: Basic platform of COVID-19.

5.5.1.4 Diagnosis for COVID-19

Machine learning is used for the detection, prediction and analysis various diseases in healthcare. ML algorithm trains the data and analyzes it statistically. Here some CV algorithm is used to analyze the 2D image or 3D image and detect whether COVID-19 image is present or not with its severity. For this analysis, it uses CT-scan, X-ray images and also there are a lot of wearable sensors through which CV can analyze patient health condition.

5.5.1.5 Avoid, management and treatment

Guideline of WHO (World Health Organization) to prevent the spread of COVID-19 infection is increasing the testing, quarantine and treatment; also to make a distance of 6 ft with always wearing face mask when you go outside. Although some vaccine has been developed still it will take time to vaccinate all the people. Those who are COVID-19 positive need to do a CT scan to see the severity of the virus infection.

Figure 5.7 is the sample computed tomography-scan images of a COVID-19 recovery patient which have been taken in a particular date. On these dates shows relative corona score which recovers from COVID-19 and in final date (February 15, 2020) that person completely recovered from COVID-19 as there is no spot identified in lungs.

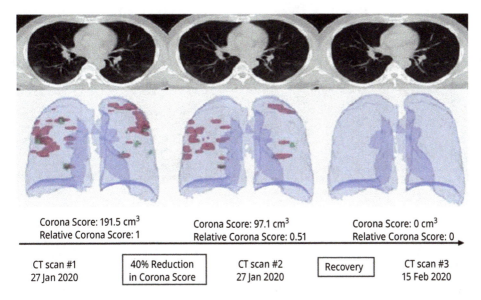

Figure 5.7: Relative corona score.

5.5.2 Facial information analysis on computer vision-based approaches

5.5.2.1 Introduction

Face is the main and vital part of human body which contains five senses and hence it has more information. Face appearance is key to identify any person and with a skilled observation can diagnose various mental and physical diseases. A lot of technology has been introduced which can detect face accurately and can predict and analyze the data. In healthcare perspective, machine learning or CV is nowadays very much useful to detect and analyze the facial data. Although there are several challenges for smart and interactive healthcare still CV gives solution of accurate diagnosis, remote monitoring with cost-effective. So, there are some applications or process through which doctors can monitor or get patient data from face.

Figure 5.8 represents the various parts of face (facial expression) analysis done by CV with specific task which is very much helpful in healthcare domain. From this figure, it is very easy to understand the functionality and requirement of healthcare domain which needs to be implemented by CV and AI.

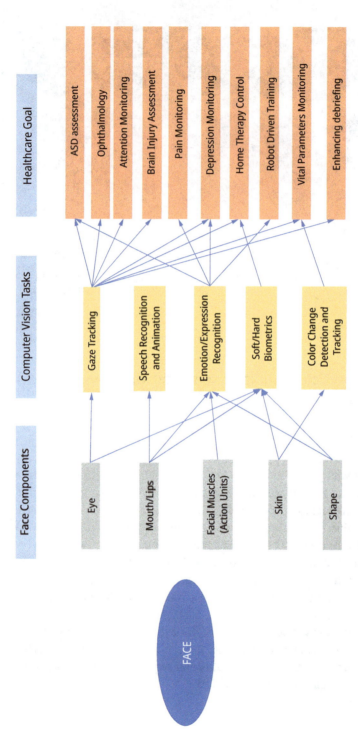

Figure 5.8: Computer vision task for face analysis in healthcare.

5.5.2.2 Eye analysis

Eye movement is a very important role in human perception and attention. Eye movement detection and tracking is now the vital research area in cognitive behavioral with the use of CV. By tracking eye movement everyone can understand the emotion of the person which can reveal many data about the person useful in detecting diseases. Some researchers provide RGB-D device which implements head-pose estimation algorithm with a system of remote-operative machine for the people of neurological problems. Also, some wearable-sensors like smart glass of CV have been used to detect or extract eye information. Table 5.3 represents comparison of different technique in healthcare [24].

The results of CV application in healthcare sector is shown in Table 5.3. It is found that, for healthcare application if the gap between the technique used and state-of-the-art method performance is very weak, still it is possible to know what research is further required from the latest research outcome.

Table 5.3: The analysis of eye movement with help of computer vision.

Healthcare work	Technology/process	Benchmark	CV application performance used	SoA CV application performance
Celiktutan et al. [22]	End-to-end system	GazeCapture	2.05 cm	1.95 cm
Cazzato et al. [23]	Active appearance model	ICT-3DHP	6.09° (own dataset)	6.2°
Wu et al. [25]	AdaBoost + Haar features	Biwi head pose	97.2% (detect acc only)	2.4°
Rudovic et al. [26]	Conditional local neural fields	MPIIGaze	9.96	4.18°
Cazzato et al. [27]	Geometric features + random forest	EYEDIAP	3.81° (own dataset)	3.23°

5.5.2.3 Facial expression

For the communication, facial expression is most vital and flexible which represents our emotion effectively. The facial expression shows the mood, nature, thought, etc. of that person which is being used in medical for the diagnosis of various diseases. AI and CV are widely popular for the detection of facial expression and also audio and video called multi-modal fusion framework has been introduced which predict human emotions [28–31]. Also, there is a cloud system which validates the user or patient and sends the facial data to emotion detection module. Then these information about emotion extracted from facial detection is sent to healthcare professionals and they analyze it and if they found it negative, then healthcare professionals can visit the patient for treatment. This facial expression is a useful diagnosis for various diseases. Detection of pain can be done automatically and also can be monitored for better treatment. Generic AU detector on Gabor and support vector machine solving the pain detection problem. Also, in the diagnosis of psychological problems facial information is used. Some module has been designed as part of human-computer interface so that the sensor can understand the emotion of human from face.

5.5.2.4 Speech monitoring recognition

In the recent development, speech recognition is tracked by CV-based app which detects the lip movement and observes the process of speech [32]. Since algorithm-based audio detection faced problem of noise a new type CV-based approach that has been developed with lip animation is lip reading which is different from traditional audio detection and processed from visual. Now deep bottle-neck feature (DBNFs) is the combination of video and audio recognition. Here DBNF used after local binary patterns which is used to reduce computational time and joint the output of discrete cosine transform for analysis. To achieve multi-modality, it adds all signals during tracking. Neural network has been trained to detect audio and video lip patterns. Some researchers used a separate learning strategy for speech reorganization to avoid over-fitting with new architecture known as Watch, Listen, Attend and Spell.

5.5.2.5 Important parameters monitoring

Nowadays it is important to check the various common signs of human body as blood pressure, heart beat, body temperature, etc. which is done by CV application of image processing with infrared and light emitting diodes which penetrates into human body detects the BP, heart rate, etc. with the identification of facial recognition. A skin classifier called Bayesian is used for segmentation and detection of skin-related problem for the detection of various skin-related problems [33]. CNN architecture is used to get spectrogram data. There is a camera-based monitoring system which is used to detect various diseases too.

5.5.2.6 Biometric

Nowadays biometric has been implemented everywhere through which robotics, CV, etc. can be used for the betterment of human beings [34]. It observes the human body patterns and takes specific action. Currently DNN has been implemented in soft biometric for race, age and gender detection. Deep regression forest is used where split node is fully connected CNN which is helpful to deal with heterogeneous data. CNN technique is very good in soft biometric problem-solving. Biometric gives various information about human body.

5.6 Conclusion

CV is now a hot topic in healthcare. Here, the application and importance of CV in healthcare have been discussed. Although a lot of development has done in medical by ML, CV and AI which make healthcare system easy, systematic, time-saving and cost-effective still more and more research are going on for the further advancement of healthcare by using CV. Nowadays CV is not only used in medical diagnosis but also in medical management which gives fluent management and efficient patient-doctor relation. Computer Vision has played a significant role in the evolution of technology implementation in the medical field, enabling smoother and higher-performing healthcare systems. Still a lot of research is required for more advancement using machine learning and CV. In this topic it is clear that in the past two decades application of CV, ML and AI significantly increased due to its technological advancement with higher benefits to our society. CNN and DNN are being used for the prediction of various types of tumor; in radiology it is used to detect various damaged tissues and bones with its severity. CV and ML also now being implemented in nuclear medicine which are beneficial for humans as it has the capability of speedy recovery. CV and AI also have a wide range of applications in cardiology and radiology due to its high-resolution imaging capability. Medical image processing is the most vital and beneficial application in healthcare domain. X-ray and MRI scan are widely used to take images of human body or anatomy. Using CV and ML or other image processing algorithm which takes 2D or 3D images as input analyze it to get the required result for diagnosis and prediction. Image processing has a wide range of applications in the detection of blood cells, in skin-related diseases (dermatology), in operation theater and surgery. In surgery it uses high level of algorithm to identify the ROI accurately and can take required action without harming the other part of the body. CV and AI have a very crucial role in healthcare management which simplified the healthcare system by using CNN and DNN models which is known as healthcare automation.

Although there are a lot of applications available for CV and AI, still some healthcare system is under process to implement CV more effectively. In nuclear medicine CV and AI need to improve the accuracy. In future CV will be implemented in cardiology, radiology, tumor detection and others with very high efficiency on which research is going on. Technology advancement is a continuous process and in the last two decades it has significantly improved.

References

[1] Chen, J., Wu, L., Zhang, J., Zhang, L., Gong, D., Zhao, Y., Hu, S., Wang, Y., Hu, X., Zheng, B. & Zhang, K. (2020). Deep learning-based model for detecting 2019 novel coronavirus pneumonia on high-resolution computed tomography: A prospective study. medRxiv.

[2] Wang, S., Kang, B., Ma, J., Zeng, X., Xiao, M., Guo, J., Cai, M., Yang, J., Li, Y., Meng, X. & Xu, B. (2020). A deep learning algorithm using CT images to screen for Corona Virus Disease (COVID-19). medRxiv.

[3] Xu, X., Jiang, X., Ma, C., Du, P., Li, X., Lv, S., Yu, L., Chen, Y., Su, J., Lang, G. & Li, Y. (2020). Deep learning system to screen coronavirus disease 2019 pneumonia. arXiv preprint arXiv:2002.09334.

[4] Song, Y., Zheng, S., Li, L., Zhang, X., Zhang, X., Huang, Z., Chen, J., Zhao, H., Jie, Y., Wang, R. & Chong, Y. (2020). Deep learning enables accurate diagnosis of novel coronavirus (COVID-19) with CT images. medRxiv.

[5] Gozes, O., Frid-Adar, M., Greenspan, H., Browning, P. D., Zhang, H., Ji, W., Bernheim, A. & Siegel, E. (2020). Rapid ai development cycle for the coronavirus (covid-19) pandemic: Initial results for automated detection & patient monitoring using deep learning ct image analysis. arXiv preprint arXiv:2003.05037.

[6] Shan, F., Gao, Y., Wang, J., Shi, W., Shi, N., Han, M., Xue, Z., Shen, D. & Shi, Y. (2020). Lung infection quantification of COVID-19 in CT images with deep learning. arXiv preprint arXiv:2003.04655.

[7] Jin, C., Chen, W., Cao, Y., Xu, Z., Zhang, X., Deng, L., Zheng, C., Zhou, J., Shi, H. & Feng, J. (2020). Development and evaluation of an AI system for COVID-19 diagnosis. medRxiv.

[8] Barstugan, M., Ozkaya, U. & Ozturk, S. (2020). Coronavirus (COVID-19) classification using CT images by machine learning methods. arXiv preprint arXiv:2003.09424.

[9] Li, L., Qin, L., Xu, Z., Yin, Y., Wang, X., Kong, B., Bai, J., Lu, Y., Fang, Z., Song, Q. & Cao, K. (2020). Artificial intelligence distinguishes COVID-19 from community acquired pneumonia on chest CT. Radiology 200905.

[10] Shi, H., Han, X., Jiang, N., Cao, Y., Alwalid, O., Gu, J., Fan, Y. & Zheng, C. (2020). Radiological findings from 81 patients with COVID-19 pneumonia in Wuhan, China: A descriptive study. Lancet Infectious Diseases. doi: 10.1016/S1473-3099(20)30086-4

[11] Jin, S., Wang, B., Xu, H., Luo, C., Wei, L., Zhao, W., Hou, X., Ma, W., Xu, Z., Zheng, Z. & Sun, W. (2020). AI-assisted CT imaging analysis for COVID-19 screening: Building and deploying a medical AI system in four weeks. medRxiv.

[12] Gaál, G., Maga, B. & Lukács, A. (2020). Attention U-net based adversarial architectures for chest X-ray lung segmentation. arXiv preprint arXiv:2003.10304.

[13] Abbas, A., Abdelsamea, M. M. & Gaber, M. M. (2020). Classification of COVID-19 in chest X-ray images using DeTraC deep convolutional neural network. arXiv preprint arXiv:2003.1381.

[14] Narin, A., Kaya, C. & Pamuk, Z. (2020). Automatic detection of coronavirus disease (COVID-19) using X-ray images and deep convolutional neural networks. arXiv preprint arXiv:2003.10849.

[15] Wang, L. & Wong, A. (2020). COVID-Net: A tailored deep convolutional neural network design for detection of COVID-19 cases from chest radiography images. arXiv preprint arXiv:2003.09871.

[16] Hemdan, E. E., Shouman, M. A. & Karar, M. E. (2020). COVIDX-Net: A framework of deep learning classifiers to diagnose COVID-19 in X-ray images. arXiv preprint arXiv:2003.11055.

[17] Asnaoui, K. E., Chawki, Y. & Idri, A. (2020). Automated methods for detection and classification pneumonia based on X-ray images using deep learning. arXiv preprint arXiv:2003.14363.

[18] Sethy, P. K. & Behera, S. K. (n.d.). Detection of Coronavirus disease (COVID-19) based on deep features.

[19] Apostolopoulos, I. D. & Mpesiana, T. A. (2020). Covid-19: Automatic detection from X-ray images utilizing transfer learning with convolutional neural networks. Australasian Physical and Engineering Sciences in Medicine, 43, 635–640.

[20] Ghoshal, B. & Tucker, A. (2020). Estimating uncertainty and interpretability in deep learning for coronavirus (COVID-19) detection. arXiv preprint arXiv:2003.10769.
[21] Farooq, M. & Hafeez, A. (2020). COVID-ResNet: A deep learning framework for screening of COVID19 from radiographs. arXiv preprint arXiv:2003.14395.
[22] Celiktutan, O. & Demiris, Y. (10–13 September 2018). Inferring human knowledgeability from eye gaze in mobile learning environments. In Proceedings of the European Conference on Computer Vision (ECCV). Munich, Germany.
[23] Cazzato, D., Leo, M. & Distante, C. (2014). An investigation on the feasibility of uncalibrated and unconstrained gaze tracking for human assistive applications by using head pose estimation. Sensors, 14, 8363–8379. [CrossRef] [PubMed]
[24] Cai, H., Fang, Y., Ju, Z., Costescu, C., David, D., Billing, E., Ziemke, T., Thill, S., Belpaeme, T., Vanderborght, B., et al. (2018). Sensing-enhanced therapy system for assessing children with autism spectrum disorders: A feasibility study. IEEE Sensors Journal, 19, 1508–1518. [CrossRef]
[25] Wu, H., Wang, B., Yu, X., Zhao, Y. & Cheng, Q. (2019). Explore on doctor's head orientation tracking for patient's body surface projection under complex illumination conditions. Journal of Medical Imaging and Health Informatics, 9, 1971–1977. [CrossRef]
[26] Rudovic, O., Lee, J., Dai, M., Schuller, B. & Picard, R. W. (2018). Personalized machine learning for robot perception of affect and engagement in autism therapy. Science Robotics, 3, eaao6760. [CrossRef]
[27] Cazzato, D., Dominio, F., Manduchi, R. & Castro, S. M. (2018). Real-time gaze estimation via pupil center tracking. Paladyn, Journal of Behavioral Robotics, 9, 6–18. [CrossRef]
[28] Roy, S. N., Mishra, S. & Yusof, S. M. (2021). Emergence of drug discovery in machine learning. Technical Advancements of Machine Learning in Healthcare, 936, 119.
[29] Tripathy, H. K., Mishra, S., Thakkar, H. K. & Rai, D. (2021). CARE: A collision-aware mobile robot navigation in grid environment using improved breadth first search. Computers & Electrical Engineering, 94, 107327.
[30] Mishra, S., Thakkar, H., Mallick, P. K., Tiwari, P. & Alamri, A. (2021). A sustainable IoHT based computationally intelligent healthcare monitoring system for lung cancer risk detection. Sustainable Cities and Society, 103079.
[31] Chattopadhyay, A., Mishra, S. & González-Briones, A. (2021). Integration of machine learning and IoT in healthcare domain. In Hybrid Artificial Intelligence and IoT in Healthcare (pp. 223–244). Springer, Singapore.
[32] Jena, L., Kamila, N. K. & Mishra, S. (2014). Privacy preserving distributed data mining with evolutionary computing. In Proceedings of the International Conference on Frontiers of Intelligent Computing: Theory and Applications (FICTA) 2013 (pp. 259–267). Springer, Cham.
[33] Mukherjee, D., Tripathy, H. K. & Mishra, S. (2021). Scope of medical bots in clinical domain. Technical Advancements of Machine Learning in Healthcare, 936, 339.
[34] Mishra, S., Dash, A. & Jena, L. (2021). Use of deep learning for disease detection and diagnosis. In Bio-inspired Neurocomputing (pp. 181–201). Springer, Singapore.

Joseph Bamidele Awotunde*, Akash Kumar Bhoi, Ranjit Panigrahi
6 Detection of COVID-19 in IoMT cloud-based system using ensemble machine learning algorithms

Abstract: Modern Cloud-IoMT-based deployments of numerous wireless equipment positions have advanced technology by delivering the full potential of digital technology. The emergence of the COVID-19 epidemic globally has had a detrimental impact on various human endeavors. Though viable vaccine has been discovered to combat the outbreak globally, various variant of the pandemic still calls for preventive measures to stop the disease from spreading. Therefore, to process the captured data from various IoMT sensors and stop the pandemic, this chapter proposes an IoMT (Internet of Medical Things) cloud-based diagnostics framework. The proposed Cloud-IoMT-based system was enabled with machine learning (ML) for the processing of the captured data. The proposed system has various levels like data reparation, processing, isolation/quarantine, and result utilization center. The proposed system utilized four ML algorithms, namely XGBoost, extra tree, random forest, and LGBM. COVID-19 signs and symptoms were captured using IoMT-based devices for the patient's diagnosis. An LGBM accuracy of 91% demonstrates that the model outperformed the other three algorithms, and the least is the RF algorithm with an accuracy of 75%. The performance of the proposed model revealed the effectiveness of ML-based algorithms in processing the capture data using IoMT-based devices and stored in a cloud database. This will help meal workers to manage COVID-19 pandemic and prevent them from contacting the disease.

Keywords: Machine learning, Internet of Things, diagnosis, cloud computing, coronavirus, ensemble algorithms, Internet of Medical Things

6.1 Introduction

Following the 1918 influenza pandemic, the COVID-19 outburst has created a universal public health concern. According to a World Health Organization report, the pandemic has really affected populace physically and economically that resulted to huge

---

*Corresponding author: **Joseph Bamidele Awotunde**, Department of Computer Science, Faculty of Information and Communication Sciences, University of Ilorin, Ilorin 240003, Nigeria,
e-mail: awotunde.jb@unilorin.edu.ng
Akash Kumar Bhoi, Directorate of Research, Sikkim Manipal University, Gangtok 737102, Sikkim, India
e-mail: akashkrbhoi@gmail.com
Ranjit Panigrahi, Department of Computer Applications, Sikkim Manipal Institute of Technology, Sikkim Manipal University, Majitar 737136, Sikkim, India, e-mail: ranjit.p@smit.smu.edu.in

https://doi.org/10.1515/9783110750942-006

amount of resources globally. People throughout the world are spending a lot of time indoors to control or sidestep individuals who are sick with the illness. There has been a swift surge in sidetracks study activities to discover a long-term resolution to this global concern up until now. Several cities and towns are experiencing major challenges, with over 10 billion individuals being confined at home due to shutdown tactics. Because of the epidemic, the demand for medical instruments and materials is increasing, and nearly all of the current ones are in desperate need of replenishing. To consult a doctor, prospective individuals must leave their homes, posing serious hazards to unaffected individuals and putting a strain on the worldwide isolation and quarantine operations [1–2]. In addition, a scarcity of medical workers, sufficient hospital instruments, and isolation centers has caused authorities to recommend persons with suspicious indications or moderate phases to remain at home. As a result, there is a crucial want for a home-based analytic test that will be cost-effective, versatile, and capable of providing important answers for various human problems. In today's telemedicine, new emerging technologies have progressively been used in analysis, forecast, remote health monitoring, diagnosis, and therapies, notably the Internet of Things (IoT), and they are becoming increasingly popular. The medical industry has embraced this quickly, with a focus on creating smart apps. Adding to this, the IoT has created platform for smart equipment to relate easily in an environment with COVID-19 outbreak and facilitated the simple interchange of data through the use of internet. When it comes to diagnosing and monitoring patients' health, the Internet of Medical Things (IoMT) has become increasingly popular, with a focus on creating smart apps in the healthcare industry. To promote seamless data and information transmission, devices and sensors are able to communicate with one another in an intelligent setting thanks to the IoMT. With the full potential that latest technological affords, modern implementations of many network gear locations Cloud-IoMT-based innovation has evolved. The IoT-based technology has gained root recently, particularly in the healthcare industries. Modern healthcare systems are altered by the IoT, which transforms the medical system's conventional practices into intelligent ones. Diagnoses, monitoring, and therapies for patients are getting more and more simple and effortless thanks to the ongoing transition from traditional healthcare systems to smart medical systems. Wearable body sensor nodes, for example, have changed the ability to modify our way of life in the medical industry, recreation, mobility, commerce, enterprise, and rescue services regulation. Combining wireless sensors, sensor technologies, simulations, and intelligent systems engineering have culminated in a multidisciplinary embedded communication concept to tackle the difficulties we encounter every day [3].

The application of IoMT-based system during any outbreak can help patients receive proper medical care at home, and healthcare experts can make use of the processed data based on the data that was captured by several IoMT-based devices. For persons with mild symptoms, diagnostic and treatment gadgets like thermometers, smart helmets, smart wrist watches, drugs, shielding masks, and disease surveillance kits can be obtained. Patients' health status may be continuously uploaded via an IoMT-based internet connection to healthcare cloud services, and their data may then be forwarded to the Centers for Disease Control and Prevention (also known as the CDC) as well as neighboring clinics or medical center facilities [4]. Following that, a healthcare professional will conduct online health evaluations depending on each patient's health state, and if required, regulators and healthcare specialists will allocate services and allocate quarantine stations to the afflicted individual. People can use the IoMT platform to continually assess their clinical diagnostic and acquire suitable medical requirements while avoiding viral spreading to others. As a result, reduce expenses, alleviate medical tool limitations, and create a systemic repository that clinicians can use to efficiently follow the progress of outbreaks, relative tool supplies become simpler, and rescue tactics are enforced.

The present pandemic is suffocating the medical industry to the point of collapse; hospitals and clinics are overflowing with observed infected patients awaiting confirmation of the diagnosis. As the number of healthcare diagnosing equipment and supplies grows, so does the scarcity of diagnostic medical equipment and materials, and as the number of patients who require care grows, so does the number of patients admitted to the hospital, exposing grassroots health professionals who perform crucial tasks at greater risk. A powerful and dependable therapy plan is necessary to preserve people's lives in order to lessen the effects of this catastrophe. Government and private donors will be able to provide supplies and equipment to clinics and hospitals more effectively thanks to this. Additionally, the approach will give information on medical facilities so that good patient care may be developed. This combination strategy can save lots of lives while also protecting stressed economies and provide a roadmap for dealing with future crises more efficiently.

Figure 6.1 presents the proposed framework used in this study. In an effort to stop the outbreak of the sickness, which would have affected millions of people, some nations were extending the lockdown. Initially, scientists questioned the initiative's practicality and warned that there was a SARS-like threat in certain nation's outbreak [5–6]. The pandemic looks to be under control in most nations at this point; however there is still criticism of what some have dubbed "draconian" measures taken to stop it from spreading. The world is currently striving to keep track of an unusual virus outbreak that has resulted in the biggest number of illnesses and deaths. Because there is no definitive medical cure for coronaviruses and attempts to restrict their blowout have so far futile [7], there is a pressing need for a global investigation of COVID-19 afflicted individuals. The IoT was born as a result of the emergence of new technological developments, and it is gaining worldwide attention for tracking, analyzing and predicting, and avoiding emerging infectious diseases. Using interconnected wearable sensors and networks, IoT in the healthcare industry has aided appropriate COVID-19 control. Infectious illness epidemiology is investigating the IoT. However, the increased risks of communicable disease transmission due to globalization, and the widespread availability of smart types of machinery, as well as the

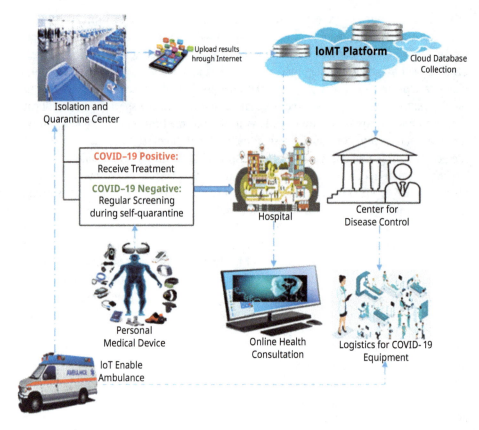

Figure 6.1: IoMT-based system for pandemic outbreak protection.

world's interconnectedness, necessitates their usage for monitoring, avoiding, anticipating, and managing transmissible infections.

The IoT is a cutting-edge method of integrating healthcare devices and applications with regard to human capabilities through the COVID-19 epidemic allowed equality to both affluent and poor populations in terms of equal access to health services, with no discrimination. The system provides a variety of cloud-based IoT administrations, including knowledge exchange, among other things. We provide report checking, inspection, assessment, therapy, and monitoring patients. This rewards diverse patients with more fulfilling treatments and diagnoses, and it develops a new medical care delivery system in operation, which is crucial in light of this pandemic. Adopting an IoT-based solution enables medical personnel to concentrate solely on the patient, identify infected individuals and those who come into touch with them, and confine them to a separate facility. Tools supplied by IoT devices, such as an alert system like the geospatial data, and monitoring devices integrated inside the body, can be utilized to control the development of the outbreak. In order to identify person's ill with the COVID-19 disease, sensors such as temperature and other indicators may be employed at airports everywhere the globe. As a result, we propose a Cloud-IoMT-based actual surveillance and therapeutic system. The suggested framework will be utilized to diagnose suspected instances based on data collected by IoMT-based devices. The proposed framework was divided into five layers: IoMT-based devices using for capture various COVID-19 data, Cloud-based database, ML model for data processing, isolation monitoring, and decision support center. The quick detection of the epidemic, as well as real-time surveillance, will lessen the strain on medical workers in terms of preventing and controlling of this infectious disease.

This chapter is arranged as follows: the use of IoMT-based cloud computing framework to combat the COVID-19 epidemic is discussed in Section 2. The related work was accessible in Section 3. The fourth section introduces the proposed framework analysis and observation system for controlling the pandemic eruption. The framework's practical applicability is discussed in Section 5, while the outcomes and conversation are offered in Section 6. Last, the conclusions and prospect work for the realization of an effective use of framework in fighting the deadly disease are discussed in Section 7.

6.2 The benefits of IoMT-based system and cloud computing in fighting COVID-19 epidemic

The healthcare system in emerging countries is rapidly evolving as a result of the dramatic rise in life expectancy during the 1990s [8]. Due to the emergence of infectious diseases, many countries' healthcare systems are under increasing strain [9]. In developed nations, life expectancy rose by roughly 30 years throughout the twentieth century. As an effect, the aging population has significantly increased [8]. In some countries, the rise of chronic diseases has also put a burden on medical institutions due to lack of funding [9]. When it comes to health care system, variety of conditions and management choices, as well as a growing patient population, rising infectious diseases, and aging populations create substantial obstacles. Successful ways have been demonstrated to prevent overloading health infrastructure and reduce healthcare expenditures [10].

Although there are many different telemedicine systems, the majority of them are created to fulfill a specific therapeutic goal, such as stroke therapy or mobile cardiac surveillance [11]. This aspect of telemedicine services' cost-effectiveness prevents medical systems from being overburdened, but it also signifies a drawback as the quantity of patients and disease type grows. The IoT-based system can satisfy the need for greater generality and dependability. It has the power to treat a wide range of illnesses that call for various kinds of rigorous monitoring and response parameters, including the aged problem and life-threatening conditions. Though the use of

IoT in highly contagious disease epidemiology is still emerging, smart technology has become widespread, as well as the through globalization and international interconnectedness, highly communicable disease hazards are magnified and disseminated to a wider audience and necessitate to predict, prevent, and manage COVID-19 pandemics as they develop [12–13]. Many countries have recently introduced Internet medical knowledge and surveillance systems techniques to increase risk controlling and early identification of events; however existing technology is not being applied methodically enough [12]. By utilizing smart healthcare monitoring in a globalized healthcare system, local health authorities would be better able to recognize, manage, and prevent infectious diseases [14].

Blood pressure monitors, blood glucose monitors, and endoscopic pills are just a few of the technologies that IoT devices, like satellites, may have in the healthcare sector [15–16]. The combination of various technologies in medical industry will revolutionize the way nations operate during pandemic outbreaks [17, 18]. The captured data using various intelligent gathering will help in real-time transmission of healthcare information to the cloud and then transmit it to healthcare IT schemes [3, 19]. There are millions of healthcare devices and sensors in use currently, and a range of biological functions are connected to and tracked to notify medical solutions [20]. To store and process data, these IoT devices are connected to cloud infrastructures like Amazon Web Services, Google Cloud, Microsoft Azure, or any other specialized web facilities. IoT services can involve tracking patients with chronic or lingering illnesses online for healthcare purposes. These technological advancements allow for the tracking of individuals utilizing wearable medical devices in hospitals as well as the observation of any patient treatment directives. The health information they've gathered can be sent to their doctor. These include inpatient beds with detectors and infusion pumps that may be connected to analyzing platforms monitor patients' IoT medical equipment such as vital signs can be incorporated or launched. The IoT realizes its full potential when used with objects, or "intelligent" commodities, that include a variety of sensing components that let them to adapt to their surroundings and embedded communication infrastructure that enables communication with any prospective substitute.

Cloud computing will be critical in absorbing healthcare transformation costs, maximizing assets, and ushering in a new era of technology. Modern policies were aimed to get data at any time and from any location, which could be accomplished by shifting medical record to the internet. This modern delivery approach will upgrade the healthcare's productivity while also cutting the cost of innovation expenditures [21]. However, due to concerns about the adherence with a specific standard, such as HIPAA, and the protection of sensitive patient data, it also poses some challenges. Taking these security and privacy concerns into account, healthcare providers may undeniably profit from cloud computing technologies, which can significantly reduce healthcare costs and improve the quality of services in healthcare systems [22, 29]. Self-service on-demand, extensive network access, resource pooling with other tenants, quick elasticity, and calculated services are all important elements of cloud computing. Clouds provide improvements in computing energy or resource availability, and ubiquitous access to services whenever, from any place, and great resource adaptability and scalability in complicated resources. These benefits have been cited as a cause for cloud computing's growing popularity in a variety of industries. In recent years, this approach has been plainly accepted in the field of healthcare. Cloud services for smart healthcare is gaining popularity in the wider literature and is offered by healthcare IT companies, but it is also gaining interest in the scientific research, with an ever-increasing number of articles and publications appearing.

One of the key benefits of cloud service would be the ability to transfer data between different platforms. This is a capability that IT desperately requires in the healthcare industry. Cloud service, for instance, can allow health care providers to share data from diverse information systems, such as EHRs, doctor's references, prescriptions, insurance data, and research reports. This already can economize on computer expenses and boost image sharing [23]. A wide range of healthcare services are available from doctors' offices to hospitals to pharmacy services. Businesses have used cloud computing to agree to collaborate and share healthcare data in order to improve service quality and cut costs. Judging by the current state of the industry, it appears that cloud-based solutions will soon overtake on-premises once the industry standard after all of the challenges is overcome.

6.3 Related work

Rath and Pattanayak [24] envisioned a smart health monitoring hospital in metropolitan settings utilizing IoT devices. A prompt medical system for individuals was tackled in the VANET district, with concerns such as cleanliness and patient safety being handled. As a result, the suggested system was tested using NS2 and NetSim simulators method [24]. Based on the associated research, Darwish et al. [25] proposed a Cloud-IoT-Health paradigm that blends cloud platform with IoT in the healthcare system. The study addressed the challenges of incorporation as well as upcoming advancements in Cloud-IoT-Health. These issues are identified at three layers: technology, connection and infrastructure, and expertise. College students' physical activity on school property was examined by Zhong [26]. The author concentrates on the physical activity recognition and monitoring (PARM) methodology. Various classifiers were used to evaluate the proposed system and the results were also compared with existing works. The classifiers used were SVM, decision tree, and neural network, and the SVM performed better when compared with the other classifiers. Din and Paul [27] developed a three-layered IoT-based system for real-time monitoring and management of patients. The architecture was separated into three layers: (i) data collecting via sensing devices, (ii) Hadoop system for processing data, and (iii) device center. Due to the limited power of sensors batteries, the proposed technique of power generation with piezoelectric equipment attached to the human body was employed. Otoom et al. [28] used ARIMA with Markov-based models to assess the insulin dosage by designing an IoT-based prototype for the monitoring and regulations of the blood sugar.

To increase safety in the outdoors, Wu et al. [30] suggested a cross IoT protection and medical monitoring. The proposed system consists of two components: the first is for data capture and gathering and the second stored the collected data through the internet collection and process and compile the data. The wearable gadgets were utilized to collect patients' clinical complaints and risk indicators from their surroundings. An actual health monitoring system based on Industrial IoT (HealthIoT) was built in 2016 by Hossain and Muhammad [31]. To negate death conditions, this gadget has a wide bandwidth for analyzing patient health information. This IoT healthcare system collects patient records using medical devices and sensors. In addition, to avoid data breaches or clinical errors by medical practitioners, safeguarding procedures like watermarking and gesture amplification have been used in this scheme. Centered on the advancements of IoT health gadgets, Gope and Hwang [32] discovered a fresh invention called as the body sensor network (BSN) in 2016. Diverse simple and compact monitoring systems can be used to keep tabs on the patient within this mechanism. Furthermore, the safety standards for implementing the BSN-medical scheme have been measured in this aspect. Verma and Sood [33] reviewed works that have been done in the areas of IoT-based applications within 2015 and proposed a U-healthcare based on IoT architecture. The IoT platform has a metadata diversity issue explained by Xu et al. [34]. Apart from that, there is a goal for resource-based data availability scheme (UDA-IoT) to process IoT data anywhere. In addition, an IoT-based system for coping with health challenges will be demonstrated to illustrate the gathering, incorporation, and interoperability of IoT data. In Banaee et al. [35], new approaches and techniques for interpreting data acquired from sensing devices in the context of health surveillance were described. Continuous time-series readings from sensing devices have been used in big data processes like outlier discovery, forecast, and assessment. In 2014, Zhang et al. [36] investigated methods for creating mHealth-based apps, with a focus on web and software development for remotely monitoring patients using IoT-based healthcare therapy systems. To let respondents (doctors) who are not in a medical environment access patient health records, web-based apps have been created. These researchers also used IoT-based health monitoring to track harmful health impacts including alcohol use and the recovery effects of medical interventions [37, 38].

A survey was conducted by Nguyen [39] discusses the employment of artificial intelligence (AI) in the COVID-19 outbreak. These strategies were grouped by their performance into numerous areas, including the utilization of IoT. Rao and Vazquez [40] proposed using machine learning (ML) methods to evaluate possible COVID-19 instances. In order to effectively exchange information across smart cities during the COVID-19 eruption, which was caused by the outbreak of COVID-19 pandemics, Allam and Jones [41] addressed the issue. For example, the sensors in smart cities that gather thermal data was used with the application of AI methods to recognize potential COVID-19 instances. A strategy centered on the IoT was proposed by Fatima et al. [42] to categorize coronavirus cases. Peeri et al. [43] utilized previously published papers to conduct a study comparison using various articles that used MERS, SARs, and COVID-19 instances. The authors proposed using IoT to track the disease outbreaks. In Mei et al. [46], the authors used three AI methods, COVID-19 (+), PTB, and SARS, to categorize CT scan pictures and individual medical data. In the first model, a chest CT scan is used; in the second, medical evidence is used; and in the third, both are used. These techniques were used to classify the data. Clinical data and CT scans integrated in the model yielded the best results, with a sensitivity of 84.3%, a specificity of 82.8%, and an AUC of 0.92.

The authors in Loey et al. [47] developed a generational neural networks to detect COVID-19 in CXR images and pneumonia microbial groups. To increase their number, they employed GAN to create more CXR images. Alexnet, Googlenet, and Restnet18 were the three algorithms that have already been trained for transmission learning. The pretrained model was used to train the GANed pictures in three phases. The images were processed using the Googlenet model with an accuracy of 80.6%. An accuracy of 85.2% was achieved using Alexnet that underwent training in the second phase. Finally, Googlenet achieved a 100% accuracy rate with just two classes (normal and non-normal). The decompose, transfer, and compose (DeTraC) approach was used by the authors in Awotunde et al. [48] to classify standard and SARS CXR images. ResNet 18 was used to train ImageNet and DeTraC for transfer learning. With the help of PCA, the feature space was made smaller. The testing results show that the DeTraC technique with 95.12% accuracy, 97.91% sensitivity, and 91.87% specificity. In a related work, Sethy and Behera [49] employed deep features (ResNet50, AlexNet, and VGG16) to analyze CXR lung pictures for features. An SVM model was then used to classify the features that were collected from the CXR images. The dataset [27–29] was contributed by Kaggle and Github and was divided into normal, pneumonia, and COVID-19.

6.3.1 The coronavirus datasets and data dashboards

In predicting and analyzing COVID-19, a centralized data platform was created to illustrate the projected and actual spread [44, 45]. These dashboards show a global picture of COVID-19 attacks as well as the growing number of them. Emerging economies, such as South Africa, have already set up their COVID-19 dashboards, and some use a Python script to show how information may be gathered from the COVID-19 data collection [50].

6.4 The proposed Cloud-IoMT-based framework

The suggested structure was illustrated and discussed in this part. The suggested design might be used to identify a probable COVID-19 case in instantaneous, and the conceptual methodology, in particular, could be used to track and forecast therapy for verified individuals with a thorough thoughtful of the landscape of the COVID-19 epidemic. The proposed system is displayed in Figure 6.2. The proposed architecture is divided into five stages, namely data capture, data processing, isolation/quarantine, evaluation, and the application layer for medical professionals. Cloud infrastructure was used to link the components.

Even when the storage capacity is quite huge, ML prototypes play a momentous part in the decision-making procedure [51–52]. The specific data categories like speed, variation, and capacity must be specified in order to apply data processing procedures for specific fields of study. Anatomy of data analysis modeling includes a description of a neural network as well as classes and clustering techniques [53–54]. Data may be created from many bases with different sorts of data, and it is also vital for the creation of systems proficient of dealing with extracted features. The architecture comprises the following essential features, as shown in Figure 6.2.

The input layer (patients data): The layer used to capture various patient physiological data using various devices and sensors like mobile and smartphone tracker attached to the users' body. Nowadays, a variety of medical gadgets are available [55–58]. Vital signs such as blood oxygen saturation, temperature, heart rate, blood sugar levels, and SPo2 are computed using these sensors. Since any abnormal data could result in illness, it is crucial to keep an eye on these signs in the patient's body [59, 60].

For instance, a drop in bodily oxygen levels can lead to sleep apnea, which raises the likelihood of dying. Before being sent to a database server, the patient's mobile app obtains the sensitive data over Bluetooth. Additionally, sensors can be programmed to calculate and transmit data continuously without the need for patient contact (IoMT), enhancing the efficiency and practicality of interface design.

The enabled IoMT-based Cloud database layer: The cloud is the place within the IoMT-based layer for keeping data captured for the purposes of analyses. The cloud enables individual information to be analyzed from their mobile device through the internet and then forwarded to doctors for evaluation. As a result, for any ailment recognition in clinical records, all records collected and distributed will be saved in the cloud, and any abnormal changes in patient data will be classified based on patient status and disease. All records generated will be either forwarded to the patient's and/or physician's webpage or to the emergency department, depending on the patient's situation. As a result, the IoMT online promotes teamwork and data transfer through its portal, allowing medical practitioners to keep patient information and records, investigates, and diagnoses the uploaded data, thus help medical professionals making useful decision

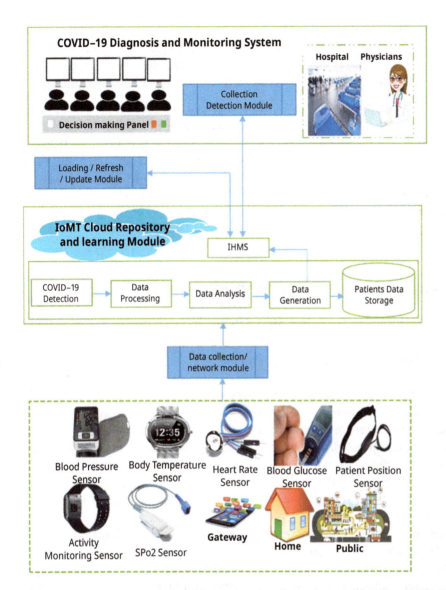

Figure 6.2: Common COVID-19 outbreak diagnostic and monitoring framework based on Cloud IoT.

concerns patients instantaneously in relation to shared data. It provides faster medications and real-time updates on patient information.

COVID-19 platform for diagnosis and tracking and warning (hospital layer): This architecture serves as a vehicle for the physician to monitor consumer information and visual information. The clinicians may evaluate and act on data generated by the application in the cloud. In this approach, in real-time base, data is replicated by deleting all data from the cloud database server. This lets firefighters make critical decisions in a critical situation before the patient's condition worsens and requires inpatient by keeping professionals updated on the patient's state. The remaining components of an enabled sensor nodes are primarily used to handle network layout setups and interactions among device phases and their entities.

Gateway: This serve as the link between the user and the IoMT-based enabled cloud computing platform. The devices and sensors wears by the patient use the gateway to communicate with the proposed framework component that is in charge of interacting with specific devices that are used to identify symptoms and carry out preliminary data processing. The situation of the patients who have been referred to medical care is summarized by this module. The structure can also respond to anomaly indications by sending a support demand, such as a call for an associate caregiver worker or a critical demand.

6.5 Applicability of the proposed model

6.5.1 The machine learning algorithms

6.5.1.1 Lightweight gradient boosting machine

The lightweight gradient boosting machine (LGBM) is a tree-based learning algorithm that uses a gradient boosting system. The tree-based algorithm, under ones' estimation, is the most intuitive because it imitates how a decision is made by humans. LGBM is a fast, distributed, and high-performance decision tree based on Microsoft's "Distributed Machine Learning Tools" R&D team frame for gradient boosting. Its distributed architecture has the advantages of speedier acceleration and high performance of training; lower memory usage; greater accuracy; parallel and GPU learning support; the ability to manage very large data.

These benefits have quickly become common in the area of ML after the release of LGBM and are commonly used in tasks such as classification, regression, and ranking. The poor learner will develop sequentially using the tree-based learning algorithm, meaning that the first tree we developed will learn how to suit the target variable, then the second tree will learn from the first tree and also learn how to fit the residual, the next tree will learn how to reduce the residual and fit the residual from the previous tree. Throughout the system, the gradient of the errors is propagated and it is called level-wise tree growth. The growth of the tree is level-wise in XGBoost, which distinguishes the LGBM from another gradient boosting algorithm, while CatBoost is more suitable for categorical variables. If you want to create a model with an abundance of data, LGBM is acceptable for use. It is safer to use other ML algorithms if you only have 100 data because your model could cause over-fitting.

6.5.1.2 XGBoost classifier

XGBoost is an effective and scalable classifier for ML, which gained popularity in 2016 by Chen and Guestrin [70]. The initial XGBoost model, which incorporates manifold decision trees in an advancing mode, is the gradient boosting decision tree. In general, a new tree is created in a manner that will reduce the gradient boosting of the previous archetypal's residual. Residual describes the differences between the actual and expected numbers. The template has been trained up till the threshold is established by the number of decision trees. Similar to gradient boosting, XGBoost uses the number of boosts, learning degree, subsampling processes scale, and ultimate tree depth to control excessive fitting and boost performance. Furthermore, XGBoost maximizes the size of the tree, the function target, and the size of the masses that are subject to regularization's normal bounds. The XGBoost achieves superior efficiency in a particular search space with multiple hyper-parameters.

Gamma $\gamma \in (0, +\infty)$ denotes minimal loss reduction, which includes a split to render the partition on a tree's leaf node, according to the hyper-parameters. The minimum child weight $w_{mc} \in (0, +\infty)$ is defined as the minimum occurrence mass total, this indicates that if the tree partition step results in a leaf node with a case weight sum smaller than w_{mc}, the tree will toss out the subsequent partition. The goal of the early stop technique is to identify the ideal number of intervals that best match the input hyper-parameters. Last, subsampling methods and $r_c \in (0,1)$ gave column subsample ratio structures for each tree. The hyper-parameters are controlled via grid search in the last stage to reduce the error in classification.

Given $X \in \mathbb{R}^{n \times d}$ as the training dataset, XGBoost object function in t-th, d features, and n samples is represented by

$$Obj^{(t)} \simeq \sum_{i=1}^{n} \left\{ \ell\left(y_i, \tilde{y}_i^{(t-1)}\right) + g_i f_t(x_i) + \frac{1}{2} h_i f_t^2(x_i) \right\} + \Omega(f_t), \qquad (6.1)$$

$$g_i = \partial_{\tilde{y}(t-1)} \ell\left(y_i, \tilde{y}_i^{(t-1)}\right), h_i = \partial^2_{\tilde{y}(t-1)} \ell\left(y_i, \tilde{y}_i^{(t-1)}\right), \qquad (6.2)$$

the first gradient g_i represents the loos function l in this instance, and h_i is the second gradient of ℓ. The process of regularization is used to gauge the level of complexity of the model $\Omega(f_t) = \gamma T + \frac{1}{2}\varphi\|\varphi\|^2$, where the number of leaf nodes is represented by T.

As demonstrated in eq. (6.3), the logistic loss ℓ of the training loss measures how well the model fits on the training data:

$$\ell\left(y_i, \tilde{y}_i^{(t-1)}\right) = y_i \ln\left(1 + e^{-\tilde{y}_i}\right) + (1 - y_i)\ln\left(1 + e^{\tilde{y}_i}\right) \qquad (6.3)$$

Given the t-th training sample $x_i \in \mathbb{R}^d$, assume that an XGBoost model of XGB contains K trees, the corresponding prediction $\tilde{y}_i$ is computed as

$$\tilde{y}_i = \sum_{k=1}^{k} F_k(x_i) \tag{6.4}$$

$$s.t. F_k \in XGB, \text{ where } XGB = \{F_1, F_2, F_3, \ldots, F_K\}. \tag{6.5}$$

6.5.1.3 Trees with extreme randomness (ET)

ET is a group of classifiers that creates a set of unpruned decision trees using a top-down approach. A random subset of the k attributes is selected for splitting at each node. Instead of choosing the best cut-point based on the local sample, each tree is formed from a discretization threshold, and a random cut-point is chosen for the entire dataset at each node to establish a break rather than using bootstrapping. As a result, regardless of the output labels from the training set, the tree's structure is determined when $k = 1$ [67–68].

6.5.1.4 Random forest

This approach builds a tree using bootstrap replication without trimming as a variation of the Bagging consortium suggested by [69]. Throughout decision tree growth, aggregation of bootstraps and unpredictability in data node selection improve the classification efficiency of a base classifier:

$$f(x) = \arg\max_{y \in y} \sum_{j=1}^{J} I(y = h_j(x)) \tag{6.6}$$

For $j = 1, \ldots, J$

6.5.2 Preprocessing

Putting the study forth as a categorization issue: Let $S = \{(x_1, y_1), (x_2, y_2), \cdots (x_n, y_n)\}$ be the set of training occurrences of dimension d. $Y = \{y_1, y_2 \cdots, y_n\}$ the group of tags where x_i is a feature and y_i is a label, we have COVID-19, PTB, and normal. The first step in photo classifiers is feature extraction. This is particularly crucial when the input data, which are the chosen features, are overly large and challenging to analyze in their original state. The selection of pertinent qualities will address this issue.

6.5.3 Systems of assessment, variables, and measurements

This segment discusses the concepts, variables, and measures that were employed in the multiclass arrangement test. The chore was completed by four students: LGBM, Extra Trees, RF, and XGBoost. The performance metrics used for the evaluation of the proposed model is discussed below. Equations (6.7) through (6.11) offer equations for metrics derived from the confusion matrix:

$$\text{Accuracy} = \frac{TP + TN}{TP + TN + FP + FN} \tag{6.7}$$

$$\text{Precision} = \frac{TP}{TP + FP} \tag{6.8}$$

$$\text{Recall (TP rate)} = \frac{TP}{TP + FN} \tag{6.9}$$

$$\text{FP rate} = \frac{FP}{FP + TN} \tag{6.10}$$

$$F1 - \text{score} = 2 \times \frac{\text{Precision} \times \text{Recall}}{\text{Precision} + \text{Recall}} \tag{6.11}$$

6.6 Results and discussion

This section presents the results and explores the chapter discussion. The experiment was run on the Anaconda platform with a Jupyter notebook and sklearn library. All tests were carried out on a Pentium Windows machine with an Intel® coreTM i5-7200 CPU running at 2.50–2.70 GHz and 8GB of RAM. To eliminate certain undesired background pictures and noise, the photographs were manually trimmed. They were resized to 128 by 128 and flattened before being converted to grayscale images and their attributes extracted. An 80:20 train:test ratio was used to divide the retrieved features. In Section 5.2, the results of the evaluation of the effectiveness of the four different ML algorithms on the extracted and reduced datasets were presented. Each statistic has a value in the range of 0 to 1. The model performs better as the measure values approach one. Table 6.1 shows the outcomes of the ML models applied to the dataset.

Table 6.1 compares the four distinct classifiers' performance in terms of the discussed metrics. The evaluation set, which makes up 20% of the entire dataset, is the foundation for the result. The results showed that LGBM had the highest classification report values (0.91%) across all criteria. In comparison to other models, its outcome value is more stable across all criteria, and its F1-score is greater. The RF had the minimum values of 0.72%, succeeded by ET, which had a value of 0.86%. With a score of 0.91%, LGBM surpassed all other models. The recall rate and accuracy of RF were the lowest, at 0.85% and 86%, respectively.

Table 6.1: The summary performance of the machine learning algorithms.

Model	Accuracy	Recall	F1-score	Precision
XGBoost	90	0.90	0.90	0.91
LGBM	91	0.91	0.91	0.91
RF	75	0.72	0.72	0.87
ET	86	0.85	0.86	0.89

6.6.1 Confusion matrix

The confusion matrix for the four models utilized in the suggested system was shown in Figure 6.3. This was utilized to assess the efficiency of the suggested system in more detail. The results obtained as shown in Figure 6.3a, LGBM has the best recall for all classes, and the model is the best in terms of accuracy. Out of 106 COVID-19 cases, 103 (97%) were correctly diagnosed by XGBoost, according to the confusion matrix results, while 3 (3%) were incorrectly classified. There were no mismatches with the PTB class, but three (4%) members of the class NORMAL were mistakenly categorized as COVID-19 whereas 78 (96%) were correctly identified as NORMAL. Additionally, although 65 instances (82%) of the class PTB were correctly classified as PTB, 14 cases (18%) of the class PTB were mistakenly classified as COVID-19. According to the results, LGBM performed better than the other three models for COVID-19 categorization.

6.6.2 ROC curves

Figure 6.4 displays the ROC curves for the four models. It has been determined to have the four models' best performance in terms of the trade-off between true positive and false-positive rate. All metrics' ROC scores are approximately one, suggesting a decent classifier, with COVID-19, NORMAL, and PTB ROC values of 0.96, 1.00, and 0.97, accordingly. The total average is 0.98, indicating a solid balance of recall and precision.

6.6.3 Comparison with the existing COVID-19 ML diagnosis systems

The suggested framework's goal is to provide scientific answers to climate change that will provide both scholars and practitioners with a working path to what is attainable epidemic utilizing an IoMT-based approach combined with ML techniques. Table 6.2 highlights the suggested system's comparison to important findings in some existing ML research projects.

6 Detection of COVID-19 in IoMT cloud-based system — 141

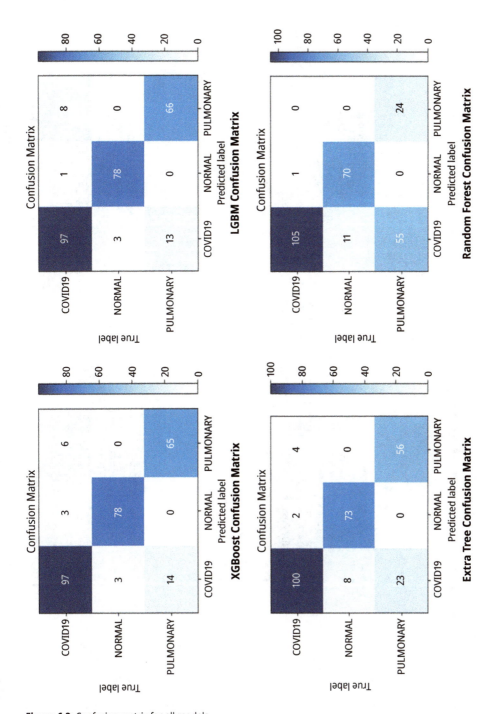

Figure 6.3: Confusion matrix for all models.

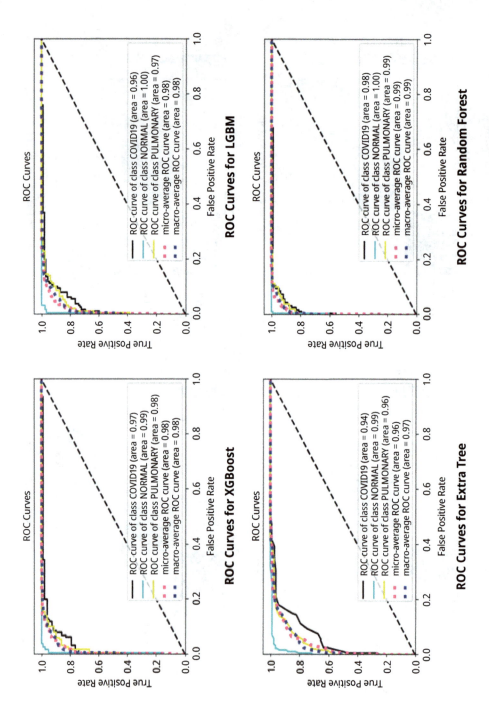

Figure 6.4: ROC for all the models.

Table 6.2: Summary of ML only approaches.

S/N	Study	Dataset, classes	Classes	Feature extraction, selection	ML	Key findings
1	Ref. [64]	Text	ARDS, COVID-19	Gini index and chi-square	LR, k-NN, DT, RF, and SVM	The SVM and k-NN models performed best having 80% accuracy for the classification of COVID-19.
2	Ref. [49]	CT scan	COVID-19, pneumonia and normal	LBP, HOG, and GLCM with deep features like ResNet50, AlexNet, VGG16, VGG19	SVM	The ResNet + SVM model has an accuracy of 95.33%, FPR of 2.33%, sensitivity of 95.03%, and F1-score of 95.34%, respectively.
3	Ref. [65]	CT scan	coronavirus/ non-coronavirus	GLCM, LDP, GLRLM, GLSZM, and DWT	SVM	There is 99.7% accuracy for the GLSZM.
4	Ref. [66]	CXR	Normal bacteria include COVID-19, MERS, SARS, Varicella, Streptococcus, and Pneumocystis.	SMOTE-B1/B2, AllKNN, ENN/RENN, LBP, EQP, LDN, LETRIST, BSIF, LPQ, oBIFs, and inception-V3 are utilized for extraction methods	k-NN, SVM, MLP, DT, and RF	The proposed model performed very well with the 89% F1-score by clustering + BSIF + EQP + LPQ + SMOTE + TL and 65% by MLP + LBP
5	Proposed system	CXR	394 PTB, 406 NORMAL, and 527 COVID-19	The HOG is used for the extraction methods applied to remove textual features	XGBoost, LGBM, RF, and extra trees	Out of the four models used for the classification of COVID-19 dataset, LGBM model performed best with an accuracy of 91%, recall of 90.78%, F1-scroe of 91%, and precision of 91.05%, respectively.

6.7 Conclusion

The most recent internet revolution is the cloud-based IoT revolution, which is a growing area of study, particularly in the field of medicine. With the increased use of smart sensors and mobile devices, such remote medical monitoring systems have emerged at such a rapid pace. IoT monitoring of health makes it possible to accurately assess one's health status even when the doctor is far away and helps to avoid the spread of disease. In healthcare, IoT is a key factor in providing improved medical treatment to people while also assisting physicians and hospitals. This study proposes a movable physiological Cloud-IoT-based diagnostic and observing scheme that can constantly screen a patient's body heat, sugar levels, pulse rate, and other specified room data. The device uses technology tools to collect biological data from patients and transmits it to a cloud-IoT server for evaluation and processing. Any discrepancy in the patient's data will therefore be communicated to the patient's carers via the COVID-19 telemonitoring platform. According to the results of the four algorithms used, LGBM performed better with an accuracy of 91%, followed by XGBoost with an accuracy of 90%, and random forest with the least accuracy of the four algorithms at 76%. The LGBM model achieved a recall rate of 0.94 in the confusion matrix, demonstrating good detection performance. Although LGBM has the highest F-score (0.91), the XGBoost and LGBM performed the best in terms of recall and precision, with 0.90 and 0.91, respectively. A patient with little symptoms may be diagnosed utilizing Cloud-IoMT-based medical devices, and information may be acquired using thermometers, drugs, customized COVID-19 infection diagnoses, and treatment kits. People can regularly upload their essential health data to the IoT-Cloud clinical server database and exchange pertinent information with clinics, the CDC, and national and local hospitals. Future developments will incorporate tougher security measures, like cloud decryption, fully holomorphic cryptography, and DNA encryption, to name a few. This is due to the fact that data protection is of utmost importance for IoT-based analysis and monitoring of medical programs. Particularly, a number of security flaws may affect cloud-based healthcare data.

References

[1] Awotunde, J. B., Ogundokun, R. O., Adeniyi, E. A. & Misra, S. (2022). Visual exploratory data analysis technique for epidemiological outbreak of COVID-19 pandemic. In EAI/Springer Innovations in Communication and Computing (2022, pp. 179–191). Springer, Cham.

[2] Folorunso, S. O., Awotunde, J. B., Adeboye, N. O. & Matiluko, O. E. (2022). Data classification model for COVID-19 pandemic. Studies in Systems, Decision and Control, 2022(378), 93–118.

[3] Joyia, G. J., Liaqat, R. M., Farooq, A. & Rehman, S. (2017). Internet of medical things (IOMT): Applications, benefits, and future challenges in the healthcare domain. J Commun, 12(4), 240–7.

[4] Yang, T., Gentile, M., Shen, C. F. & Cheng, C. M. (2020). Combining point-of-care diagnostics and the internet of medical things (IoMT) to combat the COVID-19 pandemic. Diagnostics, 224.

[5] Rahman, M. S., Peeri, N. C., Shrestha, N., Zaki, R., Haque, U. & Ab Hamid, S. H. (2020). Defending against the novel coronavirus (COVID-19) outbreak: How can the internet of things (IoT) help to save the World? Health Policy and Technology.

[6] Allam, Z. & Jones, D. S. (2020). Pandemic stricken cities on lockdown. Where are our planning and design professionals [now, then, and into the future]? Land Use Policy, 104805.

[7] Awotunde, J. B., Jimoh, R. G., AbdulRaheem, M., Oladipo, I. D., Folorunso, S. O. & Ajamu, G. J. (2022). IoT-based wearable body sensor network for COVID-19 pandemic studies in systems. Decision and Control, 2022(378), 253–275.

[8] Christensen, K., Doblhammer, G., Rau, R. & Vaupel, J. W. (2009). Aging populations: The challenges ahead. The Lancet, 374(9696), 1196-1208.

[9] Awotunde, J. B., Folorunso, S. O., Bhoi, A. K., Adebayo, P. O. & Ijaz, M. F. (2021). Disease diagnosis system for IoT-based wearable body sensors with machine learning algorithm. Intelligent Systems Reference Library, 2021(209), 201–222.

[10] Darkins, A., Ryan, P., Kobb, R., Foster, L., Edmonson, E., Wakefield, B. & Lancaster, A. E. (2008). Care Coordination/Home Telehealth: The systematic implementation of health informatics, home telehealth, and disease management to support the care of veteran patients with chronic conditions. Telemedicine and e-Health, 14(10), 1118-1126.

[11] Folorunso, S. O., Awotunde, J. B., Ayo, F. E. & Abdullah, K. K. A. (2021). RADIoT: the unifying framework for IoT, radiomics and deep learning modeling. Intelligent Systems Reference Library, 2021(209), 109–128.

[12] Christaki, E. (2015). New technologies in predicting, preventing, and controlling emerging infectious diseases. Virulence, 6(6), 558–565.

[13] Udgata, S. K. & Suryadevara, N. K. (2020) COVID-19: Challenges and advisory. In The Internet of Things and Sensor Network for COVID-19 (pp. 1–17). Springer, Singapore.

[14] Awotunde, J. B., Jimoh, R. G., Oladipo, I. D., Abdulraheem, M., Jimoh, T. B. & Ajamu, G. J. (2021). Big data and data analytics for an enhanced COVID-19 epidemic management. Studies in Systems, Decision and Control, 2021, 358, 11–29.

[15] Pramanik, P. K. D., Upadhyaya, B. K., Pal, S. & Pal, T. (2019). Internet of things, smart sensors, and pervasive systems: Enabling connected and pervasive healthcare. In Healthcare Data Analytics and Management (pp. 1–58). Academic Press.

[16] Srivastava, G., Parizi, R. M. & Dehghantanha, A. (2020). The future of blockchain technology in healthcare internet of things security. In Blockchain Cybersecurity, Trust and Privacy (pp. 161–184). Springer, Cham.

[17] Awotunde, J. B., Ajagbe, S. A., Oladipupo, M. A., Awokola, J. A., Afolabi, O. S., Mathew, T. O. & Oguns, Y. J. (2021, October). An improved machine learnings diagnosis technique for COVID-19 pandemic using chest X-ray Images. Communications in Computer and Information Science, 2021, 1455 CCIS, 319-330.

[18] Darwish, A., Ismail Sayed, G. & Ella Hassanien, A. (2019). The Impact of Implantable Sensors in Biomedical Technology on the Future of Healthcare Systems. Intelligent Pervasive Computing Systems for Smarter Healthcare, 67–89.

[19] Manogaran, G., Chilamkurti, N. & Hsu, C. H. (2018). Emerging trends, issues, and challenges on the internet of medical things and wireless networks. Personal and Ubiquitous Computing, 22(5–6), 879–882.

[20] Qadri, Y. A., Nauman, A., Zikria, Y. B., Vasilakos, A. V. & Kim, S. W. (2020). The future of healthcare internet of things: a survey of emerging technologies. IEEE Communications Surveys & Tutorials, 22(2), 1121–1167.

[21] Aarons, G. A., Hurlburt, M. & Horwitz, S. M. (2011). Advancing a conceptual model of evidence-based practice implementation in public service sectors. Administration and Policy in Mental Health and Mental Health Services Research, 38(1), 4–23.
[22] Rajabion, L., Shaltooki, A. A., Taghikhah, M., Ghasemi, A. & Badfar, A. (2019). Healthcare big data processing mechanisms: The role of cloud computing. International Journal of Information Management, 49, 271–289.
[23] Ali, O., Shrestha, A., Soar, J. & Wamba, S. F. (2018). Cloud computing-enabled healthcare opportunities, issues, and applications: A systematic review. International Journal of Information Management, 43, 146–158.
[24] Rath, M. & Pattanayak, B. (2019). Technological improvement in modern health care applications using the Internet of Things (IoT) and the proposal of a novel health care approach. International Journal of Human Rights in Healthcare.
[25] Darwish, A., Hassanien, A. E., Elhoseny, M., Sangaiah, A. K. & Muhammad, K. (2019). The impact of the hybrid platform of the internet of things and cloud computing on healthcare systems: Opportunities, challenges, and open problems. Journal of Ambient Intelligence and Humanized Computing, 10(10), 4151–4166.
[26] Zhong, C. L. (2020). Internet of things sensors assisted physical activity recognition and health monitoring of college students. Measurement, 107774.
[27] Din, S. & Paul, A. (2020). Erratum to "Smart health monitoring and management system: Toward autonomous wearable sensing for the Internet of Things using big data analytics [Future Gener. Comput. Syst. 91 (2019) 611–619]". Future Generation Computer Systems, 108, 1350–1359.
[28] Otoom, M., Alshraideh, H., Almasaeid, H. M., López-de-ipiña, D. & Bravo, J. (2015). Real-time statistical modeling of blood sugar. Journal of Medical Systems, 39(10), 123.
[29] Alshraideh, H., Otoom, M., Al-Araida, A., Bawaneh, H. & Bravo, J. (2015). A web-based cardiovascular disease detection system. Journal of Medical Systems, 39(10), 122.
[30] Wu, F., Wu, T. & Yuce, M. R. (2019). An internet-of-things (IoT) network system for connected safety and health monitoring applications. Sensors, 19(1), 21.
[31] Hossain, M. S. & Muhammad, G. (2016). Cloud-assisted industrial internet of things (iiot)–enabled framework for health monitoring. Computer Networks, 101, 192–202.
[32] Gope, P. & Hwang, T. (2015). BSN-Care: A secure IoT-based modern healthcare system using a body sensor network. IEEE Sensors Journal, 16(5), 1368–1376.
[33] Verma, P. & Sood, S. K. (2018). Cloud-centric IoT based disease diagnosis healthcare framework. Journal of Parallel and Distributed Computing, 116, 27–38.
[34] Xu, B., Da Xu, L., Cai, H., Xie, C., Hu, J. & Bu, F. (2014). Ubiquitous data accessing method in IoT-based information system for emergency medical services. IEEE Transactions on Industrial Informatics, 10(2), 1578–1586.
[35] Banaee, H., Ahmed, M. U. & Loutfi, A. (2013). Data mining for wearable sensors in health monitoring systems: A review of recent trends and challenges. Sensors, 13(12), 17472–17500.
[36] Zhang, M. W., Tsang, T., Cheow, E., Ho, C. S., Yeong, N. B. & Ho, R. C. (2014). Enabling psychiatrists to be mobile phone app developers: Insights into app development methodologies. JMIR mHealth and uHealth, 2(4), e53.
[37] Zhang, M. W., Ward, J., Ying, J. J., Pan, F. & Ho, R. C. (2016). The alcohol tracker application: An initial evaluation of user preferences. BMJ Innovations, 2(1), 8–13.
[38] Zhang, M. W. & Ho, R. (2017). Smartphone application for multi-phasic interventional trials in psychiatry: Technical design of a smart server. Technology and Health Care, 25(2), 373–375.
[39] Nguyen, T. T. (2020). Artificial intelligence in the battle against coronavirus (COVID-19): a survey and future research directions. Preprint, DOI, 10.

[40] Rao, A. S. S. & Vazquez, J. A. (2020). Identification of COVID-19 can be quicker through an artificial intelligence framework using a mobile phone-based survey when cities and towns are under quarantine. Infection Control & Hospital Epidemiology, 41(7), 826–830.
[41] Allam, Z. & Jones, D. S. (2020, March). On the coronavirus (COVID-19) outbreak and the smart city network: Universal data sharing standards coupled with artificial intelligence (AI) to benefit urban health monitoring and management. In Healthcare (Vol. 8, No. 1, p. 46). Multidisciplinary Digital Publishing Institute.
[42] Fatima, S. A., Hussain, N., Balouch, A., Rustam, I., Saleem, M. & Asif, M. (2020). IoT enabled smart monitoring of coronavirus empowered with fuzzy inference system. International Journal of Advanced Research, Ideas, and Innovations in Technology, 6(1).
[43] Peeri, N. C., Shrestha, N., Rahman, M. S., Zaki, R., Tan, Z., Bibi, S. . . . & Haque, U. (2020). The SARS, MERS, and novel coronavirus (COVID-19) epidemics, the newest and biggest global health threats: What lessons have we learned? International Journal of Epidemiology.
[44] Imran, A., Posokhova, I., Qureshi, H. N., Masood, U., Riaz, S., Ali, K. . . . & Nabeel, M. (2020). AI4COVID-19: AI-enabled preliminary diagnosis for COVID-19 from cough samples via an app. arXiv preprint arXiv:2004.01275.
[45] Yoo, S. H., Geng, H., Chiu, T. L., Yu, S. K., Cho, D. C., Heo, J. . . . & Min, B. J. (2020). Deep learning-based decision-tree classifier for COVID-19 diagnosis from chest X-ray imaging. Frontiers in Medicine, 7, 427.
[46] Mei, X., Lee, H. C., Diao, K. Y., Huang, M., Lin, B., Liu, C. . . . & Bernheim, A. (2020). Artificial intelligence-enabled rapid diagnosis of patients with COVID-19. Nature Medicine, 1–5.
[47] Loey, M., Smarandache, F. & M Khalifa, N. E. (2020). Within the lack of chest COVID-19 X-ray dataset: A novel detection model based on GAN and deep transfer learning. Symmetry, 12(4), 651.
[48] Awotunde, J. B., Folorunso, S. O., Jimoh, R. G., Adeniyi, E. A., Abiodun, K. M. & Ajamu, G. J. (2021). Application of artificial intelligence for COVID-19 epidemic: An exploratory study, opportunities, challenges, and future prospects. Studies in Systems, Decision and Control, 2021(358), 47–61.
[49] Sethy, P. K. & Behera, S. K. (2020). Detection of coronavirus disease (covid-19) based on deep features. Preprints, 2020030300, 2020.
[50] Shuja, J., Alanazi, E., Alasmary, W. & Alashaikh, A. (2020). Covid-19 open-source data sets: A comprehensive survey. Applied Intelligence, 1–30.
[51] Oladipo, I. D., Babatunde, A. O., Awotunde, J. B. & Abdulraheem, M. (2020, November). An improved hybridization in the diagnosis of diabetes mellitus using selected computational intelligence. Communications in Computer and Information Science, 2021(1350), 272–285.
[52] Lukman, A. F., Benedicta, A., Awotunde, J. B., Okon, C. E., Oludoun, O., Oluwakemi, A. . . . & Adeniyi, A. E. (2022). Robust statistical modeling of COVID-19 prevalence in African epicentres. In Studies in Systems, Decision and Control (Vol. 366, pp. 315–358). Springer, Cham, 2022.
[53] Awotunde, J. B., Ogundokun, R. O. & Misra, S. (2021). Cloud and IoMT-based big data analytics system during COVID-19 pandemic. Internet of Things, 2021, 181–201.
[54] Awotunde, J. B., Ogundokun, R. O., Adeniyi, A. E., Abiodun, K. M. & Ajamu, G. J. (2022). Application of mathematical modelling approach in COVID-19 transmission and interventions strategies. Studies in Systems, Decision and Control, 2022(366), 283–314.
[55] Chauhan, J. & Bojewar, S. (2016, August). Sensor networks based healthcare monitoring system. In 2016 International Conference on Inventive Computation Technologies (ICICT) (Vol. 2, pp. 1–6). IEEE.
[56] Ichwana, D., Ikhlas, R. Z. & Ekariani, S. (2018, October). Heart Rate Monitoring System During Physical.
[57] Pantelopoulos, A. & Bourbakis, N. G. (2009). A survey on wearable sensor-based systems for health monitoring and prognosis. IEEE Transactions on Systems, Man, and Cybernetics, Part C (Applications and Reviews), 40(1), 1–12.

[58] Nienhold, D., Dornberger, R. & Korkut, S. (2016, October). Sensor-based tracking and big data processing of patient activities in ambient assisted living. In 2016 IEEE International Conference on Healthcare Informatics (ICHI) (pp. 473–482). IEEE.

[59] Patel, S., Park, H., Bonato, P., Chan, L. & Rodgers, M. (2012). A review of wearable sensors and systems with application in rehabilitation. Journal of Neuroengineering and Rehabilitation, 9(1), 1–17.

[60] Awotunde, J. B., Bhoi, A. K. & Barsocchi, P. (2021). Hybrid cloud/fog environment for healthcare: An exploratory study, opportunities, challenges, and future prospects. Intelligent Systems Reference Library, 2021(209), 1–20.

[61] Rekatsinas, T., Joglekar, M., Garcia-Molina, H., Parameswaran, A. & Ré, C. (2017, May). Slimfast: Guaranteed results for data fusion and source reliability. In Proceedings of the 2017 ACM International Conference on Management of Data (pp. 1399–1414).

[62] Dumville, J. C., Lipsky, B. A., Hoey, C., Cruciani, M., Fiscon, M. & Xia, J. (2017). Topical antimicrobial agents for treating foot ulcers in people with diabetes. Cochrane Database of Systematic Reviews, 6.

[63] Schaper, N. C., van Netten, J. J., Apelqvist, J., Bus, S. A., Hinchliffe, R. J., Lipsky, B. A. & IWGDF Editorial Board. (2020). Practical Guidelines on the prevention and management of diabetic foot disease (IWGDF 2019 update). Diabetes/Metabolism Research and Reviews, 36, e3266.

[64] Jiang, X., Coffee, M., Bari, A., Wang, J., Jiang, X., Huang, J. . . . & Wu, Z. (2020). Towards an artificial intelligence framework for data-driven prediction of coronavirus clinical severity. CMC: Computers Materials & Continua, 63, 537–51.

[65] Barstugan, M., Ozkaya, U. & Ozturk, S. (2020). Coronavirus (Covid-19) classification using CT images by machine learning methods. arXiv preprint arXiv:2003.09424.

[66] Pereira, R. M., Bertolini, D., Teixeira, L. O., Silla Jr, C. N. & Costa, Y. M. (2020). COVID-19 identification in chest X-ray images on flat and hierarchical classification scenarios. Computer Methods and Programs in Biomedicine, 105532.

[67] Geurts, P., Ernst, D. & Wehenkel, L. (2006). Extremely randomized trees. Machine Learning, 63(1), 3–42.

[68] Geurts, P. & Louppe, G. (2011). Learning to rank with extremely randomized trees. Proceedings of Machine Learning Research, 14, 49–61.

[69] Breiman, L. (2001). Random forests. Machine Learning, 45(1), 5–32.

[70] Chen, T. & Guestrin, C. (2016, August). Xgboost: A scalable tree boosting system. In Proceedings of the 22nd ACM Sigkdd International Conference on Knowledge Discovery and Data Mining (pp. 785–794).

Idowu Dauda Oladipo, Joseph Bamidele Awotunde*,
Emmanuel Abidemi Adeniyi, Agbotiname Lucky Imoize,
Muyideen Abdulraheem, Ige Oluwasegun Osemudiame

7 Prediction of big medical data using data analytics and deep learning

Abstract: The majority of healthcare research efforts necessitate disease prevention and early detection. The use of modern technologies to collect and produce medical data triggers the use of deep learning and data analytics for prediction and classification of big medical data. This has helped greatly in receiving health risk information and warning signals. It aids in patient prediction, diagnosis, monitoring and classification using the new technologies like Internet of Things sensors, devices and smartphone applications. There is various source of big data in medical sectors like patient records, clinical notes, past illnesses in parents and family members, X-ray and scan findings, thus help in disease detection and prediction stage. The prediction of big medical data continues to improve regularly as it becomes easier for hospitals and other healthcare institutions to store larger amounts of data. Facilities like cheaper storage devices, low-cost databases and, more recently, the cloud, have made data storage in hospitals less difficult. As a result of this, several methods have been developed to allow these large amounts of medical data to be used to make predictions. Such methods include the use of machine and deep learning algorithms for the prediction of various diseases. Therefore, this chapter presents various opportunities brought by data analytics in big medical data, open research challenges and future prospects. The chapter examines contemporary research efforts toward big medical

---

***Corresponding author: Joseph Bamidele Awotunde,** Department of Computer Science, Faculty of Information and Communication Sciences, University of Ilorin, Ilorin 240003, Nigeria,
e-mail: awotunde.jb@unilorin.edu.ng
Idowu Dauda Oladipo, Department of Computer Science, Faculty of Information and Communication Sciences, University of Ilorin, Ilorin 240003, Nigeria, e-mail: odidowu@unilorin.edu.ng
Emmanuel Abidemi Adeniyi, Department of Computer Science, Precious Cornerstone University, Ibadan, Nigeria, e-mail: adeniyi.emmanuel@lmu.edu.ng
Agbotiname Lucky Imoize, Department of Electrical Engineering and Information Technology, Institute of Digital Communication, Ruhr University, Bochum 44801, Germany; Department of Electrical and Electronics Engineering, Faculty of Engineering, University of Lagos, Akoka, Lagos 100213, Nigeria,
e-mail: aimoize@unilag.edu.ng
Muyideen Abdulraheem, Department of Computer Science, Faculty of Information and Communication Sciences, University of Ilorin, Ilorin 240003, Nigeria, e-mail: muyideen@unilorin.edu.ng
Ige Oluwasegun Osemudiame, Department of Computer Science, Faculty of Information and Communication Sciences, University of Ilorin, Ilorin 240003, Nigeria,
e-mail: 16-52ha043@students.unilorin.edu.ng

https://doi.org/10.1515/9783110750942-007

data analytics. The relationship between big data analytics and big medical data is described. Furthermore, the chapter proposes a new architecture for big medical data analytics with a notable use case. A better understanding of the methods currently in place will lead to the development of better models for the prediction of medical data, as newer methods will be able to leverage the knowledge of the strengths, challenges and opportunities provided by the methods in the current literature.

Keywords: Big medical data, prediction, diagnosis, big data analytics, Internet of Things, deep learning, machine learning, diagnosis, healthcare systems

7.1 Introduction

Data analytics refers to the act of studying and discovering hidden patterns from huge amounts of data to make conclusions. In recent years, the world has experienced a great upsurge in the amount of data generated and collected daily. Because of the variety of data production sources, the flow of data is growing tremendously. This had led to the creation of the term "big data," which is used to describe collections of data that are exceedingly large. While needed data is and continues to become more easily accessible, it is necessary to find effective and efficient ways to use these data to improve current processes and to develop new ones. Companies, businesses and corporate organizations today have recognized the need to gather, store and analyze data in order to profit from this great resource. Healthcare organizations have not been left behind in this movement as big data has been used in a myriad of different ways such as treating diseases, improving patients' health quality by averting crises situations, creating novel for healthcare solutions, anticipating disease outbreaks so that they can be dealt with promptly, and optimizing the use of healthcare resources [1].

The number of large electronic health databases is growing at an exponential rate, which can no longer be managed using traditional methods. Big data analytics is an innovative approach to dealing with the massive volumes of healthcare data that are gathered every day. It consists of technologies and tools capable of navigating huge amounts of data in any given healthcare system and extracting usable information to treat patients. Many problems face the optimum use of large data sets in healthcare informatics, including the volume of data, the pace with which data is created, the variety of data kinds, the validity of data and the privacy of patient medical information [2]. Figure 7.1 depicts some of the major characteristics of big data. Old methods of handling data are often insufficient and overly expensive as data collection (which was costly to carry out) often involved collecting rather small amounts of data. As more health care businesses uncover possibilities to better understand and forecast consumer behaviors and interests, big data is becoming the primary technique for capturing data. The fast development of big data analytics technologies is becoming projected to assist the healthcare informatics sector in tackling important challenges such as knowledge representation, illness detection and clinical decision support [3] and improvements in these areas will lead to better predictions in big medical data analytics.

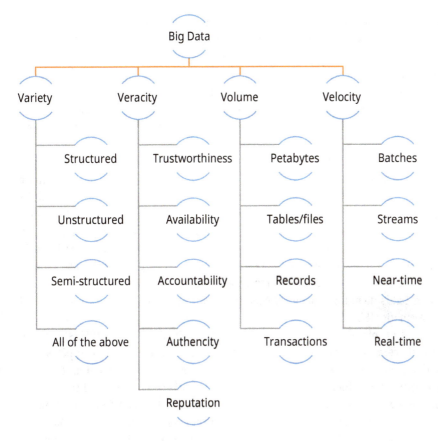

Figure 7.1: Characteristics of big data [3].

Machine learning techniques for the early identification of chronic illnesses have been developed by many researchers, including the use and analysis of data from wearable devices; yet, the field is still plagued by several challenges which include finding optimal ways to capture, store, share and interpret the collected data as it continues to attempt to answer the question: "how can knowledge in big data analysis be applied to predict disease outcomes efficiently?" Healthcare analytics has sparked interest from a variety of fields, including databases, data mining, information retrieval, image processing, medical academics and healthcare practitioners [4]. This chapter attempts to examine some of the methods in use in current literature as well as big medical data analytics opportunities and challenges.

7.2 Applications of big medical data analytics in healthcare systems

Big data has been applied in a number of different areas in medicine. The implementations of medical big data analytics cover many different aspects of healthcare. The healthcare sector may undergo a transformation thanks to big data analytics. It can increase operational effectiveness, aid in predicting and planning for disease epidemics and enhance the standard of clinical trial surveillance to reduce healthcare costs throughout all stages, including that of the government, hospital systems and patients [5, 6]. Big data analytics can develop and personalize care, enhance patient connections with providers and enhance health experiences.

Pharmacological results can be predicted using predictive modeling, recognizing patients who will benefited most from pharmacist assistance, giving pharmacists more knowledge of the dangers associated with particular medication-related issues and delivering actions that are suited to the needs of patients [7]. The acquisition and administration of data are dealt with in precision medicine (like data exchange, storage and privacy) to analytics (such as data mining, reporting and data transformation). Biotechnological advancements have made it possible to access complex biomedical data in large volumes. To leverage these diverse data, big data analytics is necessary and its application fields including image informatics, bioinformatics, sensor informatics and health informatics [8].

Analytics on big data require accuracy. Personal health records (PHRs) may include cryptic remarks, inaccuracies and approximations. Especially in comparison to clinical data, ambulatory assessments may be performed in unregulated and less dependable situations, which are gathered in a therapeutic context by qualified professionals. Making forecasts based on spontaneous, uncontrolled data from social media may not be reliable. Additionally, certain data sources can be unreliable [9]. Data that is "noise" is a huge challenge, particularly when it expands quickly. Heterogeneous results are produced by databases with different degrees of thoroughness and trustworthiness, which may raise the chance of erroneous findings and "biased fact-finding adventures." Two significant issues are poor data quality and biases brought on by the lack of standardization. The value of big data is frequently increased by connecting several databases and examining all currently available and relevant data [10]. Data pre-processing is the process of converting unstructured data into a format that can be understood, which includes (i) cleansing data, (ii) integration of data, (iii) transformation of data, (iv) data compression and (v) data discretization. In the process of using big data analytics, the pre-processing is crucial [11].

Big data streams-based systems have been created, which include computerized death certificates, patient-level post-discharge information and information on medical claims that is coded using the information on medical claims that is coded using the International Classification of Diseases (ICD) [12]. Big data streams from crowdsourcing, social media and Internet search queries have been used for surveillance operations [13, 14]. Processing medical data with big data techniques like NoSQL databases has been done, while some characteristics, such as local access and a logical connection between the distribution of logical and physical data, are crucial to enhancing the efficiency of parallelization in relational computing [15]. It was suggested to use a big data-driven strategy and procedure that includes both molecular and clinical data. The technique identifies potential treatment targets and medicines as well as candidate biomarkers. The cross-species analysis completes further clinical or preclinical confirmation; thus, the expenses and time needed for biomarker/therapeutic formulation are decreased [16, 17].

For structured data, a clinical data warehouse was developed; for analyzing unorganized data, a set of modules was also developed. The goal of the project was to create the first iteration of a structure inside the big data concept. The framework uses the distributed computing capabilities of big data to run the modules in a Hadoop cluster [18]. To manage massive data on Twitter health, a Hadoop-based architecture was created. The potential to transform how people think about healthcare

Table 7.1: The comparison of various techniques for big data analysis.

Tools	Types of databases	Platform	Advantages	Limitations
Jaql	It is a JavaScript object notation query language	It is a specific querying language	Both organized and semi-structured data is supported	No user-defined types; only conceptual model information about a domain's potential values
Hadoop	Database that is not relational	Platform that is cloud-based and open source	Stores information in any format, which including web logs	Insufficient security and technical assistance
Google Big Query	Table-based database	Platform that is cloud-based and open source	Enables data replication between various data centers	Indexes are not supported
MapReduce	Database that is not relational	Platform that is cloud-based and open source	Works well with unstructured and semi-structured data, including audio and visual information	Lacks the latest database systems' indexing abilities
Microsoft Windows Azure	Relational database	Platform based on the public cloud	Enables users to query structured, semi-structured, and unstructured files using relational methodologies	The database's size is restricted; large databases cannot be handled

through the analysis of tweets and medical professionals employs cutting-edge technology to acquire fresh clinical insights [19]. Big data analytics have made use of open sources like Hadoop, Kafka, Apache Storm and NoSQL Cassandra. For processing real-time massive data, Apache Storm has a number of fundamental components [20]. A comparison of the tools available for massive data analysis is presented in Table 7.1.

Developments in numerous clinical pathways are simultaneously manifested as fundamental pathophysiological and physiological manifestations. Strong coupling between various bodily systems is what causes this (e.g., connections between blood pressure, breathing and heart rate) resulting in possible markers for clinical evaluation. Consequently, a comprehensive strategy that uses structured data is needed for comprehending and forecasting infections, for a more thorough understanding of the illness states, and unstructured data derived from a variety of both clinical and nonclinical techniques are used. Overcoming some of the increasing pains of adding principles of big data analytics to medicine is one area of research studies that has lately garnered interest. In terms of both the properties of the data itself and the taxonomy of analytics that can be usefully applied to them, researchers are examining the complicated nature of healthcare data. Big data analytics in medicine is explored in three main areas. These three domains don't fully capture how big data analytics are used in medicine; instead, they're meant to provide readers a wide-ranging and prominent field of study where big data analytics principles are now being used.

7.2.1 Image processing

Medical images are a significant source of information that is routinely utilized for planning, evaluating and diagnosing treatments [21]. Computed tomography (CT), magnetic resonance imagery (MRI), X-ray, medical diagnostics, ultrasound, photoacoustic imaging, fluoroscopy, positron emission tomography-computed tomography (PET-CT) and mammograms are examples of imaging techniques that are widely used in clinical settings. For a single study, medical image data can be as small as a few megabytes (such as histology images) every study, up to hundreds of megabytes (e.g., investigations using thin-slice CT technology) and up to 2,500+ scans [22]. When storing such data for an extended period, huge storage capabilities are needed. If any automated decision-assistance processes were to be carried out utilizing the data, it also necessitates quick and precise techniques. Additionally, if additional sources of information obtained for each patient are also used in the processes of diagnosis, prediction and management, then, there is the issue of offering coherent storage, and creating effective strategies that can encompass the wide range of data becomes difficult [23].

7.2.2 Signal processing

Comparable to medical images, healthcare signals also present volume and velocity challenges, particularly when continuously acquiring and storing high-resolution data from a variety of devices is attached to each patient [24]. However, physiological signals also present complication of a spatial and temporal character, in addition to the problems with data size. When coupled with situational context knowledge, physiological signal analysis often has greater value. It should be incorporated into the creation of ongoing monitoring and predictive techniques to guarantee its efficiency and reliability [25].

Nowadays, healthcare organizations employ a wide variety of varying and ongoing monitoring equipment that only use a single physiological signal or discretized important information to offer warning systems in case of obvious incidents. However, such simplistic methods of development and alarm system implementation are frequently unsatisfactory, and their sheer volume may make both patients and caregivers susceptible to "alarm fatigue" [26, 27]. In this situation, previous knowledge that has often fallen short of fully exploiting high-dimensional time series data limits our ability to learn new medical information. As a result of these systems' propensity to rely on solitary information sources, these alarm strategies frequently fail while being devoid of a broader and more thorough perspective on the patients' actual physiological circumstances. In order to investigate data interactions, from heterogeneous clinical data from time-series, and correlations, it is required to give improved and detailed methodologies. This is crucial since research shows that humans struggle to make sense of changes that alter more than two signals [28, 29].

7.2.3 Genomics

Price of sequencing the human genome (consisting of 30,000–35,000 genes) is rapidly declining as high-throughput sequence alignment technology develops [30, 31]. The area of computational biology faces a substantial barrier in quickly processing genome-scale data to produce practical suggestions affecting current public health practices and healthcare delivery [32, 33]. In a clinical context, cost and turnaround time for suggestions are critical. Tracking 100,000 people over 20–30 years using the P4 (predictive, preventive, participatory and personalized) medicine paradigm is one initiative addressing this complicated issue [34, 35], with a comprehensive personal omics profile [23]. A systemic approach is being used by the P4 effort for (i) determining disease statuses by examining genome-scale datasets, (ii) utilizing blood-based diagnostic techniques for ongoing subject monitoring, (iii) investigating fresh methods for finding medication targets, creating tools to address the issues of collecting, verifying, storing, mining, integrating and finally using big data and (iv) data modeling for every individual. Biological monitoring and genomic analysis are combined in the integrative personal omics profile (iPOP) and using numerous high-throughput genomic sequencing techniques to produce a subject's comprehensive health and disease statuses [36]. The ultimate difficulty for this profession is to translate clinical recommendations into effective advice [37]. It requires unique big data methodologies and analytics to use such high density data for exploration, discovery and clinical translation.

Notwithstanding the massive amounts of money spent on the present healthcare systems, clinical outcomes are still not ideal, especially in the USA. About 96 persons per 100,000 per year pass away with ailments that are thought to be treatable [38]. The failure of the healthcare systems to efficiently obtain, distribute and use information in a more thorough manner is one of the major causes of such inadequacies [39]. This is a chance for big data analytics to support exploration in a more meaningful way, offering a way for thoroughly monitoring and assessing the complex research and discovery process, enhancing clinical practice, assisting in the formation and planning of healthcare policy, and muddled medical data. Insights from big data analytics can potentially save lives, enhance healthcare delivery, increase access to care and align payment with performance and assist in halting the aggravating rise in healthcare expenses [40].

Conventional health bioinformatics, such as "an isolated system" with only a basic analytic software, cannot analyze massive data because of their size. What is needed is a more sophisticated system that requires extensive programming and a range of abilities [41, 42]. That is frequently the case with the open-source Hadoop framework. The Hadoop distributed file system (HDFS), which Apache introduced in 2011 as a mechanism to break up enormous data sets into smaller types, is the fundamental component of Hadoop and keep them on various servers and MapReduce (parallel processing is a computational technique that uses two implementation processes) which comprises: (a) the stage of the map where authenticated key pairs are transformed into interpolated key-value pairs and (b) the reduction step, in which a key is used to group the interpolated key-value pairs. Then the values are merged to get the final output of the reductions. In order to offer storage for Hadoop distributed computing using ZooKeeper as a coordination service, HBase is a distributed database built on top of HDFS [43]. First, Google launched MapReduce, allowing for the mapping and reducing of large amounts of data on clusters. Hadoop was created by Yahoo as an open-source MapReduce framework [44, 45]. Hadoop map/reduce jobs, which may also be created on Hive (a Hadoop execution compatibility infrastructure), give a method for projecting structure onto these data and enable queries Map. When necessary, fewer employment are needed in other languages [46, 47].

Researchers assess business analytic tools in terms of their availability, sustainability and other factors due to the numerous issues they confront, simpleness of use, scalability, flexibility in manipulation, privacy and security enablement, or quality control [47, 48]. For instance, in order to address Hadoop's primary drawback of tight coupling between the programming model and using the resource management framework, a new architecture known as YARN was created. YARN separates the programming interface from the physical infrastructure for resources development and assigns numerous scheduling duties [49]. Additionally, the Apache Pig dataflow architecture was created to make it simple for users to combine various data processing methods. Due to the fact that Hadoop MapReduce was only available to professionals with excellent technological capabilities because multi-step data transfers and concurrent processing are difficult [50].

Overall, Apache Hadoop is the computer platform that is most frequently used for BDA applications in general and for healthcare in particular [51, 52]. Furthermore, the Mapreduce framework scales across numerous servers in a Hadoop framework and has a wide range of practical implementations. [53, 54].

The research by authors in [55] provides one use of the Hadoop framework as an example that reads EHR and presented a "user-friendly" technology named CHESS that was created in Visual Studio for C# and give analysts tools to conduct queries and tests. The input datasets are transferred by CHESS to Hadoop and consolidated data are settled to an SQL server for examination with significantly fewer rows. Users can then access them using their preferred statistics software (such as Excel, Tableau and R) and can do statistical tests to look into, after rearranging the data in the required way, the significance of particular factors, for instance (consider demographics), over specific medical disorders. For managing huge data challenges, the application uses Hadoop, and users can only query smaller data sets through statistical tools. To enable the execution of statistically significant tests, the program could have benefitted from more comprehensive clustering techniques to more automatically discover critical elements in healthcare.

As the emphasis of biology has begun to move from identifying genomes to evaluating the enormous amount of data arising from workable genomics research, the post-genomic age, [56, 57] to undertake biomedical ontology reliability, detail the development of using Hadoop and MapReduce in a scalable and capable cloud computing environment [58, 59]. The usual progressive methodology for deploying ontology quality assurance (OQA) techniques has been shortened from weeks to hours thanks to this functionality. Large ontological hierarchy can be structurally analyzed more thoroughly with this speed and careful tracking of transformation between iterations for evolutionary analysis. The creation of better user interfaces for reviewing OQA findings is an area that needs more study and the functionality of the graphical interface by intelligently pre-computing laborious tasks, and demonstrating ontological compatibility and progression while engaging the user in conversation.

Using a novel method, the authors [60] unlocked the information of unstructured healthcare data and enables inquiries, processing and diagnosis of personalized health using both structured and unstructured health data. This is a step in the right direction because most applications can only query structured medical data, such as a component of a population's EHR databases. For instance, when it comes to processing medical images and EHR, software and systems that operate in the cloud, for sharing and retrieving big data medical images and other health records, consider LifeImage and

Nuance mPower; however, they can only use organized data (for instance, conduct a patient gender search) to find all pertinent photographs and documents; however, it is unable to process unstructured data (for instance, a search based on a brain structure's dimensions).

Models are included in other initiatives, even in a Hadoop/Map lessen the environment [61], that concern pattern recognition in medical image data. This denotes the uploading of a picture for input and extraction of features and resemblance pattern matching methods are employed to find related images [62]. The studies in our dataset demonstrate several technological limitations, such as the fact that the Hadoop and MapReduce environments sometimes struggle with handling unstructured content from health data and in the desired manner, and medical images. To solve the issue, researchers develop specialized tools (instead of, say, a Hive component from Hadoop) [60]. Such methods let medical professionals make decisions with the use of computerized algorithms.

One major aspect in which medical big analytics have been applied is in the field of analyzing medical data from several different sources simultaneously [63]. Big medical data has also been used in assisting healthcare workers in determining their training requirements, ongoing education and scientific research, among other things [64]. Some of the significant applications of health informatics are data management in hospitals systems, telemedicine and medical and managerial decision support systems [64].

Prediction has been a major research area in big medical data analytics. Support vector machine (SVM) and tongue pictures have been used to predict diabetes outcomes [65]. A Spark-based machine learning model was also used to predict health status from large data streams [66]. Diagnosis of chronic kidney disease using feature selection techniques and SVM [67] has also been studied. Another area of importance in big medical data research has been the development of a smart ambulance system based on big data and the Internet of Things (IoT) has also been developed [68]. SVM and dynamic time warping have also been used to develop a smart healthcare system based on speech recognition [69]. Perhaps, most importantly, several studies have shown that scientists have reduced rates of death, healthcare costs and medical difficulties at numerous institutions by using clinical data analytics software [70].

7.3 Big medical data analytics and deep learning methods in healthcare systems

7.3.1 The spectrum of big medical data analytics

Analytics of substantial amounts of medical data using all available AI techniques (i.e., methods that are both data- and knowledge-driven) provides a wide range of data analytics alternatives to gain insights into healthcare decision and knowledge discovery [71]. The alternatives for health data analytics that are applicable for particular analytics scenarios are discussed below.

7.3.1.1 Decision analytics

Decision analytics recommends patient-specific diagnostic and/or treatment solutions based on an analysis of medical data from the entire population in order to help health workers [72]. The decision rationale could show up as (a) employing machine learning techniques, developing a mathematical decision model and (b) ontology with a collection of logic-based decision rules make up a knowledge-based decision methodology. The most well-known and frequently used analytics in healthcare is providing a variety of outcome functions is decision informatics based on a patient's characteristics [73, 74]. These includes (a) suggest individualized diagnostic and therapeutic choices, (b) suggest the most effective and scientifically supported strategies, (c) develop care strategies, (d) raise alarms for possible negative developments and (e) organize patients according on disease risk, treatment response and medical results.

7.3.1.2 Predictive analytics

The creation of data-driven models using a set of multidimensional prognostic qualities is a key component of predictive analytics [75, 76] and can identify the historical trend present in a collection and use the discovered pattern to make predictions (i.e., evaluate the possibility of something happening) given the input values of the predictor qualities, a future value, outcome or event [77, 78]. As a result, using a trend from the history, forecast models infer in the time-frequency domain potential degree of an attribute's forecast [79]. There are various applications for predictive analytics in healthcare, such as predicting the rate of antibiotic susceptibility in a particular populace based on historical antimicrobial tolerance data based on prior data for individuals with comparable conditions, forecast the likelihood of renal deterioration in specific diabetic patients and forecast the effectiveness of a medication using data on rehospitalization, follow-ups and other trends.

7.3.1.3 Prescriptive analytics

The goal of prescriptive analytics is to determine what should be done to minimize the anticipated disaster. Prescriptive analytics is a process that recommends actions by simulating the results of "what-if" circumstances [80, 81]. Prescriptive analytics is difficult because it necessitates thorough and accurate understanding of the process being replicated [82]. The extensive collection of decision criteria and domain-specific restrictions needed for prescriptive analytics can only be developed from the vast amount of health data and intricate domain expertise. Prescriptive analytics often uses rule-based argumentation, constraints compliance and decision optimization strategies [83, 84]. Healthcare prescriptive analytics is still in its infancy, simply because it is difficult to generate and validate what-if situations for complicated medical problems.

7.3.1.4 Comparative analytics

Based on a collection of associated properties, compare and contrast offers an unbiased and comprehensive assessment of two objects/results. Comparative analytics is therefore more comprehensive and well-informed than evaluating focused on a single feature, which is very common in the present healthcare system [85, 86]. In order to express an established causal connection amongst a set of qualities leading to a particular event, comparative analytics creates deterministic comparative algorithms. Comparative analytics has the advantage that, when used exploratorily, the full set of attributes is impartially examined by machine learning algorithms to find a combination of features that can be used to both characterize and performance measurement based on a single property is not as effective as comparing the value of a specified comparator attribute [87, 88]. The medical field can benefit from the use of technology to assess the ordering patterns of doctors treating patients with comparable case mixes for pathology tests utilizing managerial and clinical data [89, 90]. The price of hospitalization in relation to various specialties, as well as the impact of diagnostic tests on diagnostic procedures can be greatly reduce.

7.3.1.5 Semantic analytics

A knowledge-driven method called semantic analytics recognizes and uses the underlying semantic connections between the data elements to (a) find out additional knowledge and (b) respond to intricate and specific questions [91]. Sentiment analysis uses approaches for logic-based cognitive on large datasets and subject-specific information (signified as an ontology or information chart) to guess the responses to a challenging question [92]. The semantic web foundation is utilized by semantic analytics to (a) expanding the scope of the data for query response requires the integration of heterogeneous data utilizing linked data concepts and (b) by creating fresh, logical semantic connections between the well-known notions, one might deduce viable explanations through reasoning that is logical. Operating as an integration of insights that are informed by data and data sources techniques, semantic analytics is predominantly well suitable for evaluating "big" biological, genomic, using drug datasets to discover earlier undiscovered response to therapy, genotype-phenotype, gene-drug response, drug sickness, the effects of drug rehabilitation and so forth.

7.3.2 The prospects of big medical data analytics in healthcare systems

To obtain relevant information, medical data (like any other data to be used in prediction) must always be analyzed after they have been obtained and processed. This analysis usually occurs in three phases (see Figure 7.2). First, researchers must use the benefit of hindsight to look into past events, similar to the event to be predicted in order to find what transpired previously to get us where we are at the moment. Secondly, researchers must get insight from the data being used for prediction. This insight should give an understanding of what caused past events and an idea of what future events should look like. Finally, researchers will be able to predict, to some extent, what would happen in future events and might even be able to make adjustments to improve possible outcomes.

Figure 7.2: Processes for analyzing big data.

Prediction in data analytics cannot be carried out alone. It is an activity which is preceded by a number of processes. First among these processes is data collection as it is impossible to predict future occurrences without inferences from the past. These inferences can be gathered from a study of past events which is put together into a dataset usually containing features (information about past observations) and a target variable (what is to be predicted). After the data is collected, a number of processes may be carried out to make the data suitable for analytics. These processes are together referred to as *data pre-processing* and can include cleaning missing data, data transformation, normalization and dimensionality reduction. The operations carried out will depend on the condition of the data gathered. Sometimes, to improve prediction accuracy, feature selection/engineering may be carried out. Feature engineering refers to the process of creating new features out of those which already exist in the dataset while feature selection has to do with choosing which features to use and which ones can be ignored among those in the dataset and a number of these exist such as forward elimination, backward elimination and stepwise selection.

After these processes have been carried out, the predictive model to be used is then deployed on the dataset. Many different models exist and a lot of them can be fine-tuned to improve prediction capabilities. Some of the existing models are considered in this section. After the models have been deployed, they are usually tested using several parameters including correctness, precision, recall, area under receiver operating characteristic (ROC) curve and kappa statistic to see how well they perform with the data on which they were trained. If the models are seen to perform well enough, they can then be used to predict future occurrences; if not, some more work may need to be done on the data or a different predictive model may be chosen instead. Figure 7.3 describes the process that usually occurs before prediction takes place.

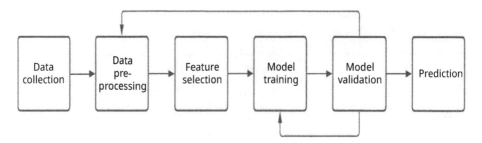

Figure 7.3: Prediction process.

Big medical data analytics is a field that has now been in existence for several years due to their ability to predict medical outcomes quite accurately as inaccurate predictions can lead to incorrect diagnosis, which can be catastrophic and disastrous. Many different methods have been used in predicting medical data outcomes. Some of these methods will be discussed in this section.

7.3.2.1 Support vector machine (SVM) classifier

A learning technique called a support vector machine (SVM) makes an effort to categorize objects by looking at examples [93]. Examining a vast collection of handmade zeros, ones and other symbols that have been scanned, you may develop an SVM to recognize the different data numbers. Additionally, by analyzing thousands or hundreds of fraudulent and legitimate credit card transaction records and by identifying fraudulent debit card usage, an SVM can be trained. SVM can be a strong technique for creating classifiers and is extremely effective at detecting subtle trends in large datasets [94].

SVMs are already being successfully applied in an increasing variety of biological domains. One of the automated analyses of microarray profiling of gene expression is a biological usage of SVM [95]. SVMs are also employed in biology to categorize items like mass spectra, microarray expression patterns and DNA and protein sequences [96]. SVM has recently been used to forecast the likelihood that patients may have cardiac disorders with an accuracy of 90.6% [63]. Due to its capability to manage data streams from multiple sources, including the IoT, Apache Spark was used in this work in order to continue analyzing the data and to provide insights into the data. It was suggested that the use of feature selection along with SVM played a part in improving the accuracy of the system.

7.3.2.2 Neural networks

A network of linked basic processing units, nodes or units that are inspired by animal neurons is referred to as a neural network. The weights or strengths of an internet connection created by a process of adaptation to, or the network's processing power is stored by using, or learning from, a collection of training patterns [97]. A "network" can be any collection of synthetic neurons. The complexity of this could range from a single node to a vast network of nodes, and every node in the network is connected to every other node.

Neural networks are commonly used as an alternative to nonlinear regression or cluster analysis approaches in statistical analysis and data modeling [98]. Using abstraction, neural networks are used to create computer models of the animal brain. Neuroscientists and psychologists are interested in the components of real nerve tissue that are thought to be essential for information processing. Additionally, physicists and mathematicians with an interest in automata theory, statistical mechanics and nonlinear dynamical systems are curious about neural networks. Engineers and computer scientists seek to develop intelligent devices, and mathematicians want to understand the underlying features of neural networks as complex systems; all these are reasons why neuroscientists want to know how animal brains work. Neural networks are also useful in our attempts to understand and analyze massive, poorly understood datasets that naturally occur in work environments [99].

In recent years, neural networks have been employed in healthcare systems. They have been supporting a large number of medical experts and analysts in extracting useful information from clinical data and enhancing medical facilities. Assessing patients' risk of anticipating disease and providing personalized treatment is a prominent study subject for neural network researchers. Neural networks are currently widely utilized for drug development and the detection of life-threatening conditions like cancer and diabetes mellitus using a medical imaging method [100].

To diagnose diabetes, neural networks have been used to construct a diabetes prediction system [101]. The experiment was carried out using WEKA software and medical data on diabetes from University of California, Irvine (UCI) machine learning repository which comprised eight characteristics of the people including the number of times they were pregnancy, heart rate, skin fold thickness, insulin level, BMI, functioning of the diabetic lineage, age and the outcomes, such as if they had diabetes (positive) or not (negative). In this study, several machine learning algorithms and methodologies for improving diabetes prediction accuracy using medical data were investigated. For data pre-processing, the correlation-based feature selection technique was used to remove irrelevant information. Test methods used included 10-fold cross validation (FCV), 66% split (PS) and using the training dataset (UTD) as the test dataset. During this experiment, it was observed that, when compared to other approaches (such as Naïve Bayes and random forests), without using a pre-processing method, the UTD test method produced higher accuracy with the multilayer perceptron neural network. Furthermore, it was noted that, except for the UTD test technique, using the pre-processing method even improved the accuracy of the MLP machine learning algorithm.

Another method, which uses gradients strategies and back propagation approaches, one can anticipate cardiac disease before a stroke or heart attack occurs, was recently developed [102]. The proposed system's accuracy (98.5%) was compared to traditional classifier models and found to be superior to the existing systems. Also, by retraining the attributes of deep neural networks in 5- and 10-FCV, effective methods for the diagnosis of diabetes have been created, with predictive performance of 98.3% and 97.11%, respectively [103]. Based on convolutional long short-term memory, a new diabetes classification model (Conv-LSTM) was also created [104]. When compared to other common models like convolutional neural networks (CNN), traditional long-short term memory (LSTM) and CNN-LSTM, the suggested model has a highest precision over the Pima Indians Diabetes Database of 97.26%. Furthermore, to diagnose glaucoma, a new feature extraction using an optic disc (OD) and an optic cup (OC) was developed [105]. To produce more accurate results, the suggested system uses two alternative CNN structures to divide the OD and OC. A lung cancer prediction convolutional neural network (LCP-CNN) that can categorize benign pulmonary nodules with the aid of US testing data obtained 94.5% accuracy was constructed [106]. Finally, using a correlation neural network (CorrNN), a 98.6% accurate automatic diagnostic technique for chronic renal disease has been established [107]. Each of these studies shows the efficacy of neural networks in medicine.

7.3.2.3 Random forests

Random forest (RF) is a classification and regression ensemble learning system. The strategy, which was developed over a decade ago [108], combines a bagging sample approach with the autonomous introduction of a haphazard assortment of elements by some researchers [109, 110] to assemble a set of monitored decision trees. The bagging technique and a specimen with substitution from the training set are used to construct each decision tree in the ensemble. Statistics indicate that about 64% of occurrences will appear in the samples at least once. Examples in the collection are known to as in-bag examples, while the remaining examples (about 36%) are alluded to as out-of-bag examples. To increase variety, a best split feature is chosen from a collection of randomly selected features at each node in all trees using a goodness measure (e.g., Gini index) (usually $\sqrt{n}$, where n is the overall quantity of attributes). Each tree is developed to its full potential and is unpruned. In high-dimensional data sets, an extreme deepness is frequently permitted to avert trees from expanding out of recall.

The use of decision tree (C4.5) algorithms to forecast chronic renal disease has been examined [111] and it performed well in relations of correctness (63%) and completing time. Researchers have also looked into using RF as one of the classifiers for the prognosis of three diseases: leukemia, lung cancer and heart disease [112] and they claimed to have better accuracy scores than existing systems.

A recent study, which tried to develop a system for detecting heart problems, discovered that the random forest classifier method was the best machine learning algorithm for predicting heart disease, with a 94.9% accuracy rate among other classification algorithms like SVM, DT and logistic regression [113]. The univariate feature selection and relief algorithms are used to identify essential characteristics from the dataset. Another experiment was implemented to use data mining to build predictive models for postoperative complications, test their reliability and to choose the best model for predicting postoperative problems in older head and neck squamous cell carcinomas (HNSCC) patients [114]. Before building the models, the researchers enrolled a sample of elderly individuals with HNSCC in a retrospective cohort trial that was developed and implemented and also altered the study's data mining protocols. The researchers concluded that the RF algorithm paradigm was a promising method in this field.

In a variety of applications, RFs have demonstrated their efficiency as a strategy for classification and regression [115]. CLUB-DRF has also been offered as a new method for selecting varied tree clustering and are used to create decision trees from groupings of related trees in order to create a pruning RF ensembles that is considerably lesser than the original and typical RF ensemble while performing at least as well [116] and it has demonstrated its usefulness with a pruning level accuracy of at least 92% or higher, while maintaining or beating the RF accurateness (before pruning).

Another method, entailing using a trimmed RF regression methodology on health records sets from a variety of disorders, has been proposed [117] and clustering was the primary diversity strategy used for identifying varied trees that comprised the pruned RF ensemble. To test their approach, the researchers prepared their training and test datasets, with CLUB-DRF receiving the training data set as input and generating a primary RF of 500 trees. CLUB-DRF subsequently generated pruned RFs of sizes 5–50, which were following which each occurrence of the data set's aim feature's value was forecasted. The crucial evaluation metrics MAE (mean absolute error) proved CLUB-accuracy. DRF's outperformed not just the parent RF but also a regular RF of the same size. Furthermore, this method appeared to be unconcerned about the dimensions and sizes of the datasets. A notable finding in the results is that as the dimension count and original dataset length grow, CLUB-DRF operates much better. The results showed that R-squared for CLUB-DRF attained 0.9 in both the breast cancer and Parkinson's data sets; this means that 90% of the variation in the data was explained and the researchers contended that the main reason for this speed improvement was the heterogeneity that the clustering process supplied. With more than or equal to 30 trees, CLUB-DRF was able to explicate a portion of the variation in the diabetes data set (6% when the number of trees is 40).

7.3.2.4 Bayesian networks

The Naïve Bayesian classifier has been shown to be one of the most effective predictors around [118]. Using the class label as input, the classifier determines the conditional distribution of each attribute from training data. The observation is then classified by using the Bayes method to determine the likelihood of the class label given a specific instance of some attributes choose the category with the greatest likelihood function after that. A high independence assumption – that given the class value, all of the characteristics are conditionally independent – is used to make this computation possible. This represents the key assumption of the naive Bayesian classifier, which is that each feature (considering the state of the classification model, each leaf in the network) is distinct of the other properties (the root in the network).

The Naive Bayesian network is different from the other predictors that have been examined so far in that it is a form of unsupervised learning (we are not predicting something we already know) while the others have primarily been supervised learning approaches. A network (or collection of layers) should be created with the intention of "best describing" the probability distribution over the training dataset. In actuality, heuristic search strategies are used to carry out this optimization procedure to choose the best option from a set of possible networks. The search is based on a scoring algorithm that evaluates the worthiness of each candidate network.

The corpus of literature on Bayesian networks in healthcare is enormous and growing quickly, reflecting a high level of interest in the field. They have been used to predict the severity of burn-related pathological scarring [114] with an error rate of 24.83%. The system was able to show a set of relationships between the type of scar and features like the size of the burn, burn therapies used, the age and gender of the patient. Bayesian networks have also been used to predict one-year survival in patients with bone sarcomas [119] and the network showed excellent forecasting accuracy with an area under ROC curve value of 0.767. They were also able to describe relationships between the features and the target variable to varying degrees. Furthermore, there has been an attempt to predict complications in patients suffering from type 2 diabetes using Bayesian networks [120]. Bayesian networks have also been used to forecast the patterns of organ failures in ICU patients [121].

7.4 Opportunities and challenges in medical data analytics

Predictive medical data analytics has become quite a popular field of research and as a result of the amount of research that has been done, we can discuss some of the visible opportunities and challenges in the area.

7.4.1 Opportunities

One of the major opportunities that is easily noticeable in medical data analytics is the advent of cloud computing. The cloud makes it possible to store and access data remotely and to run predictive models anywhere and at anytime. This is a big benefit for healthcare organizations as it eliminates the need for having data centers in other to leverage the power of predictive analytics. Other benefits of the cloud are shown in Figure 7.4.

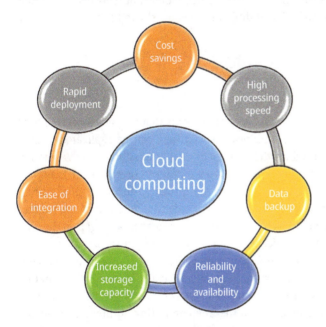

Figure 7.4: Benefits of cloud computing.

Another big opportunity in predictive medical data analytics today is the number of tools that have been developed for use in this field. These tools cover a wide array of activities in the data analytics process such as data storage, data pre-processing, data mining and data visualization. Also, the development of different programming languages, most notably Python and R, allows for easier development of predictive models.

Also, the continued growth of IoT devices has made it easier for medical data to be gathered. The IoT is a cutting-edge technology that combines several specialties, including sensor development, data acquisition, management and processing, as well as communication and networking, in which subjects (e.g., objects and people) with distinct characteristics can connect to a remote server and form local networks. Older methods such as questionnaires, which can be bulky and difficult to put together and analyze, can now be dropped in favor of wearable devices and sensors that can easily gather and send data without much human effort. Because IoT-based systems' connectivity allows objects to exchange and fuse data to get a more comprehensive understanding of their functionality and the attributes of their surrounding environments, it provides superior, intelligent and well-organized services. Furthermore, they have led to an increase in the ability of predictive models to make predictions accurate to the individual rather than the more generalized predictions that can be made from older data collection methods. Another key benefits of IoT technologies is that they increase people's quality of life through continuous remote monitoring systems rather than having them come to healthcare centers for data collection. This is more important for older patients who might find it difficult or even risky to have to make hospital trips regularly.

7.4.2 Challenges

A major challenge in predictive medical data analytics is that the developed methods are rarely described in such detail in literature that they can be replicated. If peer researchers are unable to reproduce these methods, it is impossible to know whether the results gotten are just one-off or specific to the dataset in use. Another issue that could easily occur when developed methods are not properly documented is that errors made during development are likely to be repeated in subsequent works. Furthermore, new researchers will be unable to address current research gaps if they are focused on already implemented which were simply not properly reported.

Another challenge that we can see in literature is the amount of time and processing power predictive models might require to run, especially in cases where neural networks are used. Some corporate healthcare organizations might be unwilling to make the necessary investments in top-of-the-line computing equipment to ensure that the more complex predictive models run quickly enough that even in emergency situations, they can be used to take critical care decisions in short spaces of time. It must be noted however that the field of predictive data analytics has generally seen a decline in the cost of equipment with time as the field becomes more accessible. Also, the use of cloud computing can also enable healthcare organizations to have access to extremely powerful virtual machines at relatively lower cost.

Also, there is a need for nurses and primary healthcare workers to receiving some more training especially as regards new equipment such as IoT devices being used to gather. To a lesser extent, using cloud computing for predictive medical data analytics (while it has many benefits) also comes with its own challenges. One of the major challenges involved is in the area of inadequate bandwidth; one cannot leave major decision about patients' lives aside because of an inability to connect to the cloud. Another issue is that of security. Medical information can be extremely sensitive and that makes it dangerous to store such information off-premises where access to the data cannot be monitored; although it must be said that the major cloud providers have extremely well setup security systems, a breach in these systems can lead to catastrophic data loss.

7.5 Proposed architecture for big medical data analytics for healthcare systems

Having studied the various methods in current use, we proposed an architecture for big medical data analytics that can be used generally in healthcare systems. The proposed system can be used for the prediction of various diseases like heart attack, diabetes, cancers, malaria among others enabled with machine learning and deep learning [101]. The big medical data analytics architecture involves an efficient structure of data modeling, assessment and handling stages. Figure 7.5 demonstrates a distinctive big medical data analytics structure.

The proposed framework are the two characteristics of healthcare information analytics approaches: (a) data-driven procedures and (b) knowledge-driven techniques. Deep learning and pattern recognition algorithms are two examples of data-driven analytics techniques [122]. Data-driven model's' fundamental goal is to first separate the intricate patterns and asymmetric relationships that are present in the data and then develop multifaceted data-driven models based on these pathways. These models fit into the category of (a) categorization models are examples of supervised learning methods that link a pattern of selected features to a certain result, (b) clustering methods are unsupervised learning algorithms that can group together comparable data elements and (c) the artificial intelligence models like artificial neural network (ANN), deep neural network (DNN) and convolutional neural network (CNN) among others. Data-driven models are typically "black boxes," meaning their decision-making logic cannot usually be understood [123]; however, the results of these models are consistent with current medical understanding. A certain amount of ambiguity results from their incapacity to describe the reasoning behind a solution, particularly in cases where medical decision-making is generally based on established guidelines, facts and justifications [124, 125].

Logic-based knowledge modeling and cognitive procedures are examples of knowledge-driven analytics techniques [126]. These techniques first entail creating knowledge models based on logic (like production rules and ontologies) based on the problem description, symbolize the sphere information and then use cognitive techniques to extrapolate new information/resolutions from the information model [71]. Using a patient profile, for instance, clinical criteria can be used to determine the most effective therapy approach. Examples of knowledge-based systems are expert systems, and they have become very prominent in the healthcare industry because to their clarity in laying out the reasons for the suggested course of action. The most advanced information technologies are web information methodologies right now [71].

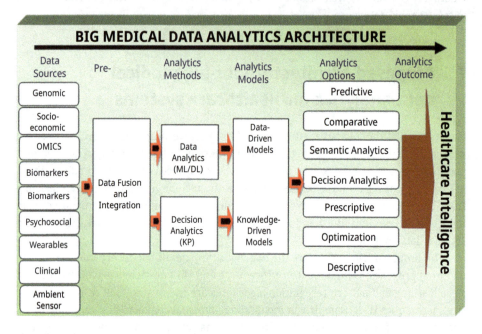

Figure 7.5: A big medial data analytics architecture, showing the sequences of data science steps to perform healthcare data analytics.

7.6 Conclusion and future directions

Big data analytics is a novel approach to dealing with the massive amounts of healthcare data that are streamed on a daily basis. It consists of technologies and tools capable of navigating huge amounts of data in any given healthcare system and extracting usable information to treat patients. Big data tools can now anticipate, prevent and recommend the best evidence-based treatment regimens for patients based on data from several sources. In today's data-driven environment, care managers are critical for personalizing medicine. It is critical for developed predictive healthcare data analytics programs to be as precise as possible in order to reduce misdiagnosis, which can be fatal at times. To ensure accurate disease diagnosis, we have described some of the major methods in use in recent literature. This is aimed at aiding researchers who intend to build programs for predictive healthcare data analytics in having a clear understanding of the major methods in current use, their advantages and their limitations so they can make decisions on what method would be suitable for their use and what improvements could be made in subsequent novel methods. The researchers also proposed a pruned big medical data analytics approach for various diseases prediction which is expected to produce faster and more accurate models for predicting different diseases. In future research, many more statistical and deep learning methods can be reviews and discusses as this chapter only focuses on a few of the major methods. Also, the proposed model will be fully implement to diagnose and predict various health challenges like heart attack diabetes, arthritis, dementia, cancer, malaria among others. Furthermore, the proposed architecture can be improved by enhancing its security and privacy so as to be trusted and accepted by physicians and patients. It can also be applied in predicting other health challenges such as cancers.

References

[1] Yang, C. C. & Veltri, P. (2015). Intelligent healthcare informatics in big data era. Artificial Intelligence in Medicine, 65(2), 75–77. https://doi.org/10.1016/J.ARTMED.2015.08.002.

[2] Elhoseny, M., Ramírez-González, G., Abu-Elnasr, O. M., Shawkat, S. A., Arunkumar, N. & Farouk, A. (2018). Secure medical data transmission model for IoT-based healthcare systems. IEEE Access, 6, 20596–20608. https://doi.org/10.1109/ACCESS.2018.2817615.

[3] Herland, M., Khoshgoftaar, T. & Wald, R. (2014). A review of data mining using big data in health informatics. Journal of Big Data, 1(2), 374–380. https://doi.org/https://doi.org/10.1186/2196-1115-1-2.

[4] Reddy, C. K. & Aggarwal, C. C. (2015). Healthcare data analytics. In Healthcare Data Analytics. CRC Press. https://doi.org/10.1201/b18588.

[5] Nambiar, R., Bhardwaj, R., Sethi, A. & Vargheese, R. (2013, October). A look at challenges and opportunities of big data analytics in healthcare. In 2013 IEEE international conference on Big Data (pp. 17–22). IEEE.

[6] Awotunde, J. B., Oluwabukonla, S., Chakraborty, C., Bhoi, A. K. & Ajamu, G. J. (2022). Application of artificial intelligence and big data for fighting COVID-19 pandemic. International Series in Operations Research and Management Science, 2022(320), 3–26.

[7] Hernandez, I. & Zhang, Y. (2017). Using predictive analytics and big data to optimize pharmaceutical outcomes. American journal of health-system pharmacy, 74(18), 1494–1500.

[8] Wu, P. Y., Cheng, C. W., Kaddi, C. D., Venugopalan, J., Hoffman, R. & Wang, M. D. (2016). Omic and electronic health record big data analytics for precision medicine. IEEE Transactions on Biomedical Engineering, 64(2), 263–273.

[9] Andreu-Perez, J., Poon, C. C., Merrifield, R. D., Wong, S. T. & Yang, G. Z. (2015). Big data for health. IEEE journal of biomedical and health informatics, 19(4), 1193–1208.

[10] Sacristán, J. A. & Dilla, T. (2015). No big data without small data: Learning health care systems begin and end with the individual patient. Journal of Evaluation in Clinical Practice, 21(6), 1014.

[11] Farid, D. M., Nowe, A. & Manderick, B. (2016, December). A feature grouping method for ensemble clustering of high-dimensional genomic big data. In 2016 Future Technologies Conference (FTC) (pp. 260–268). IEEE.

[12] Wang, L. & Alexander, C. A. (2019). Big data analytics in healthcare systems. International Journal of Mathematical, Engineering and Management Sciences, 4(1), 17.

[13] Simonsen, L., Gog, J. R., Olson, D. & Viboud, C. (2016). Infectious disease surveillance in the big data era: Towards faster and locally relevant systems. The Journal of Infectious Diseases, 214(suppl_4), S380–S385.

[14] Awotunde, J. B., Jimoh, R. G., Ogundokun, R. O., Misra, S. & Abikoye, O. C. (2022). Big data analytics of iot-based cloud system framework: Smart healthcare monitoring systems. In Internet of Things, Vol. 2022. Springer, Cham, 181–208.

[15] Salavati, H., Gandomani, T. J. & Sadeghi, R. (2017, September). A robust software architecture based on distributed systems in big data healthcare. In 2017 International Conference on Advances in Computing, Communications and Informatics (ICACCI) (pp. 1701–1705). IEEE.

[16] Panigrahi, R., Ghose, M. & Pramanik, M. (2013). Cloud computing: A new era of computing in the field of information management. International Journal of Computer Science Engineering, 2(5).

[17] Awotunde, J. B., Jimoh, R. G., Oladipo, I. D., Abdulraheem, M., Jimoh, T. B. & Ajamu, G. J. (2021). Big data and data analytics for an enhanced COVID-19 epidemic management. In Artificial Intelligence for COVID-19. Springer, Cham, 11–29.

[18] Istephan, S. & Siadat, M. R. (2015, November). Extensible query framework for unstructured medical data-a big data approach. In 2015 IEEE International Conference on Data Mining Workshop (ICDMW) (pp. 455–462). IEEE.

[19] Cunha, J., Silva, C. & Antunes, M. (2015). Health twitter big bata management with hadoop framework. Procedia Computer Science, 64, 425–431.

[20] Vanathi, R. & Khadir, A. S. A. (2017, February). A robust architectural framework for big data stream computing in personal healthcare real time analytics. In 2017 World Congress on Computing and Communication Technologies (WCCCT) (pp. 97–104). IEEE.

[21] Ritter, F., Boskamp, T., Homeyer, A., Laue, H., Schwier, M., Link, F. & Peitgen, H. O. (2011). Medical image analysis. IEEE pulse, 2(6), 60–70.

[22] Seibert, J. A. (2009). Modalities and data acquisition. In Practical Imaging Informatics. Springer, New York, NY, 49–66.

[23] Panigrahi, R., Pramanik, M., Chakraborty, U. K. & Bhoi, A. K. (2020). Survivability prediction of patients suffering hepatocellular carcinoma using diverse classifier ensemble of grafted decision tree. International Journal of Computer Applications in Technology, 64(4), 349–360.

[24] Borah, S., Singh, N. K., Yolmo, P. U., Kumar, R. & Panigrahi, R. (2022). Document classification using genetic algorithm. In Advances in Data Science and Management. Springer, Singapore, 253–261.

[25] Chidinma, O. A., Borah, S. & Panigrahi, R. (2021). Suicidal intent prediction using natural language processing (bag of words) approach. In Soft Computing Techniques and Applications. Springer, Singapore, 147–153.

[26] Drew, B. J., Harris, P., Zegre-Hemsey, J. K., Mammone, T., Schindler, D., Salas-Boni, R. . . . Hu, X. (2014). Insights into the problem of alarm fatigue with physiologic monitor devices: A comprehensive observational study of consecutive intensive care unit patients. PloS one, 9(10), e110274.

[27] Cvach, M. (2012). Monitor alarm fatigue: An integrative review. Biomedical instrumentation & technology, 46(4), 268–277.

[28] Rothschild, J. M., Landrigan, C. P., Cronin, J. W., Kaushal, R., Lockley, S. W., Burdick, E. . . . Bates, D. W. (2005). The critical care safety study: The incidence and nature of adverse events and serious medical errors in intensive care. Critical Care Medicine, 33(8), 1694–1700.

[29] Carayon, P. & Gürses, A. P. (2005). A human factors engineering conceptual framework of nursing workload and patient safety in intensive care units. Intensive and Critical Care Nursing, 21(5), 284–301.
[30] Lander, E. S. (2001). Initial sequencing and analysis of the human germane. Nature, 409, 860–921.
[31] Drmanac, R., Sparks, A. B., Callow, M. J., Halpern, A. L., Burns, N. L., Kermani, B. G. . . . Reid, C. A. (2010). Human genome sequencing using unchained base reads on self-assembling DNA nanoarrays. Science, 327(5961), 78–81.
[32.] Caulfield, T., Evans, J., McGuire, A., McCabe, C., Bubela, T., Cook-Deegan, R. . . . Wilson, B. (2013). Reflections on the cost of" low-cost" whole genome sequencing: Framing the health policy debate. PLoS biology, 11(11), e1001699.
[33] Dewey, F. E., Grove, M. E., Pan, C., Goldstein, B. A., Bernstein, J. A., Chaib, H. . . . Quertermous, T. (2014). Clinical interpretation and implications of whole-genome sequencing. Jama, 311(10), 1035–1045.
[34] Hood, L. & Friend, S. H. (2011). Predictive, personalized, preventive, participatory (P4) cancer medicine. Nature reviews Clinical oncology, 8(3), 184–187.
[35] Hood, L. & Flores, M. (2012). A personal view on systems medicine and the emergence of proactive P4 medicine: Predictive, preventive, personalized and participatory. New biotechnology, 29(6), 613–624.
[36] Chen, R., Mias, G. I., Li-Pook-Than, J., Jiang, L., Lam, H. Y., Chen, R. . . . Snyder, M. (2012). Personal omics profiling reveals dynamic molecular and medical phenotypes. Cell, 148(6), 1293–1307.
[37] Fernald, G. H., Capriotti, E., Daneshjou, R., Karczewski, K. J. & Altman, R. B. (2011). Bioinformatics challenges for personalized medicine. Bioinformatics, 27(13), 1741–1748.
[38] Oyelade, J., Soyemi, J., Isewon, I. & Obembe, O. (2015). Bioinformatics, healthcare informatics and analytics: An imperative for improved healthcare system. International Journal of Applied Information System, 13(5), 1–6.
[39] Kannampallil, T. G., Franklin, A., Cohen, T. & Buchman, T. G. (2014). Sub-optimal patterns of information use: a rational analysis of information seeking behavior in critical care. In Cognitive Informatics in Health and Biomedicine. Springer, London, 389–408.
[40] Belle, A., Thiagarajan, R., Soroushmehr, S. M., Navidi, F., Beard, D. A. & Najarian, K. (2015). Big data analytics in healthcare. BioMed research international, 2015.
[41] Raghupathi, V. & Raghupathi, W. (2014). An unstructured information management architecture approach to text analytics of cancer blogs. International Journal of Healthcare Information Systems and Informatics (IJHISI), 9(2), 16–33.
[42] Ravichandar, H., Polydoros, A. S., Chernova, S. & Billard, A. (2020). Recent advances in robot learning from demonstration. Annual Review of Control, Robotics, and Autonomous Systems, 3, 297–330.
[43] McClay, W. A., Yadav, N., Ozbek, Y., Haas, A., Attias, H. T. & Nagarajan, S. S. (2015). A real-time magnetoencephalography brain-computer interface using interactive 3D visualization and the Hadoop ecosystem. Brain Sciences, 5(4), 419–440.
[44] Poucke, S. V., Zhang, Z., Schmitz, M., Vukicevic, M., Laenen, M. V., Celi, L. A. & Deyne, C. D. (2016). Scalable predictive analysis in critically ill patients using a visual open data analysis platform. PloS one, 11(1), e0145791.
[45] Awotunde, J. B., Ogundokun, R. O. & Misra, S. (2021). Cloud and IoMT-based big data analytics system during COVID-19 pandemic. In Internet of Things, Vol. 2021. Springer, Cham, 181–201.
[46] Knipe, D., Evans, H., Marchant, A., Gunnell, D. & John, A. (2020). Mapping population mental health concerns related to COVID-19 and the consequences of physical distancing: A Google trends analysis. Wellcome open research, 5.

[47] Conboy, K., Mikalef, P., Dennehy, D. & Krogstie, J. (2020). Using business analytics to enhance dynamic capabilities in operations research: A case analysis and research agenda. European Journal of Operational Research, 281(3), 656–672.
[48] Sivarajah, U., Irani, Z., Gupta, S. & Mahroof, K. (2020). Role of big data and social media analytics for business to business sustainability: A participatory web context. Industrial Marketing Management, 86, 163–179.
[49] Khallouli, W. & Huang, J. (2021). Cluster resource scheduling in cloud computing: Literature review and research challenges. The Journal of Supercomputing, 1–46.
[50] Sahoo, S. S., Wei, A., Valdez, J., Wang, L., Zonjy, B., Tatsuoka, C. . . . Lhatoo, S. D. (2016). NeuroPigPen: A scalable toolkit for processing electrophysiological signal data in neuroscience applications using apache pig. Frontiers in Neuroinformatics, 10, 18.
[51] De Silva, D., Burstein, F., Jelinek, H. F. & Stranieri, A. (2015). Addressing the complexities of big data analytics in healthcare: The diabetes screening case. Australasian Journal of Information Systems, 19.
[52] Dinov, I. D. (2016). Methodological challenges and analytic opportunities for modeling and interpreting Big Healthcare Data. Gigascience, 5(1), 13742–016.
[53] Honar Pajooh, H., Rashid, M. A., Alam, F. & Demidenko, S. (2021). IoT big data provenance scheme using blockchain on Hadoop ecosystem. Journal of Big Data, 8(1), 1–26.
[54] Addisie, A. & Bertacco, V. (2020). Collaborative accelerators for streamlining MapReduce on scale-up machines with incremental data aggregation. IEEE Transactions on Computers, 69(8), 1233–1247.
[55] Batarseh, F. A. & Latif, E. A. (2016). Assessing the quality of service using big data analytics: With application to healthcare. Big Data Research, 4, 13–24.
[56] Doyle, T., Jimenez-Guri, E., Hawkes, W. L., Massy, R., Mantica, F., Permanyer, J. . . . Wotton, K. R. (2022). Genome-wide transcriptomic changes reveal the genetic pathways involved in insect migration. Molecular Ecology.
[57] Lombardo, S. D., Wangsaputra, I. F., Menche, J. & Stevens, A. (2022). Network approaches for charting the transcriptomic and epigenetic landscape of the developmental origins of health and disease. Genes, 13(5), 764.
[58] Alashhab, Z. R., Anbar, M., Singh, M. M., Leau, Y. B., Al-Sai, Z. A. & Alhayja'a, S. A. (2021). Impact of coronavirus pandemic crisis on technologies and cloud computing applications. Journal of Electronic Science and Technology, 19(1), 100059.
[59] Awotunde, J. B., Bhoi, A. K. & Barsocchi, P. (2021). Hybrid cloud/Fog environment for healthcare: An exploratory study, opportunities, challenges, and future prospects. Hybrid Artificial Intelligence and IoT in Healthcare, 1–20.
[60] Istephan, S. & Siadat, M. R. (2016). Unstructured medical image query using big data-an epilepsy case study. Journal of biomedical informatics, 59, 218–226.
[61] Selvi, R. T. & Muthulakshmi, I. (2021). Modelling the map reduce based optimal gradient boosted tree classification algorithm for diabetes mellitus diagnosis system. Journal of Ambient Intelligence and Humanized Computing, 12(2), 1717–1730.
[62] Toews, M., Wachinger, C., Estepar, R. S. J. & Wells, W. M. (June, 2015). A feature-based approach to big data analysis of medical images. In International Conference on Information Processing in Medical Imaging. Springer, Cham, 339–350.
[63] Ismail, A., Abdlerazek, S. & El-Henawy, I. M. (2020). Big data analytics in heart diseases prediction. Journal of Theoretical and Applied Information Technology, 98(11), 1970–1980.
[64] Kamran, M. & Javed, A. (2015). A survey of recommender systems and their application in healthcare. Technical Journal, University of Engineering and Technology (UET) Taxila, Pakistan, 20(4), 111–119.
[65] Zhang, J., Xu, J., Hu, X., Chen, Q., Tu, L., Huang, J. & Cui, J. (2017). Diagnostic method of diabetes based on support vector machine and tongue images. BioMed Research International. https://doi.org/10.1155/2017/7961494.

[66] Nair, L. R., Shetty, S. D. & Shetty, S. D. (2018). Applying spark based machine learning model on streaming big data for health status prediction. Computers and Electrical Engineering, 65, 393–399. https://doi.org/10.1016/J.COMPELECENG.2017.03.009.

[67] Polat, H., Danaei Mehr, H. & Cetin, A. (2017). Diagnosis of chronic kidney disease based on support vector machine by feature selection methods. Journal of Medical Systems, 41(4). https://doi.org/10.1007/s10916-017-0703-x.

[68] Dumka, A. & Sah, A. (2019). Smart ambulance system using concept of big data and internet of things. Healthcare Data Analytics and Management, 155–176. https://doi.org/10.1016/B978-0-12-815368-0.00006-3

[69] Ismail, A., Abdlerazek, S. & El-Henawy, I. M. (2020). Development of smart healthcare system based on speech recognition using support vector machine and dynamic time warping. Sustainability (Switzerland), 12(6). https://doi.org/10.3390/su12062403.

[70] Panigrahi, R., Borah, S. & Mishra, D. (2021). A proposal of rule-based hybrid intrusion detection system through analysis of rule-based supervised classifiers. In Intelligent and Cloud Computing. Springer, Singapore, 623–633.

[71] Abidi, S. S. R. & Abidi, S. R. (July, 2019). Intelligent health data analytics: a convergence of artificial intelligence and big data. In Healthcare management forum, Vol. 32(4), 178–182. Sage CA, Los Angeles, CA, SAGE Publications.

[72] Awotunde, J. B., Adeniyi, E. A., Kolawole, P. O. & Ogundokun, R. O. (2022). Application of big data in COVID-19 epidemic. In Data Science for COVID-19. Academic Press, 141–165.

[73] Awotunde, J. B., Folorunso, S. O., Bhoi, A. K., Adebayo, P. O. & Ijaz, M. F. (2021). Disease diagnosis system for IoT-based wearable body sensors with machine learning algorithm. In Intelligent Systems Reference Library, Vol. 2021(209), 201–222, Springer, Singapore.

[74] Moreira, M. W., Rodrigues, J. J., Korotaev, V., Al-Muhtadi, J. & Kumar, N. (2019). A comprehensive review on smart decision support systems for health care. IEEE Systems Journal, 13(3), 3536–3545.

[75] Khumprom, P. & Yodo, N. (2019). A data-driven predictive prognostic model for lithium-ion batteries based on a deep learning algorithm. Energies, 12(4), 660.

[76] Massaad, E., Fatima, N., Hadzipasic, M., Alvarez-Breckenridge, C., Shankar, G. M. & Shin, J. H. (2019). Predictive analytics in spine oncology research: First steps, limitations, and future directions. Neurospine, 16(4), 669.

[77] Smith, T. C. & Frank, E. (2016). Introducing machine learning concepts with WEKA. In Statistical Genomics. Humana Press, New York, NY, 353–378.

[78] Stachl, C., Au, Q., Schoedel, R., Gosling, S. D., Harari, G. M., Buschek, D. . . . Bühner, M. (2020). Predicting personality from patterns of behavior collected with smartphones. Proceedings of the National Academy of Sciences, 117(30), 17680–17687.

[79] Parmezan, A. R. S., Souza, V. M. & Batista, G. E. (2019). Evaluation of statistical and machine learning models for time series prediction: Identifying the state-of-the-art and the best conditions for the use of each model. Information sciences, 484, 302–337.

[80] Soltanpoor, R. & Sellis, T. (September, 2016). Prescriptive analytics for big data. In Australasian Database Conference. Springer, Cham, 245–256.

[81] Poornima, S. & Pushpalatha, M. (2020). A survey on various applications of prescriptive analytics. International Journal of Intelligent Networks, 1, 76–84.

[82] Gupta, S., Drave, V. A., Dwivedi, Y. K., Baabdullah, A. M. & Ismagilova, E. (2020). Achieving superior organizational performance via big data predictive analytics: A dynamic capability view. Industrial Marketing Management, 90, 581–592.

[83] Pienaar, C. (2021). Machine learning in predictive analytics on judicial decision-making (Master's thesis, Faculty of Science).

[84] Joshi, M., Mecklai, K., Rozenblum, R. & Samal, L. (2022). Implementation approaches and barriers for rule-based and machine learning-based sepsis risk prediction tools: A qualitative study. JAMIA open, 5(2), ooac022.

[85] Tarride, J. E., Cheung, M., Hanna, T. P., Cipriano, L. E., Regier, D. A., Hey, S. P. . . . Mittmann, N. (2022). Platform, basket, and umbrella trial designs: Issues around health technology assessment of novel therapeutics. Canadian Journal of Health Technologies, 2(7).

[86] Lee, D. & Yoon, S. N. (2021). Application of artificial intelligence-based technologies in the healthcare industry: Opportunities and challenges. International Journal of Environmental Research and Public Health, 18(1), 271.

[87] Chey, S. W., Chey, W. D., Jackson, K. & Eswaran, S. (2021). Exploratory comparative effectiveness trial of green kiwifruit, psyllium, or prunes in US patients with chronic constipation. Official journal of the American College of Gastroenterology| ACG, 116(6), 1304–1312.

[88] Steele, J., Malleron, T., Har-Nir, I., Androulakis-Korakakis, P., Wolf, M., Fisher, J. P. & Halperin, I. (2022). Are trainees lifting heavy enough? Self-selected loads in resistance exercise: A scoping review and exploratory meta-analysis. Sports Medicine, 1–15.

[89] Kaur, S., Singla, J., Nkenyereye, L., Jha, S., Prashar, D., Joshi, G. P. . . . Islam, S. R. (2020). Medical diagnostic systems using artificial intelligence (AI) algorithms: Principles and perspectives. IEEE Access, 8, 228049–228069.

[90] Pablo, R. G. J., Roberto, D. P., Victor, S. U., Isabel, G. R., Paul, C. & Elizabeth, O. R. (2022). Big data in the healthcare system: A synergy with artificial intelligence and blockchain technology. Journal of Integrative Bioinformatics, 19(1).

[91] Mohammadhassanzadeh, H., Van Woensel, W., Abidi, S. R. & Abidi, S. S. R. (2017). Semantics-based plausible reasoning to extend the knowledge coverage of medical knowledge bases for improved clinical decision support. BioData mining, 10(1), 1–31.

[92] Tu, S. W., Tennakoon, L., O'Connor, M., Shankar, R. & Das, A. (2008). Using an integrated ontology and information model for querying and reasoning about phenotypes: The case of autism. In AMIA Annual Symposium Proceedings (Vol. 2008, p. 727). American Medical Informatics Association.

[93] Boser, B., Guyon, I. & Vapnik, V. (1992). A training algorithm for optimal margin classification. COLT '92: Proceedings of the Fifth Annual Workshop on Computational Learning Theory, 144–152. https://doi.org/https://doi.org/10.1145/130385.130401

[94] Aruna, S. & Rajagopalan, P. (2011). A Novel SVM based CSSFFS Feature Selection Algorithm for Detecting Breast Cancer. International Journal of Computer Applications, 31(8), 14–20.

[95] Noble, W. S. (2006). What is a support vector machine?. Nat Biotechnol, 24(12), 1565–1567. https://doi.org/10.1038/nbt1206-1565.

[96] Noble, W. S. (2004). Support vector machine applications in computational biology. In Kernel Methods in Computational Biology (pp. 71–92).

[97] Gurney, K. (2017). An Introduction to Neural Networks. CRC Press. https://doi.org/https://doi.org/10.1201/9781315273570

[98] Cheng, B. & Titterington, D. (1994). Neural networks: A review from a statistical perspective. Statistical Science, 9(1), 2–30. https://www.jstor.org/stable/2246275.

[99] Folorunso, S. O., Awotunde, J. B., Ayo, F. E. & Abdullah, K. K. A. (2021). RADIoT: The unifying framework for Iot, radiomics and deep learning modeling. In Intelligent Systems Reference Library, Vol. 2021(209), 109–128, Springer, Singapore.

[100] Panigrahi, R., Borah, S. & Chakraborty, U. K. (2021). WEKA result reader – a smart tool for reading and summarizing WEKA simulator files. In Evolution in Computational Intelligence. Springer, Singapore, 159–167.

[101] Gnana, A., Leavline, E. & Baig, B. (2017). Diabetes prediction using medical data. Journal of Computational Intelligence in Bioinformatics, 10(1), 1–8.

[102] Ali, F., El-Sappagh, S., Islam, S. M. R., Kwak, D., Ali, A., Imran, M. & Kwak, K. S. (2020). A smart healthcare monitoring system for heart disease prediction based on ensemble deep learning and feature fusion. Information Fusion, 63, 208–222. https://doi.org/10.1016/J.INFFUS.2020.06.008.

[103] Ayon, S. I. & Milon Islam, M. (2019). Diabetes prediction: A deep learning approach. International Journal of Information Engineering and Electronic Business, 11(2), 21–27. https://doi.org/10.5815/ijieeb.2019.02.03.

[104] Rahman, M., Islam, D., Mukti, R. J. & Saha, I. (2020). A deep learning approach based on convolutional LSTM for detecting diabetes. Computational Biology and Chemistry, 88(December), 107329. https://doi.org/10.1016/j.compbiolchem.2020.107329.

[105] Veena, H. N., Muruganandham, A. & Senthil Kumaran, T. (2021). A novel optic disc and optic cup segmentation technique to diagnose glaucoma using deep learning convolutional neural network over retinal fundus images. Journal of King Saud University – Computer and Information Sciences. https://doi.org/10.1016/j.jksuci.2021.02.003.

[106] Heuvelmans, M. A., Van ooijen, P. M. A., Ather, S., Silva, C. F., Han, D., Heussel, C. P., Hickes, W., Kauczor, H. U., Novotny, P., Peschl, H., Rook, M., Rubtsov, R., Von stackelberg, O., Tsakok, M. T., Arteta, C., Declerck, J., Kadir, T., Pickup, L., Gleeson, F. & Oudkerk, M. (2020). Lung cancer prediction by Deep Learning to identify benign lung nodules. Lung Cancer, 154 (November 2020), 1–4. https://doi.org/10.1016/j.lungcan.2021.01.027.

[107] Bhaskar, N. & Suchetha, M. (2021). A computationally efficient correlational neural network for automated prediction of chronic kidney disease. IRBM, 42(4), 268–276. https://doi.org/10.1016/j.irbm.2020.07.002.

[108] Breiman, L. (1996). Bagging predictors. Machine Learning, 24, 123–140. https://doi.org/10.1007/BF00058655.

[109] Amit, Y. & Geman, D. (1997). Shape quantization and recognition with randomized trees. Neural Computation, 9(7), 1545–1588. https://doi.org/10.1162/neco.1997.9.7.1545.

[110] Ho, T. (1998). The random subspace method for constructing decision forests. IEEE transactions on Pattern analysis and Machine Intelligence, 20(8), 832–844. https://doi.org/10.1109/34.709601.

[111] Boukenze, B., Mousannif, H. & Haqiq, A. (2016). Predictive analytics in healthcare system using data mining techniques. Computing and Information Technology, 1, 01–09. https://doi.org/10.5121/csit.2016.60501.

[112] Nagarajan, V. R. & Kumar, V. (2018). An optimized sub group partition based healthcare data mining in big data. International Journal for Innovative Research in Science & Technology, 4(10), 79–85.

[113] Ahmed, H., Younis, E. M. G., Hendawi, A. & Ali, A. A. (2020). Heart disease identification from patients' social posts, machine learning solution on Spark. Future Generation Computer Systems, 111, 714–722. https://doi.org/10.1016/j.future.2019.09.056.

[114] Chen, Y. M., Cao, W., Gao, X. C., Ong, H. S. & Ji, T. (2015). Predicting postoperative complications of head and neck squamous cell carcinoma in elderly patients using random forest algorithm model. BMC Medical Informatics and Decision Making, 15(1), 1–10. https://doi.org/10.1186/s12911-015-0165-3.

[115] Berchialla, P., Gangemi, E. N., Foltran, F., Haxhiaj, A., Buja, A., Lazzarato, F., Stella, M. & Gregori, D. (2014). Predicting severity of pathological scarring due to burn injuries: A clinical decision making tool using Bayesian networks. International Wound Journal, 11(3), 246–252. https://doi.org/10.1111/j.1742-481X.2012.01080.x.

[116] Fawagreh, K. & Gaber, M. M. (2020). Resource-efficient fast prediction in healthcare data analytics: A pruned Random Forest regression approach. Computing, 102(5), 1187–1198. https://doi.org/10.1007/s00607-019-00785-6.

[117] Fawagreh, K., Gaber, M. M. & Elyan, E. (2014). Random forests: From early developments to recent advancements. Systems Science and Control Engineering, 2(1), 602–609. https://doi.org/10.1080/21642583.2014.956265.

[118] Fawagreh, K., Gaber, M. M. & Elyan, E. (2015). CLUB-DRF: A Clustering Approach to Extreme Pruning of Random Forests. Research and Development in Intelligent Systems XXXII, November, 59–73. https://doi.org/10.1007/978-3-319-25032-8.

[119] Friedman, N., Geiger, D. & Goldszmidt, M. (1997). Bayesian network classifiers. Machine Learning, 29, 131–163. https://doi.org/10.1023/A:1007465528199.

[120] Nandra, R., Parry, M., Forsberg, J. & Grimer, R. (2017). Can a Bayesian belief network be used to estimate 1-year survival in patients with bone Sarcomas? Clinical Orthopaedics and Related Research, 475(6), 1681–1689. https://doi.org/10.1007/s11999-017-5346-1.

[121] Yousefi, L., Tucker, A., Al-Luhaybi, M., Saachi, L., Bellazzi, R. & Chiovato, L. (2018). Predicting disease complications using a stepwise hidden variable approach for learning dynamic bayesian networks. Proceedings – IEEE Symposium on Computer-Based Medical Systems, 2018 -June, 106–111. https://doi.org/10.1109/CBMS.2018.00026

[122] Darcy, A. M., Louie, A. K. & Roberts, L. W. (2016). Machine learning and the profession of medicine. Jama, 315(6), 551–552.

[123] Awotunde, J. B., Adeniyi, E. A., Ajamu, G. J., Balogun, G. B. & Taofeek-Ibrahim, F. A. (2022). Explainable artificial intelligence in genomic sequence for healthcare systems prediction. In Studies in Computational Intelligence, 2022,, Vols. 1021,. Springer, Cham, 417–437.

[124] Dauda, O. I., Awotunde, J. B., AbdulRaheem, M. & Salihu, S. A. (2022). Basic issues and challenges on explainable artificial intelligence (XAI) in healthcare systems. Principles and Methods of Explainable Artificial Intelligence in Healthcare, 248–271.

[125] Abiodun, K. M., Awotunde, J. B., Aremu, D. R. & Adeniyi, E. A. (2022). Explainable AI for fighting COVID-19 pandemic: Opportunities, challenges, and future prospects. Computational Intelligence for COVID-19 and Future Pandemics, 315–332.

[126] Abidi, S. S. R. (July, 2007). Healthcare knowledge management: The art of the possible. In AIME Workshop on Knowledge Management for Health Care Procedures. Springer, Berlin, Heidelberg, 1–20.

Niyati Mishra, Sushruta Mishra

8 Impact of deep learning applications in medical hyper spectral imaging

Abstract: In the past few years, deep learning (DL) algorithms and its applications have been used for research and study in various developing fields including medical hyper spectral imaging (HSI) as one of the most prominent domain. In this paper, we have focused on various DL techniques that have been researched as promising tools that aid the medical hyper spectral image analysis. This paper widely discusses about the different ways in which HSI has been used in the medical field and how the use of DL techniques for classification, detection and segmentation have enhanced the disease diagnosis techniques and surgical procedures. Toward the end of the paper, we have also discussed the various future challenges that researchers might face in this domain and also the probable ways to mitigate them.

Keywords: Medical image analysis, hyper spectral or HS, deep learning, medical hyper spectral imaging or MHSI

8.1 Introduction

Hyper spectral imaging (HSI) is a technology dedicated to help tackle the imaging limitations of the human eye which is restricted to the RGB spectrum. HSI combines the features provided by two prominent technologies: digital imaging and spectroscopy [1]. Digital imaging is the creation of a representation of the visual characteristics of an object and spectroscopy mainly focuses on the interaction between the electromagnetic (EM) radiation and matter. HSI provides information in regions of the EMS that cannot be perceived by the human eye. The human eye is only capable of distinguishing three different wavelengths such as blue light, green light and red light (RGB), while HS cameras can capture the EMS in hundreds of narrow wavelengths, thereby largely increasing the resolution beyond what humans can perceive. The entire EM spectrum is portrayed in Figure 8.1. It refers to the EM radiation's entire distribution based on wavelength or frequency. The different ranges of EM spectrum include all radio waves, visible light, infrared radiation, UV radiation, gamma rays and X-rays.

Niyati Mishra, School of computer engineering, Kalinga Institute of Industrial Technology, Bhubaneswar, Odisha, India, e-mail: 2050005@kiit.ac.in
Sushruta Mishra, School of computer engineering, Kalinga Institute of Industrial Technology, Bhubaneswar, Odisha, India, e-mail: sushruta.mishrafcs@kiit.ac.in

https://doi.org/10.1515/9783110750942-008

Only the reflections in the visible (RGB) band can be perceived by the human eye, but a hyper spectral image comprises reflections in bands such as infrared and near-infrared, which cannot be seen by the human eye.

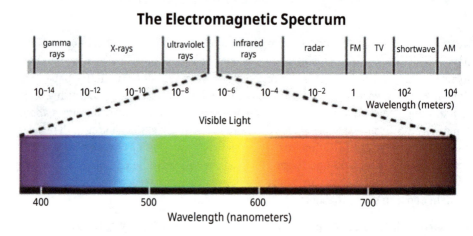

Figure 8.1: Electromagnetic spectrum.

An HS image is captured in the form of an HS cube as can be seen in Figure 8.2, comprising both spatial and spectral information of the corresponding image [2]. There are various ways in which we can visualize an HS cube. It shows the depiction of an HS cube which comprises both spatial and spectral information of the corresponding HS image. We can also see a visual comparison between the information that can be visualized using HSI and the naked human eye which is only capable of distinguishing three different wavelengths such as blue light, green light and red light (RGB)

We can either examine a spectrum related to a single pixel or we can visualize the entire spatial information for the respective wavelength. The information gathered at various wavelengths gives a proper understanding of the various properties of the matter.

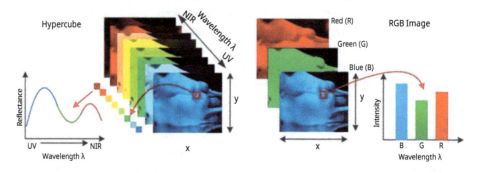

Figure 8.2: HS image captured in the form of an HS cube.

The spectral signature, as seen in Figure 8.2, is the curve representing the variation of reflectance or emittance of material with respect to wavelengths. Each material has a distinguished interaction with EMS; therefore each material has a unique spectral signature. In-depth analysis and studies of the spectral signature belonging to an HS image can help in differentiating different elements present in the captured image [3].

With hyper spectral camera, we are measuring thousands or hundreds of thousands of spectra.

A complete spectrum is included in each image pixel which helps us in forming an image of the target using the collected spectra as can be seen in Figure 8.3.

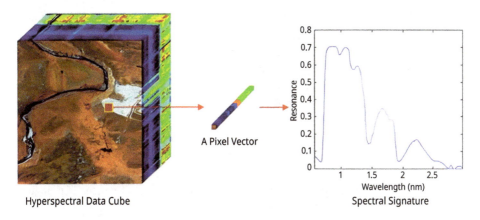

Figure 8.3: HS data cube, spectral signature and pixel vector.

8.2 Role of hyper spectral imaging in healthcare

Hyper spectral imaging (HSI) provides great potential for non-invasive diagnosis and surgical guidance. While light travels through tissues, multiple scattering occurs due to the heterogeneous structure of the tissue and absorption also occurs mainly in hemoglobin, melanin and water. There are changes observed in the absorption, fluorescence and scattering properties of tissue during the advancement of a disease [4]. Thus, by analyzing the fluorescent, reflected and transmitted light from tissue recorded by HSI, we can uncover various diagnostic information about tissue pathology.

HSI helps in delivering real-time images of biomarker information, such as oxyhemoglobin and deoxyhemoglobin, and also helps in assessment of tissue pathophysiology based on the spectral characteristics of different tissue. Hence, we can find increased use of HSI for medical diagnosis and image-guided surgery [5–7]. Next, we will uncover various applications of HSI to cancer, cardiac disease, retinal disease, image-guided surgery, etc.

8.2.1 Disease diagnosis

HSI can be used for disease screening, detection and diagnosis as it has the ability to detect biochemical changes that might occur with the progression of disease. Next, we will be dealing with how HSI system can be used for the diagnosis of various diseases such as different types of cancer, cardiac disease, retinal disease and diabetes.

8.2.1.1 Cancers

The main idea behind cancer detection by using optical imaging is that biochemical and morphological changes associated with lesions might cause changes in the absorption, scattering and fluorescence properties. Thus various optical features of tissue can provide prominent diagnostic knowledge [8].

Images of large area of tissues can be captured using HIS and thus HIS has manifested great probabilities in the diagnosis of cancer in the cervix, breast, solon, lymph nodes, brain, etc.

The main aspects that are followed in the HSI cancer studies are:
- Identifying genomic modifications and protein biomarkers on single tumor cells in vitro
- Examination of the structural and morphological aspects of cancer histological specimens to categorize the cancer grades
- Investigating the tissue surface to pin point malignant and precancerous lesions in vivo
- Estimating the blood oxygenation and tissue blood volume to gauge the tumor metabolism and tumor angiogenesis

Certain research studies performed on some types of cancer have been mentioned in the following section.

Cervical cancer: Pap smear tests are the mostly widely used screening method to identify cervical cancer. But these tests have been found to exhibit a false-positive rate ranging from 15% to 40%. Various studies have demonstrated that both fluorescence and reflectance spectroscopy are capable of detection of increased angiogenesis coexists with pre-cancer. A clinical study was performed by Ferris et al. [26] on a varied population of women which included both women with and without the disease by using an MHSI system and measured tissue reflectance and fluorescence of the cervical epithelium on the ectocervix. This study proved that the said system could help properly distinguish between severe cervical lesions and less severe cervical lesions, thus providing better results in cervical cancer detection in comparison to pap smear test.

Breast cancer: Hypoxia is caused due to insufficient oxygen supply in tumor cells. Many studies have demonstrated the fact that hypoxia has great prognostic value in various clinical trials concerning chemotherapy, radiation and surgery. In order to obtain serial spatial maps of blood oxygenation in accordance to hemoglobin saturation at the microvascular level on the mouse mammary carcinoma in vivo, Sorg et al. [27] applied HSI. For the identification purpose of mouse mammary carcinoma cells, RFP was used and for the identification of the hypoxic fraction, hypoxia-driven GFP was used. The said study holds the promise of improvement of the treatment as well as the protocols that can help address the tumor behavior.

Skin cancer: MHSI is primarily focused on two varieties of skin cancers – Kaposi's sarcoma (KS) and melanoma. The deadliest form of skin cancer is melanoma as it catered to almost 75% skin cancer-related deaths in the year of 2012. KS is a highly vascularized tumor which is responsible for the cause of cutaneous lesions. A six band multi-spectral NIR imaging system was constructed by Hattery's team [28] for the identification of the thermal signatures of blood volume on patients suffering from KS and were just getting started with anti-angiogenesis therapy. It was observed from the results of the said study that blood oxygen saturation and relative spatial tissue blood volume values can serve as promising indicators of tumor metabolism and tumor angiogenesis.

Head and neck cancer: The head and neck region with the inclusion of oral cavity, lip, nasal cavity, hypopharynx, oropharynx, larynx, etc. is the area where head and neck cancer (HNC) may occur. Majority of HNCs stem from the epithelial region. Thus, HSI with restricted penetration depth can be used to detect the cancerous tissue.

Colon cancer: Colon cancer or colorectal cancer is a deadly disease that affects the rectum or colon or appendix. Cancer diagnosis and its corresponding treatment are based on pathological analysis. Variation in nuclei shape and size is caused by malignant tumor. Conventionally, pathologists investigate the specimens under the microscopes and observe the deviations in the cell structures and distribution of the cells across the tissue being examined in order to identify the presence of any tumor or cancerous cells. But, the said technique is subjective, cumbersome and inconsistent as there is a limited field of view. Thus multiple images are to be taken and put together in order to build the entire image of the tissue specimen. To provide a solution for this problem, a confocal scanning macroscope embedded with prototype HSI mode was developed by Constantinou's [29] team for the detection of fluorescently labeled antibodies and the removal of autofluorescence in formalin-fixed, paraffin-integrated tissues with linear unmixing method. The said MHSI model boasts the capability to concurrently image-diverse fluorescently labeled tissue-specific markers in huge biological samples in a timely and cost-effective fashion.

8.2.1.2 Heart and circulatory pathology

An extensive exploration of HSI has been done in heart and circulatory pathology both in vivo and in vitro.

In vivo study: Peripheral artery disease (PAD) is a circulatory disorder in which blood flow to the limbs is reduced due to the presence of narrowed arteries. Various symptoms of this disease include painful cramping of limbs, numbness in limbs, color change in legs, no pulse or a weak pulse in legs and feet. Proper diagnostic techniques are required for timely detection and treatment to avoid further complications [9].

Traditional methods such as ankle-brachial index and Doppler waveform analysis could not provide proper prediction of healing of tissue loss in patients suffering from PAD.

HSI can cater to non-invasive measurement of oxyhemoglobin and deoxyhemoglobin concentrations which in turn helps form an anatomic oxygenation map.

Various studies have indicated that HSI can be helpful in observing the distinction between oxygenation levels in patients who are affected or patients who are not affected by PAD, thus proving to be a distinguished instrument for the diagnosis of patients affected by PAD.

In vitro study: Coronary artery disease attributes to congestion of coronary arteries due to the development of a fatty substance known as plaque. It results in chest pain, shortness of breath, nausea, weakness, etc.

Coronary disease mostly results from atherosclerosis through a gradually developing lesion formation and constricting of arteries. Traditionally, atherosclerosis is diagnosed by using angiography, but this technique is stunted to the identification of stenotic plaques. Spectroscopic techniques have been tried as instruments for diagnosing atherosclerosis. But, further research showed that due to spatial variation of plaque, the use of traditional spectroscopic measurements for the accurate classification of plaque becomes extremely arduous.

But with the help of HSI, atherosclerosis can be diagnosed by examining large area of tissue under study and thereby contributing spectral data for each pixel in the area of study. Wight-light reflectance and UV-excited fluorescence HS images can help in determining various plaque features, thus providing better results in comparison to histology.

8.2.1.3 Retinal diseases

Present diagnostic techniques for retinal diseases is highly dependent on optical imaging methods. Generally a fundus camera is combined with an HSI system to activate optical imaging of the eyes.

Cohen's team in 1999 revealed that HSI can help in quantifying retinal images as HSI can be used for mapping wavelength resolved reflectivity in 2D and thus provides prospects for rapid detection and proper monitoring of efficacy of treatment.

A snapshot HSI system with stationary parts was developed by Johnson and his team for delivering functional mapping of the human retina. Qualitative and quantitative oxygen saturation maps were obtained with the help of hemoglobin spectral signatures, which are in turn used for the treatment of diseases such as retinal ischemia and diabetes, which if not properly treated might lead to incurable blindness [10].

8.2.1.4 Diabetes foot

One of the major threats posed to diabetes patients is diabetic foot ulceration. If not properly treated these ulcers might get infected and lead to total or partial amputation of the leg. Deterioration of the condition of existing ulcers preceded by advancement of diabetic foot ulceration has great dependability on the variation in the large vessels and microcirculation of the diabetic foot. As shown by a study, risk assessment of diabetic foot ulcer growth and estimation of the probability of non-invasive treatment could be accomplished by using HSI between 450 and 700 nm. Analysis of in vivo hyper spectral measurements can be accomplished using two methods. The preliminary method helped in forming a map of oxyhemoglobin and deoxyhemoglobin density in the dermis of the foot. Another method deals with the retrieval of oxyhemoglobin and deoxyhemoglobin density along with epidermal thickness and melanin density [11].

Another study revealed that hyper spectral tissue oximetry can be used for risk evaluation of diabetic foot ulceration formation with high levels of sensitivity and specificity.

8.2.1.5 Shock

Skin is the largest and hence the most reachable organ of the body, which is often prone to variations in the systemic circulation, and this aspect is quite crucial for the diagnosis of shock affected patients. MHSI provides fresh techniques for the measurement of both temporal and spatial variations in skin hemodynamics.

Gillies et al. [30] have gauged the capability of MHSI for the quantification and depiction of the cutaneous illustrations of shock by making use of a porcine model. Shock was generated by chest trauma which after which hemorrhage occurred. During shock and recovery, both qualitative and quantitative variations in the level of skin oxygenation were noted. During hemorrhagic shock, a mottled pattern of oxygen saturation was detected. This study provided a firm insight regarding the use of non-invasive imaging of skin oxygen saturation in keeping track of the how the microvasculature responds to shock and further treatment. Fresh insights regarding the treatment of shock can be offered by the use of MHSI in the measurement of variation in hemoglobin saturation and cutaneous blood flow distribution.

8.2.2 Surgical guidance

A surgeon's senses of vision and judgment making skills with regard to identification of the lesion and its margins help determine the success of the surgery. Medical HSI can be useful in enhancing a surgeon's view point at molecular, cellular and tissue levels.

One of the most important components of microsurgery is proper visual inspection. Blood spillage during surgery is one of the inevitable factors that might compromise the visual aspect of surgery thereby posing a threat to the life of patients. One of the prominent ways to picture the tissue layers immersed in blood is NIR HIS spectrograph [12].

One of the most effective treatments for cancer is the removal of cancerous or tumor tissues while posing no threat to the surrounding non-cancerous or normal tissue. Differentiating between cancerous and non-cancerous tissues is often difficult thereby leading to residual tumor cells in patients. MHSI helps in the detection of residual tumor by helping in distinguishing between normal and cancerous tissue based on their spectral signatures almost real time during the surgery. The tissue oxygen level saturation helps in identifying healthy tissues that might be compromised during tumor removal, and this oxygen saturation level is monitored with help of HSI.

A surgeon is facilitated with the capability to uphold investigation and gauge evolving surgical procedures in the operating theater with the help of MHSI which has the scope of real-time imaging since MHSI can capacitate the perception of the anatomy of vasculatures and organs. MHSI has been used in various surgeries such as mastectomy, cholecystectomy, renal surgery and abdominal surgery.

8.2.2.1 Mastectomy

Nearly 45% of the victims of breast cancer choose to opt for primary surgical procedure with mastectomy, yet the absolute resection rate is almost as low as 40%, as has been reported by certain studies. The residual tumors that were not identified at the time of the surgery were discovered in the marginal areas in the resected case subject. This aspect of the procedure makes intraoperative assessment of residual tumor quite crucial for the absolute resection. By making use of MHSI in an intraoperative procedure conducted using a rat specimen, Panasyuk et al. [31] were successful in detecting residual tumors ranging from 0.5 to 1.0 mm (as can be seen in Figure 8.4) which were left deliberately during the said procedure. Initially the rat breast tumors were exposed and further imaged using HS camera, and then it was partly resected and further imaged once again using HS camera. Thus MHSI technique was successful in the identification and differentiation of blood vessels, tumors, connective tissue and muscles. The discussed model was able to a specificity of 94% and a sensitivity of 89% for the residual tumor detection. Thus, MHSI can prove to be of utmost importance for large-scale resection and also for the identification of essential and promising biopsy sites.

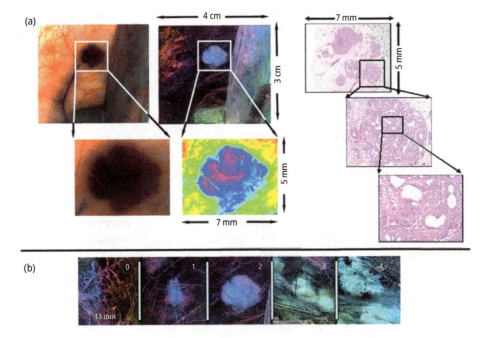

Figure 8.4: (a) Image of on the spot breast tumor (4 × 3 cm) taken through a microscope by hyper spectral camera and equivalent hyperspectral imaging image (left upper and middle upper positions). After removal of tumor, the neighboring tissue along with the eviscerated tumor was soaked with hematoxylin and eosin and assessed by biopsy. The right panels exhibit higher resolution microscopic histopathological depictions of the same; (b) prototypes of normal tissue (grade 0), benign tumor (grade 1), intraductal carcinomas (grade 2), papillary and cribriform carcinoma (grade 3), and carcinoma with invasion (grade 4).

8.2.2.2 Gall bladder surgery

Gall bladder-related ailments mostly seek surgical assistance which more often than not entails the removal of the organ from the body. Laparoscopic cholecystectomy was one such conventionally used surgical procedure. The said procedure requires several small incisions of diameter ranging from 5 to 10 mm, in the abdominal region. Through these incisions, a video camera and the essential surgical tools are inserted into the abdominal cavity. More often than not solid feedback is lost by surgeons as traditionally used camera in this procedure through an endoscope for the biliary tree identification lacks wider image contrast. For the identification purpose of molecular and anatomy constituent of tissue an endoscope-based HSI model was used by Zuzak's [32] team while conducting laparoscopic procedure on a pig. The observations made from the said study confirmed the fact that near infrared laparoscopic HSI procedure can prove to be of heavy use for not only non-invasive interrogation but also for tissue identification purposes depending on their respective chemical constitution instantaneously in an intraoperative fashion and also in the absence of a radioactive contrast agent. This study confirms the fact that lipids with absorption potential of 930 nm have the capability to be efficient biomarkers in order to image the bile ducts having lipid that connect the gall bladder in the duration of the cholecystectomy procedure.

8.2.2.3 Abdominal surgery

Reduced blood flow in the intestine also known as intestinal ischemia results in diminished supply of oxygen and also in the accumulation of waste products and deoxygenated blood. The said condition brings about necrosis and cell death, thus resulting in ulcers and inflammations. Proper visibility is quite crucial to identify the aforementioned issues during a surgery as there might be structural variations and surgeries can also prove to be quite unpredictable. To help surgeons improve the visibility and examination of greater regions during the surgical procedure Akbari et al. [33–37] used MHSI as a critical tool in aiding the detection of anatomical variations in organs and intestinal ischemia while conducting abdominal surgery on swine specimen. While doing do, they landed on discovering a crucial wavelength spectrum ranging from 765 to 830 mm that helps in providing the most accurate distinction between ischemic and normal intestine. This study and many others helped in demonstrating the fact that MHSI proves to be a critical tool to enhance the visibility of anatomy of artery and veins and thus helps distinguishing them from each other during surgical procedures.

8.3 Use of deep learning in hyper spectral imaging

Primitive learning techniques for interpretation of HSI data rely heavily on handspurn attributes which were fed to a classifier. Initially it started with simple and easy to understand low-level attributes and then gradually the attribute set along with the classifiers became more and more complicated. Hints related to deep learning (DL) were already implanted in the track of digital signal processing and computer vision. For instance, neural networks can easily do the task done by a primitive bag of features model associated with convolutional filters. The forte of DL-based solutions heavily relies on the hierarchical and automatic learning derived from data which has the ability to form a model with progressively higher interpretation layers as long as we reach a proper representation for our current task (e.g., regression, detection and classification). Despite all these advantages, special attention needs to be given when DL is used for HS data. Due to the huge number of attributes or parameters used in DL models, a substantially larger data set is required to steer clear of overfitting [13].

Limited attainability of labeled or public datasets is one of the most prominent disadvantages in the coming together of DL and HSI. Lack of availability of labeled training data is magnified due to the high data dimensionality. This might have severe negative effects compassing from classification performance degradation to the lack of the models' capacity to generalize or critical overfitting.

Another major limitation is the availability of researched solutions which may be restricted to the sphere of dataset. This in turn leads to work with the possibility of using unsupervised algorithms to relatively dial down the effects of unattainability of labeled data. Certain DL models (e.g., CNN and auto-encoders) along with data augmentation procedures can also help in tackling the aforementioned issues [14].

8.3.1 What is deep learning?

Deep learning is a class of machine learning and artificial intelligence which takes inspiration from the way humans gain insights and knowledge by imitating the human brain's structure and function by not just complementing its capability but also "learning" from large-scale data. It is substantially a neural network with multiple layers, minimum being three. Neural networks with a single layer can also make broad projections but to achieve greater accuracy and enhanced predictions, multiple hidden layers are recommended. Weights, bias and data inputs collectively work together to perceive, categorize and report targets in the data.

Various techniques can be implemented to create strong, predictive models with good levels of accuracy.

These include
a) Learning rate decay: Learning rate is a hyperparameter, that is, its value is used to manage the learning process by guiding the change percentage in the model based on the approximate error occurring with each modification of model weights. Higher learning rates lead to unbalanced learning processes while smaller learning rates lead to long-drawn-out learning processes. In order to elevate performance levels and decrease training times, learning rate needs to be adjusted through a process called learning rate annealing which comprises various approaches.
b) Transfer learning: This entails refining a previously trained model and thus necessitates an interface to the intramurals of the prior-developed network. On the existing model, new data with undisclosed categorizations is fed and the model is retrained. After the network is adapted based on the new training, more predictions can be made with the classification categories widened. The computational time also gets reduced to hours or minutes.
c) Training from scratch: For new applications or applications that have massive brackets for objects to be grouped into, to prepare a model it is required to accumulate a huge labeled data set and design a network architecture to grasp the characteristics and develop a model.

d) Dropout: In order to decode the issue of overfitting in networks caused by the large number of variables taken into consideration, dropout method can be incorporated. It involves randomly removing inter-connected components from training and co-relating the resulting accuracy.

8.3.2 Deep learning methods

ML techniques are mainly divided into two categories: unsupervised and supervised learning algorithms. Supervised algorithm is fed with a dataset containing an input attribute or feature set and an output label to predict the output of a given unlabeled attribute set. Supervised model can be a classification or a regression model. The output is grouped into discrete values in case of classification while a regression model portrays the output in the form of continuous values. Supervised learning model is focused on discovering optimal parameters that helps in minimizing the cost function, thus resulting in a best-fit model according to the provided bias, input and learning rate. Once the model is created, a dummy dataset is used to evaluate the accuracy of the model by checking whether the real output from the given dataset matches the result provided by the model [15].

The main goal behind testing is to check the robustness of the model. An unsupervised learning algorithm focuses on finding the label for an unlabeled attribute set while being fed with a dataset containing an input attribute or feature set and no output label, that is, unlabeled data is fed into the model in case of an unsupervised learning algorithm. So, in this case almost every time there is variation in the output as the initial parameters are chosen in an ambiguous fashion.

In the subsequent section, we will be reading about some famous supervised and unsupervised models.

8.3.1 Supervised learning methods

8.3.1.1 Neural networks

Multilayer perceptron or neural network is a type of learning algorithm that owns it origins to the human brain as it was developed with the idea of mimicking a human brain in all aspects and thus is the founding father of maximum number of DL techniques. A single NN, as can be seen in Figure 8.4, comprises many neurons which serve as the foundation unit that consists of weights W, bias b and an activation number.

A simple activation function can be represented as

$$a^{(1)} = \sigma\left(Wa^{(0)} + b\right),$$

where $a^{(0)}$ refers to the input attributes or features, $a^{(1)}$ represents the input numbers for the next layer and σ represents the transfer function. In order to form an entire complete layer at each interim, the dot product between the input attribute vector and the weight vector is obtained. This portrays a single layer comprising several neurons following a feed forward technique, which means that one neuron intakes a single input and after executing the operation and passes on the result of the operation to the next layer in the network [16]. Two or more neuron layers (otherwise referred to as hidden layers) combine to form a multi-layer perceptron or MLP. These MLP layers come together to form the foundation of deep neural network or DNN which can be viewed in Figure 8.4. The first part portrays a single layer comprising several neurons following a feed forward technique, which means that one neuron intakes a single input and after executing the operation, passes on the result of the operation to the next layer in the network. In the second part, two or more neuron layers (otherwise referred to as hidden layers) combine to form a multi-layer perceptron or MLP. These MLP layers come together to form the foundation of deep neural network or DNN.

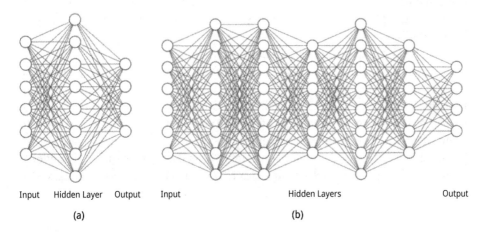

Figure 8.5: Schematic diagram of (a) simple NN; (b) DNN.

8.3.1.1.1 Convolutional neural networks (CNN)

CNN helps in identifying features and patterns and thus helps in classifying objects that are fed as inputs to the model. Instead of performing convolution techniques on the features, the weights are designed to carry out the operations on the input image itself [17]. The temporal dependencies and spatial structure are preserved in a convolution layer by using kernels or filters. CNN, as seen in Figure 8.5, is designed in such a way that it instinctively learns a large variety of filters that are particular to a given training dataset simultaneously under the constraints of a particular prediction problem, for instance, image classification.

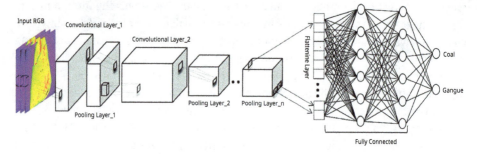

Figure 8.6: A convolutional neural network (CNN).

8.3.1.1.2 U-net

U-net came into existence in order to help with Bio Medical Image Segmentation. The U-net architecture, as can be seen in Figure 8.6, mainly comprises two pathways. It is a sequential fully convolutional network of FCN, as it comprises only convolutional layers and not any dense layer due to which it can take up images of varied sizes. It was invented for Bio Medical Image Segmentation where the requirement was fixated upon classification of whether there was presence of infection along with the identification of the area affected by the infection [18].

Contraction path or the encoder is the initial path which is devoted to record the subject matter of the input image. The encoder or the contraction path is a conventional stack of max pooling and convolutional layers. The other path is known as the decoder or the symmetric expanding pathway. This path helps enable accurate localization with the use of transposed convolutions. Finally we can conclude that the U-net is a sequential fully convolutional network of FCN, as it comprises only convolutional layers and not any dense layer due to which it can take up images of varied sizes.

8.3.1.1.3 Recurrent neural networks (RNNs)

RNNs came into existence to tackle the advancement of vectors as time passes, as this could not be accomplished by CNNs as their ability is limited to deal with vectors of a certain size and thus in turn provided results of a fixed type as well [19]. While CNN can work with only a certain number of layers, RNNs can have variable-sized output and input vectors, thus making RNNs a promising tool for helping with natural language processing or NLP problems as in these applications, the input vector is continuously evolving. RNNs, as seen in Figure 8.7, are not feed forward in nature as the output of each individual hidden layer is put in loop to itself. This is another aspect in which RNNs and traditional CNNs are different. It depicts a structure of RNN which belongs to a category of neural networks where a directed graph is formed by the connections formed between different nodes along a temporal sequence. RNNs are not feed forward in nature as the output of each individual hidden layer is put in loop to itself. This is an aspect in which RNNs and traditional CNNs are different.

8 Impact of deep learning applications in medical hyper spectral imaging — 193

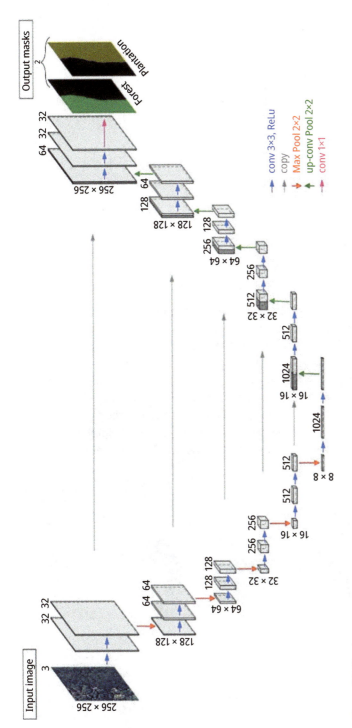

Figure 8.7: U-net.

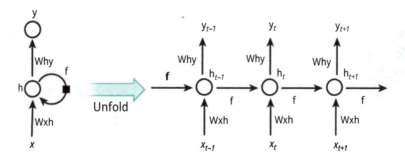

Figure 8.8: A structure of RNN.

8.3.2 Unsupervised learning methods

8.3.2.1 Auto-encoders

Auto-encoder primarily deals with generating a duplicate copy of the given input after going through a sequence of operations. The model, as seen in Figure 8.8, is concerned with encoding followed by decoding of the input in order to produce the corresponding output and all these operations take place in every individual hidden layer. This process provides a proper mapping as to the way in which the data is estimated for a lower dimension as the hidden layer comprises all data that helps in the reconstruction of the output for a particular input class and it also has the smallest dimension in the entire network [20]. This aspect proves to be the most helpful for anomaly detection due to the fact that the mapping attributes would give rise to an unclear

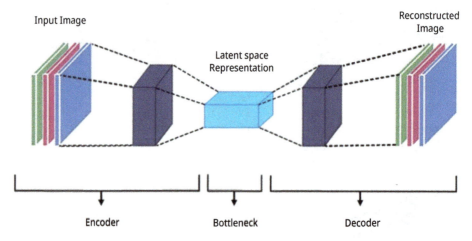

Figure 8.9: An auto-encoder.

result in respect of the auto-encoder hidden layer, thus leading to the easy discovery of the anomalies.

8.3.2.2 Generative adversarial networks (GANs)

GANs are a type of generative architecture based mostly on probability-oriented fix up to deal with unlabeled datasets, thus proving as a proper surrogate to maximum likelihood estimators. This GAN puts one neural network against another so that synthetic labels are generated with can be compared to real data. The two NNs go on improving successively for each iteration run. This process, as depicted in Figure 8.9, goes on till the generated result has resemblance with the real sample data to a maximum extent.

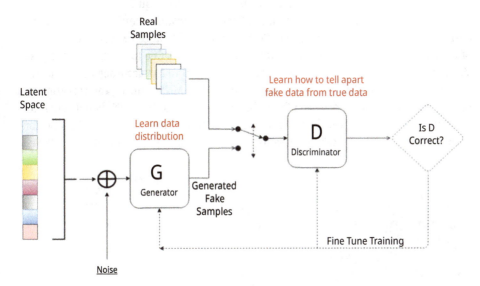

Figure 8.10: A generative adversarial networks (GANs).

8.4 Deep learning methods for MHSI

8.4.1 Classification

Deep learning techniques have had a notable impact on the classification of pathological images. General processes used the processing of MHSI with the help of classification techniques mostly encompasses cell classification applications to help in the identification and classification of cancerous cells. MHSI classification procedures mostly apply transfer learning as in the computer field vision there are large datasets with millions of sample images while MHSI mostly uses comparatively smaller datasets generally comprising hundreds or thousands of sample images [21].

The origin of DL implementations in MHSI started with classification of malignant and benign cell samples by making use of artificial neural networks such as MLPs. One study focusing on HSI for the characterization of kidney stones applied principal component analysis or PCA to decide suitable variables that are put to use for a simple ANN model made up of a single hidden layer comprising four nodes. This was applied to the classification of different categories of kidney stones from the HSI and an identical process was also used for the classification of different types of cancer [22].

These days CNNs are primarily used for cell or tissue classification as can be seen in Figure 8.10. A study made use of PCA to facilitate the transfer learning for CNNs by making use of kernel fusion to finish the process of classification in MHSI. This study also discussed a model that made use of both CNN kernel and Gabor kernel to improve the conventional CNN operation in MHSI classification, which showed a considerable improvement in performance. Classification of blood cell MHSI also made use of CNN implementation in an almost identical manner as due to increase in the pixel size for MHSI demonstrated better output with regard to the accuracy of the classification, thereby solidifying the prospective for CNN in MHSI. During the classification of HNC, the CNN model portrayed favorable prospects. Another CNN model generated solid outputs for the classification of diagnosis of oral cancer and the model's performance was substantiated when the same dataset was also applied for DBN and SVM.

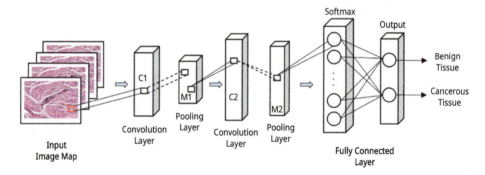

Figure 8.11: Classification of a cancerous tissue sample through convolutional neural network (CNN).

8.4.2 Detection

The detection of an object for an image given as input are mostly depicted as detection techniques [23]. Figure 8.11 shows a standard depiction of the how the combined use of DL and MHSI is used in cancer detection. In case of MHSI, detection techniques are mostly focused on malignant cancerous cell detection. Detection of malignancy has been done using ANN, but almost all detection procedures used for MHSI make use of CNN implementation initially for classification of pixels in an image following which it is used for malignancy detection of the cells or tissues concerned. One study made use of CNN-based implementation for the purpose of tissue surface reconstruction with the help of an endoscopic probe and this set up displayed promising future for practical applications. Another study followed an almost similar procedure to examine tissue surface by applying FCN techniques. CNN and AEN implementation have been put the use for detection of head and neck squamous cell carcinoma and have also proved to be successful.

Brain tumor surgeries are also being aided by CNN implementation that to in real time. CNN implantation has also provided good results in the detection of skin cancer. Many studies have pressed upon the fact that even though CNN has been very helpful for classification procedures, it also portrays as a solid potential tool for the detection techniques used in MHSI and also holds scope for further research in the detection area in the future.

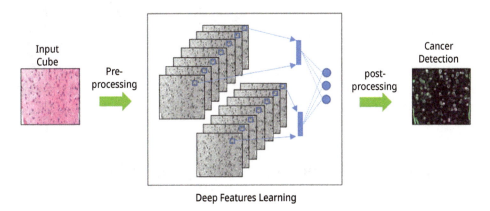

Figure 8.12: A generalized workflow used for the detection of cancer by combining medical image analysis and deep learning techniques.

8.4.3 Segmentation

Segmentation helps provide a synopsis for the segments an image that determine the volume, size and position of the respective objects present in a given image [24]. This is very useful for medical image diagnosis as it focuses on providing a clear outline of particular organs or important aspects of a given medical image, thus being of notable significance in the medical diagnosis involving from distinction among the important organs such as liver and brain. A study highlighted the use of segmentation technique in retinal image analysis in which they used a dense-FCN-based implementation for the segmentation of the retinal image as can be seen in Figure 8.12. This figure depicts how FCN is used in the segmentation process. FCN is one of the most progressive and successful DL technique that is used for the purpose of semantic segmentation. By using K-means clustering on the input, the aforementioned study helped minimize the complexity and thus ensured the smooth running of the segmentation process, thereby providing better validation in comparison to other ML approaches like random forest and SVM. The discoveries made by the said study discussed that spectral information help provide a better chance for extemporizing of segmentation outputs for macula and optic disc segmentation that serves as a critical component for retinal imaging analysis, thus providing scope for future research for segmentation procedures in MHSI field.

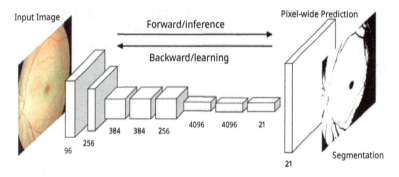

Figure 8.13: FCN used in the segmentation process.

8.5 Use of hyper spectral imaging and adaptive deep learning techniques for the detection of head and neck cancer

This study discussed an optical biopsy method based on HSI operated with CNN. This said method helped provide diagnostic information over a variety of categories for thyroid carcinomas, head-and-neck tissue and squamous cell carcinoma. Analysis of hyper spectral images was done using a model based on a CNN implementation for the HNC detection purposes using an animal model. Squamous cell carcinoma detection techniques made use of an advanced inception v4 CNN model. Some CNN-based implementation such as SegNet, FCN and U-net, having pixel-wise prediction, have shown efficient results in detection and segmentation procedures. U-net deep NN has been used for the purpose of detection of breast tumor and segmentation of tumor present in the input HS images.

The tumor margin can lack clarity and regularity sometimes due to the presence of system noise and the image-related data that are a result of irregular surface fluorescence. This makes the task of differentiation between a tumor and adjacent normal tissues an arduous task. A proposition for a self-operating cancer detection algorithm was made in a research study for emphasizing the tumor by using the adaptive auto-encoder network learning approach. Auto-encoder falls under the category of an unsupervised DNN that boasts the ability to learn intrinsic features and also the ability to draw out fitting representation from complicated datasets intuitively [25]. Auto-encoder network was used in this study for learning and subsequently recognizing the profound features of pixels in HS images for the initial stage of cancer detection. A weight was assigned to each pixel based on its corresponding classification output. The adaptive auto-encoder learning technique discussed in the said study was applied on the aforementioned weighted pixels and were further trained to rectify the wrongly classified pixels in order to improve the performance associated with the detection techniques. The aforementioned study helped in demonstrating the effectiveness and efficacy of the adaptive DL and auto-encoder usage in HSI for the detection of HNC in an animal subject.

8.5.1 Methods

- HSI system: A wavelength-scanning CRI Maestro in vivo imaging system was used to obtain HS images. The said tool mostly composes of a solid-state liquid crystal filter, a pliable fiber optic lighting system, a 16-bit charge-coupled high resolution device and a spectrally developed lens. The wavelength setting may be specified in the limit ranging from 450 to 950 nm with an increment of 2 nm for image acquisition purposes.
- The discussed adaptive deep learning method: The discussed model for the detection of cancer mainly comprised four major steps such as:
  - Pre-processing
  - Deep feature learning
  - Adaptive weight learning
  - Post-processing

An overview of the discussed model is shown in Figure 8.13. It depicts outline of the adaptive DL technique that was discussed for the detection of cancer using HSI techniques. It mainly comprised four major steps such as pre-processing, deep feature learning, adaptive weight learning and post-processing. Once the pre-processing of the input hypercube is over, then the extraction and learning of the deep feature takes place for the initial stage of cancer detection. Basing on the result supposition of the pixels, the calculation of the adaptive weights takes place followed by the construction of the upgraded hypercube. Re-extraction and re-learning of the discriminant deep feature take place on the newly constructed hypercube. Thereby, the newly trained model is both discriminative and adaptive. Now the process of identification of the cancerous tissue present in a test hypercube can be carried out with the help of the adaptive model, following which the detected or identified cancerous tissue can undergo purification in the post-processing step.

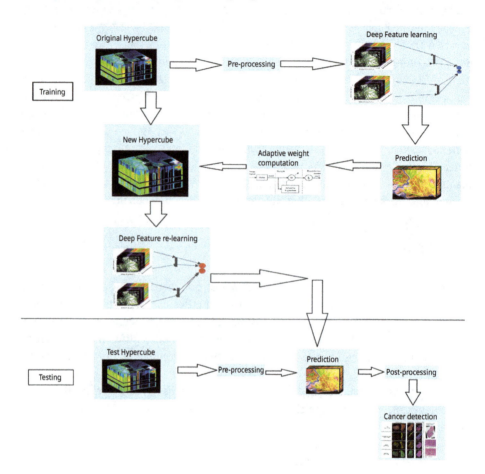

Figure 8.14: Outline of adaptive deep learning technique.

8.5.2 Results

The quantitative assessment results of the model that was discussed in this study involving 12 mice subjects can be visualized by the graphs in Figures 8.14, 8.15 and 8.16. Figure 8.14 depicts the accuracy results for 12 mice specimen model. Figure 8.15 depicts the sensitivity results for 12 mice specimen model. Figure 8.16 depicts the specificity results for 12 mice specimen model. The average specificity, accuracy and sensitivity were found to be 91.31%, 91.33% and 92.32%, respectively. Based on these results, the said model was found to be effective. The poor performances depicted by the last two mice specimen could be attributed to the invasion of the neighboring tissues and the tissue artifacts. Even though when certain parts of tumors vanished, the discussed model did not get satisfactory outcomes. Still the said model was successful

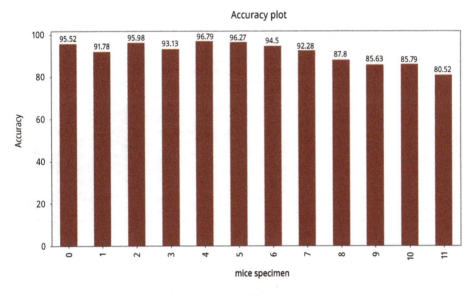

Figure 8.15: Accuracy results for 12 mice specimen model.

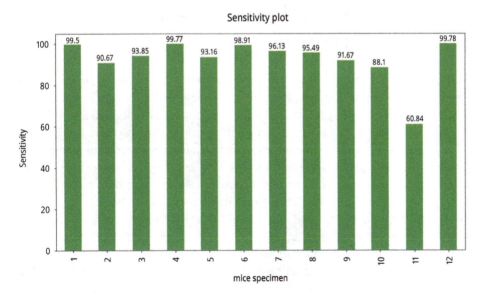

Figure 8.16: Sensitivity results for 12 mice specimen model.

in reaching an accuracy greater than 80%. Had the last two mice specimen been eliminated, the average specificity, accuracy and sensitivity would have been 92.26%, 92.97% and 94.72%, respectively as shown in figure 8.17.

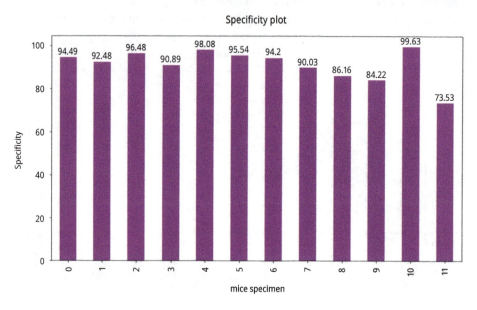

Figure 8.17: Specificity results for 12 mice specimen model.

8.6 Future challenges in deep learning and MHSI integrated domain

Various medical fields have been profoundly impacted by the use of prominent DL-based applications, for instance, the field of radiology as it has negatively impacted numerous radiologists in practice, still MHSI field has yet to be impacted in a similar fashion which could be due to deficiency of experienced researchers in this field. After thorough investigation of the various trends followed by numerous publications that have focused on the implementation of deep learning techniques in MHSI, we could expect similar results in the near future as well. As the general medical image analysis has reached a deadlock while the DL techniques have been providing efficient and accurate outcomes, MHSI field might also get affected. Progress in research in the MHSI field would help in fulfilling the need for large obtainable datasets, which has been a prominent setback for DL for the last few years.

Even if there are many prominent DL techniques which are being thoroughly studied and researched, we cannot say that one technique is fairly better than others as it depends on the requirements and needs of the given situation. CNNs happen to be one of the most popular DL technique as many studies are focused on them. Various types of CNN implementation are available which is mostly depending on the situation which requires the use of these implementations. Majority of the issues associated with the use of DL in MHSI can be attributed to wide ranging problems faced by detection and classification techniques, for instance, disparity of classification when it is used for the purpose of object detection.

8.7 Conclusion

In this paper, we have put forward the concept of hyperspectral imaging as well as its role and impact in various domains, prominent among which is in healthcare. We have also discussed in depth about what DL is and how it can help medical professionals in unearthing the hidden and promising opportunities in data and be of use to the healthcare industry. We have then attempted to combine these two, that is, use DL in the field of HSI. The abundance of information present in HSI data is used by DL which is transforming the world of digital data analysis. We have discussed the various DL methods that are being used to study the data presented by MHSI like classification and segmentation the accuracy of the models developed through the DL networks and how they can be used in future prediction of diseases more efficiently and conveniently. We have also shed light on the impediments that are faced while using these technologies. The obstacles include fewer availability of quality publicly available data sets, thus impacting the research of accurate, more efficient and broad scope solutions. This new era of DL-HSI integration and application in health care opens a wide range of exciting opportunities for further research in this domain.

References

[1] Calin, A., Parasca, S. V., Savastru, D. & Manea, D. (2014). Hyperspectral imaging in the medical field: Present and future. Applied Spectroscopy Reviews, 49(6), 435–447.
[2] Ren, J., Zabalza, J., Marshall, S. & Zheng, J. (2014). Effective feature extraction and data reduction in remote sensing using hyperspectral imaging. IEEE Signal Processing Magazine, 31(4), 149–154.
[3] Jena, L., Kamila, N. K. & Mishra, S. (2014). Privacy preserving distributed data mining with evolutionary computing. In Proceedings of the International Conference on Frontiers of Intelligent Computing: Theory and Applications (FICTA) Vol. 2013 (pp. 259–267). Springer, Cham.
[4] Mishra, S., Tripathy, H. K. & Acharya, B. (2021). A precise analysis of deep learning for medical image processing. In Bio-Inspired Neurocomputing (pp. 25–41). Springer, Singapore.
[5] Teke, H. D., Halilog Iu, O., Gürbüz, S. & Sakarya, U. (2013). A short survey of hyperspectral remote sensing applications in agriculture. In 2013 6th International Conference on Recent Advances in Space Technologies (RAST) (pp. 171–176). IEEE.

[6] Lorente, N. A., Gomez-Sanchis, J., Cubero, S., Garcia-Navarrete, O. L. & Blasco, J. (2012). Recent advances and applications of hyperspectral imaging for fruit and vegetable quality assessment. Food & Bioprocess Technology, 5(4), 1121–1142.

[7] Sabine, M. R., Thomas, S., Manuel, R., Paula, E., Marta, P. & Alicia, P. (2014). Potential of hyperspectral imagery for the spatial assessment of soil erosionstages in agricultural semi-arid spain at different scales. In 2014 IEEEGeoscience and Remote Sensing Symposium (pp. 2918–292). IEEE.

[8] Mishra, S., Mishra, B. K. & Tripathy, H. K. (December, 2015). A neuro-genetic model to predict hepatitis disease risk. In 2015 IEEE International Conference on Computational Intelligence and Computing Research (ICCIC) (pp. 1–3). IEEE.

[9] Sylvain, G. M. (2014). A novel maximum likelihood based method for mapping depth and water quality from hyperspectral remote-sensing data. Remote Sensing of Environment, 147, 121–132. https://doi.org/10.1016/j.rse.2014.01.026.

[10] Paheding, Y. D., Arigela, S. & Asari, V. K. (2014). Visibility improvement of shadow regions using hyperspectral band integration. In Proc. SPIE 9244, Image and Signal Processing for Remote Sensing XX. Amsterdam.

[11] Sahoo, S., Das, M., Mishra, S. & Suman, S. (2021). A hybrid DTNB model for heart disorders prediction. In Advances in Electronics, Communication and Computing (pp. 155–163). Springer, Singapore.

[12] Fischer, & Kakoulli, I. (2006). Multispectral and hyperspectral imaging technologies in conservation: current research and potential applications. Studies in Conservation, 51, 3–16.

[13] Pike, S. K. P., Lu, G., Halig, L. V., Wang, D., Chen, Z. G. & Fei, B. (2014). A minimum spanning forest based hyperspectral image classification method for cancerous tissue detection. SPIE Medical Imaging, 9034, 15–20.

[14] Vincent, H. L., Bengio, Y. & Manzagol, P. (2008). Extracting and composing robust features with denoising autoencoders. In International Conference on Machine Learning (pp. 1096–1103).

[15] Archibald & Fann, G. (2007). Feature selection and classification of hyperspectral images with support vector machines. IEEE Geosience and Remote Sensing Letters, 4(4), 674–677.

[16] Ray, C., Tripathy, H. K. & Mishra, S. (2019). A review on facial expression based behavioral analysis using computational technique for autistic disorder patients. In Singh M., Gupta P., Tyagi V., Flusser J., Ören T. & Kashyap R. (eds.) Advances in Computing and Data Sciences. ICACDS 2019. Communications in Computer and Information Science. 1046, Springer, Singapore. https://doi.org/10.1007/978-981-13-9942-8_43.

[17] Jena, L., Mishra, S., Nayak, S., Ranjan, P. & Mishra, M. K. (2021). Variable optimization in cervical cancer data using particle swarm optimization. In Advances in Electronics, Communication and Computing (pp. 147–153). Springer, Singapore.

[18] Vyas, A. B., Garza, L., Kang, S. & Burlina, P. (2013). Hyperspectral signature analysis of skin parameters. In Proc. SPIE, Medical Imaging 2013: Computer-Aided Diagnosis. Lake Buena Vista.

[19] Halicek, G. L., Little, J. V., Wang, X., Patel, M., Griffith, C. C., El-Deiry, M. W., Chen, A. Y. & Fei, B. (2017). Deep convolutional neural networks for classifying head and neck cancer using hyperspectral imaging. Journal of Biomedical Optics, 22(6).

[20] Mishra, S., Thakkar, H., Mallick, P. K., Tiwari, P. & Alamri, A. (2021). A sustainable IoHT based computationally intelligent healthcare monitoring system for lung cancer risk detection. Sustainable Cities and Society, 103079.

[21] Tripathy, H. K., Mallick, P. K. & Mishra, S. (2021). Application and evaluation of classification model to detect autistic spectrum disorders in children. International. Journal of Computer Applications in Technology, 65(4), 368–377.

[22] Khatami, A. K., Nguyen, T., Lim, C. P. & Nahavandi, S. (15 November, 2017). Medical image analysis using wavelet transform and deep belief networks. Expert Systems with Applications, 86, 190–198.

[23] Huang, Q., Li, W. & Xie, X. (2018). Convolutional neural network for medical hyperspectral image classification with kernel fusion. In International Conference on Biological Information and Biomedical Engineering. Shanghai.
[24] Chattopadhyay, A., Mishra, S. & González-Briones, A. (2021). Integration of Machine Learning and IoT in Healthcare Domain. In Hybrid Artificial Intelligence and IoT in Healthcare (pp. 223–244). Springer, Singapore.
[25] Mallick, P. K., Mishra, S., Mohanty, B. P. & Satapathy, S. K. (2021). A deep neural network model for effective diagnosis of melanoma disorder. In Cognitive Informatics and Soft Computing (pp. 43–51). Springer, Singapore.
[26] Ferris, D. G., et al. (2001). Multimodal hyperspectral imaging for the noninvasive diagnosis of cervical neoplasia. Journal of Lower Genital Tract Disease, 5(2), 65–72.
[27] Sorg, B. S., et al. (2005). Hyperspectral imaging of hemoglobin saturation in tumor microvasculature and tumor hypoxia development. Journal of Biomedical Optics, 10(4), 44004.
[28] Hattery, D., et al. (2002). Hyperspectral imaging of Kaposi's sarcoma for disease assessment and treatment monitoring. In Proc. 31st Applied Imagery Pattern Recognition Workshop (pp. 124–130). Washington, DC.
[29] Constantinou, P., Dacosta, R. S. & Wilson, B. C. (2009). Extending immunofluorescence detection limits in whole paraffin-embedded formalin fixed tissues using hyperspectral confocal fluorescence imaging. Journal of microscopy, 234(2), 137–146.
[30] Gillies, R., et al. (2003). Systemic effects of shock and resuscitation monitored by visible hyperspectral imaging. Diabetes Technology and Therapeutics, 5(5), 847–855.
[31] Panasyuk, S. V., et al. (2007). Medical hyperspectral imaging to facilitate residual tumor identification during surgery. Cancer Biology and Therapy, 6(3), 439–446.
[32] Zuzak, K. J., et al. (2007). Characterization of a near-infrared laparoscopic hyperspectral imaging system for minimally invasive surgery. Analytical Chemistry, 79(12), 4709–4715.
[33] Akbari, H., et al. (2010). Detection and analysis of the intestinal ischemia using visible and invisible hyperspectral imaging. IEEE Transactions on Biomedical Engineering, 57(8), 2011–2017.
[34] Akbari, H., et al. (2008). Hyperspectral imaging and diagnosis of intestinal ischemia. In 30th Annual Int. Conf. of the IEEE Engineering in Medicine and Biology Society (pp. 1238–1241). Vancouver, BC.
[35] Akbari, H., et al. (2008). Wavelet-based compression and segmentation of hyperspectral images in surgery. In Medical Imaging and Augmented Reality (pp. 142–149). Springer, Berlin Heidelberg.
[36] Ma, L., Lu, G., Wang, D., Qin, X., Chen, Z. G. & Fei, B.(2019). Adaptive deep learning for head and neck cancer detection using hyperspectral imaging.
[37] Chaudhury, P., Mishra, S., Tripathy, H. K. & Kishore, B. (March, 2016). Enhancing the capabilities of student result prediction system. In Proceedings of the Second International Conference on Information and Communication Technology for Competitive Strategies (pp. 1–6).

M. Ganeshkumar, V. Sowmya*, E. A. Gopalakrishnan, K. P. Soman

9 Disease prediction mechanisms on large-scale big data with explainable deep learning models for multi-label classification problems in healthcare

Abstract: Deep learning models have been prominently applied for the automatic detection of various cardiovascular conditions using ECG signals. The concept of explainable artificial intelligence is all about finding whether the deep learning framework has captured the appropriate characteristics for the detection task instead of learning some unsolicited approaches (learning features that do not reflect the properties of the instance being classified). So that the health care professionals who use the artificial intelligence system can be confident about the diagnosis obtained from the model. In this chapter, we establish an explainable artificial intelligence method through the multi-label ECG classification. Our proposed method employs a convolutional neural network (CNN) trained using 2D matrices constructed from various leads of ECG recordings. In this work, we show that training the CNN with only a single label per ECG recording is sufficient for the CNN to capture the characteristics of multi-label ECG points. The proposed model when tested with ECG signals containing multi-label information was found that the output probabilities of the correct labels obtained from the softmax layer are in the same order of magnitude. This leads to an explainable framework of how the proposed network correctly gets activated when it sees multiple features pertaining to different heart diseases in the same ECG signal despite having trained only with a single label for each ECG recording. This establishes the fact that the CNN has captured the correct features for the categorization of ECG instead of some undesirable features which are local to our dataset. Further, thresholding is applied to the probabilities from the softmax layer of the proposed CNN, leading to the multi-label categorization of ECG containing up to two labels. The number of ECG records in the training and test set is 6,311 and 280, respectively. The proposed model is evaluated with common performance metrics analyzed in the multi-label classification problem. The model achieved the following scores in different metrics considered: subset accuracy – 0.962, hamming loss – 0.037, precision – 0.986, recall – 0.949 and F1-score – 0.967.

***Corresponding author: V. Sowmya**, Center for Computational Engineering and Networking (CEN), Amrita School of Engineering, Amrita Vishwa Vidyapeetham, Coimbatore, Tamil Nadu, India, e-mail: v_sowmya@cb.amrita.edu

M. Ganeshkumar, E. A. Gopalakrishnan, K. P. Soman, Center for Computational Engineering and Networking (CEN), Amrita School of Engineering, Amrita Vishwa Vidyapeetham, Coimbatore, Tamil Nadu, India

https://doi.org/10.1515/9783110750942-009

Thus, our proposed model is an explainable artificial intelligence-based approach for the multi-label classification of ECG recordings of patients which can be used for computer-aided diagnosis of heart diseases confidently.

Keywords: Explainable artificial intelligence, ECG classification, heart disease identification, multi-label classification

9.1 Introduction

Artificial intelligence (AI) has been used in a wide spectrum of biomedical and health applications such as heart disease identification [1, 2], brain tumor diagnosis [3], myeloma detection [4] and diabetic retinopathy identification [5]. One of the important challenges in the application of AI to automated disease diagnosis is the lack of explainability on how a particular diagnosis is made by the model. This makes the decisions from AI difficult to justify to the end-users or domain experts. ECG analysis is a widely utilized diagnostic method for evaluating different cardiovascular conditions. Variations in the normal ECG pattern are an indicator of numerous cardiac abnormalities, which are analyzed by doctors manually to diagnose various cardiovascular diseases. This diagnosis method, however, is dependent on the availability of a trained doctor, and as a result, it may be time inefficient and even sometimes unreliable. Many times, the patient suffers from more than one cardiovascular disease and the automated identification of these multiple cardiovascular diseases in a patient using ECG signals is a very difficult task. Therefore, an automated method that can identify different cardiovascular diseases present in one ECG recording will be very much helpful to aid doctors in a timely and precise diagnosis.

So, in this chapter, we introduce a new approach for the multi-label classification of ECG recordings. We also demonstrate an explainable artificial intelligence method through the multi-label classification of ECG signals. Our proposed approach incorporates a CNN trained on 2D matrices created from ECG recordings. 2D ECG matrices are created by clipping the ECG signals of heartbeats from different leads and arranging them row-wise in a matrix. During our experiments, we found that training the deep learning model with only a single label per ECG recording is sufficient for the CNN to capture the characteristics of multi-label ECG recordings. This was evident from the fact that for a multi-label ECG, the probabilities outputted by the softmax layer pertaining to the right labels were in the same order of magnitude (this is further validated in the results section). During the classification phase, simple thresholding was applied to softmax layer probabilities for selecting the appropriate class labels for the ECG recording. This also leads to an explainable artificial intelligence framework of how our model has captured the appropriate features of various cardiovascular diseases considered.

Our proposed method is capable of identifying the following cardiovascular conditons: (1) atrial fibrillation (AF); (2) ST-segment depression (STD); (3) premature atrial contraction (PAC); (4) ST-segment elevated (STE); (5) first-degree atrioventricular block (I-AVB); (6) left bundle brunch block (LBBB); (7) premature ventricular contraction (PVC); (8) right bundle brunch block (RBBB) and the normal heart condition.

9.2 Other works in literature for the multi-label classification of ECG

Sun et al. [6] used an ensemble method for the multi-label categorization of ECG recordings. The authors used the 12 lead ECG data from the CCDD dataset. The authors first pre-processed the ECG signals to remove noise using various filters. Further, using the WFDB toolbox the authors extracted 169 features from the ECG signals. The extracted features were used to train several multi-label machine learning classification algorithms like BR, HARAM and ML-kNN [6]. Final multi-label classification is obtained by computing the weighted average of the individual classifier's results. Their method obtained an F1-score of 0.752 and a hamming loss of 0.062.

Cai et al. [7] developed multi-ECGNet, a new CNN model for the multi-label categorization of 55 different categories of arrhythmia. Multi-ECGNet combines the benefits of multiple CNN architectures, such as ResNet, depthwise convolution and SENets module [7]. The first stage of feature extraction was done using multi-channel 1d convolution, considering various leads of the ECG recordings as different channels. Multi-ECGNet finally outputs 55 sigmoid probability distributions that are trained with binary cross-entropy loss, thereby enabling the multi-label classification of ECG recordings into 55 different categories of arrhythmia. During testing, their method obtained an F1-score of 0.863.

Jia et al. [8] used an ensemble CNN for the multi-label classification of ECG signals. The first module is a sequence generator that uses an LSTM network to generate multiple labels for ECG signals. The second module uses a separate linear classifier for identifying each label independently. The final results are generated using a voting ensemble strategy on the predictions from both modules. Twelve lead ECG recordings from First China ECG Intelligent Competition were used in this work. Pre-processing is done using a band-pass Butterworth filter to eliminate high-frequency noises and baseline wandering. The authors used 6,500 ECG data points in both the training and the test set. During testing, their model obtained a macro average F1-score of 0.872.

Cheng et al. [9] used a 1D CNN for the multi-label classification of ECG recordings into four categories of arrhythmia. Their 1D CNN generates a binary vector with four values. Each value in the binary vector indicates the presence of a particular category of arrhythmia. Finally, the summation of binary cross-entropy loss over each of these individual identifications is used to train the CNN. All the leads of the ECG signal are taken individually and they are segmented to a length of 2 s, and 80% of them were utilized for training, while 20% were used for testing the model. When trained and tested with ECG signals without compressing them, their model obtained a macro average F1-score of 0.9848 and a hamming loss of 0.0031.

Luo et al. [10] used a model that combines a neural network and long short-term memory architecture for the multi-label categorization of ECG signals into nine disease classes (one normal and eight abnormal). The authors used an 18-layer one-dimensional CNN added with skip connections and a bi-directional long short-term memory layer [10]. The authors reported an F1-score of 85.11%.

Zhu et al. [11] used the SE-ResNet model for the categorization of ECG recordings into normal rhythm and arrhythmia. Further, individual binary classifiers were utilized for the multi-label classification of arrhythmia into its different categories. Also, the authors used DCGANs and WGAN-GP generative adversarial networks to create new synthetic ECG data belonging to the arrhythmia class [11] to solve the inherent data imbalance problem present in the arrhythmia detection task. The authors used the dataset from the ECG Intelligence Challenge 2019, which had 6,500 12-lead ECG recordings. Their model was validated with a dataset consisting of 500 ECG signals and obtained an F1-score of 0.862.

None of the existing methods described above (except [10], which uses the same dataset as ours) include the detection of ST-segment depression and elevation. Detection of both ST-segment depression and elevation is critically important, as they are characteristic variations found in serious cardiovascular diseases like myocardial infarction (MI) [12]. Our proposed method includes the identification of both ST-segment depression and elevation in the multi-label classification of ECG signals. Also, a comparison of the performance of our proposed method with that of the method in [10] (which uses the same dataset as that of ours) and also with the other existing methods available for the multi-label classification of ECG recordings is given in Section 9.7.

9.3 Proposed method

As described in Figure 9.1, the proposed method comprises four major steps: (1) preprocessing of ECG recordings, (2) ECG matrix construction, (3) training the CNN and (4) multi-label classification of ECG recordings by employing thresholding on softmax probabilities. Further, the explainable artificial intelligence framework for the ECG classification is established in the results section (Section 7.6.3), using the results obtained from our experiments.

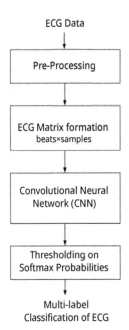

Figure 9.1: Flow diagram of the proposed method for the multi-label classification of ECG signals.

9.3.1 Pre-processing of ECG signals

Two of the frequently occurring noises in the ECG recordings are (1) low-frequency noise-causing baseline wander; (2) power line interference. These two noises sometimes make it challenging for the neural network to capture the right characteristics of various diseases. So, the pre-processing step aims to remove these noises from our ECG signals.

9.3.1.1 Baseline wander removal

Baseline wander is a common noise that is introduced in the ECG recordings mainly due to body movements of patients while recording like coughing or breathing [13]. It is usually a low-frequency noise [13]. So we used a Butterworth high pass filter to eliminate baseline wander from our ECG recordings [14]. The cut-off frequency of the filter was set to 0.5 Hz. For a zero-phase shift, we applied the filter in forward and backward directions consecutively. The built-in functions from the SciPy package[1] are used to implement the filter.

---

[1] https://www.scipy.org/.

9.3.1.2 Power line interference removal

During ECG recording, electromagnetic interference from the power line is a primary source of the noise. It is usually a 50 Hz noise (50 Hz is the frequency of the power line) [15]. So, we used a Butterworth low pass filter. The cut-off frequency of the filter was set to 50 Hz.

9.3.2 ECG matrix construction

Once pre-processed, we further construct an ECG matrix by clipping the heartbeats from various leads of the ECG recording and arranging them row-wise in the matrix. Figure 9.2 visualizes our ECG matrix. Our dataset had ECG recordings with 12 leads. Sujadevi et al. [16] established that only three leads (aVF, V5 and V6) out of the 12 leads in an ECG signal are sufficient for the precise detection of various cardiovascular diseases. So only those three identified leads: aVF, V5 and V6 were used in our study. This reduced the data that we needed to process by a good amount, leading to reduced training time of the CNN. Thirty beats were extracted in total to construct the ECG matrix (10 beats from each one of the three selected leads). Each of the extracted beats is period normalized to 400 ms (milliseconds). Finally, a matrix of dimension: 30 × 400 is constructed. The procedure we adopted for the beat extraction and period normalization is described in Section 3.2.1.

9.3.2.1 Extraction of beats from ECG and period normalization of beats

The first step in the beat extraction process is to locate the R-peaks in the various leads of an ECG recording. We used multiple R-peak detection methods available in the literature [17–22]. During our experiments, we found that some of the above R-peak detection methods performed better for some ECG signals, but did not for others. So we applied all of the R-peak detection methods sequentially until the number of R-peaks detected for a particular ECG signal is close to the ratio of that ECG's length to the standard duration of a heartbeat. Once the R-peaks are detected, we use the following criteria to extract the beats from any lead of an ECG signal: signal that extends between 170 ms left from any R-peak to 170 ms left of its successive R-peak. This criterion is derived from the fact that the PR interval (time interval between the beginning of the P wave and the beginning of the QRS complex) in a standard ECG signal varies between 120 and 200 ms. We analyzed some random ECG signals in the dataset used and we discovered that fixing the PR-interval to be 170 ms was effective for our dataset during beat extraction. Once the beats are extracted we do the following to normalize the time period of all the beats to 400 ms: align all the R-peaks at 200 ms and append zeros in the front and the end of the beat appropriately.

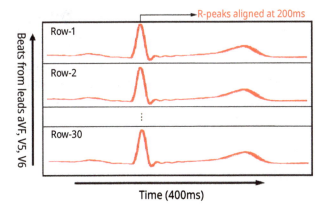

Figure 9.2: ECG matrix constructed.

9.3.3 Training the CNN

Following the creation of ECG matrices for all of the patient's records, a CNN is trained using the constructed matrices. The CNN architecture used was derived from the standard VGG-16 architecture. Since one of the dimensions of the input ECG matrix is very small (dimension of input ECG matrix: 30 × 400), one convolutional block is removed from the standard VGG-16, thereby making the CNN architecture suitable to the dimensions of our input. The detailed architecture of the CNN used is given in Figure 9.3. The number of convolutional filters in each layer of the CNN and their size are also specified in Figure 9.3 (e.g., 3 × 3 Conv 64). Also, "Fc" in Figure 9.3 denotes fully connected layers, given along with the number of neurons present in them (e.g., Fc-1024). All the convolutional layers and fully connected layers utilize the ReLU non-linearity function. The final fully connected layer outputs nine scores pertaining to the nine disease classes considered in our study. The Soft-max layer utilizes the Soft-max function defined in eq. (9.1) to normalize the output of the last fully connected layer into probabilities:

$$\sigma(\vec{z})_i = \frac{e^{z_i}}{\sum_{j=1}^{K} e^{z_j}} \tag{9.1}$$

where $\vec{z}$ is the vector from the last fully connected layer, containing the scores pertaining to the different disease classes. All the max-pooling layers in our CNN had a stride of 2 × 2. We also introduced dropout layers with a dropout rate of 0.5 between our fully connected layers to prevent overfitting. The derived CNN is trained using only one label (the first label), out of the multiple labels each ECG data point has got.

9.3.4 Multi-label classification of ECG recordings by employing thresholding on softmax layer probabilities

Once the CNN is trained, during the classification phase, we apply some simple thresholding on the probabilities outputted from the softmax layer of the CNN to select the correct labels for each ECG data point in the test set. With the help of many experiments, we carefully developed the thresholding approach. The formulated thresholding technique is presented in the Results section (Section 9.6.1), along with the results of experiments that were used to arrive at it.

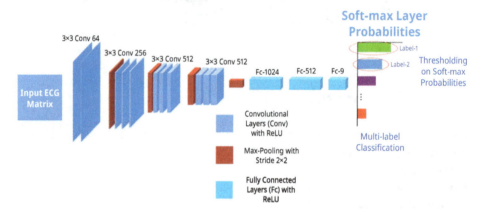

Figure 9.3: The architecture of the CNN used for the multi-label classification of ECG recordings.

9.4 Experimental setup

The dataset we utilized for our experiments is described in this section along with the experimental setup we had while training the CNN.

9.4.1 Dataset

The data set hosted in the China Physiological Signal Challenge 2018 is utilized in our experiments [23]. The ECG recordings in the dataset were originally collected from 11 hospitals. The dataset had 12 lead ECGs with a duration of 6 to 60 s sampled at 500 Hz [23]. The majority of the ECGs had only one label and some recordings had two labels. Around six ECG recordings had three labels with them, which we had to remove, as our proposed model was unable to capture the characteristics of ECG signals with three labels. The dataset also contains a separate validation set with around 300 ECG recordings for testing. Few ECG recordings were removed from both training and validation sets, due to their shorter duration, as we couldn't extract the required number of beats from them. Finally, we used 6,311 ECG recordings for training and 280 ECG recordings for testing the proposed model.

9.4.2 Experimental setup for CNN

Our proposed CNN is implemented using the Keras package[2] with the TensorFlow[3] backend. All the experiments were run in runtimes provided by the Google Collab cloud service.[4] Google Collab provides an NVIDIA Tesla K80 GPU with 12 GB of memory and 12 GB of RAM. The CNN is trained with an Adam optimizer. The learning rate of the optimizer is set to 0.0001. In the Adam optimizer [24], the exponential decay rate for the first-moment estimates and second-moment estimates were set to 0.9 and 0.999, respectively. The loss function used was the traditional categorical cross-entropy loss [25]. Keras's Callback API is used for model checkpointing. The model is trained for 200 epochs. The model obtained from every epoch was saved and the best performing model out of them was picked.

9.5 Evaluation metrics

This section describes the evaluation metrics adopted for evaluating our multi-label ECG classification model. Let N be the number of ECG recordings in the test set. L is the maximum possible labels any ECG datapoint can have.

9.5.1 Hamming loss

Hamming loss is the ratio of the number of incorrectly predicted labels to the total number of labels the ECG data point can belong to:

$$\text{Hamming loss} = \frac{1}{N \cdot L} \sum_{i=1}^{N} \sum_{j=1}^{L} \text{xor}(p_{i,j}, g_{i,j}),$$

where $p_{i,j}$ is the prediction and $g_{i,j}$ is the ground truth.

---

2 https://keras.io/.
3 https://www.tensorflow.org/.
4 https://colab.research.google.com.

9.5.2 Exact match ratio or subset accuracy

The exact match ratio or subset accuracy is the percentage of ECG recordings in the test set for which all their labels are correctly identified by the model. Exact match ratio or subset accuracy is the most stringent evaluation metric; it ignores all the partially correct predictions by the model:

$$\text{Exact match ratio/subset accuracy} = \frac{1}{N} \sum_{i=1}^{N} I(P_i = G_i)$$

where P_i is the prediction by the model for a particular ECG data point and G_i is its ground truth.

9.5.3 Precision

Precision is the measure of: out of all the identifications made by the model, classifying an ECG signal into a particular class of disease (positive identification), how many of them were actually correct. Precision is given by

$$\text{Precision (h)} = \frac{\sum_{j=1}^{L} t_{p_j}}{\sum_{j=1}^{L} \left(t_{p_j} + f_{p_j} \right)}$$

where t_p is the number of true-positive identifications and f_p is the number of false-positive identifications.

9.5.4 Recall

Recall is the quantification of: out of all the test ECG signals belonging to any particular disease class (positive points), how many of them were identified correctly by the model. Recall is given by

$$\text{Recall (h)} = \frac{\sum_{j=1}^{L} t_{p_j}}{\sum_{j=1}^{L} \left(t_{p_j} + f_{n_j} \right)}$$

where f_n is the number of false-negative identifications. A false-negative identification happens when the model fails to identify the particular disease class the ECG data point belongs to.

9.5.5 F1-score

F1-score combines precision and recall and gives a single consolidated performance score for the model by taking the harmonic mean between precision and recall.

9.6 Results

This section describes the findings from the experiments, which were used to formulate the softmax probability thresholding technique we adopted for the multi-label classification task. Also establishes the explainable artificial intelligence framework, validating the fact that our CNN has captured the correct features of various cardiovascular diseases identified in the classification task. Further, this section provides a thorough analysis of the proposed model's performance on the multi-label ECG classification task.

9.6.1 Formulating the softmax probability thresholding technique

During the classification of test ECG data points, it was found that for a multi-label ECG, the softmax layer probabilities of its correct labels are the largest and also they are in the same order of magnitude. But for a single label point, the largest probability corresponds to its correct label, and no other probabilities are in the same order magnitude as that of the largest one. Figure 9.4 further validates this by showing the softmax layer probabilities of some sample test ECG points. In Figure 9.4, the red ellipse indicates the probabilities of the correct labels for each of the sample points shown. Sample test point-1 and sample test point-2 are multi-label points; from Figure 9.4, we can see that the softmax probabilities of their correct labels are the largest and also they are in the same order of magnitude. Sample test point-3 and sample test point-4 are single label points; from Figure 9.4, we can see that the probability of the correct label is the largest and none of the other probabilities are in the same order of magnitude as that of the correct label.

So we adopted the following thresholding technique to select the correct class labels for any test ECG data point:
1. If the first and the second largest probabilities of the softmax layer are in the same order of magnitude, then assign both the labels to the ECG recording.
2. If not, assign only the label of the largest softmax probability.

With the above thresholding technique applied to all the test ECG data points, we were able to classify them with up to two labels accurately.

Sample Test Point-1
[9.1371854e − 05   1.4661181e − 02   3.6171664e − 04   1.4042368e − 04   4.1600552e − 01
5.6366813e − 01   2.9123572e − 03   1.9757694e − 03   1.8353252e − 04]
Correct Class Labels: 6,5

Sample Test Point-2
[3.57838280e − 06   6.39685214e − 01   1.09759836e − 04   2.02141047e − 04
3.56797814e − 01   7.15703878e − 04   1.69493153e − 03   6.47477165e − 04
1.43371857e − 04]
Correct Class Labels: 5,2

Sample Test Point-3
[9.9999881e − 01   3.1207674e − 16   3.2661405e − 09   2.6036834e − 15   1.2367628e − 06
4.8828590e − 14   2.6376254e − 13   1.9792063e − 08   1.3414558e − 11]
Correct Class Labels: 1

Sample Test Point-4
[1.8525486e − 04   1.6536933e − 06   1.3984331e − 04   4.0575983e − 06   9.9897492e − 01
6.3378643e − 04   3.1597324e − 06   1.4806805e − 05   4.2486154e − 05]
Correct Class Labels: 5

Figure 9.4: Softmax layer probabilities of sample ECG test points.

9.6.2 Performance on the multi-label ECG classification task

To gauge the efficacy of our proposed method, various evaluation metrics described in Section 7.5 are calculated using our test set. Table 9.1 represents the class-wise performance of the proposed method in evaluation metrics: Precision, Recall and F1-score, also giving the number of test points belonging to that particular class (support column). From the F1-score values given in Table 9.1 we can see that our proposed method worked very effectively in identifying all the disease classes considered in our study. Also, Table 9.2 represents the confusion matrix achieved by the proposed method. The confusion matrix is computed considering the classification of the first

Table 9.1: Class-wise performance of the proposed method.

Class	Precision	Recall	F1-score	Support
Normal	1.0	1.0	1.0	43
Atrial fibrillation (AF)	1.0	0.978	0.989	46
First-degree atrioventricular block (I-AVB)	1.0	0.977	0.988	23
Left bundle branch block (LBBB)	1.0	1.0	1.0	11
Right bundle branch block (RBBB)	1.0	0.923	0.960	65
Premature atrial contraction (PAC)	0.961	0.961	0.961	26
Premature ventricular contraction (PVC)	0.962	0.866	0.912	30
ST-segment depression (STD)	0.971	0.944	0.957	36
ST-segment elevated (STE)	0.937	1.0	0.967	15

Table 9.2: Confusion matrix achieved by the proposed method.

Total number of points = 280	Predicted normal	Predicted (AF)	Predicted (I-AVB)	Predicted (LBBB)	Predicted (RBBB)	Predicted (PAC)	Predicted (PVC)	Predicted (STD)	Predicted (STE)
Actual normal	43	0	0	0	0	0	0	0	0
Actual (AF)	0	42	0	0	0	0	0	0	0
Actual (I-AVB)	0	0	21	0	0	1	0	0	0
Actual (LBBB)	0	0	0	10	0	0	0	0	0
Actual (RBBB)	0	2	0	0	58	0	1	0	0
Actual (PAC)	0	0	0	0	0	24	0	0	0
Actual (PVC)	0	0	0	1	0	0	26	1	1
Actual (STD)	0	0	0	0	0	0	0	33	0
Actual (STE)	0	0	0	0	0	0	0	0	15

label of ECG test points. The diagonal elements of the confusion matrix give the number of correct classifications and from Table 9.2 we can see that majority of the classifications on the test set are correct.

Table 9.3 represents the overall performance of the model on evaluation metrics: subset accuracy, average hamming loss, average precision, average recall and average F1-score. From Table 9.3 we can see that our model performed extremely well in all the metrics.

Table 9.3: Overall performance of the prosed method.

Evaluation metric	Score obtained
Subset accuracy	0.962
Average hamming loss	0.037
Average precision	0.986
Average recall	0.949
Average F1-score	0.967

9.6.3 Explainable artificial intelligence framework

From Figure 9.4 and its inference given in Section 7.6.1, we can see that our proposed method can learn the features of multi-label points automatically, having trained with only one label for each ECG recording. This also validates the fact that the model has captured the correct features for each of the individual diseases being classified. As the model rightly figures out the features of diseases when they occur together in a combination in a single ECG signal. Further, the values of performance metrics described in Section 7.6.2 infer that the proposed method has captured such features very accurately for all the diseases considered in our study. With this, we can be confident that CNN has not learned some undesirable tricks which are local to the dataset but captured the features of all the individual diseases accurately.

9.7 Comparative study

Table 9.4 gives the comparison of the proposed method's performance to that of other approaches in the literature. From Table 9.4, we can see that our proposed method performed better than all the existing approaches, except the approach in [9]. The approach in [9] surpassed the performance of our method by a very small margin. However, the method in [9] includes the identification of four categories of arrhythmia only. The authors in [10] used the same dataset as ours and from Table 9.4, we can see that our proposed method outperformed the method in [10] significantly.

Table 9.4: Comparison of the proposed method's performance to that of other approaches.

Reference	Performance
[6]	F1-score: 0.752 and hamming loss: 0.062
[7]	F1-score: 0.863
[8]	F1-score: 0.872
[9]	F1-score: 0.9848 and hamming loss: 0.0031
[10]	F1-score: 0.8511
[11]	F1-score: 0.862
Proposed method	F1-score: 0.967 and hamming loss: 0.037

9.8 Conclusion

In this chapter, we devise an explainable artificial intelligence approach through the multi-label classification of ECG recordings. This work introduces a new approach for the multi-label classification of ECG recordings and further establishes an explainable artificial intelligence framework, making the diagnosis from the model highly confident. This chapter also provides a thorough review of the available methods for the multi-label ECG classification task. A detailed study on the efficacy of the proposed method is done using different evaluation metrics for multi-label classification. Our proposed method performed better than almost all the existing methods available. Thus, our proposed method can act as a practical support system for doctors/cardiologists and make their diagnosis more precise.

9.9 Future works

Currently, our proposed model is capable of identifying only eight heart conditions. In the future, the model can be trained with an extended dataset, which combines other multi-label datasets containing ECG recordings belonging to different varieties of heart diseases. Experiments can be performed to analyze whether the proposed method is capable of identifying these wider varieties of diseases without compromising on performance. A retrospective clinical study can also be conducted to further study the efficacy of the model in handling real-world data.

References

[1] Sanjana, K., Sowmya, V., Gopalakrishnan, E. A. & Soman, K. P. (2021). Performance improvement of deep residual skip convolution neural network for atrial fibrillation classification. In Evolution in Computational Intelligence. Springer, Singapore, 755–763.

[2] Gopika, P., Sowmya, V., Gopalakrishnan, E. A. & Soman, K. P. (January, 2019). Performance improvement of residual skip convolutional neural network for myocardial disease classification. In International Conference on Intelligent Computing and Communication Technologies. Springer, Singapore, 226–234.

[3] Kurup, R. V., Sowmya, V. & Soman, K. P. (January, 2019). Effect of data pre-processing on brain tumor classification using capsulenet. In International Conference on Intelligent Computing and Communication Technologies. Springer, Singapore, 110–119.

[4] Vyshnav, M. T., Sowmya, V., Gopalakrishnan, E. A., Vv, S. V., Menon, V. K. & Soman, K. P. (July, 2020). Deep learning based approach for multiple myeloma detection. In 2020 11th International Conference on Computing, Communication and Networking Technologies (ICCCNT) (pp. 1–7). IEEE.

[5] Balasubramanian, R., Sowmya, V., Gopalakrishnan, E. A., Menon, V. K., Variyar, V. S. & Soman, K. P. (July, 2020). Analysis of adversarial based augmentation for diabetic retinopathy disease grading. In 2020 11th International Conference on Computing, Communication and Networking Technologies (ICCCNT) (pp. 1–5). IEEE.

[6] Sun, Z., Wang, C., Zhao, Y. & Yan, C. (2020). Multi-label ECG signal classification based on ensemble classifier. IEEE Access, 8, 117986–117996. 10.1109/ACCESS.2020.3004908.

[7] Cai, J., Sun, W., Guan, J. & You, I. (2020). Multi-ECGNet for ECG arrythmia multi-label classification. IEEE Access, 8, 110848–110858.

[8] Jia, D., Zhao, W., Li, Z., Yan, C., Wang, H., Hu, J. & Fang, J. (2019). An ensemble neural network for multi-label classification of electrocardiogram. In Machine Learning and Medical Engineering for Cardiovascular Health and Intravascular Imaging and Computer Assisted Stenting. Springer, Cham, 20–27.

[9] Cheng, Y., Ye, Y., Hou, M., He, W. & Pan, T. (July, 2020). Multi-label arrhythmia classification from fixed-length compressed ECG segments in real-time wearable ECG monitoring. In 2020 42nd Annual International Conference of the IEEE Engineering in Medicine & Biology Society (EMBC) (pp. 580–583). IEEE.

[10] Luo, C., Jiang, H., Li, Q. & Rao, N. (2019). Multi-label classification of abnormalities in 12-lead ecg using 1d cnn and lstm. In Machine Learning and Medical Engineering for Cardiovascular Health and Intravascular Imaging and Computer Assisted Stenting. Springer, Cham, 55–63.

[11] Zhu, J., Xin, K., Zhao, Q. & Zhang, Y. (2019). A multi-label learning method to detect arrhythmia based on 12-lead ECGs. In Machine Learning and Medical Engineering for Cardiovascular Health and Intravascular Imaging and Computer Assisted Stenting. Springer, Cham, 11–19.

[12] Thygesen, K., Alpert, J. S., Jaffe, A. S., Chaitman, B. R., Bax, J. J., Morrow, D. A., White, H. D., Mickley, H., Crea, F., Van de werf, F. & Bucciarelli-Ducci, C. (2019). Fourth universal definition of myocardial infarction. European Heart Journal, 40(3), 237–269.

[13] Weng, B., Blanco-Velasco, M. & Barner, K. E. (April, 2006). Baseline wander correction in ECG by the empirical mode decomposition. In Proceedings of the IEEE 32nd Annual Northeast Bioengineering Conference (pp. 135–136). IEEE.

[14] Haritha, C., Ganesan, M. & Sumesh, E. P. (March, 2016). A survey on modern trends in ECG noise removal techniques. In 2016 International Conference on Circuit, Power and Computing Technologies (ICCPCT) (pp. 1–7). IEEE.

[15] Thalkar, S. & Upasani, D. (2013). Various techniques for removal of power line interference from ECG signal. International Journal of Science and Engineering Research, 4(12), 12–23.

[16] Sujadevi, V. G. & Soman, K. P. (2020). Towards identifying most important leads for ECG classification. A Data driven approach employing Deep Learning. Procedia Computer Science, 171, 602–608.
[17] Pan, J. & Tompkins, W. J. (1985). A real-time QRS detection algorithm. IEEE Transactions on Biomedical Engineering, 3, 230–236.
[18] Kalidas, V. & Tamil, L. (October, 2017). Real-time QRS detector using stationary wavelet transform for automated ECG analysis. In 2017 IEEE 17th International Conference on Bioinformatics and Bioengineering (BIBE) (pp. 457–461). IEEE.
[19] Christov, I. I. (2004). Real time electrocardiogram QRS detection using combined adaptive threshold. Biomedical Engineering Online, 3(1), 28.
[20] Hamilton, P. (September, 2002). Open source ECG analysis. In Computers in cardiology (pp. 101–104). IEEE.
[21] Engelse, W. A. H. & Zeelenberg, C. (1979). A single scan algorithm for QRS-detection and feature extraction. Computers in Cardiology, 6, 37–42.
[22] Elgendi, M., Jonkman, M. & De Boer, F. (2010). Frequency bands effects on QRS detection. Biosignals, 2002.
[23] Liu, F., Liu, C., Zhao, L., Zhang, X., Wu, X., Xu, X., Liu, Y., Ma, C., Wei, S., He, Z. & Li, J. (2018). An open access database for evaluating the algorithms of electrocardiogram rhythm and morphology abnormality detection. Journal of Medical Imaging and Health Informatics, 8(7), 1368–1373.
[24] Kingma, D. P. & Ba, J. (2014). Adam: A method for stochastic optimization. arXiv preprint arXiv:1412.6980.
[25] Koidl, K. (2013). Loss functions in classification tasks. School of Computer Science and Statistic Trinity College, Dublin.

Idowu Dauda Oladipo, Muyideen Abdulraheem,
Joseph Bamidele Awotunde*, Sulaimon Olayinka Dauda,
Roseline Oluwasenu Ogundokun, Muiz Olalekan Raheem,
Ige Oluwasegun Osemudiame

10 Application of big data analytic techniques for healthcare systems

Abstract: The digital age has brought in massive amounts of high-speed data that resulted in big data in healthcare system. This data contains hidden knowledge in the form of inherent features and patterns that should be obtained and used. Businesses would be able to obtain essential data and knowledge, undertake comprehensive analysis and develop new opportunities and benefits as a result. The healthcare system's success especially in the areas of medical diagnosis, prediction and classification depends basically on the amount of data generated. Big data analytics (BDA) is critical in areas of healthcare diagnostics, early detection of epidemics and better patient management. Data analytics is the process of analyzing raw data to derive useful insights. However, experts have emphasized the necessity for analytics in order to improve healthcare quality and patient care coordination. As a result, this chapter addresses how big data and analytics can be used to improve traditional public health techniques in the areas of diagnosis of diseases, forecast, categorization and management in the healthcare system. The chapter presents the significant application of BDA in healthcare systems, challenges and future research directions. Leveraging on

---

***Corresponding author: Joseph Bamidele Awotunde,** Department of Computer Science, Faculty of Information and Communication Sciences, University of Ilorin, Ilorin, Kwara State, Nigeria,
e-mail: awotunde.jb@unilorin.edu.ng
Idowu Dauda Oladipo, Department of Computer Science, Faculty of Information and Communication Sciences, University of Ilorin, Ilorin, Kwara State, Nigeria, e-mail: odidowu@unilorin.edu.ng
Muyideen Abdulraheem, Department of Computer Science, Faculty of Information and Communication Sciences, University of Ilorin, Ilorin, Kwara State, Nigeria, e-mail: muyideen@unilorin.edu.ng
Sulaimon Olayinka Dauda, Department of Computer Science, Faculty of Information and Communication Sciences, University of Ilorin, Ilorin, Kwara State, Nigeria,
e-mail: olawoyinolayinka20@gmail.com
Roseline Oluwasenu Ogundokun, Department of Multimedia Engineering, Kaunas University of Technology, 51368 Kaunas, Lithuania, e-mail: rosogu@ktu.lt
Muiz Olalekan Raheem, School of Built Environment, Engineering and Computing, Leeds Beckett University, Leeds LS1 3HE, United Kingdom, e-mail: raheemolalekan2@gmail.com
Ige Oluwasegun Osemudiame, Department of Computer Science, Faculty of Information and Communication Sciences, University of Ilorin, Ilorin, Kwara State, Nigeria,
e-mail: 16-52ha043@students.unilorin.edu.ng

https://doi.org/10.1515/9783110750942-010

big data and intelligent analytics becomes expedient in other to enjoy their use for healthcare system especially in the area of public health. Various machine learning and deep learning algorithms have been used to uncover knowledge and patterns in healthcare systems.

Keywords: Big data, big data analytics, machine learning, deep learning, data mining, healthcare system

10.1 Introduction

The medical sector provides a copious volume of patient information, medicines, illness, treatments, research and several others [1, 2]. By recordkeeping, compliance and regulatory requirements, patterns have been recognized in the use of healthcare analytics to automate all these kinds of data for care delivery [3]. A record that supports medical practice or healthcare issues is referred to as an electronic health record (EHR). Some of the advantages of EHR include earlier detection of disease, improved patient treatment, better accurate prediction and greater medical research advancement. The main difficulties with providing valuable insights from huge amounts of data include intricacies in the data, variability, immediacy, distortion and omissions. In general, big healthcare analytics is no exception. The procedures that must be undertaken include the gathering, connection, cleaning, storage, evaluation and reporting of EHR data. Focus is placed on certain specialized objectives throughout the entire evaluation process of digital infrastructure, which integrates a number of techniques or platforms to generate an all-encompassing solution [4].

The view may be something like a software stack, with various options for each phase and the real choice obtained from data type [5]. There are two sorts of EHRs: data from sensors and electronic medical records (EMR). Sensor or EMR data can only be sent through one of two methods. Basic understanding of EMR from hospitals is one step in the right manner. The second option is to collect additional health information using devices like smartphones and wearables [6]. EMRs from hospitals are often gathered and processed to provide useful information, and this data is timestamped. Diagnostic tests, prescriptions, laboratory tests, unclassified text data like doctors' notes and images such as magnetic resonance imaging (MRI) data are all examples of unstructured text data found in EMR. EMR data is useful for disease classification, disease progression modeling and phenotyping [7]. Despite the fact that EMR data is a vital resource for healthcare applications, it is fraught with difficulties. One issue is that EMR data has a high dimensionality as a result of the sheer amount of clinical variables it contains. Second, EMR data is frequently unclean or partial since it is collected in a rather disconnected manner and over a lengthy time period [8].

Third, data from EMRs tend to be inconclusive as patients often go to clinics only when it is really necessary. By assessing the impulses from sensors, readings may also be used to assess patient health. When seen through the lens of big data, sensor readings have numerous different features [9]. In real time, millions of sensors users and mobile devices signals generate heterogeneous data streams from varied sources and circumstances. Monitoring and analyzing those streams will be an excellent way to learn about patients' psychological, physiological and physical health issues. As an example, pressure sensors set within a patient room can remotely monitor the activities of elderly individuals and assist in any emergency situation; ECG and EEG sensors are used to monitor people's emotions, stress levels and depression [10]. Carbon nanotube sensors, which are used to treat patients with cancer tissues, can monitor their oxygen and pH levels [11].

Regarding healthcare, big data storage provides the prospect to improve quality while simultaneously cutting costs. Clinical decision support, illness monitoring and population health management are just some of the medical and healthcare tasks it might assist with. According to sources, health data in the United States exceeded 150 exabytes in 2011 and has the potential to reach zettabytes (1,021 bytes) and yottabytes (1,024 gigabytes) [12, 13].

The systematic application of analytical models, such as statistical, contextual, quantitative, predictive, cognitive and other models, to drive fact-based decision making for healthcare planning, management, measurement and learning is referred to as healthcare analytics [14]. The application of big data analytics (BDA) has the potential to anticipate epidemics, treat diseases, raise the standard of living and minimize needless deaths in addition to increasing profits and reducing waste [15]. Among these applications, predictive analytics is expected to be the next revolution in medicine and statistics around the globe [16]. The use of empirical procedures (statistical and non-statistical) to produce predictions based on data, along with ways of measuring prediction strength, are all part of predictive modeling [17]. It analyzes current and past data to create forecasts for the future using various statistical approaches such as data mining, machine learning and modeling. For example, forecasting might be used to identify high-risk individuals and treat these to minimize unnecessary hospitalizations and readmissions. The diverse data forms, enormous size and related uncertainties in big-data sources make it challenging to turn data into useful information. Because medical data contains so many health variables, identifying them and choosing classification features for health informatics necessitates highly advanced and architecturally particular frameworks [18].

Big data's architectural analytics in healthcare is conceptually similar to classical healthcare informatics [19]. When we evaluate how processing is carried out, we can see the key distinction. Traditionally, healthcare projects entailed the use of a stand-alone business intelligence technology. When dealing with "big data," processing must be separated into several nodes for execution, resulting in distributed processing [20]. Because data comes from both internal and external sources and is stored in numerous locations, healthcare networks must be redefined (IBM Centre for Applied Insights, the IoT healthcare network [21, 22] exemplifies this endeavor).

The remainder of this paper is organized as follows: Section 2 describes various applications of big data analytics of healthcare systems. Section 3 focuses on the challenges of BDA in healthcare systems. Section 4 discusses the proposed architecture for big data analytics in the healthcare system. Section 5 concludes and reflects the future vision.

10.2 Application of big data analytics of healthcare systems

The information produced and stored digitally is massive and growing. Consequently, the science of managing and analyzing data is progressing, allowing organizations to transform this immense resource into knowledge and information that aids in achieving the goals. In this point of view, the research is looking at how big data can be used in healthcare, applying an economic framework in emphasizing its benefits and applications. Using patient and practitioner data to enhance the standard of healthcare provision is seen to be a helpful technique.

The growing use of EHRs has resulted in massive data collections. According to a survey done by the American Hospital Association, EHR utilization quadrupled between 2009 and 2011, owing in part to funding provided by the Health Information Technology for Economic and Clinical Health Act of 2009 [23]. Quantitative data such as laboratory values, textual files and demographic data and records like insurance information are all currently included in most EHRs documentation of delivery of drugs. Nevertheless, a lot of these collected data is now viewed as a byproduct of care provision rather than a strategic tool for increasing performance. The transformation of data out of garbage to gold has been crucial in other sectors' big data revolutions.

Improvement in computer science analytic methods, particularly machine learning, has been a critical accelerator in handling these huge data volumes. Unstructured data, including textual files that did not match relational data models, is difficult to analyze using conventional analytical techniques developed from the physical and social sciences. Similarly, most text-based healthcare data is said to be unstructured. Healthcare, unlike other customer service sectors, has embraced the idea of counselling patients and clinicians through innovative randomized clinical trials and semi-experimental studies. Scientific study is preferred over expert opinion and personal testimony, according to the evidence-based movement.

Unlike many other businesses, medicine understood the importance of data and expertise in making reasonable decisions. Nonetheless, healthcare has been slow to adopt innovative strategies for using the wealth of data included in EHRs [24]. In four ways, big data may aid the economic objective of healthcare delivery by boosting quality and efficiency [25]. To begin with, big data has the ability to greatly enhance the capacity to create new data. Obtaining organized data to address many health questions prospectively, or even retrospectively, is too expensive. Employing computational tools to examine the complex data in EHRs (for example, natural language processing to derive medical ideas from free-text files) enables improved data collection in an optimized way. Computerized recognition inside EHRs using natural language processing was more successful at identifying postsurgical issues than discharge coding-based drug safety signals [26].

Second, big data may aid in the sharing of knowledge. Most doctors find it difficult to stay up to date on the most recent evidence-based guidelines for clinical practice. Medical literature has been digitized, which has substantially increased access; nonetheless, knowledge translation is difficult due to a large number of studies. This problem might be handled through the analysis of current EHRs and developing a platform to assist physicians in making better decisions. In contrast to traditional expert systems, the big data strategy delivers suggestions relating to current patient data analysis instead of rule-based decision trees. Longitudinal diagnostic data, for example, was shown to accurately estimate a patient's likelihood of receiving a domestic violence diagnosis in the future [27, 28].

Third, by allowing analysts to connect systems biology (e.g., genomics) with EHR data, big data can possibly assist medical care in adopting personalized medicine [29]. Natural language processing is used by the electronic medical records and genomics network to profile patients and simplify genomics research. Fourth, big data aids in the improvement of medical treatment by quickly communicating information to patients and so involving them in their own treatment. Patients' records are currently inactive and maintained with healthcare providers.

Medical records may be preserved with patients in the future. Big data combines traditional care data such as prescription records and genealogy with other user data such as earning, schooling, community, military experience available on other websites, food patterns, workouts and types of entertainment, which can all be obtained without requiring an in-depth conversation with the patient [30].

Nearly every single aspect of healthcare administration may benefit from big data. Detection of fraud, outbreak development forecasting, omics, treatment outcomes, medical device research, insurance business, personalized patient care and factory production, as well as pharmaceutical research, are some of the possible industry sectors [31]. Furthermore, big data is being more widely employed in customized healthcare, which emphasizes a patient-centered approach [32].

10.2.1 Applications of big data in "omics"

Huge amounts of data are referred to as omics in the organic and molecular sciences (such as metabolomics, proteomics, genomics and macrobiotics). The goal of this study using big data is to discover illness strategies and increase the accuracy of therapies (e.g., "precision medicine") [33]. In previous ages, the development of genomics, proteomics, metabolomics and other forms of omics knowledge resulted in vast amounts of molecular biology data [34]. Genomic science is the study of genes and how they function [35].

Big data in genomics will assist in illness prevention and cure as well as the provision of personalized care to each patient [36]. This domain is very much in its infancy, with presentations in highly concentrated research fields such as leukemia, diabetes and cancer [37]. Pathway analysis is primarily utilized for large amounts of genome-scale data [38], and it uses three generations of the same structures [39]. The references of [40, 41] are examples of first-generation tools. GSEA [42] is the most prominent second-generation tool, and Pathway-Express [43] shows the use of a third-generation tool.

Proteomics is the exploration of the development and function of the proteome. The whole collection of cellular proteins is referred to as the proteome. ExPASy has over 100 tools and dozens of databases on proteomics. The utilization of large datasets in proteomics will play a key part in the detection and prevention of human cancer [44]. For PTMs prediction, Find Mod [45] and CSS-Palm [46] are often employed. The systematic idea of chemical procedures, including metabolites, is known as metabolomics. For systems biology, the BiGG data sources use a simulation of human metabolism based on genetic data [47].

10.2.2 Insurance industry/payer

Healthcare insurance businesses and consumers use big data in underwriting, fraud detection and claim management. As indicated by person-centric actions, insurance firms are looking at more than simply computational fraud [48, 49]. For example, how many similar claims were made by the same person or indicated the same service across many insurance carriers?

10.2.3 Medical device design and manufacturing

The use of big data allows for the evaluation of a greater range of device materials, distribution mechanisms, tissue interfaces and anatomical designs. In the planning and manufacturing of healthcare systems, computational techniques and big data can be quite useful [50].

10.2.4 Pharmaceuticals

Big data is employed throughout the pharmaceutical research process, especially during the development of a medication [51]. Pfizer has launched the Precision Medicine Analytics Environment initiative, which draws the connections between EHRs, clinical trial data and genetic data to find new methods to administer breakthrough drugs to particular treatment populations.

10.2.5 Personalized patient care

Big data will enable the greatest and most customized patient care to be provided. New big data-derived implications will drive essential improvements in diagnostic support, clinical recommendations and patient triage in the not-too-distant future, allowing for more focused and individualized therapy to enhance patient outcomes [52].

10.2.6 Fraud detection and prevention

Fraud can be identified, predicted and minimized through the use of modern analytical tools for the identification of fraud and evaluating the correctness as well as the integrity of claims. Healthcare payers can employ big data predictive modeling to combat fraud. Analysis of veterans claims and benefits, as well as academic fraud, can be done using fraud waste and abuse analytics [1, 53].

10.2.7 Asthmapolis

The market has developed a GPS-enabled monitor that tracks patients' inhaler consumption, resulting in more effective asthma therapy. By placing a small cap-cover device with a GPS sensor upon an inhaler, the organization may collect user data. When a patient has an asthma attack and has to use their inhaler, the small gadget records the time and place and sends the information to a website. This data is then combined with data from the Centers for Disease Control and Prevention (CDC) [54]. The data from CDC contains details including the most common asthma triggers in the area as well as where the highest pollen count is found. The final output will show how patients with asthma and other people who have had comparable reactions to specific allergens reacted as well as whether or not an inhaler was needed [55]. When making travel selections, a patient can become more conscious of whether or not to prepare for an asthma attack. This vast quantity of data may be used by a clinician to create a tailored plan for a patient, concentrating on certain periods during which the danger of an asthma attack is highest and reacting by raising or reducing the dose [56].

10.3 Challenges of big data analytics in healthcare systems

Big data's enormous quantity, tempo and diversity have posed significant issues in terms of memory, generation, search, recovery and presentation. Big data variability and truthfulness are inherently unstable and unclear, making BDA problematic. The following are the major issues with big data in clinical use and healthcare:

i. Several healthcare organizations, particularly hospitals, segregate or segment data. The EHR stores healthcare records such as patients' medical history, vital signs, progress notes and routine diagnostic results. Effectiveness and outcome data, such as surgical site infections, return-to-surgery rates and patient falls, are kept in the quality and risk management sections. Data validation, consolidation and processing standards are required [57].

ii. Aggregating and analyzing unstructured data is difficult. In the patients' EHR, unstructured data comprises lab results, scanned papers, photographs and case notes [26, 58]. Managing vast volumes of medical imaging data, deriving theoretically relevant information and biomarkers, and assessing unorganized case records in the correct setting are all difficult tasks [59].

iii. Telemetry obtained via patient-owned gadgets as well as similar data provided by patients is a developing new source of information. As feedback from automatic monitoring devices is included, big data becomes even more complex. Weight, motion, sugar, blood pressure and pulse oximetry are examples of patient-reported outcomes, as well as device telemetry [60]. Fine-grained temporal data that is constantly flowing (and potentially annotated) is challenging to capture, index and analyze [51].
(iv) For clinicians who are oriented toward the biological paradigm, in which the goal is to discover the source of the sickness so that it may be adequately treated. Big data is difficult since it focuses on correlations rather than causes. Big data entails greater information, but it also entails the presence of noisy or erroneous data [61].

iv. Combining genetic data with conventional clinical data increase the difficulty of genomic data analysis [59].

v. Privacy concerns raised by the Health Insurance Portability and Accountability Act (HIPAA) are frequently highlighted as roadblocks to large data collection [63]. In telecardiology and teleconsultation, data confidentiality in the cloud, data compatibility across hospitals and transmission delay and accessibility are all challenges [62].

vi. Suppose that the patient's privacy can be safeguarded, many healthcare professionals are cautious to exchange information due to market competitiveness. It is tough to strike the right balance between securing information about the patient and preserving the usability and integrity of the data. It is difficult to achieve integration, standardization and open access of usable and accessible data [53].

vii. Data hackers have become more hazardous in the era of big data. Data leaks may be expensive. Hackers got access to Utah's Department of Health data set in March 2012, stealing private information from 780,000 individuals (including 280,000 patients' Social Security numbers) [82]. Fingerprint identification helps in the protection of information and the prevention of information leaks. Total data security, on the other hand, is practically impossible to obtain.

viii. Both providers and payers cited a lack of resources, such as infrastructure, budget and staffing as major roadblocks to big data implementation. A lack of infrastructure, as well as policies, practices and standards that make use of big data in healthcare, was also mentioned as a source of worry [83].

ix. De-identification involves deleting personally identifiable information from health data so that it can no longer be connected to a specific person. Expert determination and a safe zone are the two techniques HIPAA mandates for de-identification of data. For cost savings and quality improvement, the capacity to gather and assess de-identified data is crucial. Data cannot be properly de-identified, according to certain worries [62, 63].

The storage, processing and classification of a piece of data present several issues. The first and most pressing issue is the speed with which data may be browsed and processed. We cannot afford to wait till the essential data is obtained in today's industry, where time is of the essence. As the level of granularity rises, so does the difficulty. We can address this by using parallel processing or better technology to scan vast amounts of data quickly.

With developments in computer science, scientific computation and other disciplines, data integration, data visualization and information security are just a few of the big data technology issues that need to be overcome. Data privacy and ownership, data sharing and cross-disciplinary collaboration are all issues that need to be addressed, among other issues, requiring policy support from organizations and governments. To achieve big data continuity, it is critical to combine e-infrastructures as permanent platforms.

10.3.1 Big data and healthcare informatics

Healthcare informatics is a multifaceted discipline that brings together computer science, medicine and social science. Clinical informatics, biomedical informatics, nursing informatics, medical informatics and healthcare informatics are all different terms for the same area. Healthcare informatics uses cutting-edge information technology to improve data storage, retrieval, collection and application in biomedicine and healthcare. Because of the ongoing development of hardware and software such as wireless sensor networks (WSN), radio frequency identification (RFID), cloud services and IoT sensors, clinical and healthcare informatics have gained more capabilities during the previous decade [64–67]. Remote patients monitoring and other health care assistants are generating massive amounts of data using IoT medical devices and environmental sensors in real time. Cloud repositories are used to hold patient medical data and retrieve it using various analysis methodologies, such as assessing patients' health status and creating novel methods for diagnosing and treating illnesses. This development gave birth to a new age for biomedical informatics, which will be employed to cope with massive data and gain unparalleled information in the area of medicine. These technologies contribute to the creation of prototypes for monitoring, assisting and curing patients [67].

The key problem in this area is the ever-increasing volume of data created in the healthcare sector, which needs complicated analysis of the data in order to get information. Patients get contemporary healthcare services, lives are saved and innovative diagnosis and treatment techniques for a range of ailments are developed using big data analysis tools to acquire meaningful information from patient care data [68].

10.3.2 Applications of healthcare using big data

Table 10.1 shows the potential of this technology and classifies the usage of healthcare analytics, while Table 10.2 shows medical applications that leverage BDA gadgets and methodologies [69]. There are five different categories of big data usage according to authors in [70].

Table 10.1: Categorization of various uses of big data in healthcare.

S/N	Categories	Uses
1	Behavior/ consumer	Big data (BDA) approaches are employed for demographic examination. Varieties of information employed in this type comprise advertising data, consumer, marketing, public and individual behavior data and so on.
2	Medical decision support	BDA approaches assist to deal with healthcare interrelated verdict making procedure. Information such as precise medical forecasting, e-health annals, genomics, R&D and medicine institutions which could assist in healthcare verdicts is categorized here.
3	Management and delivery	This deals with the organization of budget on medical services offered on treatment provided including insurance. This comprises information about patient's data and treatment. BDA could be employed to examine data management and delivery separately.
4	Medical information	This indicates data that is accessible via different types of information systems and medical information systems for BDA. Information here comprises treatment of diseases data such as genomics and data from biomedical sensors.
5	Support information	BDA usage which cannot be put in any of the four previously discussed kinds is convened into this type. Efficiencies of treatment, lab and investigation records, medication and detection of errors are situated in these types.

Table 10.2: Medical applications using BDA devices and approaches.

S/N	Medical application	BDA approaches
1	Early diagnosis of disease	Predictive data analytics tools can diagnose the disease early, before the patient begins to experience symptoms of the condition [14]. Stream mining and pattern detection for disabled and elderly persons can assist physicians to comprehend the dynamic health factors by using wearable sensors.
2	Health data usage	It is feasible to uncover intuitions such as patient identification with respect to his ailment, treatment remedies and hospital performance analysis by gathering and storing clinical data such as patient data, administrative data records from hospitals and government data.
3	Conscripting public strategy	BDA solutions can aptly provide tangible summarized data basis for effective conscripting of the public strategies.
4	Peoples' health	The consequences of BDA can be employed on making choices for handling the populace health and upcoming medical advancement
5	Treatment policy based on history	Investigational data, outcomes and individual's details can assist for statistical researches as well as similarly assist medical practitioners to identify the illnesses. This implies that it enables medical practitioners to make verdicts and likewise study the obtainable indications.
6	Image processing	Therapeutic pictures, which are generated using techniques, such as X-ray, ultrasound, MRI scanning and molecular imaging, are a major source of data used for identification and planning.
7	Signal processing	In addition to the images, each patient has a monitor attached to them that generates continuous, high-resolution waveforms or discrete digital data that aids in understanding the patient's behavior and response to the treatment. BDA has the capacity to hold and evaluate a wide range of data types.
8	Genomics	Due to the advancement of effective sequencing technology, the cost of constructing the animal genome is decreasing. In the biological world, analyzing genome data in conjunction with time data is becoming a serious difficulty. This task necessitates BDA.
9	Data analytics for multi-modal data	A patient data includes data from various aspects like the doctor's prescriptions, patient's biological history, scanning, blood test reports, X-ray and billing information. All these data which are in different formats can be analyzed to generate a consistent dataset semantically using BDA devices and approaches [26].
10	Data analytics from different perspectives	Health data analytics can be approached from a variety of angles. For example, the outcome of the analytics varies depending on the stakeholder.

10.4 The proposed architecture for big data analytics in the healthcare system

Big data is a relatively new topic in information technology, arising as a result of the exponential increase in the volume of data in the last couple of years. Big data is a concept that describes datasets that are larger than standard data processing and storage methods can handle. Because of the need to process and evaluate such large datasets, a new type of data analytics dubbed BDA has emerged [71]. According to studies, the current surge in health information is essential to enhancing population health, cutting the ever-increasing cost of health care and handling the large amounts of data created by patients in healthcare today. This section gives an introduction of the exploratory approach for using predictive analytics in medicine as well as a description of some of the most often used techniques for evaluating big data that are accessible on a variety of platforms.

10.4.1 Healthcare architectural framework for big data analytics

A traditional health informatics or analytics design framework is similar to a full suggested architecture framework for healthcare big data analytics design. The key difference is how the processing is done. To conduct analysis in a typical health analytics project, a business intelligence product installed on a standalone device, such as a desktop or laptop, can be employed. According to authors in [72], the growing usage of mobile and wearable sensor technologies has flooded the healthcare industry with a vast quantity of data, resulting in a rapid growth in the number of data sources. As a result, typical techniques to healthcare data analysis, which are unable to manage the vast number of diverse medical data, become impossible to implement.

Generally, there are four types of analytics in the healthcare domain: descriptive, diagnostic, predictive and prescriptive analytics; a brief overview of each is provided below.

i. Descriptive analytics: Descriptive analytics is a type of data analysis that is used to describe anything. It entails summarizing and reporting current occurrences. This degree of analysis is accomplished in a number of ways. Among the approaches utilized in descriptive analytics are descriptive statistics tools such as histograms and charts.
ii. Diagnostic analysis: Analyze the situation. Its goal is to explain why specific events happened and what variables caused them. Diagnostic analysis, for example, uses approaches like clustering and decision trees to figure out why some patients are readmitted regularly.
iii. Predictive snalysis: It demonstrates one's capacity to predict future occurrences; it can also help with pattern detection and probability prediction for uncertain

events. Its role can be illustrated by predicting whether or not a patient would develop complications. Machine learning techniques are frequently used to create predictive models.
iv. Prescriptive analysis: Its purpose is to recommend appropriate behaviors that lead to optimal decision-making. For example, if there is a high risk of a harmful side effect, prescriptive analysis may advocate refusing a treatment. Methods used to undertake prescriptive analytics include decision trees and Monte Carlo simulation.

The phases of analytics in medicine are depicted in Figure 10.1. Integration of big data technology in healthcare analytics may result in improved medical system performance.

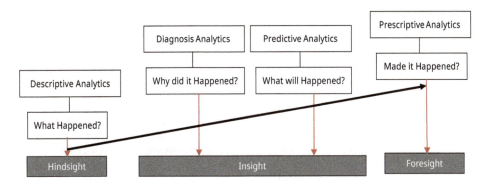

Figure 10.1: The ecosystem of analytics in the healthcare systems.

10.4.2 A big data architecture

In terms of technology, big data refers to datasets that require more computing power than is currently accessible. They represent a new business strategy for generating actionable insights that enable firms to perceive and adapt to a quickly changing environment. The benefits of BDA have been recognized in a variety of industries, with the healthcare system emerging as one with a lot of potential [73, 74]. The differentiating qualities of big data, including volume (hugeness of data availability), velocity (coming of data in a flood of fashion) and variety (presence of data from numerous sources in a variety of formats), all have their properties in the plentiful streams of medical data [75].

10.4.3 Big data frameworks in healthcare system

Various authors have proposed several architectures for big data in medical systems in the past works of literature. Table 10.3 lists some of these methods.

Table 10.3: Summary of big data analytics frameworks in healthcare system.

S. no.	Authors	Source of data	Proposed framework	Application(s) area	Merits/highlight
1	[76]	Radio-frequency identification (RFID) tags	Privacy-preserving framework for RFID-based healthcare systems	Securing healthcare services	It proposed an improvement to RFID-based healthcare systems
2	[77]	Electronic health records, biometric data, diagnosis reports and surveillance data	Big data-enabled smart healthcare system framework	Intelligent systems for healthcare services	Integration of a knowledge discovery method for healthcare with smart-service infrastructure was highlighted
3	[78]	Protein data bank dataset	Big data framework for structure prediction of proteins using ensemble learning	Designing of drugs	The study presented a more accurate distributed spark-based framework
4	[79]	RFID data, ECG data and patient biometrics	Policy enforcement frameworks for Internet of things (IoT) applications in smart health	Securing large-scale heterogeneous healthcare systems	A flexible enforcement framework alongside policy definition language was proposed
5	[80]	Health informatics dataset	A cloud-based data analytics and visualization framework for the prediction of health shocks	Public healthcare services	The authors presented an AWS-based cloud framework for integrating, capturing and visualizing big healthcare *data
6	[81]	Patient data from laboratories, radiology information system and hospital records	Cyber-physical system-based healthcare framework	Data analytics in smart health	Integration of sensor technologies, cloud computing, and big data analytics to improve healthcare services

10.5 Conclusion and future directions

A study of big data analytics in the health sector is presented in this work, with illness diagnosis and prediction, categorization and management among the topics covered. It also discusses the use of big data in a variety of health-related sectors such as genomics, pharmaceuticals and medicine. There were also some issues and excellent frameworks for big data in healthcare discussed. Finally, future research in the smart-health system sector should look at the analytics process for complex data such as photos and streams of images (video).

References

[1] Raghupathi, W. & Raghupathi, V. (2014). Big data analytics in healthcare: Promise and potential. Health Information Science and Systems, 2(1), 3.
[2] Folorunso, S. O., Awotunde, J. B., Ayo, F. E. & Abdullah, K. K. A. (2021). RADIoT: The unifying framework for IoT, radiomics and deep learning modeling. Intelligent Systems Reference Library, 209, 109–128.
[3] Awotunde, J. B., Jimoh, R. G., Ogundokun, R. O., Misra, S. & Abikoye, O. C. (2022). Big data analytics of IoT-based cloud system framework: Smart healthcare monitoring systems. In Internet of Things (pp. 181–208). 2022, Springer, Cham.
[4] Ismail, A., Shehab, A. & El-Henawy, I. M. (2019). Healthcare analysis in smart big data analytics: Reviews, challenges and recommendations. In Hassanien A., Elhoseny M., Ahmed S. & Singh A. (eds.) Security in Smart Cities: Models, Applications, and Challenges. Lecture Notes in Intelligent Transportation and Infrastructure. Springer, Cham. https://doi.org/10.1007/978-3-030-01560-2_2.
[5] Saiod, A. K., van Greunen, D. & Veldsman, A. (2017). Electronic Health Records: Benefits and Challenges for Data Quality (pp. 3–319). Springer International Publishing AG, Midtown Manhattan, New York City.
[6] Darwish, A., Hassanien, A. E., Elhoseny, M., Sangaiah, A. K. & Muhammad, K. (2017). The impact of the hybrid platform of internet of things and cloud computing on healthcare systems: Opportunities, challenges, and open problems. Journal of Ambient Intelligence and Humanized Computing, https://doi.org/10.1007/s12652-017-0659-1.
[7] Kuang, Z., Thomson, J., Caldwell, M., et al. (2016). Computational drug repositioning using continuous self-controlled case series. arXiv preprint arXiv: 1604.05976.
[8] Avendi, M. R., Kheradvar, A. & Jafarkhani, H. (2016). A combined deep-learning and deformable model approach to fully automatic segmentation of the left ventricle in cardiac MRI. Medical Image Analysis, 30, 108–119.
[9] Cort, R., Bonnaire, X. & Marin, O. (2015). Stream processing of healthcare sensor data: Studying user traces to identify challenges from a big data perspective. In: Proceedings of the 4th international workshop on body area sensor networks.
[10] Sioni, R. & Chittaro, L. (2015). Stress detection using physiological sensors. IEEE Computer, 48(10), 26–33.
[11] Kumar, S., Willander, M. & Sharma, J. G. (2015). A solution processed carbon nanotube modified conducting paper sensor for cancer detection. Journal of Materials Chemical B, 3, 9305–9314.
[12] Shafqat, S., Kishwer, S., Rasool, R. U., et al. (2020). Big data analytics enhanced healthcare systems: A review. Journal of Supercomputing, 76, 1754–1799. https://doi.org/10.1007/s11227-017-2222-4.
[13] Awotunde, J. B., Adeniyi, E. A., Ogundokun, R. O. & Ayo, F. E. (2021). Application of big data with fintech in financial services. In Fintech with Artificial Intelligence, Big Data, and Blockchain (pp. 107–132). Springer, Singapore.
[14] Cortada, J. W., Gordon, D. & Lenihan, B. (2012). The value of analytics in healthcare: from insights to outcomes. IBM Global Business Services, Life Sciences and Healthcare, Executive Report.

[15] Marr, B. (2015). How big data is changing healthcare. http://www.forbes.com/sites/bernardmarr/2015/04/21/how-big-data-is-changing-healthcare/print/. Accessed 8 Aug 2021.

[16] Winters-Miner, L. A. (2014). Seven ways predictive analytics can improve healthcare. Elsevier Connect. https://www.elsevier.com/connect/seven-ways-predictive-analytics-can-improve-healthcare. Accessed 8 Aug 2021.

[17] Shmueli, G. & Koppius, O. R. (2011). Predictive analytics in information systems research. MIS Quarterly, 35(3), 553–572.

[18] Kumar, S. & Singh, M. (2019). Big data analytics for healthcare industry: Impact, applications, and tools. Big Data Mining and Analytics, 2(1), 48–57, March 2019. 10.26599/BDMA.2018.9020031.

[19] Rehman, A., Naz, S. & Razzak, I. (2021). Leveraging big data analytics in healthcare enhancement: Trends, challenges and opportunities. Multimedia Systems, 1–33.

[20] Cloud Security Alliance. (2013). Big data analytics for security intelligence. Big Data Working Group.

[21] IBM Centre for applied insights. (2014). Raising the game: The IBM business tech trends study.

[22] Islam, S. R., Kwak, D., Kabir, M. H., Hossain, M. & Kwak, K-S. (2015). The internet of things for health care: A comprehensive survey. IEEE Access, 3, 678–708.

[23] Khairat, S., Burke, G., Archambault, H., Schwartz, T., Larson, J. & Ratwani, R. M. (2018). Focus section on health IT usability: Perceived burden of EHRs on physicians at different stages of their career. Applied Clinical Informatics, 9(02), 336–347.

[24] Safran, C., Bloomrosen, M., Hammond, W. E., Labkoff, S., Markel-Fox, S., Tang, P. C. & Detmer, D. E. (2007). Toward a national framework for the secondary use of health data: An American Medical Informatics Association White Paper. Journal of the American Medical Informatics Association, 14(1), 1–9.

[25] Abiodun, M. K., Awotunde, J. B., Ogundokun, R. O., Arowolo, M. O. & Jaglan, V. (2021). Cloud and big data: A mutual benefit for organization development. Journal of Physics: Conference Series, 1767(1), 012020.

[26] Awotunde, J. B., Jimoh, R. G., Oladipo, I. D., Abdulraheem, M., Jimoh, T. B. & Ajamu, G. J. (2021). Big data and data analytics for an enhanced COVID-19 epidemic management. In Studies in Systems, Decision and Control (pp. 11–29). Vol. 2021(358), Springer, Cham.

[27] Barak-Corren, Y., Castro, V. M., Javitt, S., Hoffnagle, A. G., Dai, Y., Perlis, R. H. & Reis, B. Y. (2017). Predicting suicidal behavior from longitudinal electronic health records. American Journal of Psychiatry, 174(2), 154–162.

[28] Miller, A. C., Koeneman, S. H., Arakkal, A. T., Cavanaugh, J. E. & Polgreen, P. M. (September, 2021). Incidence, duration, and risk factors associated with missed opportunities to diagnose herpes simplex encephalitis: A population-based longitudinal study. In Open Forum Infectious Diseases (pp. ofab400). 8(9), Oxford University Press, US.

[29] White, J. V., Guenter, P., Jensen, G., Malone, A., Schofield, M., Group, A. M. W. & Force, A. M. T. (2012). Consensus statement of the Academy of Nutrition and Dietetics/American Society for Parenteral and Enteral Nutrition: Characteristics recommended for the identification and documentation of adult malnutrition (undernutrition). Journal of the Academy of Nutrition and Dietetics, 112(5), 730–738.

[30] Awotunde, J. B., Adeniyi, A. E., Ogundokun, R. O., Ajamu, G. J. & Adebayo, P. O. (2021). MIoT-based big data analytics architecture, opportunities and challenges for enhanced telemedicine systems. Studies in Fuzziness and Soft Computing, 2021(410), 199–220. Springer, Cham.

[31] Wang, L. & Alexander, C. A. (2015). Big data in medical applications and health care. American Medical Journal, 6(1), 1. 10.3844/amjsp.2015.1.8.

[32] Shah, R., Echhpal, R. & Nair, S. (2015). Big data in healthcare analytics. International Journal on Recent and Innovation Trends in Computing and Communication, 10, 134–138.

[33] Hansen, M. M., Miron-Shatz, T., Lau, A. Y. S. & Paton, C. (2014). Big data in science and healthcare: A review of recent literature and perspectives. Contribution of the IMIA social media working group. Yearbook of Medical Informatics, 9, 21–26. 10.15265/IY-2014-0004.

[34] Li, S., Kang, L. & Zhao, X-M. (2014). A survey on evolutionary algorithm based hybrid intelligence in bioinformatics. BioMed Research International, 2014, 8. 10.1155/2014/362738.362738.

[35] Genomics and World Health: Report of the Advisory Committee on Health research. Geneva, WHO (2002). http://www.who.int/genomics/geneticsVSgenomics/en/.

[36] Belle, R. T., Soroushmehr, S. M. R., Navidi, F., Beard, D. A. & Najarian, K. (n. d.). Big Data Analytics in Healthcare. 10.1155/2015/370194.

[37] van Allen, E. M., Wagle, N. & Levy, M. A. (2013). Clinical analysis and interpretation of cancer genome data. Journal of Clinical Oncology, 31, 1825–1833.

[38] Andre, F., Mardis, E., Salm, M., Soria, J. C., Siu, L. L. & Swanton, C. (2014). Prioritizing targets for precision cancer medicine. Annals of Oncology, 25, 2295–2303.

[39] Huang, D. W., Sherman, B. T. & Lempicki, R. A. (2009). Bioinformatics enrichment tools: paths toward the comprehensive functional analysis of large gene lists. Nucleic Acids Research, 37, 1–13.

[40] Khatri, M. S. & Butte, A. J. (2012). Ten years of pathway analysis: Current approaches and outstanding challenges. PLoS Computational Biology, 8, e1002375.

[41] Draghici, S., Khatri, P., Martins, R. P., Ostermeier, G. C. & Krawetz, S. A. (2003). Global functional profiling of gene expression. Genomics, 81, 98–104.

[42] Subramanian, P. T. & Mootha, V. K. (2005). Gene set enrichment analysis: A knowledge-based approach for interpreting genome-wide expression profiles. Proceedings of the National Academy of Sciences of the United States of America, 102, 15545–15550.

[43] Draghici, S., Khatri, P. & Tarca, A. L. (2007). A systems biology approach for pathway level analysis. Genome Research, 17, 1537–1545.

[44] Yalamanchili, H. K., Xiao, Q. W. & Wang, J. (2012). A novel neural response algorithm for protein function prediction. BMC Systems Biology, 6, S19.

[45] Wilkins, M. R., et al. (1999). High-throughput mass spectrometric discovery of protein post-translational modifications. Journal of Molecular Biology, 289, 645–657.

[46] Ren, J., et al. (2008). CSS-Palm 2.0: An updated software for palmitoylation sites prediction. Protein Engineering, Design, and Selection, 21, 639–644.

[47] Issa, N. T., Byers, S. W. & Dakshanamurthy, S. (2014). Big data: The next frontier for innovation in therapeutics and healthcare. Expert Review of Clinical Pharmacology, 7, 293–298. 10.1586/17512433.2014.905201.

[48] Awotunde, J. B., Adeniyi, A. E., Ajagbe, S. A. & González-Briones, A. (2022). Natural computing and unsupervised learning methods in smart healthcare data-centric operations. In Cognitive and Soft Computing Techniques for the Analysis of Healthcare Data (pp. 165–190). Academic Press.

[49] Bharal, P. & Halfon, A. (2013). Making sense of big data in insurance. ACORD and MarkLogic.

[50] Erdman, G. & Keefe, D. F. (2013). Grand challenge: Applying regulatory science and big data to improve medical device innovation. IEEE Transactions on Biomedical Engineering, 60, 700–706. 10.1109/TBME.2013.2244600.

[51] Schultz, T. (2013). Turning healthcare challenges into big data opportunities: A use-case review across the pharmaceutical development lifecycle. Bulletin Association for Information Science and Technology, 39, 34–40.

[52] Awotunde, J. B., Jimoh, R. G., Folorunso, S. O., Adeniyi, E. A., Abiodun, K. M. & Banjo, O. O. (2021). Privacy and security concerns in IoT-based healthcare systems. Internet of Things, 2021, 105–134. Springer, Cham.

[53] White, S. E. (2014). A review of big data in health care: Challenges and opportunities. Open Access Bioinformatics, 6, 13–18. 10.2147/OAB.S50519.

[54] Awotunde, J. B., Ajagbe, S. A., Oladipupo, M. A., Awokola, J. A., Afolabi, O. S., Mathew, T. O. & Oguns, Y. J. (October, 2021). An improved machine learnings diagnosis technique for COVID-19 pandemic using chest X-ray images. Communications in Computer and Information Science, 2021, 1455 CCIS, 319–330.

[55] Awotunde, J. B., Folorunso, S. O., Bhoi, A. K., Adebayo, P. O. & Ijaz, M. F. (2021). Disease diagnosis system for IoT-based wearable body sensors with machine learning algorithm. Hybrid Intelligent Systems Reference Library, 2021(209), 201–222. Springer, Singapore.

[56] Nambiar, R., Bhardwaj, R., Sethi, A. & Vargheese, R. (2013). A look at challenges and opportunities of big data analytics in healthcare. 2013 IEEE International Conference on Big Data, 17–22. 10.1109/BigData.2013.6691753.

[57] Adriaens, T., Tricarico, E., Reyserhove, L., De Jesus Cardoso, A., Gervasini, E., Lopez Canizares, C. & Tsiamis, K. (2021). Data-validation solutions for citizen science data on invasive alien species. In Publications Office of the European Union. Luxembourg.

[58] Folorunso, S. O., Awotunde, J. B., Adeboye, N. O. & Matiluko, O. E. (2022). Data classification model for COVID-19 pandemic. Studies in Systems, Decision and Control, 2022(378), 93–118.

[59] Priyanka, K. & Kulennavar, N. (2014). A survey on big data analytics in health care. International Journal of Computer Science and Information Technology, 5, 5865–5868.

[60] Halamka, J. D. (2014). Early experiences with big data at an academic medical center. Health Affairs, 33, 1132–1138. 10.1377/hlthaff.2014.0031.

[61] Bottles, K. & Begoli, E. (2014). Understanding the pros and cons of big data analytics. Physician Executive, 40, 6–12.

[62] Hsieh, J. C., Li, A. H. & Yang, C. C. (2013). Mobile, cloud and big data computing: Contributions, challenges and new directions in telecardiology. International Journal of Environmental Research and Public Health, 10, 6131–6153. 10.3390/ijerph10116131.

[63] Warner, D. (2013). Safe de-identification of big data is critical to health care. Health Information Management.

[64] Awotunde, J. B., Chakraborty, C. & Adeniyi, A. E. (2021). Intrusion detection in industrial internet of things network-based on deep learning model with rule-based feature selection. Wireless Communications and Mobile Computing, 2021, 7154587.

[65] Elsayed, W., Elhoseny, M., Sabbeh, S. & Riad, A. (2017). Self-maintenance model for wireless sensor networks. Computers and Electrical Engineering, https://doi.org/10.1016/j.compeleceng.2017.12.022.

[66] Elhoseny, M., Yuan, X., Yu, Z., Mao, C., El-Minir, H. K. & Riad, A. M. (2015). Balancing energy consumption in heterogeneous wireless sensor networks using genetic algorithm. IEEE Communication Letter, 19, 2194–2197. https://doi.org/10.1109/LCOMM.2014.2381226.

[67] Awotunde, J. B., Bhoi, A. K. & Barsocchi, P. (2021). Hybrid cloud/fog environment for healthcare: An exploratory study, opportunities, challenges, and future prospects. Intelligent Systems Reference Library, 2021(209), 1–20.

[68] O'Donoghue, J. & Herbert, J. (2012). Data management within mhealth environments: Patient sensors, mobile devices, and databases. Journal of Data and Information Quality, 4(5), 1–5, 20. https://doi.org/10.1145/2378016.2378021.

[69] Awotunde, J. B., Ogundokun, R. O. & Misra, S. (2021). Cloud and IoMT-based big data analytics system during COVID-19 pandemic. Internet of Things, 2021, 181–201.

[70] Groves, P., Kayyali, B., Knott, D. & Kuiken, S. V. (2016). The 'big data' revolution in healthcare: Accelerating value and innovation.

[71] Kumari, S. (February, 2018). Big data analytics for healthcare system. 2018 IADS International Conference on Computing, Communications & Data Engineering (CCODE), 7–8.

[72] Benhlima, L. (2018). Big data management for healthcare systems: Architecture, requirements, and implementation. Advances in Bioinformatics, 2018.

[73] Andreu-Perez, J., Poon, C. C. Y., Merrifield, R. D., Wong, S. T. C. & Yang, G. Z. (2015). Big Data for health. IEEE Journal of Biomedical and Health Informatics, 19, 1193–1208. https://doi.org/10.1109/JBHI.2015.2450362.

[74] Palanisamy, V. & Thirunavukarasu, R. (2019). Implications of big data analytics in developing healthcare frameworks–A review. Journal of King Saud University-Computer and Information Sciences, 31(4), 415–425.

[75] Martin-Sanchez, F. & Verspoor, K. (2014). Big data in medicine is driving big changes. Yearbook of Medical Informatics, 9, 14–20. https://doi.org/10.15265/IY-2014-0020.

[76] Rahman, F., Bhuiyan, M. Z. A. & Ahamed, S. I. (2017). A privacy preserving framework for RFID based healthcare systems. Future Generation Computer Systems, 72, 339–352.

[77] Pramanik, M. I., Lau, R. Y., Demirkan, H. & Azad, M. A. K. (2017). Smart health: Big data enabled health paradigm within smart cities. Expert Systems with Applications, 87, 370–383.

[78] Xavier, L. D. & Thirunavukarasu, R. (2017). A distributed tree-based ensemble learning approach for efficient structure prediction of protein. Training, 227.

[79] Sicari, S., Rizzardi, A., Grieco, L., Piro, G. & Coen-Porisini, A. (2017). A policy enforcement framework for Internet of Things applications in the smart health. Smart Health, 3, 39–74.

[80] Mahmud, S., Iqbal, R. & Doctor, F. (2016). Cloud enabled data analytics and visualization framework for health-shocks prediction. Future Generation Computer Systems, 65, 169–181.

[81] Sakr, S. & Elgammal, A. (2016). Towards a comprehensive data analytics framework for smart healthcare services. Big Data Research, 4, 44–58.

[82] Schmitt, C., Shoffner, M., Owen, P., Wang, X., & Lamm, B. (2013). Security and privacy in the era of big data. The SMW, a Technological Solution to the Challenge of Data Leakage, 1(2).

[83] Awotunde, J.B., Panigrahi, R., Shukla, S. et al. Big data analytics enabled deep convolutional neural network for the diagnosis of cancer. Knowl Inf Syst (2023). https://doi.org/10.1007/s10115-023-01971-x.

Jay Patel
11 Big data security and privacy in healthcare

Abstract: The rapidly growing technology in the field of biomedical and healthcare, medical and also after the introduction the digitizing medical records there has been the flood in the amount of data in terms of complexity, diversity and timeliness in the healthcare industry. If the data can be utilized potentially then we can see the valuable health outcomes, lowering costs, gaining important insights and many more. This revolutionary shift from reactive to proactive healthcare can play a valuable role by increasing economic growth as overall healthcare costs decrease. But the privacy and security issues assigned with data have become hurdles in the way of the healthcare industry and we are unable to capitalize on it up to its potential. In this paper, we will analyze some of the state-of-art methods and techniques used to tackle the privacy and security issues in the field of the healthcare industry and also discuss the limitation associated with the methods.

Keywords: Big data, security, healthcare, privacy

11.1 Introduction

The current trend of digitizing healthcare workflows and transferring to digitalized patient records had brought a revolution in the healthcare industry. Due to this, the quantity of data will increase as more and more people will follow this path in terms of diversity, complexity and timeliness which can be known as big data [1]. Big data exploit the traditional methods of computing, storage and communication capabilities as it refers to the mass collection of a complex and large data set. A recent study states that the major six use cases of big data that will decrease the cost for adverse events are monitoring, readmissions, patients, triage, health insurance and treatment optimization for several diseases of the organs [2]. In the last two decades, several factors are leading to the urge of big data that can fulfill like the healthcare expenditures are estimated at around 17.6 GDP which is increased at an alarming rate. In such a case big data can come up as a feasible solution to make the profound change that can improve the management, care process and delivery while also lowering the overall healthcare cost. McKinsey Global Institute estimates that if we can capitalize on the use of big data up to its potential then a $100 billion increase in profits annually for healthcare industries [33]. This can give the doctor power to make them more accu-

Jay Patel, Department of Information and Communication Technology, School of Technology, Pandit Deendayal Petroleum University, Gandhinagar, 382007, Gujarat, India, e-mail: jay.hict19@sot.pdpu.ac.in

rate decisions on patient treatment by accessing the real-time data generated by big data analytics.

An increase in the health insurance premium and increasing healthcare services cost urge for proactive healthcare management and wellness. This revolutionary shift from reactive to proactive healthcare can play a valuable role by increasing economic growth as overall healthcare costs decrease. The recent technological advancement has played a crucial role in empowering proactive healthcare. For example, with IoT, the sensors are attached to the patient's body which provides real-time health-related data that can allow the health workers to act appropriately in case of emergency. Electronic health records (EHRs) which can be used to digitalize healthcare with integrated analytics can be the next research area in healthcare information technology. With the use of EHR, a healthcare organization can provide enhanced patient care due to access to shareable, accurate and sharable healthcare records [34].

Big data can provide the healthcare industry an endless opportunity from diagnosis to treatment, to population health management and eventually capital and strategic planning. Data can play a very crucial role as with the trend many healthcare leaders are transferring from volume-based to value-based business models [35]. As the name suggests big data has the data in mass volume so from it the first task for the healthcare industry is to fetch accurate and actionable real-time data also to integrate the health management system with social, environmental, financial, clinical and genomic data to make it actionable will be crucial for real-time analytics and patient care. The next step in the value-based model is to adapt the new all-inclusive scale for monitoring the wellness and health-related data of patients like social, environmental, psychological, physical, clinical and many more. As there can be a case in which the vital signs of a patient can be seen as normal but the environmental and psychological can derive to some consequence due to this there is a need of considering the various factor from multiple domains that can be crucial for the patient condition in the real-time holistic model for healthcare.

The important factor due to which big data can be a boosting factor for healthcare is the real-time availability and to achieve it, we need IoT devices that can provide real-time monitoring. As Gartner estimates that there is an explosion in the IoT devices the amount of data generated by it will be large enough to be placed in big data [36]. There can be many types of IoT devices but the primary focus will always remain on low-cost and low-powered constraint resource usage [37]. With the introduction of the body sensor network (BSN) [38] it can provide healthcare workers extra privilege to monitor the parameters affecting the patient and act accordingly. Thus, from all the above facilities that big data can provide it will be a revolutionary change if we can use it up to its extent. Nevertheless, such changes can only be enjoyed if privacy and security are kept at the core of any design and development.

When we talk about data, security and privacy are the two important factors that are always attached to it. As we saw above big data can bring a major transformation still the adoption of it is not up to that much extent due to concern over security and privacy. The concern over security and privacy of sensitive information not only in healthcare but also in some other fields is increasing day by day. Also, some studies found that the top-bottom, reactive, technology-centric approach is not enough to protect the sensitive information of organizations and patients [3]. In 2013, 49,000 patient records had been compromised due to theft of an unencrypted USB flash drive containing patient records at Kaiser Permanente [39]. In 2012, Verizon's data breach investigation report found 621 confirmed data breaches from 47,000 reported security incidents [40]. A study performed on patient data security and privacy showed that 94% of hospitals had at least one data breach in the past couple of years [41]. In most of these cases, it was seen that the breach has been performed from the inside rather than the outside and the external breach was mostly performed from China, USA and European countries.

As there are technological advancements the threats and vulnerabilities associated with it also came and are expected to grow in the upcoming years. Due to the Affordable Care Act [42] there will be an increase in healthcare insurance which can become an attractive point for hackers which will open the floodgate of various security breaches in the healthcare industry. Thus, to protect the data a preventive, proactive approach must be taken by the organization by keeping future security and privacy need in mind.

In this paper, we will discuss some of the techniques and methods used in this domain with its main goal and use case and also find out all are the drawbacks related to those methods. We will start by exploring the security concern and some of the studies carried out till now for big data in healthcare. Then we will also explore the privacy-related concern for big data in the healthcare domain. Finally, we will state the limitation associated with the proposed methods and the necessary steps that can be taken to deal with security and privacy risks before concluding the paper and highlighting the future work.

11.2 Related works

In this section, we will see some of the inventions in which big data is assisting factor to improve the overall healthcare experience for the patient implemented by some of the profound healthcare organizations.

Institute name	Functionality	Reference
South Tyneside NHS Foundation	It provides the acute community health service in England which aims to provide high quality, compensate and safe care for the patient in real time but needs improvement in resource allocation and wait-time to act early on any situation.	South Tyneside NHS Foundation Trust. Harnessing analytics for strategic planning, operational decision making and end-to-end improvements in patient care. IBM Smarter Planet brief, 2013.

(continued)

Institute name	Functionality	Reference
UNC Health Care (UNCHC)	It has implemented that the system based on natural language processing in which health worker gets instant access to analyze the unstructured patient data. It aims to provide safe care to a high-risk patient by analyzing a high quantity of unstructured data to fetch insightful information and predict the readmission risk promptly.	UNC Health Care relies on analytics to better manage medical data and improve patient care. IBM Press release, 2013.
Indiana Health Information Exchange	It had implemented a robust and secured system that can provide healthcare information linking more than 90 hospitals, rehabilitation centers, and other healthcare providers in that area in such a way that the information of any patient is only accessible to doctor office or the hospital in which patient is hoisted.	Indiana Health Information Exchange. http://www.ihie.org/. Accessed 24 March 2016.
Kaiser Permanente medical network	It had implemented a medical network-based system which estimate to manage a large volume of data ranging from 26.5 petabytes to 44 petabytes with more than 9 million members.	Transforming healthcare through big data, strategies for leveraging big data in the healthcare industry. Institute for Health, 2013.
Institute of Technology Ontario	It is made in collaboration between IBM and the Institute of Technology Ontario launches Artemis project which monitors the new borns by real-time analysis, data mining and retrospective analysis on the psychological and clinical information of the patient.	Artemis. http://hir.uoit.ca/cms/?q=node/24. Accessed 21 May 2016.
Italian medicines agency	It analyzes a large amount of clinical data due to expensive new medicine and reassesses the medicine price based on the result obtained.	Groves P, Kayyali B, Knott D, Kuiken SV. The big data revolution in healthcare, accelerating value and innovation, 2013.
World Health Organization	It has launched the project named "Be Healthy Be mobile" under the mDiabetes initiative in which text messaging and apps are used to control, prevent and manage non-communicable diseases such as cancer, diabetes and heart disease.	WHO. Mobile phones help people with diabetes to manage fasting and feasting during Ramadan. Features, 2014.

11.3 Big data security in healthcare

11.3.1 Introduction

If we visualize any Healthcare organization in terms of data management then its primary workflow would be to store, maintain and make the data flow between entities efficient in a proper manner. At most places, the patient records are stored at the outside data centers that possess varying levels of security. Although most of the data centers have HIPAA certification but it is not fully reliable as it focuses more on policies and procedures rather than implementing them. To make it more complicated the data flow came from diverse sources which bring extra complexity to storage, processing and communication. As shown in Figure 11.1 the various data of patients like social, financial, environmental, clinical, physical, genomic and physiological are coming from various sources to the data centers.

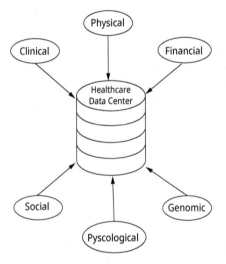

Figure 11.1: Various data of patients.

Providing security to this data has been the main hurdle to the industry over the decades. If we also go through the history then healthcare is the prime suspect for publicly disclosed data breaches. In a data breach usually hacker uses the data mining approach to carry out sensitive information and disclosed it publicly. Thus, it has become an important concern for the organization to implement healthcare data security and also satisfy healthcare compliance needs.

11.3.2 Data security techniques in healthcare

There are numerous technologies used for protecting data of the healthcare industry but we will discuss the main four widely used technologies.

11.3.2.1 Authentication

It can be defined as confirming or establishing the claim that is made by one are true and authentic. It plays an important role in any organization that protects the user details by securing the success of the corporate network and validating that a user is who he claims to be.

Certain cryptographic protocols help to prevent men-in-the-middle (MITM) attacks when we want to transfer something between two endpoints. For example, the transport layer security (TLS) and its other forms [4]. Then there is the secure sockets layer (SSL) which provides security for over the internet communications. In these protocols, the segments of the network get encrypted end-to-end at the transport layer. These protocols along with its variant are being used widely over web applications such as faxing, messaging, email services and web browsing.

Somu et al. [5] proposed the one pad algorithm which uses a simple authentication model which eliminates the password communication over the serves. Thus, we need such a system in the healthcare industry that should verify the identity of both the providers and consumers to ensure the security of data and systems.

11.3.2.2 Encryption

It ensures to prevent unauthorized access to sensitive data by encoding the data into a form that cannot be decoded between entities. The main aim of it is to protect and maintain the ownership of the data throughout the lifecycle which is from passing one endpoint to other. This can also provide the protection of exposing the data breaches such as packet sniffing and theft of storage devices.

Organizations should ensure to use the efficient encryption algorithm which is not only stronger but also feasible for the consumer and provider to use and easily scalable to add new records. To make in the way in which the keys held by both entities should be minimum. There are various types of encryption algorithm like RSA, AES and RC6 [7–9], DES, 3DES, Blowfish, RC4 [6], IDEA and Rijndael but choosing the most efficient algorithm according to their need is also an important factor required to look by an organization.

11.3.2.3 Data masking

It replaces the sensitive data information with unreadable values and the only difference between encryption and masking is that we can't retrieve the original information after masking it out while we can decrypt the encrypted text to get the original value. The information like name, security number, zip code and date of birth is masked by using a de-identifying strategy. It is used for live data anonymization.

Swaney and Samrati [10, 11] proposed the k-anonymity algorithm which performs well against identity disclosure but breaks against attribute disclosure. Truta and Vinay [12] came up with p-sensitive anonymity which performs well against both the disclosure. There are also other methods in which noises are added to data, replacing rows with a column, replacing a group of k records with single representing k copies, etc. But the only problem with these methods is difficulty in anonymizing high-dimensional data sets [13, 14]. The main advantage this technology gives is that it reduces to apply any other security layer after masking the data.

11.3.2.4 Access control

After the authorization, the user can enter the information system; still the access given to the user is controlled by the admin. It is used to grant several levels of permission to the user. It ensures to keep control over the user activity according to the specific rights and permission given to that specific user.

Various solutions can be used to provide access control with ease and can be efficient. Attribute-based access control (ABAC) [15, 16] and role-based access control (RBAC) [17] are the most popular and widely used model though they have shown certain limitation challenges while used alone in the medical area.

Zhou and Wen [18] proposed the efficient dynamic access control system on cloud-oriented storage which also used the ciphertext based on any symmetric encryption algorithm and (CP-ABE).

Han et al. [32] proposed a robust zero-watermarking scheme to tackle the security concern of the teledermatology healthcare framework which is based on federated learning.

Due to the diversity and complexity of the data, the traditional method cannot be applied directly to the data set. Also, with the increase in trend in the healthcare industry to move forward with healthcare cloud solutions, to secure the software as a service (SaaS) architecture is challenging with diversified data and its format. Hence before exposing data to analytics data governance is an important step.

11.3.3 Data governance

Data governance is the first step in managing and regulating healthcare data as the healthcare industry moves to a value-based business model. As the data gets generated by BSN it will be diverse in terms of nature so our main goal is to have common data representation that also confines with industry standards by normalization, standardization and data governance.

11.3.4 Real-time security analysis

Currently, there has been a flood of elegant attacks ranging from distributed denial of service (DDoS) to stealthy malware experienced by the healthcare industry which urges the need of analyzing security risk and predicting threat sources in real-time. To make the situation even worse the social engineering attacks are also increasing rapidly and it is difficult to predict such attacks as it is based on human cognitive behavior. For example, cognitive bias: "it is a pattern of deviation in judgment, whereby influences about other people and situations may be drawn in an illogical manner" [43, 44] and it can happen mainly with an elderly aged patient. So, all the above scenarios should be taken into consideration while designing or developing any end-to-end system.

In IoT resource-constrained devices security implementation can be challenging and as the number of devices increases, it will become more and more complex. Also, the state-of-the-art method of symmetric and asymmetric key distribution system is unable to scale to a greater number of IoT devices. So, there is a demand to form a new scalable key management system that can transfer the data between networks securely to integrate IoT with big data in the cloud.

As the healthcare industry going to enjoy the power that comes with big data to make an accurate decision, security will always remain the core for any system. Real-time security intelligence can play a crucial role in better risk management as it provides the real-time monitoring of the threat so the necessary steps can be taken before affecting the vulnerability to the system.

11.3.5 Inference

We have discussed the four widely used technology that has been used till now for protecting the data in the healthcare sector. After analyzing all the techniques, we can conclude that although all methods are capable to protect sensitive information with the development of the technologies and attackers coming with new attacks the conjunctions of all technology would give another layer of protection to the data. For example, encryption with access control, authorization, data masking, etc.

11.4 Big data privacy in healthcare

11.4.1 Background

Data security refers to control the access of the data throughout the data lifecycle while data privacy is to set the access to a user based on privacy policies and laws. Privacy referred to who can view which type of data like financial, personal, confidential or medical information. The challenges in patient privacy are growing concerns in the medical field as attackers target the information systems to smuggle sensitive data. A baby-care coup got sent to a teenage baby girl without knowing of the parents by Target Corporation was mentioned in one of the *Forbes* magazines which can be considered as an alarm over patient privacy [19]. Developers and analytics should get awareness from this incident to verify that their application should stick to the privacy agreements and that sensitive data should be kept secured regardless of a change in application and privacy guidelines.

To make the sensitive information of the user in safe hands various countries had established their data protection laws and policies in the healthcare domain. We will discuss some of the laws and features of some countries in the below section.

11.4.2 Data protection laws and policies

Country	Law	Features
USA	HIPAA Act Patient Safety and Quality Improvement Act (PSQIA) HITECH Act	HIPAA Act in which any e-transaction related to healthcare are required to establish the national standards. Patient Safety and Quality in which before giving any information related to healthcare to anyone one has to sign a disclosure and the Safety Work Product of a patient should not be disclosed. [20] Improvement Act (PSQIA) in which civil penalty should be paid if anyone violates the confidentiality provisions HITECH act in which establishment should be made to protect and secure the privacy of electronic health information.
India	IT Act IT (Amendment) Act	IT Act and IT (Amendment) Act in which if the information of any person gets compromised then the organization has to pay him compensation. Also, if anybody is found doing unethical things like leaking or providing sensitive information of the user to another person then imprisonment and/or fine punishment will be taken against the person.

(continued)

Country	Law	Features
Canada	Personal Information Protection and Electronic Documents Act ("PIPEDA")	Personal Information Protection and Electronic Documents Act ("PIPEDA") in which everyone has given right to know the reason behind the collection or using any of their personal information which also indirectly makes the organization think about protecting the information of the user [21]
UK	Data Protection Act (DPA)	Data Protection Act (DPA) provides the way to users for full control over their data and the organization should not transfer the data to any country which is outside the European Economic Area unless they provide the assurance to protect and keep the data right of the user secured.
Russia	Russian Federal Law on Personal Data	Russian Federal Law on Personal Data in which the organization has to take full responsibility to make all the technical measures in order to protect the data against any attack or accidental access.
EU	Data Protection Directive	Data Protection Directive protects the right of people's privacy in terms of processing their personal information [45]
Morocco	The 09-08 act, dated on 18 February 2009	Data controllers are used to limit the usage of personal and sensitive information in any data processing task and protect one's privacy [46].
Brazil	Constitution	Sensitive information like the image, honor and private life of any individual is impregnable and any material or moral damage to it without assured right will be resulting in violation.
Angola	Data Protection Law	Authorization from ADP is required before any collection and processing of any sensitive data is to be performed.

11.4.3 Big data privacy preserving techniques

In this section, we will discuss a few state-of-art methods that were being used for privacy-preserving in big data for patient privacy and some other methods with some medication to older methods to get a better result.

11.4.3.1 De-identification

This is the traditional information in which sensitive data prevent getting exposed by eliminating the information that can identify the patient which can be done within two ways: one is to remove specific parameter that identifies the patient or with a static method in which the patient verifies that all the identifiers get off recorded. The de-identification in big data will not work in that extant because the attacker might find the sensitive information from big data. Thus, the methods like k-anonymity, l-diversity and t-closeness have been introduced that eliminate the drawback of the de-identification method and provide a better result.

11.4.3.2 k-anonymity

Here the probability of re-identification is inversely proposal to the value k. The greater the value of k (i.e., replacement of the group) the lesser are the chances to retrieve the sensitive information back by an attacker. The only problem in this method is that if we take a higher value of k then there is a possibility of distortions of the data which can lead to higher information loss through this method. Also, for the re-identification of an individual if quasi-identifiers data is used to make a connection to publicly available data then there is a risk to reveal sensitive attributes like a disease of the patient. Various other methods based on k-anonymity are been proposed to eliminate the cons of this method but none of them are efficient [22, 23].

11.4.3.3 L-diversity

It is used the protect the privacy of the data by hiding the small groups of the data. This model can be considered as an extension of k-anonymity in which the granularity of the data is reduced by suppression and generalization such that the records get maps to at least k various records. The cons of k-anonymity which is k referred to as a level of protection of an individual corresponds to securing the sensitive data that was suppressed or generalized gets eliminated with other few weaknesses in l-diversity. If the sensitive attributes of data fell under similar ranges then as the l-diversity depends on the range of attributes, the fiction data gets added; though by implementing this the security of the data gets increased which may create a challenge in the analysis of data at later stages [24].

11.4.3.4 T-closeness

It is an extension of the l-diversity method as the model (hierarchical/equal distance) [25, 26] handles the value of attribute distinctly from the distribution of data values for that attribute. Handling the distinct data increases the size and variety of the data and also the probability of re-identification gets increased.

11.4.3.5 HybrEx

Cloud computing is also one of the fields through which the big data associated with the healthcare industry can be managed with ease through the data lifecycle method in the cloud that encounters security issues [31]. The hybrid execution model ensures that cloud computing happens with confidentiality and privacy [27]. This model uses two clouds: first one is the public cloud when an organization declares that the specific amount doesn't require confidentiality and privacy then the model execute computation happens on the public cloud, while if there is any sensitive information that requires privacy and security then the model executes its computation in the private cloud. The model is also capable to provide the data from both the public and private cloud to an application as per its requirement with safety and privacy.

The drawback of this model is that it does not handle any key that is generated in the private and public cloud in the linking phase and manage the things with an only cloud [28].

11.4.3.6 Identity-based anonymization

Intel created the open-source architecture for anonymization to extract the maximum number of benefits of cloud storage which gives accessibility for both de-identifying and re-identifying weblog records [29, 30]. The anonymized data containing sensitive information which were masked were found defenseless against the attacks by Intel. The reason behind this vulnerability is that the User-Agent information is strongly connected to specific users. Thus, from this evaluation, we can conclude that only the data masking and generalized data are also required to be examined carefully before checking if they are capable of resisting any attacks that may get carried out.

11.4.4 Inference

Thus, from the above discussion, we can conclude that there are many flaws in the traditional data privacy methods though the method derived from it with some modification performs better than the state-of-art one but still more research can be carried out in this domain and the methods that give more accurate result need to be founded. The laws applicable by the government also restrict the organization to follow the guidelines of the government in terms of the privacy of their users.

11.5 Future work

Apart from this above-discussed methods there are many other methods like haystack-hiding a needle, storage path encryption, attribute-based encryption access control and homomorphic encryption, but still, there is always a risk of imposing the data. Thus, this domain is currently not that much explored by the researcher and furthermore study to find out the effective method in this area can be considered as a future work for the researcher. As technological advancement always comes with threats and vulnerabilities it will always be going to be a challenging task to keep sensitive information secured. Though there are various big data security and privacy techniques used in other domains can also be reviewed to see the impact factor it brings if used in the healthcare industry.

11.6 Conclusion

The power that big data gives in the healthcare domain is immense to clinical care, knowledge discovery, personal health management and drive research in the healthcare domain. Numerous hurdles and challenges are restricting the industry to make use of big data with great extant. Security and privacy can be considered as the major barrier for the researcher in this domain.

In this paper, we started by investigating the challenges and hurdles that the current healthcare industry is facing in terms of big data security. Then we moved on to some of the techniques and methods that can be beneficial for the healthcare industry in order of security and privacy of their big data with their main aim and also some of the drawbacks. From the above discussion we can conclude that big data if used at its potential then can be the boosting factor in the healthcare industry as from some of the related work, we can see that although to date we are not utilizing the big data up to its extent still it has increased the overall healthcare experience. The major hurdle to achieving this is the privacy and the security concern assigned to the data but proper implementation of the robust and secured system can help to achieve our goal and bring the major revolution in the healthcare industry.

References

[1] Burghard, C. (2012). Big data and analytics key to accountable care success. IDC Health Insights.
[2] Bates, D., Saria, S., Ohno-Machado, L., Shah, A., et al. (2014). Big Data in health care: Using analytics to identify and manage high-risk and high-cost patients. Health Affairs, 33(7), 1123–1131. https://doi.org/10.1377/hlthaff.2014.0041.
[3] Houlding, D., MSc, CISSP: Health information at risk: Successful strategies for healthcare security andprivacy Healthcare IT Program Of ce Intel Corporation, white paper 2011.

[4] Rui Zhangand Ling Liu Security models and requirements for healthcare application clouds in IEEE 3rd International Conference on Cloud Computing, (2010).
[5] Somu, N., Gangaa, A. & Sriram, V. S. (2014). Authentication service in hadoop using one time pad. Indian Journal of Science and Technology, 7, 56–62.
[6] Fluhrer, S., Mantin, I. & Shamir, A. (2001). Weakness in the Key schedualing algorithm of RC4, 8th Annual International Workshop on Selected Areas in Cryptography, Springer-Verlag London, UK.
[7] Federal Information Processing Standards Publication 197. (2001). Specification for the Advanced Encryption Standards (AES).
[8] Shafer, J., Rixner, S. & Cox, A. L. (March, 2010). The hadoop distributed file system: Balancing portability and performance. Proc. of 2010 IEEE Int. Symposium on Performance Analysis of Systems & Software (ISPASS), White Plain, NY, pp. 122–133.
[9] Somu, N., Gangaa, A. & Sriram, V. S. (2014). Authentication service in hadoop using one time pad. Indian Journal of Science and Technology, 7, 56–62.
[10] Sweeney, L. (2002). Achieving k-anonymity privacy protection using generalization and suppression. international Journal on Uncertainty, Fuzziness and Knowledge-based Systems, 10, 571–588.
[11] Samrati, P. (2001). Protecting respondents' identities in microdata release. IEEE Transactions on Knowledge and Data Engineering, 13, 1010–1027.
[12] Truta, T. M. & Vinay, B. (2006). Privacy protection: p-sensitive k-anonymity property, in Proceedings of 22nd International Conference on Data Engineering Workshops, p. 94.
[13] Spruill, N. (1983). The confidentiality and analytic usefulness of masked business microdata, in Proceedings on survey research methods, pp. 602–607.
[14] Chawala, S., Dwork, C., Sheny, F. M., Smith, A. & Wee, H. (2005). Towards privacy in public databases, in Proceedings on second theory of cryptography conference.
[15] Science Applications International Corporation (SAIC). (May, 2004). Role-Based Access Control (RBAC) Role Engineering Process Version 3.0.
[16] Mohan, A. & Blough, D. M. (2010). An attribute-based authorization policy framework with dynamic conflict resolution, Proceedings of the 9th Symposium on Identity and Trust on the Internet.
[17] Hagner, M. (2007). Security infrastructure and national patent summary. In Tromso Telemedicine and eHealth Conference.
[18] Zhou, H. & Wen, Q. (2014). Data security accessing for hdfs based on attribute-group in cloud computing, in International Conference on Logistics Engineering, Management and Computer Science (LEMCS 2014).
[19] Hill, K. (2012). How target figured out a teen girl was pregnant before her father did, Forbes, Inc.
[20] Data Protection Laws of the World. (2017). DLA Piper. [Online]. Available: http://www.dlapiperdataprotection.com
[21] Fluhrer, S., Mantin, I. & Shamir, A. (2001). Weakness in the Key schedualing algorithm of RC4, 8th Annual International Workshop on Selected Areas in Cryptography, Springer-Verlag London, UK.
[22] Iyenger, V. (2002). Transforming data to satisfy privacy constraints. Proceedings of the ACM SIGKDD, 279–288.
[23] LeFevre, K., Ramakrishnan, R. & DeWitt, D. J. (2006). Modorian multidimensional k-anonymity, in Proceedings of the ICDE, p. 25.
[24] Sweeney, L. (2002). K-anonymity: A model for protecting privacy. International Journal of Uncertainty, Fuzziness, 10(5), 557–570.
[25] Li, N., et al. (2007). t-Closeness: Privacy beyond k-anonymity and L-diversity. In: Data engineering (ICDE) IEEE 23rd international conference.
[26] Samarati, P. & Sweeney, L. (1998). Protecting privacy when disclosing information: K-anonymity and its enforcement through generalization and suppression. Technical Report SRI -CSL-98–04, SRI Computer Science Laboratory.

[27] Ko, S. Y., Jeon, K. & Morales, R. (2011). The HybrEx model for confidentiality and privacy in cloud computing. In: 3rd USENIX workshop on hot topics in cloud computing, HotCloud'11, Portland.
[28] Priyank, J., Manasi, G. & Nilay, K. (2016). Big data privacy: A technological perspective and review. Journal of Big Data.
[29] Sedayao, J. & Bhardwaj, R. (2014). Making big data, privacy, and anonymization work together in the enterprise: Experiences and issues. Big Data Congress.
[30] Yong, Y., et al. (2016). Cloud data integrity checking with an identity-based auditing mechanism from RSA. Future Generation Computer Systems, 62, 85–91.
[31] Patel, A. D., Jhaveri, R., Parmar, J. & Shah, S. (2010). Security Issues and Recommendations for the Lifecycle of Data in Cloud Computing. https://www.academia.edu/35389344/Security_Issues_and_Recommendations_for_the_Lifecycle_of_Data_in_Cloud_Computing
[32] Han, B., Jhaveri, R., Wang, H., Qiao, D. & Du, J. (2021). Application of robust zerowatermarking scheme based on federated learning for securing the healthcare data. IEEE Journal of Biomedical and Health Informatics, 1. https://doi.org/10.1109/jbhi.2021.3123936
[33] Groves, P., Kayyali, B., Knott, D. & Kuiken, S. V. (2013). The 'Big Data' Revolution in Healthcare. McKinsey & Company.
[34] EHR incentive programs. (2014). [Online]. Available: https://www.cms.gov/Regulations-and-Guidance/Legislation/EHRIncentivePrograms/index.html.
[35] Brown, M. M., Brown, G. C., Sharma, S. & Landy, J. (2003). Health care economic analyses and value-based medicine. Survey of Ophthalmology, 48(2), 204–223.
[36] Middleton, P., Kjeldsen, P. & Tully, J. (2013). Forecast: The Internet of Things, Worldwide, Gartner.
[37] Atzori, L., Iera, A. & Morabito, G. (2010). The internet of things: A survey. Computer Networks, 54(15), 2787–2805.
[38] Hanson, M., Powell, H., Barth, A., Ringgenberg, K., Calhoun, B., Aylor, J. & Lach, J. (2009). Body area sensor networks: Challenges and opportunities. Computer, 58–65.
[39] McCann, E. (2013). Kaiser reports second fall data breach, Healthcare IT News.
[40] Verizon. (2013). Data breach investigation report, Verizon.
[41] P. Institute. (2012). Third annual benchmark study on patient privacy and data security, Ponemon Institute LLC.
[42] Public Law 111 – 148 – Patient Protection and Affordable Care Act, U.S. Government Printing Office (GPO), (2013).
[43] Haselton, M. G., Nettle, D. & Andrews, P. W. (2005). The evolution of cognitive bias. In The Handbook of Evolutionary Psychology. John Wiley & Sons Inc, 724–746.
[44] Health insurance portability and accountability act. (1996). U.S. Government Printing Office. [Online]. Available: http://www.gpo.gov/fdsys/pkg/PLAW104publ191/html/PLAW-104publ191.htm
[45] Privacy and Big Data – Terence Craig & Mary, E.Ludloff.
[46] Data protection overview (Morocco) – Florence Chafiol-Chaumont and Anne-Laure Falkman, (2013).

Arpan Maity, Sushruta Mishra

12 Healthcare encryption using augmented intelligence

Abstract: In the present generation of technical and industrial revolution, augmented intelligence has become part of every day's life. No doubt this technology is also being used in modern healthcare system. The use of augmented intelligence along with the help of machine learning and neural networks has made the medical science more advanced than ever before. But with the goods of advancement, there comes the threats from the attackers, who are ready to break into any systems from the weakest point they can find. So we have attempted to build a neural network model for brain tumor detection, and storing the data in such a way that it becomes secure from the attackers. For model building, we have used ResNetV2 model and for security purpose, we have encrypted the classified data using elliptical curve cryptography (ECC) algorithm. To make the algorithm suitable for scanned MRI images, we have also modified the algorithm and used the modified version. In this way we contributed in the encryption of healthcare system using ML and neural networks.

Keywords: Cryptography, image processing, image cropping, artificial neural network (ANN), preprocesing, dataset, augmented intelligence, encryption, healthcare system, IOT

12.1 Introduction

In the recent times, various methods of machine learning and augmented intelligence have changed the way we look into medical science and healthcare systems. Not only that, this has started a conversation of replacing human doctors with artificial intelligence (AI) physicians! Though this kind of imagination is extremely far-fetched, we can safely say that, in near future, ML and AI can assist physicians to make better clinical decisions [1] or even replace human judgment in certain functional and critical areas of healthcare like cancerous cells, radiology and brain tumor detection. The increasing availability of data related to healthcare and the swift advancement of big data analytical methods has made possible the recent successful applications of AI and ML in healthcare systems. With the help of relevant clinical questions, powerful AI techniques can unlock medically relevant information hidden in the massive

---

Arpan Maity, KIIT Deemed to be University, Bhubaneswar, Odisha, India,
e-mail: maityarpan797@gmail.com
Sushruta Mishra, KIIT Deemed to be University, Bhubaneswar, Odisha, India,
e-mail: sushruta.mishrafcs@kiit.ac.in

https://doi.org/10.1515/9783110750942-012

amount of data [2], which in turn can help clinical decision-making in various critical conditions, in which humans are unaware of making the fruitful decision.

Augmented intelligence can use complex algorithms to "learn" variety of features from a large volume of healthcare-related data and then use the obtained details to help in medical practice. It can also be related with learning and correcting abilities [3] to enhance the accuracy of the model with the help of various feedback from the users. An AI system can assist the medical teams and nurses by providing up-to-date information related to medicine and surgery from various publications, books, journals, etc. and clinical practices to inform patient and proper care. This not only helps the medical system to improve but also the researchers to find new cures. Moreover, an AI system can also help to reduce therapeutic and diagnostic errors that are inevitable in the medical practice done by human. Not only that, an AI system extracts useful information from a large group of patients to help in making real-time inferences for health risk alert and health outcome prediction [4].

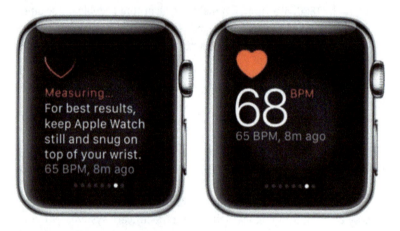

Figure 12.1: IOT wearables for healthcare (shutterstock 2018).

Not only in the case of doctors, the features of augmented intelligence are also implemented in various IOT devices like smartwatches (Figure 12.1), smart bands and other wearables so that all the fitness and health-related data of the person can be tracked and stored online or in cloud. It also helps to give proper notification of health-related issues to the users so that it can be prevented, much before it is too late. For example, if a person has unusually high heart rates, for no specific reason, the wearable will give him/her a high heart rate alert and warn them to prevent any serious threats like heart attack and much more.

This paper offers an ML-based model to further enhance the success of current healthcare system. Not only that, the importance of security of the healthcare-related data is also taken care of, as the data regarding the health of various patients is extremely confidential and needs proper encryption to make it safe. Also, special attention has been given in the space and time constraints so that the overall process does not become very much bulky and slow.

Our main contribution can be summarized as follows:

- We have taken the example of brain tumor detection for our model building.
- For that we have collected the MRI scan images from various open source libraries such as Kaggle, UCI machine learning repository, Microsoft Azure Public Datasets, CMU libraries and many more.
- We have used certain preprocessing techniques so that the scanned images can be tweaked and can be made best suitable for our model to give the most accurate results.
- After classification, the images need to be stored, but the normal disk storage of images is vulnerable to various attackers.
- That's why we encrypted the images using the modified version ECC algorithm as it is both fast and more secure than other cryptographic methods like RSA.
- Modified ECC algorithm is used because, traditionally this method is used to encrypt text files, but we have to encrypt images using this. So we modified the ECC algorithm according to our needs. As a bonus, the modification also tweaked the performance of the overall method.

Figure 12.2: Role of augmented intelligence in healthcare (DataFlair.training).

12.2 Implementation of ML and artificial neural network (ANN) in healthcare system

Machine learning is nothing but a simple application of augmented intelligence and mathematics that gives systems the opportunity to automatically learn, improve and predict results from past experience, without forming separate logic or being explicitly programmed. The learning process starts with the gathering of data, analysis of information through certain instructions [5], so as to make better decisions to form and predict patterns in data through the examples that we offer. The first aim is to make the computers learn all by itself without any human interference or support and can adjust their actions according to the information they learn. The focus of the sector is learning, that is, acquiring skills or knowledge from experience. Most ordinarily, this suggests synthesizing useful concepts from historical data. For building complex models, specially the models which deals with images (more specifically MRI scans), it is better to use artificial neural networks (ANN). A very simple diagram of ANN is portrayed in Figure 12.3.

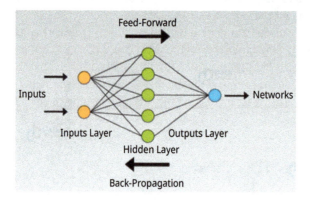

Figure 12.3: Layered structure of artificial neural networks.

ANN is programmed like a human brain, which contains thousands of neurons, network of nerves interconnected sort of a web. The processing units of an ANN are made of input and output units and have hundreds or thousands of artificial neurons, which are actually connected with each other by nodes. Various structures and forms of data supported by an inside weighting system [6] are received by input units, and the neural network attempts to be told about the data presented to supply one output report. By feeding the ANN models, with hundreds of MRI-scanned images, the model will detect some patterns among the classes. More the images fed, more will be the accuracy and the end results will be better.

12.3 Augmented intelligence in healthcare system

Augmented intelligence is the part of AI and machine learning, which focus on increasing the capability of human intelligence rather than operate independently or outright replace the humans. Basically it is a design pattern for an environment

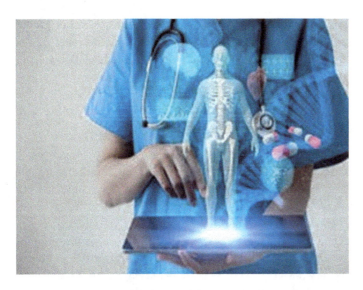

Figure 12.4: Digital medical facility (simplelearn.com 2018).

where both the human brain and AI work together to enhance cognitive performance including learning, decision-making and gaining [7] new experiences. It is a self-learning design, where it gets more and more better when it gets into different kinds of scenarios.

No doubt it has a vast application over the field of medical science, some of the applications are cited below:
- Care coordination command center: This command center will offer assistance and suggestion on various emergency situations and alerts to help hospitals, nursing homes and heath care centers track the progress report of their patients, prevent and accurate prediction of their future risks and maintain and manage staff workload.
- AI-based app for mental health tracking: It is one of the biggest tools that uses big data and various analytical methods to give behavioral health support (mental training and behavioral therapy) to patients by their therapists, physicians, trainers and psychiatrists. The app uses augmented intelligence and other ML methods that we see tracking how several patients use their mobiles and other smart devices to identify various patterns and make plans that are related to mental health [8].
- Diagnosis using augmented intelligence: This method is also used worldwide in all the modern hospitals. Here the diagnostic data of the patients is fed to the AI engines to predict the result in a very efficient and accurate ways. In busy hospitals, thousands of patients come, with different problems. So difficulty increases and often it becomes time-consuming to deal with each one of it accurately. This is the scope where augmented intelligence makes its way into healthcare system

Likewise there are several other uses of augmented intelligence which will be gradually discussed later on in this paper. For the sake of simplicity, we have taken an example of brain tumor detection, for this paper, but we must remember that we can use AI in almost any fields in healthcare system.

12.4 Need of encryption in healthcare system

In the previous sections, we discussed about the role of ML and augmented intelligence in healthcare system. They also explain about how ML and AI help the physicians to diagnose diseases efficiently and more accurately. This diagnostic data which is classified [9] with the help of various ML models needs to be stored for the future use. This is where data encryption comes in healthcare system. Figure 12.5 is a demonstration of how encrypted data looks like. With the advancement of computing capabilities, the attackers have also become very powerful. So there is an increasing risk of that diagonistic data, which is stored in local server or cloud, to be attacked by them.

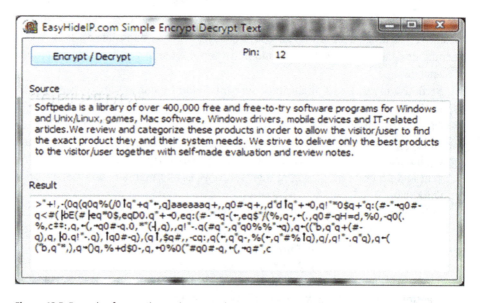

Figure 12.5: Example of encryption and encrypted text.

The healthcare data is often very much sensitive and confidential to all the hospitals/ nursing homes. So it is very essential to preserve and secure this data effectively with the help of encryption. Details of how the healthcare data is encrypted are discussed in later sections. In this section, let's discuss a bit about what encryption is.

Before knowing about encryption, we must know about two terms: plain text and cipher text. Plain text can be any data which is human readable. This can be normal

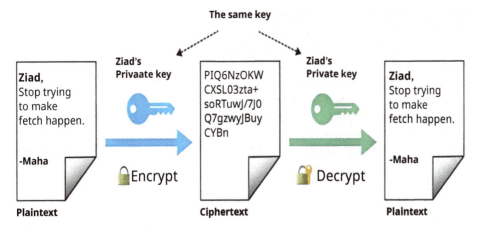

Figure 12.6: Plain text, cipher text and the concept of key (medium.com).

text document, audio, video, photo or anything. Cipher text in simple terms is the unreadable form of that plain text and the conversion of plain text to cipher text is known as encryption. This is done with the help of two keys: the public key and the private key, as shown in Figure 12.6. Like its name, the public key is the key [10], which is known to all, but the private key is known only by the specific user. During encryption, user 1 has to use to public key of user 2 and his own private key and during decryption (i.e., conversion of cipher text back to plain text), and user 2 has to use his own private and public key.

But to convert plain text into cipher text, we need certain algorithms and methods so that when the cipher text is reconverted back to plain text, then the original plain text and the new plain text must be equal.

There are several algorithms in the field of cryptography, for serving the same purpose, each having different complexities and different time constraints. Examples of such algorithms are affine cipher, poly-alphabetic cipher, playfair method, Rivest, Shamir, Adleman (RSA) method, ECC method, data encryption standard (DES) method and many more [11]. For this paper, we have chosen ECC method to implement, whose detailed explanation is to be provided in the following sections.

12.5 Role of augmented intelligence in encryption

We all know that how encryption and security of data are essential for the large organizations and reputed enterprises. For that, to ensure the maximum security, the institutions and organizations begin with all over defense, which built a first round of strong security around the stored data. However, the perimeter defense mechanism was later proved to be ineffective as several crimes like spoofing and snooping and their unique methodologies became more advanced and complex over time. Various institutions started buying various security products to reduce the risk of data being stolen. They used several analytics from the various security information and event management (SIEM) [12] systems to assess and collect the necessary data. But cybercriminals, spoofers, snoopers and attackers are well organized, well trained, very well-funded and often had powerful personalities behind them. To stay ahead of the good guys and cyberpolice, criminals on the Dark Web got united and worked together and shared experiences, methods and algorithms that led to cybercrime for hire [13]. Figure 12.7 shows different ways, where encryption is used in healthcare system.

For this kind of chaotic scenario, the role of augmented intelligence came into play. This technology increases the analysts' performance by providing them methods, techniques and with highly focused knowledge of threat. It minimizes the lack of highly skilled security analysts by increasing their ability and improving their effectiveness.

The main problem is that the knowledge of data security analysts is limited to a small fraction of available threat data, while security systems of the organizations consume structured data from fully instrumented and automated enterprises. The reason behind this is that, every day, more and more modern techniques are evolving. Unfortunately, the large amount of security content is both unstructured and human-generated [14].

Let us give a statistical view of the rate of cybercrimes. On an average over 17,000 malware and spoofing alerts per day is captured by various organizations, and some of them are spending as hefty as $1.3 million in response to the very misleading or inaccurate malware alerts, according to the Ponemon Institute report, "The Cost of Malware Containment." Just 19% of all malware alerts are considered to be true and reliable and out of that only 4% are ever investigated [15]. This causes a huge amount of economic loss for the companies. Not only that, the cost of incident mitigation and breaching is increasing more and more as organizations continue to use methods to overburden the limited number of security personnel.

The following facts will be enough to prove it:
- The number of several software vulnerabilities and bugs reported in National Vulnerability Database is more than 75,000.
- The number of articles and publications related to information security and network security is more than 15,000 per month.
- More than 10,000 research papers and journals, related to cybercrimes, information security, cryptography and network security that are published every year, are all classified as unstructured content.

Augmented intelligence is the key answer to that. AI is the most powerful way and perhaps the only way to consume and prioritize a large collection of data related to security by providing diagnostic, predictive and prescriptive analytics. IBM is one of the earliest companies to offer this kind of chances [16] with Watson for Cyber and

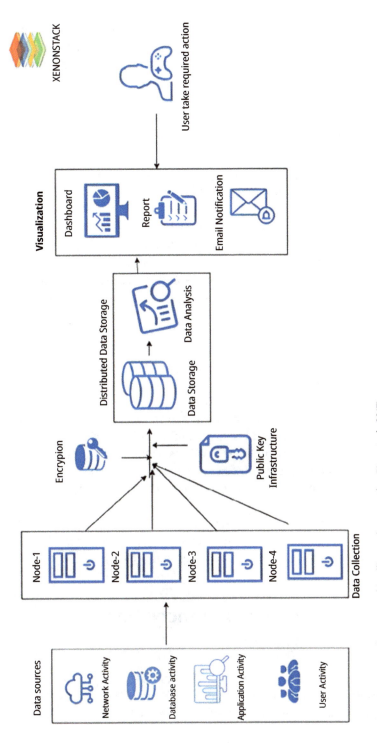

Figure 12.7: Use of augmented intelligence in encryption (Xenostack, 2017).

Network Security. It is achieved by rigorous training and testing a modern generation of systems to comprehend and learn about rapidly developing security threats [17]. Watson could very quickly understand and analyze the research works, texts on website, video and threatening data at an increasingly high speed and scale [18–21].

12.6 Brief description of brain tumor

As said earlier, ML and augmented intelligence can be applied in any field of medical science. But discussing each and every scenario in one paper will be next to impossible. So, we chose a particular case for the sake of discussion – brain tumor.

A brain tumor is a group or a mass of abnormal cells, inside human brain (in Figure 12.8). The human skull, also known as the "brain-box" which encloses the brain, is very tough. Any abnormal growth inside such a small space can cause various complexities. Brain tumors are of two types: malignant (cancerous) and benign (non-cancerous). When any of these two kinds of tumor starts growing, they cause a very high pressure inside the skull. This can cause permanent brain damages, coma and even death.

Brain tumors can again be classified into primary or secondary tumors. A primary brain tumor has its origination inside brain. Maximum primary brain tumors are non-cancerous. A secondary brain tumor, also known as a metastatic brain tumor, occurs when cancer cells spread to the brain from another organ of the body, like lungs or breasts. These tumors are often cancerous.

The only way of getting read of brain tumor is, whenever the patient gets any symptom of it like headaches, blurred vision, loss of balance, blood vomiting, then immediately, he must do a MRI scan of brain. The doctors must confirm the scan to be of a brain tumor and then a surgery must be done to remove it entirely. But sometimes, due to work pressure, and other human errors, the diagnosis of the scan becomes inaccurate.

That's why, the modern-day hospitals take the help of machine learning models. A well-trained ML or ANN model can reach to an accuracy level of almost 95–99% and since they are self-learning, this method can be trusted undoubtedly.

12.7 Proposed work related to encryption in healthcare system

So, as it is said earlier, we are taking the example of brain tumor for our work. Though all the detailed explanations are provided in the later sections (Sections 10.8–10.10) of this chapter, for the easiness of the readers, a brief overview of the whole work is given below.

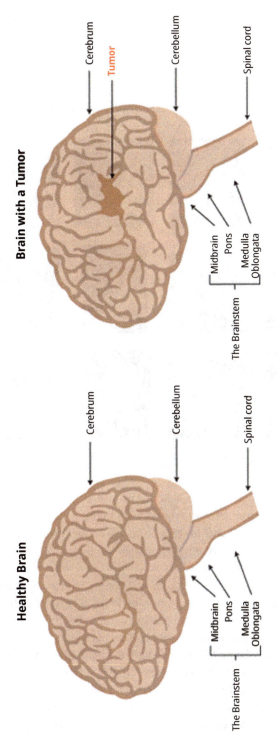

Figure 12.8: Structure of brain tumor (shutterstock 2018).

Now, from the example we have considered, it is very much clear that this is a classifier model, in which there will be two classes: the has_tumor class and no_tumor class. So, at first, the dataset is collected from various open sources (details in Section 10.8), and some basic preprocessing is done to eliminate all the outliers. Our aim was to first create the model, which will classify the test images into two classes accurately and then use encryption method to encrypt the images in both the classes.

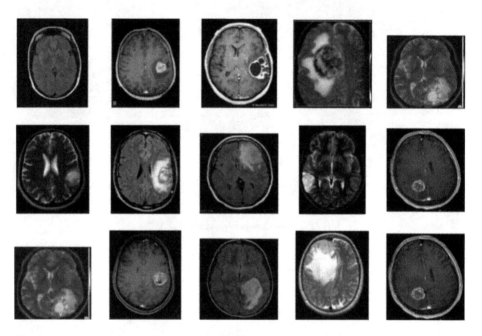

Figure 12.9: Snippet of the dataset used in the algorithm.

So, as our dataset was ready (shown in Figure 12.9), we needed a model to fit it into. Several machine learning and neural network models were there, which we can use. But we needed is simple yet accurate model to work on. So we chose ResNetV2 (details given in Section 10.9), which is a deep-layered, ANN model. We used 60 epochs there and got an average accuracy of 82–89%.

Satisfied with the work, we wrote a function that would store the classified file in two different folders for further processing. Now since the first job of classification of MRI scans was over, we were into the more vital portion of the work that is encrypting those MRI scans. Now, as said earlier there are hundreds of methods in modern cryptography for encrypting texts. Some of them are very efficient, but is oversimplified, and can be broken very easily and others are very difficult to break, but at a cost of being very much complex, and hence very time-consuming. We needed to think of a method which was neither so easy to break as the others nor so much complex and hence was very much secured and efficient. Hence we chose the ECC algorithm, which is a secure, easy to use, symmetric key algorithm, which works on basic mathematical formulae.

But our obstacle for proper encoding of the images was far from over. Most of the encrypting algorithms, which are developed, including ECC, are made for the text files. They can easily convert any text (including spaces and special characters) into cipher text format. But we needed to make it run for MRI-scanned images. So we needed to tweak and modify the algorithm as per our needs.

We wrote three functions to modify the algorithm. While doing it, special care was given so that the time and space constraint remains as it is, just like the text.

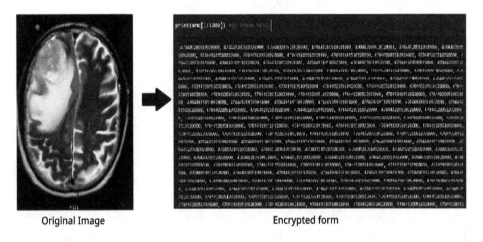

Figure 12.10: Original image and its corresponding cipher text.

Otherwise, the whole purpose of choosing ECC algorithm over any other algorithm will go in vain. So, we wrote the functions, and the encoding and decoding were done as we had expected. The example image of the original MRI scan and its cipher text format are provided in Figure 12.10.

So, as the modification of the algorithm was successful, we applied the same algorithm over all the images in the two folders, which was classified previously, and the whole test dataset was perfectly and efficiently encrypted.

12.8 Dataset collection and preprocessing

In our model, we wanted to use images of various forms and from various sources so that the overall accuracy of our model becomes good. So we used images from various open sources like Kaggle, UCI machine learning repository, Microsoft Azure Public Datasets and many more.

Kaggle is a renowned website created in 2010 created by a team of data scientists. It helps developers to find, analyze, publish and work on the several data sets, explore them and build models in a web-based data-science environment. Not only that, it also allows to collaborate and work together with other data scientists and ML experts. The UCI machine learning repository is also a combination of several databases, domain theories and data generators that are used by the communities of data scientists machine learning professionals for the analysis and development of several machine learning and neural networks algorithms. The aim was to create an ftp archive in 1987 by David Aha and fellow graduate students at UC Irvine and it is the second most popular dataset collection after Kaggle.

We needed to use several image processing algorithms for this project. But the main problem of that was as follows:

Photos were of various shapes and sizes: To implement the same algorithm for all the images, we need to get all the photos into same shape and size. Hundreds of photos having different sizes could increase the overall complexity of our program. So we analyzed all the images to find an optimal size so that all the images can be resized, without much distortion. We chose 300 × 350 as the optimal size and wrote an algorithm so that all the images can be resized at once.

Second most important problem was the object-to-frame ratio: As we selected our dataset from different sources, the object to frame ratio varied vastly. In some images, the main scan occupied about 90% of the frame, and in some other the object occupied as low as 65% of the total frame. Though this scenario will not create any errors, but will adversely affect the accuracy of our model. So we needed to improve that. We observed all the images closely to get the optimal coordinates so that each and every image can be cropped using the same values, without much data loss. We crop 8% of the image from all diagonals. As a result our average object-to-image ratio increased from about 67% to 85%. We wrote an algorithm to perform the cropping of all the images at once and the time taken for doing all of this was 16.94 s, which is considered quite good. An example image after preprocessing is given below in Figure 12.11.

12.9 Experimental setup and methodology for building the ML model

12.9.1 Experimental setup

All the members who participated in this work used the same device. We used an HP ProBook laptop with Intel(R) Core(TM) i5-8250U processor, CPU @ 1.60 GHz 1.80 GHz. RAM available was 16 GB. So the processing time may vary a bit from device to device.

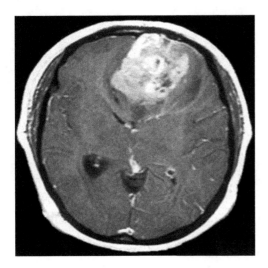

Figure 12.11: Test image after preprocessing.

In our work we had used TensorFlow, which is a machine learning platform that provides a distributed, in-memory, open source, ML and predictive analytic allowing the user to build ML models. TensorFlow allows developers to visualize and work with medium-to-large-sized data sets. It also helps us analyze how the data moves through a graph by using dataflow graphs or a series of processing nodes. A mathematical operation is represented by each node in the graph, and each connection or edge between nodes is a multidimensional data array or tensor.

To make this project really light weight, yet efficient, we used ResNetV2 (residual network Version 2, cleanly demonstrated in Figure 12.12) as our ANN algorithm. It is the special type of ResNet algorithm. It uses a neural network architecture, which is used specifically for the classification of image files. It uses the simplicity and advantages of linear and logistic regression and uses its feature extraction method. It uses skip connections to add the input of a group of convolutions to its output.

The idea and motivation behind to create and develop ResNetV2 model was to build a network consisting of several branches and subbranches with a large number of skip connections. This will increase the accuracy as for each and every branch, the difference between them is analyzed and the residual activation-map between the input and the output of each of the branch is predicted. After that the residual activation-map is added together with the previously found activation-maps making the "collective knowledge" of the ResNet, which is the heart and soul of the framework.

But for that, the neural networks become more and more deep. The deeper neural networks are always very difficult to train due to its large number of layers. With the increasing number of layers, the overall complexity increases exponentially. The residual learning with skip connections made it easy to train deeper models successfully, with much more ease than ever before. Example can be made of networks,

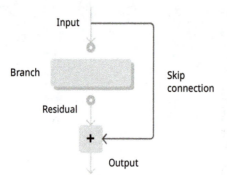

Figure 12.12: Working of ResNetV2 model.

which performed extremely well with a very high accuracy with more than 1,000 layers. For most recent models, now it is observed that the deeper models are becoming increasingly powerful, with the help of this model.

Hence the choice of ResNetV2 as our go-to ML algorithm due to the low execution time and high accuracy is proved right and this is confirmed even more from the confusion matrix given below.

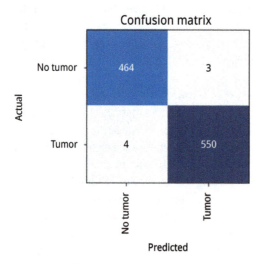

Figure 12.13: Confusion matrix.

12.9.2 Class imbalance problem

While choosing the datasets, we kept a keen eye on equality of all the datasets so that we can prevent the class imbalance problem. By doing so we kept 460–550 images in both of the classes and successfully prevented the problem.

12.9.3 Model building

We split our dataset into three classes: test, train and test data frame into ratio of whole numbers 8:1:1. We used the general train_test_split() function for doing this. We introduced 30 epochs for gaining better accuracy over time. We executed our code several times both before and after preprocessing and the result of continuous change of epoch, with number of iterations, is demonstrated below in Figure 12.14.

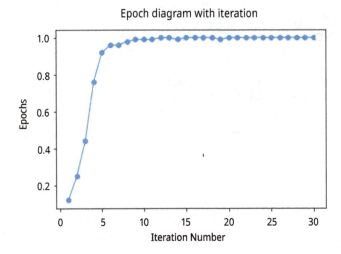

Figure 12.14: No. of epochs vs no. of iteration graph.

12.9.4 Model accuracy

As discussed earlier in Section 12.4, the more the epoch line is parallel or undeviated to the X-axis, the more accurate is the model. Though this reason of this result was not only the resNetV2 model, but also the preprocessing, which was applied to each and every image, before fitting into the model (discussed in Section 10.8). The preprocessing increased the accuracy of the model to about 8%.

But, the good accuracy was not the only factor to be taken care of, more important than that was the consistency of the result. So we ran the code for 20 times continuously and the accuracy ranged from 89% to 95%, which is considered quite consistent. The test result is given below in Figure 12.15.

The total accuracy is calculated with the help of the following equation:

$$\text{Accuracy} = \frac{\text{True Positives} + \text{True Negatives}}{\text{True Positives} + \text{False Negatives} + \text{True Negatives} + \text{False Positives}}$$

where

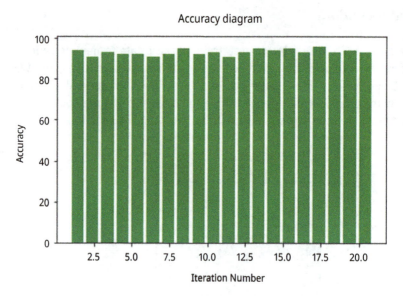

Figure 12.15: Accuracy percentage vs number of iteration graph.

- True positive means, Predicted: Tumor present, Actually: Tumor present
- True negative means, Predicted: Tumor not present, Actually: Tumor not present
- False positive means, Predicted: Tumor present, Actually: Tumor not present
- False negative means, Predicted: Tumor not present, Actually: Tumor present

This accuracy rate is also confirmed by the confusion matrix shown in Figure 12.13.

12.10 Encryption of the classified images

12.10.1 Choice of encryption algorithm

In the world of cryptography, there are hundreds of encrypting algorithms, each having different use cases and has their own advantages. So it would seem like choosing an encrypting algorithm was very easy. But the reality is far from different. Each algorithm comes with the disadvantages of their own along with the advantages. We had to choose that algorithm, which fits as per our needs. In Table 12.1, we showed different types of encrypting algorithms.

Encrypting algorithms can be broadly classified into symmetric key (SK) and asymmetric key (ASK) algorithms. SK algorithms are ones, whose encrypting and decrypting keys are same, and for ASK, it is the opposite.

Table 12.1: Different types of encrypting algorithm.

Class or interface	Description
Symmetric	The top level abstraction for all symmetric cryptographic algorithms
Assymmetric	The top level abstraction for all symmetric cryptographic algorithms
RC2	The RC2 abstraction, a subclass of symmetric algorithm
DES	The DES algorithm abstraction, a subclass of symmetric algorithm (DES.cs)
Triple DES	The triple DES algorithm abstraction, derived from symmetric algorithm
Rijndael	The Rijndael algorithm abstraction, derived from symmetric algorithm
RSA	The RSA public key cipher abstraction, derived from assymmetric algorithm
DSA	The DSA public key cipher abstraction, derived from assymmetric algorithm

But for SK there were different types of algorithms. Example can be made like affine cipher, poly-alphabetic cipher, playfair method, RSA, elliptic curve cryptography (ECC), DES, double and triple DES, AES, Rijndael algorithm, Blowfish and many more. Out of this, affine cipher and polyalphabetic cipher was too simple and is very easy to be cracked by the attackers. Playfair method, though a very efficient encrypting algorithm, which works very well in texts, was not so easy to modify to work for images. DES, AES and Blowfish were much complex and also text-oriented. So we searched for an algorithm, which is fast, efficient, secure and will be easy to modify. For that reason we came across an ECC algorithm due to its modular in nature. Details about ECC algorithm and how we modified are given in the following sections.

12.10.2 Basic concepts of ECC model

ECC, which was created as an alternative algorithm to RSA, is a very much powerful, yet simple cryptographic approach. It helps to form the private and public keys with high security using ellyptic curve methods. As ECC method is a trapdoor function, breaking it is very difficult and the security provided is higher than RSA.

RSA executes the process similarly as ECC. But RSA works with prime numbers and ECC works with elliptic curves. That's why complexity of ECC is more and breaking it with brute force attack is much more difficult than that of RSA. ECC has gradually been growing in popularity in recent times due to its simplicity, efficiency and mainly due to its much smaller key size than RSA and its ability to ensure a high level of security. This trend of success will surely continue as the demand of smart devices to remain more and more security increases. This is why it is so necessary to understand ECC in this context.

Unlike RSA, ECC mainly depends on its unique approach toward public key cryptographic systems, as using which method the elliptic curves are structured algebraically over the finite fields, in specific range. All these calculations are done with the help of a special kind of mathematics known as ECC mathematics. Therefore, ECC creates keys which are more difficult to break using brute force attack and computationally expensive to crack. For this reason, ECC is considered to be the next generation implementation of public key cryptography and is much more secure than RSA by using keys of very less size. It is much more feasible than other assymmetric methods.

Few points on ECC algorithm are:
- It is a asymmetric public key cryptosystem
- It provides equal security with smaller key size
- It makes the use of elliptical curves
- It used the formula $y^2 = x^3 + ax + b$ for key generation

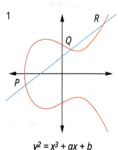

Figure 12.16: Example of an ellyptic curve (avinetworks.com).

- The elliptic curve is drawn symmetric to X-axis (shown in Figure 12.16)
- If we draw a line, it would cut through a maximum of three points through the elliptic curve
- It uses trapdoor function
- On an average it is 256 times more secured than RSA algorithms
- It also takes 20–25 times less time than RSA algorithm

Trapdoor function is a kind of function, which is easy to compute in one direction, but nearly difficult to compute through the other direction if won't have a special value called trapdoor value (key in case of ECC algorithm). In other words, if $f(n)$ is a trapdoor function, then calculating $f(n)$ would be easy, but calculating $f-1(n)$ is very difficult without the key (shown in Figure 12.17).

12.10.2.1 Encryption

Now, let na and nb are the private keys of user A and user B.

Let Pa and Pb are their public keys of user A and user B. Let G is the point on that elliptic curve on Figure 12.16, such that

$$Pa = na \cdot G$$

If f is a trapdoor function

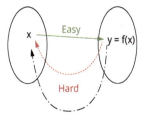

Figure 12.17: Trapdoor function (quora.com 2020).

$$Pb = nb.G \quad \text{and}$$
$$Pa = Pb$$

To generate the secret key K, we can use any of the two formulae $K = na . Pb$
Or $K = nb . Pa$, both will give the same result.

Now, for ECC encryption, let the message length be m. Let another point in the same elliptic curve be p, whether the message m is embedded.

Therefore, the cipher point c will be in $K.G, p + K.Pb$ – (a). And this point will be transmitted to the receiver.

12.10.2.2 Decryption

Now, decrypting in the receivers' side. He will first multiply his private key with the value $(K.G)$

So he will get $K.G.nb$ – (b)

Now he will subtract this (b) with the y coordinate of a, to get the original point p $(p + K.Pb) - K.G.nb$

$$= p + K.Pb - K.G.nb$$

But we know that,

$$Pb = G.nb$$
$$= p + K.Pb - K.Pb$$
$$= p$$

Now from the original point p, the whole message m can be retrieved. So this is in nutshell, the working procedure of ECC algorithm.

12.10.3 Procedure of application of ECC model in image data

So from the discussions in Section 10.10.2, it must be clear that how ECC algorithm works. But the main obstacle for us now was that ECC algorithm is used only for text files. So we had to modify the ECC algorithm to make it work for images. So we wrote two functions, whose details are given below step by step:

- The images are composed of pixels, which contain RGB values of that images. Each pixel can have 256 different values ranging from 0 to 255
- Using image processing by PIL library we got all the values of the pixels in array form, e.g. [122,56,212]
- The output we got was in 3D matrix. But implementing any operation in 3D matrix was very difficult, so we converted the 3D matrix into 1D array using numpy library functions. 1D array is known as lists in python

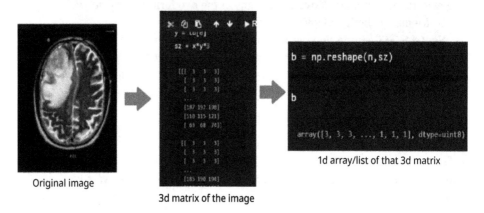

Figure 12.18: Image to text conversion using PIL.

- After converting it into list, the size of the list became huge. It could be calculated with the help of the formula (height × length × 3) of the image.
- We then converted the digits into characters using type casting and eventually we converted the image into text, which can now be encrypted using ECC algorithm (shown in Figure 12.18).
- So after encryption and decryption, we got back the same characters. Then we did just the reverse of the previous steps.
- First converted the characters into numbers by type casting.
- Then converted the 1D array into 3D array using numpy method.
- Then eventually at the end we converted the 3D matrix into the image used PIL method

12.10.4 Performance of the modified ECC algorithm

Unlike ML/DL models, testing the performance of any encryption algorithm is much simpler. We don't need to consider, space constraint, accuracy or have to find out any confusion matrix. We have to check only two things:
– The decrypted and original image are same or not and
– The time constraint

Obviously the decrypted and original images were the same; otherwise, there would be no point in writing the paper. And talking about time constraint, the whole algorithm took less than 2 s to encrypt a file of 400 × 300 size (shown in Figure 12.19).

Figure 12.19: Time constraint for image encryption.

So from the above discussion, we can confidently say that, our modified ECC algorithm performed accurately and efficiently.

12.11 Future works

Though we are satisfied with the performance, security, efficiency and accuracy of our model, but we can't deny the fact that there are some chances of improvement. In Section 10.10.1, we talked about why we chose ECC algorithm over anything else. There we mentioned that playfair is also an efficient and secure algorithm (in Figure 12.20), perhaps more efficient than ECC also!! But the main problem with that was it only worked with text files and was very difficult to be modified and make it to work with image files. In future, we will definitely try to modify the playfair technique and implement it in our model to make our model even more secure.

Another thing that we need to work is on security of transfer of the keys from the sender to receiver. It may be possible that the attackers do not directly attack the images, but attack on the keys by which the image is encrypted. So the secure transfer of the keys is very much essential. Block chain mechanism is a very popular and effective way of transferring keys and other texts, so in the future we can certainly think of using that in our algorithm.

Figure 12.20: Example of playfair cipher method (wikipedia.com).

12.12 Conclusion and limitations

We live in twenty-first century, the age of automation. In this age with the progress of computation power, the risk of spoofing and hacking has also increased exponentially [22–24]. Though hundreds of encrypting algorithms are available, which are claimed to be very secure, not a single algorithm is attack proof!! Each and every algorithm can be attacked, but the difference arises on the time, the attacker needs to attack the system. More the time needed by the attacker for a successful attack, more secure the system is. In 1992, the most popular encrypting algorithm, DES [25], which was considered unbreakable was attacked and broken in just 112 h! A whole lot of chaos started from then, as at that time most of the computers used DES. So the company upgraded their algorithm to double and triple DES to make the algorithm more secure. Also some new methods, like Blowfish algorithm and AES, were also introduced to combat the chaotic situation. So the only way to make our system safe is to upgrade the security system on a regular interval and keep on developing new cryptographic algorithm.

Talking about limitations, as we discussed in Section 11, the only limitation we observed in our work is key transferring mechanism. Only the Diffie Hellman procedure is used for the key transfer, which is very basic and can be easily broken. So we are thinking of applying block-chain method (demonstrated in Figure 12.21), in addition to Diffie Hellman, to make the overall model even more secure.

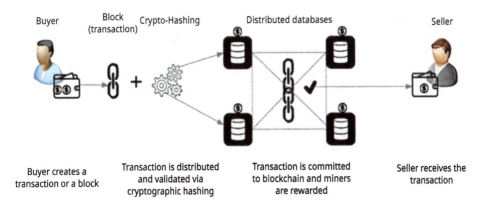

Figure 12.21: Block-chain method and secure folder (mlsdev.com).

References

[1] Pathak, A. & Aurelia, S. (2020). Mobile-based indian currency detection model for the visually impaired. In Convergence of ICT and Smart Devices for Emerging Applications. Springer, Cham, 67–79.
[2] Patil, V. & Sirsat, A. (2020). Artificial Intelligence Digital Assistant For Visually Im- paired People. International Journal of Future Generation Communication and Networking, 13(1s), 24–31.
[3] Tripathy, H. K., Mishra, S., Thakkar, H. K. & Rai, D. (2021). CARE: A Collision-Aware Mobile Robot Navigation in Grid Environment using Improved Breadth First Search. Computers & Electrical Engineering, 94, 107327.
[4] Yang, Q., et al. (2019). Federated machine learning: Concept and applications. ACM Transactions on Intelligent Systems and Technology (TIST), 10(2), 1–19.
[5] Ghosh, D. & Singh, J. (2020). A novel approach of software fault prediction us- ing deep learning technique. In Automated Software Engineering: A Deep Learning-Based Approach. Springer, Cham, 73–91.
[6] Singh, J. & Sahoo, B. (2011). Software effort estimation with different artifi- cial neural network.
[7] Li, L., et al. (2020). A review of face recognition technology. IEEE Access, 8, 139110–139120.
[8] Ciocca, G., et al. (2007). Self-adaptive image cropping for small displays. IEEE Transactions on Consumer Electronics, 53(4), 1622–1627.
[9] A somewhat recent survey of research on decision trees: Sreerama K. Murthy: Automatic Construction of Decision Trees from Data: A Multi-Disciplinary Survey. (1998). Data Mining and Knowledge Discovery, 2(4), 345–389.
[10] Chakraborty, K., et al. (2013). Recent developments in paper currency recognition system. International Journal of Research in Engineering and Technology, 2, 222–226.
[11] Kamesh, D. B. K., et al. (2016). Camera based text to speech conversion, obstacle and currency detection for blind persons. Indian Journal of Science and Technology, 9(30), 1–5.
[12] Vishnu, R. & Omman, B. (2014). Currency detection using similarity indices method. International Conference for Convergence for Technology. IEEE.

[13] Hartigan, J. A. & Wong, M. A., Algorithm AS 136: A k-means clustering algorithm in Wiley global publications.
[14] Xiaojiang, D., Guizani, M., Xiao, Y. & Chen, H.-H. .Transactions papers a routing-driven Elliptic Curve Cryptography based key management scheme for Heterogeneous Sensor Networks, 1223–1229.
[15] Maria Celestin Vigila, S. & Muneeswaran, K., Implementation of text based cryptosystem using Elliptic Curve Cryptography, NSPEC Accession Number: 11059820 Publisher IEEE.
[16] Azarderakhsh, R., Järvinen, K. U. & Mozaffari-Kermani, M., Efficient algorithm and architecture for elliptic curve cryptography for extremely constrained secure applications, 1144–1155, IEEE.
[17] Liu, Z., Seo, H., Castiglione, A. & Raymond Choo, K.-K., Memory- Efficient Implementation of Elliptic Curve Cryptography for the Internet-of-Things, 521–529.
[18] Malan, D. J., Welsh, M. & Smith, M. D., A public-key infrastructure for key distribution in TinyOS based on elliptic curve cryptography, Print ISBN:0-7803-8796-1, Publisher IEEE.
[19] The majorization approach to metric MDS via stress minimization is reviewed and analyzed by Jan de Leeuw, Convergence of the Majorization Method for Multidimensional Scaling. (1988). Journal of Classification, 5, 163–180.
[20] Chaudhury, P., Mishra, S., Tripathy, H. K. & Kishore, B. (March, 2016). Enhancing the capabilities of student result prediction system. In Proceedings of the Second International Conference on Information and Communication Technology for Competitive Strategies (pp. 1–6).
[21] Jena, L., Patra, B., Nayak, S., Mishra, S. & Tripathy, S. (2021). Risk prediction of kidney disease using machine learning strategies. In Intelligent and Cloud Computing. Springer, Singapore, 485–494.
[22] Rath, M. & Mishra, S. (2019). Advanced-level security in network and real-time applications using machine learning approaches. In Machine Learning and Cognitive Science Applications in Cyber Security. IGI Global, 84–104.
[23] Mishra, S., Tripathy, H. K., Mallick, P. K., Bhoi, A. K. & Barsocchi, P. (2020). EAGA-MLP – an enhanced and adaptive hybrid classification model for diabetes diagnosis. Sensors, 20(14), 4036.
[24] Mishra, S., Thakkar, H., Mallick, P. K., Tiwari, P. & Alamri, A. (2021). A Sustainable IoHT based Computationally Intelligent Healthcare Monitoring System for Lung Cancer Risk Detection. Sustainable Cities and Society, 103079.

Navod Neranjan Thilakarathne*, Rohan Samarasinghe,
Rakesh Kumar Mahendran

13 Security system design for medical big data: layered security framework for protecting medical big data

Abstract: Owing to the rapid development and the evolvement of technology in the twenty-first century many domains such as agriculture, surveillance, military, healthcare and manufacturing are transforming with underlying technologies to cater to this growing demand. As a consequence the input data is becoming a vital component and strategic asset of every organization that ultimately maximizes the value of data, transferring them into meaningful information, which eventually helps in effective decision-making. This vast amount of vital and complex data which is also known as big data is becoming an integral part of every application domain including healthcare. Owing to the current demand and the latest trends, medical big data is growing day by day enormously, posing a variety of challenges. The big data in medical care has a considerable impact on improving the quality of healthcare, gaining insights about the patient's condition and reducing the overall cost and time of patient care, where it is a vital and successful factor for driving medical organizations to the next level. Even though big data in healthcare offer many advantages, the security and privacy of big data are becoming a tedious challenge among many other prevailing challenges, owing to the rapid demand for big data and as a result of its ever-growing endless nature. Nevertheless, as per the time being the security and privacy of medical data are overseen by many acts and regulations, where the medical big data should be protected from getting into the wrong hands, which if not endanger the lives of patients. Owing to the growing threats that target healthcare and to the further development of healthcare, the security and privacy aspect of medical big data needed to be concerned and solutions should be provided to make sure the trustworthiness of the environment. To go deeper into this topic, it's crucial to examine the critical components in the creation of security solutions for protecting medical big data from security and privacy risks. In this paper, we examine the present state of security and privacy problems in medical big data, as well as

---

*Corresponding author: **Navod Neranjan Thilakarathne**, Department of ICT, Faculty of Technology, University of Colombo, Sri Lanka, e-mail: navod.neranjan@ict.cmb.ac.lk
Rohan Samarasinghe, Department of ICT, Faculty of Technology, University of Colombo, Sri Lanka, e-mail: rohan@ict.cmb.ac.lk
Rakesh Kumar Mahendran, Department of Electronics and Communication Engineering, Vel Tech Multitech Dr. Rangarajan Dr. Sakunthala Engineering College, Tamil Nadu, India, e-mail: rakeshkumarmahendran@gmail.com

https://doi.org/10.1515/9783110750942-013

the current state of safe solution development, and propose a tiered framework for securing and preserving medical big data security and privacy.

Keywords: Security, privacy, big data, artificial intelligence, data analytics, healthcare, encryption, IoT

13.1 Introduction

Big data refers to the large volume of complex and enormous data sets that cannot be analyzed using traditional computing techniques, in which data can be in structured, unstructured or semi-structured formats [1]. The exact definition for the term "Big Data" is continuously evolving, where a data collection is considered "Big" if it has a size ranging from a few terabytes to several petabytes [2]. On the other hand, even though the data can be apportioned into three categories as abovementioned, the main focus is toward unstructured big data [2]. When the data becomes unstructured and complex they cannot be maintained and handled by traditional relational databases where it necessities novel mechanisms to analyze this large volume of complex data [3–5]. In simple terms, big data refers to the ever-changing nature of our world [4], as everything changes around us, in every fraction of second we spend. For an instance, according to the latest statistics during one single day more than 500 terabytes of data get ingested into the databases of Facebook, a social media networking company, owing to the billions of user transactions that are happening daily (audio and video uploads, content creations, message exchanges and user comments) [4]. Moreover, the New York Stock Exchange is a one another example, which generates one terabyte of trade data per single day [4, 5]. Modern businesses/organizations use the insights from this big data to discover consumer shopping habits/patterns for targeted marketing and advertising, to offer personalized medical plans for patients, to monitor the health condition from wearable devices and to real-time monitoring of networks for cyber security attacks [6]. One of the most significant thing is, every industry, nowadays, uses big data for their future planning of businesses and to predict what happened next and to identify their customer behavior by inferring insights from the past data [4, 5]. According to recent estimates [5, 6], the big data analytics (BDA) industry would be worth $103 billion by 2023. Furthermore, it is clear that in 2020, each individual created 1.7 megabytes in only one second, whereas daily internet users generate around 2.5 quintillion bytes of data, altogether. Furthermore, to acquire a competitive edge and stay in the market, 97.2% of modern corporate organizations are investing in big data and artificial intelligence-based BDA approaches for the time being [4–6].

Medical big data is a complex collection of digital medical data acquired from a number of sources that is challenging to handle with standard technology and software owing to its large volume and complexity [1]. According to [1, 2], this medical big data can also interchangeably call as multimedia medical big data (MBD), as the data is acquired from a variety of sources. This medical big data mainly consist of patient data in the form of electronic health records (EHRs), data from written notes and prescriptions of physicians, medical imaging, insurance, laboratories, medical journals, pharmacy, other administrative and medical environmental data, data collected from machines and sensors (Internet of Things (IoT) devices), and social media data (for instance, data from social networking sites and blog entries) [6–12]. All these massive amounts of data have enormous potential in improving efficiency and quality of healthcare, detecting health hazards before they are onset, predict outbreaks of epidemics [4], controlling human health by diagnosing diseases at an early stage and aiding in improved decision-making. Even though medical big data offer greater benefits for the goodness of mankind, there are a variety of challenges that hinder the optimal growth of technology, in which the key challenges are data storage, data standards, data transport and security and privacy [1, 2]. According to recent study [13], the worldwide healthcare big data industry is expected to develop at a compound annual growth rate (CAGR) of 22.07% to reach roughly $34 billion by 2022, with a CAGR of 36% by 2025 [10–12].

According to [1–5], the majority of researchers that used artificial intelligence and BDA in medical diagnosis did not place priority on data privacy and security, which could eventually jeopardize the lives of patients. Even though collecting data in healthcare may be highly beneficial for diagnosing the patient's condition and further research, we must also consider the security and privacy issues that technology brings, which could endanger the lives of patients. Digitalization in the medical industry is reaching a tipping point where the rapid use of new technologies like IoT, mobile computing and cloud computing has posed new difficulties and dangers to big data in healthcare. As a result, it is essential to address cyber security concerns throughout the generation, collection, storage, sharing, exchange and use of medical big data [1, 2]. Medical big data, on the other hand, is composed of three types of physical states [2], that is, files and images, video and data flow, and text and language which clearly indicate the unstructured nature of all these medical data. As medical big data often consist of patient pathological information and personal identification information (PII), protecting the privacy of medical big data is a deemed essential thing. Otherwise, if the patient's personal information is revealed by any means, it will affect the patient's reputation and life as well as pose severe moral and ethical issues [2–5].

As previously said, medical big data has many advantages and has a lot of potential for revolutionizing healthcare, but it also has lot of drawbacks and problems, in which security and privacy is the utmost concern. The security and privacy concerns, which target medical big data, are being increased annually, posing a doubt in the mind of researchers and medical organizations about the reliability of medical care. Nevertheless, healthcare organizations have discovered that current security and privacy measures are not adequate for safeguarding their big data repositories and pervasive environment [3]. As a result, no matter how beneficial to medical science and critical to the success of all healthcare organizations, big data can only be utilized if security and privacy concerns are addressed [5–7]. Thus it is essential to recognize the limitations of present security and privacy solutions and envisage future research paths in order to maintain a safe and trustworthy medical big data environment.

13.1.1 Contributions of the study

It has been highlighted that the use of big data and analytics techniques is constantly assisting in the administration and control of huge volumes of data created in the healthcare business [1–6], raising concerns about the security and privacy of this medical big data. In this respect, this research provides a brief overview of security and privacy problems as well as the current state of security and privacy solution deployment for medical big data as well as a security framework for protecting the security and privacy of medical big data. The following is a list of our study's significant contributions.

- First, a quick overview of the function of big data in medical care is offered.
- Second, for a better understanding, a quick review of the security and privacy of medical big data is offered.
- Third, we look at possible tactics and methodologies for dealing with security and privacy challenges in medical big data as well as the important components of security solution creation, as reported in the literature.
- Next the related work is highlighted in the form of a summary.
- Finally we highlight our proposed framework and the study ends with conclusions and future directions.

13.1.2 Outline of the study

The remainder of the research is structured as follows. The second section provides a brief explanation of big data, highlighting major aspects and offering significant information about medical big data. Following that, we give a brief discussion on the security and privacy of medical big data in Section 11.3. The protective methods are highlighted in Section 11.4, with a brief description of these preventative measures and associated studies. Our suggested security framework is given in Section 11.5. Finally, we come to a conclusion to our research in the last section.

13.2 Big data

The purpose of this section is to emphasize the fundamental aspects of big data and offer a prelude on medical big data, emphasizing how it differs from "Big Data" in general.

13.2.1 Big data characteristics

In general, big data can be categorized based on the following characteristics which are earlier known as three Vs. Now, this has extended toward five Vs to ten Vs [1–5].
1. *Volume*: Refers to the amount/volume of data, and the volume/amount of data may be used to classify the data as big data. As a result, while evaluating large data, this is a vital issue to consider [1–5].
2. *Variety*: Refers to a wide range of data sources and nature of data, which could be in many forms such as *unstructured, semi-structured* or *structured* [1–5].
3. *Velocity*: The pace at which data is created or processed is referred to as the data generation or processing rate. How rapidly data is produced and processed to meet demands determines its actual potential [1–5].
4. *Variability*: Refers to data inconsistencies that hinder the process of effectively handling and maintaining data [1–5].
5. *Veracity*: Refers to the capacity to trust data or the data source's reliability [1–5].
6. *Validity*: Relates to how the work will be completed with proper and valid/accurate data [1–5].
7. *Vulnerability*: When data is compromised, it raises a lot of worries about how vulnerable it is to security and privacy assaults [1–5].
8. *Volatility*: This is related to the life cycle of data, which refers to how long outdated data should be preserved before being discarded [1–5].
9. *Visualization*: This involves meaningful visualization of big data which is often not an easy [1–5].
10. *Value*: Refers to the conversion of data into money and represents the scientific worth assigned to the data [1–5].

Since 2010, big data has been in the limelight, and it is increasingly being employed in a variety of economic, social and professional settings [10–20]. For a better understanding, Table 13.1 outlines some of the important areas and applications where big data is now used [1, 5–10].

Big data allows a company to store and handle enormous amounts of data at rapid speeds in order to get the most useful information/insights from them. To examine diverse and abundant data and turn raw data into information to improve decision-making processes, several tools and approaches are necessary which is known as BDA, which refers to the tools and methods for transforming large amounts of data into in-

Table 13.1: Big data applications.

Application category	Applications
Healthcare	Disease prediction, improve the quality of patient care, medical research, cost reduction of medical treatments, identify the diseases at early stages and identify the best possible treatment plans, pandemic surveillance
Public sector	Surveillance, environmental protection, power generation and consumption (smart grid), tax reduction, public welfare
Education	Track student performance, improve student learning, provide student guidance
Entertainment	Manage content for a target audience, measure the performance, measure the feedback
Banking	Analyzing business, customer habit analysis, prognostic analytics
Industry	Improve the manufacturing process, improve the quality of products, reduce the errors
Transportation	Intelligent transport systems, traffic control, traffic congestion management, identify the best possible route (Google Maps), revenue management

formation that can be used for further analysis. BDA is a technology that combines IT, business professionals and data scientists, where it is concerned with gaining deeper insights from the underlying data. Different big data tools can be employed depending on the problem and the type of data to be examined, in a typical big data environment, Table 13.2 provides a summary of this various tools and approaches [1–5].

Table 13.2: Big data analytics tools and techniques.

Technique	Tools
Map reduce	Oozie, Flume, Pig, Hive
NoSQL	Cassandra
Storage	HDFS

Having provided a preamble on what is big data, characteristics and application areas, and analytical tools, in the next section we aim to provide a brief discussion on big data in the healthcare environment.

13.2.2 Big data in healthcare

Big data in healthcare has increased over the recent years owing to the increased adoption of IoT devices in healthcare, where most data comes from medical records [2]. This vast amount of data has the potential to revolutionize healthcare assisting disease diagnosis, clinical decision support systems, pandemic surveillance, population health management, food safety management, and so on [2–4]. As an example for detecting cancerous situations, it necessitates the collection of petabytes of data from multiple sources from the patient in order to determine the stage of the disease and the patient's chances of survival [5]. Furthermore, by focusing more on the preventative aspect and offering customized care, and based on continuous monitoring, the medical big data paradigm is decreasing the overall healthcare costs while increasing the quality of care. Based on the literature related to medical big data [1–17], big data is assisting and involving with medical care in various aspects by offering big data analytical capabilities, such as for offering patient-centric care, offering predictive analysis of disease, real-time patient condition monitoring and improving medical treatments. For better understanding the following highlights the benefits of big data in healthcare.

- **Offer patient-centric care:** In patient-centric care, medical big data assist in getting timely decisions based on the evidence inferred from the clinical data [1–3].
- **Offering predictive analysis of diseases:** Based on the evidence inferred from the underlying medical data, this helps to predict the spread of diseases and virus outbreaks and offers ample time to take necessary actions [1, 4–7].
- **Real-time patient condition monitoring:** Through the data collated from the IoT devices such as sensing devices and wearable devices, this helps to monitor the condition of patients in real time [3–7].
- **Improving medical treatments and quality of care:** Based on the current condition and the status inferred from the medical big data, this provides opportunities for medical staff to review the treatment plans and revise the plans considering the current condition of the patient. On the other hand, providing decisions, taken from real-time up to date medical data aid in improving the quality of care in a healthcare setting [3–7].
- **Reduction of mortality rate:** As big data ensures identification and diagnosis of diseases at the early stages, it guarantees that the right decisions are taken at the right time in a timely manner, which reduces patient morbidity and mortality [5–8].
- **Better communication between patient and healthcare provider:** Big data improves the communication amongst healthcare providers and patients by allowing them to share their ideas/prescriptions/advice/views through social medical sites, telemedicine tools [5–8].
- **Improves public health surveillance and response:** With the involvement of artificial intelligence and high-end data analytics tools and platforms, big data helps in the analysis of patterns of diseases, tracking and tracing of disease out-

breaks and spread, which would help in public health surveillance and having speedy responses [5–8].
- **Detection of security anomalies and fraud in medical care:** Big data with the collaboration of artificial intelligence tools help in identifying the presence of security anomalies and frauds in healthcare which comes from the internet facing devices and through the medical networks [5–8].
- **Improved patient participation:** Owing to the up-to-date and real-time insights provided by the medical big data, it gives a sense of satisfaction for patients and facilitates them to take any decisions of their wellbeing [7–10].
- **Reduced cost of care:** By enabling patients and medical staff to take timely and up-to-date and optimized decisions, big data allows to cut down unnecessary cost which involves patient care and medical environment [7–10].

In terms of medical big data applications, all big data-related medical applications can be apportioned into four key application types; that is, applications for providing patient-centric care, applications for predictive analysis, applications for real-time monitoring and applications for improving patient treatment as denoted in Table 13.3.

Table 13.3: Big data application in healthcare.

Category	Reference or the source
Patient-centric care	Raghupathi and Raghupathi [37], Kim et al. [38], Patel and Patel [39]
Predictive analysis	Chawla and Davis [40], Kuriyan and Cobb [41], Abinaya [42], Wang and Alexander [43]
Real-time monitoring	Shinde [44], Luo et al. [45], Balladini et al. [46], Boukenze et al. [47]
Improving patient treatment	Herland et al. [48], Belle et al. [49]

13.2.3 Sources of medical big data

The sources of medical big data come from a variety of sources and may vary depending on the context [10–17]. As it is essential to get to know the origin source of this big data, in the following we highlight the key origin sources that the big data are currently originated in a healthcare setting.
- **Sensors/machine-generated data:** Examples for machine/sensory data include data obtained for IoT sensing devices, wearable devices such as fitness trackers and other devices that measure vital signs of patients [1, 3].

- **Human-generated data:** This comprises data created by people interacting with medical systems, which frequently includes semi-structured and unstructured data such laboratory test results, clinical notes and hospital admission notes [2–4].
- **Social media and behavioral data:** this includes the data generated from social medic sites such as Twitter, Facebook and data generated as a result of social interactions [1–5].
- **Biometric data:** Biometric data often involves data that may be obtained from individuals such as signature, fingerprint, genetics, blood pressure, retinal scan, heart rate as well as medical images [1–5].
- **Epidemiological data:** This includes various sources of statistical data and data from medical surveys [1–5].
- **Transactional data:** This data includes transactional data happening across medical organizations such as billing [1–5].

Next, having provided a brief discussion on big data in the healthcare environment, we intended to discuss the security and privacy of medical big data as the focal point of this study.

13.3 Security and privacy of big data

When it comes to the security and privacy aspect of medical big data many studies, whitepapers and business reports [1–12] suggested if properly applied big data can be used to determine the correct treatments plans based on the patient condition, assurance of public and community health, improve the diagnosis process and improve the accuracy of clinical decisions, ensure proper management within medial organizations and ensure long-term sustainability of medical industry. However, several researchers have pointed out that this would be somewhat difficult owing to the security and privacy challenges, among many other challenges such as needed expertise and technological skills, heterogeneity and complexity pertained to the medical big data [10–12]. According to [2], the researchers pointed that in the medical industry security and privacy issues pertained to the big data can see on four stages that is data collection, data transmission, data storage, data usage and sharing stages.

Security of medical big data often involves having protection against unauthorized access, while ensuring fundamental information security concepts that is confidentiality, integrity and availability, where the focus is totally on protecting the data from a variety of cyber attacks. On the other hand, privacy is defined as protecting sensitive information from unauthorized disclosure, such as PII included with medical data. Further privacy focus on developing appropriate policies and authentication and authorization procedures toward guaranteeing that patient private data is collected, shared and used in an appropriate manner [17–20].

In Youssef [9], the researchers proposed a secure BDA framework for healthcare information system (HIS) as shown in Figure 13.1, which is composed of five components, which can be used to manage the medical big data in typical healthcare environment.

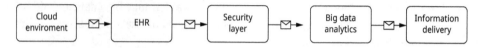

Figure 13.1: HIS framework proposed in [9].

The first component of the proposed HIS framework is composed of a cloud environment that provides various user services and allows data sharing between authorized users. The second component is electronic health record (EHR), which is used to collate and integrate patient data from various data sources in a typical medical environment. The third component is the security layer which is used to manage various security and privacy issues pertaining to the underlying medical big data such as authentication, authorization, data confidentiality and availability. In order to provide such medical services, the security layer is composed of cryptographic encryption algorithms such as RSA, RC4, AES and authentication techniques such as two factor authentication (2FA), one time password (OTP) for allowing access only to authorized users. Further, it also comprises access control mechanisms for authorizing users to execute tasks based on the granted access control privileges. The fourth layer comprises BDA tools to get insights from the raw medical data collated. Finally, the fifth component which is the information delivery layer takes care of delivering this medical information to relevant destinations and providing information services [9]. With this what we have understood is the security and privacy protection mechanisms should be an integral part of the medical big data life cycle from the point of data generation to the data processing and information dissemination stage, where we can provide optimal protection to underlying medical big data [21, 22]. In this regard in the next section, we intend to provide a brief summary of what actions can be taken against protecting the security and privacy of medical big data, followed by our derived security framework.

13.4 Security and privacy protection mechanisms

Having discussed the security and privacy pertained to the big data in healthcare, the main aim of this section is to outline a brief summary of available security and privacy protecting mechanisms for protecting medical big data based on the literature [22–30].

13.4.1 Encryption

Encryption involves transforming original data into an encoded form which is known as cipher text to hinder unauthorized access into the original data and this is the most commonly used method in protecting the confidentiality and integrity of data at rest or in transit. Once the data is encrypted using appropriate encryption algorithm, using decryption the cipher text can be transferred back to the original data as depicted in Figure 13.2. This encryption can be performed at different levels such as data base level, protocol level, disk level and file level to protect the underlying data. In this regard in a typical medical setting, a variety of private key cryptographic algorithms and public key algorithms are used to encrypt medical records [20–23].

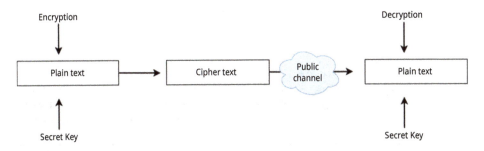

Figure 13.2: The encryption and decryption flow.

Even though encryption appears to be the most common solution for protecting the confidentiality and integrity of data, when they are deployed in a resource constrained environment, particularly in the resource constrained medical IoT environment, these algorithms may place an additional load on these resource-constrained IoT devices, which may sometimes affect data communication and proper device functioning. As previously said, these cryptographic algorithms may be divided into two categories based on the algorithm and the amount of keys. In private key cryptography or symmetric key cryptography, one key is used wherein the public key cryptography or asymmetric key cryptography two keys known as public and private are used [25], where it is believed that public-key cryptographic algorithms are more secured than the private ones.

Table 13.4 depicts the commonly used encryption algorithms that are already available for protecting medical big data in resource-constrained healthcare environment.

Based on these common encryption algorithms it is evident that there are already algorithms capable of effectively work on resources constrained medical applications such as Twofish and ECC algorithms.

Table 13.4: Common encryption algorithms that can apply for protecting data in medical environments.

Algorithm	Technology	Details
Data encryption standard (DES)	Symmetric key encryption	As DES is a symmetric key algorithm, it uses the same key for both encryption and decryption.
Advanced encryption standard (AES)	Symmetric key encryption	As AES is a symmetric key algorithm, it uses the same key for both encryption and decryption and often the key length can be vary.
Triple data encryption standard (3DES)	Symmetric key encryption	3DES is introduced for superseding the DES where in 3DES each block of data receives three passes unlike in DES.
RSA encryption	Asymmetric key encryption	This employs public-key encryption, which uses two keys: public and private key.
Twofish encryption	Symmetric key encryption	This employs symmetric key encryption, which proved to be really efficient with medical IoT devices with lower processing power.
Elliptic curve cryptography (ECC)	Asymmetric key encryption	This employs asymmetric key encryption which is based on the elliptic curve theory. This has been proved to be really efficient in working with resource-constrained IoT devices owing to the low resources consumption nature which result in improved security when dealing with IoT healthcare applications.

13.4.2 Implementation of access control mechanisms

Users have the ability to manage their own data thanks to access control, which determines their identity based on preset regulations that prohibit unauthorized users from accessing resources. Only approved devices and persons have access to medical servers as well as vital medical equipment and data, which are safeguarded by access control mechanisms [1, 5]. Access control may be utilized with a variety of encryption schemes, including symmetric and asymmetric encryption as well as attribute-based encryption [10, 12].

13.4.3 Data masking

By encrypting crucial aspects of PII, such as personal information, data masking ensures the confidentiality of medical data. To save the original data, it muddles or obscures the sensitive data by substituting it with unrelated data. To safeguard medical data from illegal disclosure, data obfuscation, data perturbation, data exclusion, data hashing and other EHR masking approaches can be used [20–23].

13.4.4 Data auditing

Personal health information (PHI) comprises a variety of pathological facts about patients, such as mental health, medical history and test findings, which might be used for profit by attackers [3]. As a result of the high value of this data, a simple data breach might threaten consumer's privacy. As a result, any action that included the creation or processing of this medical data, as well as its receiving, storage or transfer is required to be audited on a regular basis in order to detect any security flaws. Because the cloud cannot be entirely trusted, cloud data should be audited as well, as data in the untrusted cloud might be damaged and inadvertently erased without the data owner's explicit authorization [12–15].

13.4.5 Network layer defense mechanisms

Because of the ever-changing nature of advanced threats, most medical networks are now designed on a contained domain with a network defensive perimeter to protect against outside assaults and threats [6]. A network defense layer safeguards a healthcare institution by preventing external threats from infiltrating the medical network. For example, a private medical network might be outfitted with firewalls, intrusion detection systems and honeypots to secure the underlying data from outside network-level threats [15, 17, 18].

13.4.6 Data governance

The practice of appropriately controlling and managing medical data is referred to as data governance in healthcare. The objective is to provide a consistent data format that integrates industry standards as well as local and regional norms, allowing for successful data management, across all sorts of medical organizations [24, 26].

13.4.7 Compliance with the regulations

Patient pathology data is often maintained in the form of electronic medical records (EMR) in digital archives. This EMR may contain patient privacy information such as personal identifiers and mental health information, also known as PHI. In the recent years, we've seen an increase in the number of invaders targeting patient privacy information, and based on recent research, we've noticed that access breaches to medical data are growing more common owing to sophisticated cyber-attacks like ransomware [1–5]. As a result, securing the privacy of medical data while ensuring high availability for genuine users who need access has become a major concern. Several policies have been implemented across the world to increase medical data stewardship. The Health Insurance Portability and Accountability Act (HIPAA) of 1996 in the United States and the General Data Protection Regulation (GDPR) of 2016 in Europe are two examples of laws that require data to be stored and shared in a secure and privacy-preserving manner and may impose severe penalties in the event of a healthcare data breach [10, 21]. The HIPAA legislation, in particular, mandates the development of national standards to secure sensitive patient health information from disclosure without the patient's agreement or awareness. It states that all required safeguards are in place to ensure the security of patient data anytime it is accessed, kept or transferred. Failure to comply with HIPAA security rules can result in large penalties and, in certain situations, the revocation of a medical license [21–28].

13.4.8 Authentication

The process of authenticating a user's identification is known as authentication. Insufficient authentication protection schemas might allow intruders to enter the system and obtain access to the users' confidential healthcare data. All medical information systems should only be accessible by authorized and authenticated users or devices. This user and device authentication is critical for medical systems because it guarantees that data is properly ascribed and that information in the system is only available to authorized parties. The capacity to authenticate users of medical equipment might be utilized to ensure the integrity of data in healthcare systems. Authentication would also be used to protect patients' privacy by ensuring that sensitive information, such as EMR, is only available to those who are authorized and authenticated [20–27].

13.4.9 Data minimization

Data minimization advises limiting the collection of PHI to only the medical data that is required, as well as retaining medical data only for as long as it is required to provide the services that the users have requested [2–4]. Effective data minimization techniques in healthcare include reducing the overall amount of patient personal data collected, collecting only the personal data that is adequate and relevant for the intended purpose, deleting or masking obsolete or unnecessary personal data that is no longer needed and performing periodic checkups to ensure the adequacy and relevance of data collected. Because too much personal data may lead to increased dangers, effective data reduction can assist to reduce risks while also lowering storage costs [25–30].

13.4.10 Data anonymization

Data anonymization is the process of safeguarding private or sensitive information by eliminating or encrypting identifiers that link an individual to stored data. For example, you may run PII data such as your name, social security number and address through a data anonymization technique that keeps the data but hides the source [26].

13.4.11 Real-time security analytics

Because of the increasing threats, analyzing security and privacy threats and forecasting threat sources in real time is critical in the healthcare industry. The healthcare business is currently dealing with a slew of sophisticated threats, including ransomware, distributed denial of service and all sorts of malware [9, 12]. Furthermore, social engineering attacks are becoming more common, and the hazards associated with them are difficult to forecast without taking human cognitive behavior into account. As the healthcare industry embraces developing big data technologies to make better decisions, real-time security analytics should be a major component of any security solution for detecting security and privacy breaches before they occur [26].

13.5 Proposed security framework

Having discussed the security and privacy issues pertained to the medical big data including preventive mechanisms, this has motivated us to come up with a security framework that we can adopt for designing security solutions for protecting the security and privacy of medical big data, where the holistic overview of framework is shown in Figure 13.3.

According to the proposed security framework, as shown in Figure 13.3, general big data security system should comprise four layers that is data source, data storage, security and the application layer. In general, in a typical healthcare environment, environment itself is a distributed environment where data sources are located in distributed locations. Nevertheless the data may acquire from heterogeneous data sources such as from IoT sensing devices, EHR systems, wearable devices, medical imaging devices and clinical reports, where data from these sources are often in an unstructured format [7]. The second layer, depending on the type of data, is in charge of storing this diverse medical data. To improve data storage, retrieval and archiving functions, the data may be stored as data files or in a data warehouse depending on the data type. The third layer comprise security layer which provides various security and privacy protection mechanisms. In order to protect the underlying medical data various encryption mechanisms, data anonymization, masking and minimization mechanism and access control

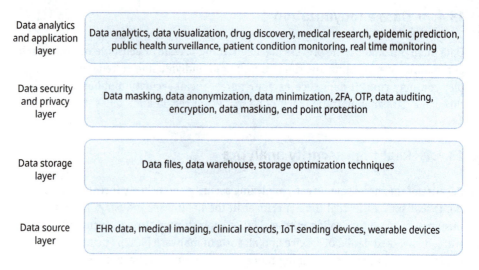

Figure 13.3: Design of secure medical big data framework.

mechanisms such as role-based access control, monitoring and auditing modules are embedded into this security layer, which we have discussed in the previous section. The fourth and the final application layer is responsible for providing data analytics and application services for end users. The data analytics part may comprise machine learning and deep learning methods such as neural networks, decision tree, support vector machine and naive Bayes algorithm in order to provide data analytical services which aid in accurate decision-making using various data classification and clustering techniques [7, 30–36]. Based on this proposed framework, we emphasize that security should be an integral part of medical big data [40–50], which should become an essential part of a big data life cycle in healthcare, where it will ensure optimal security.

13.6 Related work and discussion

After providing an overview of medical big data, security and privacy of medical big data, and protection mechanisms with our proposed framework, we provide a brief summary of related work carried out by other researchers in terms of security and privacy of medical big data, as shown in Table 13.5, to highlight the importance of our study.

Table 13.5: Comparison of related work.

Reference and year	Survey/ review	Research	Scope of the study
Kaur et al. [1]		✓	The authors present a brief overview of big data and its role in medical care in this study. Further, they also propose a design of a novel secure medical information system to handle medical data in a healthcare environment.
Jiang et al. [2]		✓	In an urban computing environment, the researchers looked at the danger of security and privacy leaks across the life cycle of medical big data.
Hamid et al. [3]		✓	The researchers in this study focused on deploying a fog computing facility to secure medical confidential data in the cloud.
Abouelmehdi et al. [7]	✓		In this research, the researchers evaluated the security and privacy aspect of medical big data and explored potential solutions.
Siddique et al. [8]	✓		The researchers discuss the state-of-the-art security and privacy problems pertaining to medical big data highlighting existing data privacy, data security and users' access control methodologies.
Youssef [9]		✓	The researchers presented a framework for a mobile cloud-based medical information system based on big data analytics.
Manogaran, et al. [10]		✓	The researchers proposed a secure industrial IoT architecture toward processing the big data collated from sensors for medical applications.
Manogaran et al. [11]		✓	In this study, the researchers proposed a knowledge management system based on big data to infer accurate clinical decisions.
Jee et al. [12]	✓		The researchers provide an overview of the current state of big data applications in medical care as well as the problems that governments and healthcare stakeholders face and the opportunities and possibilities that medical big data presents.
Price et al. [16]	✓		In the study, the researchers discuss the legal and ethical challenges that big data brings to patient privacy and importance of preserving this patient privacy.
Olaronke and Oluwaseun [17]	✓		The study looked at the fragmentation of healthcare data as well as ethical and usability issues as well as security and privacy concerns, as some of the roadblocks to successful big data application in healthcare.

Table 13.5 (continued)

Reference and year	Survey/ review	Research	Scope of the study
Sarkar [18]		✓	The researchers present a brief overview of medical big data and proposed a distributed model for protecting the patient data.
Patil et al. [26]	✓		The researchers present a brief review of security and privacy issues in terms of healthcare big data.
Rao et al. [27]	✓		In this study the research highlights the viable security solutions for medical big data.
Kuo et al. [28]	✓		In this study, the researchers discuss the characteristics of health big data as well as the challenges and solutions in terms of healthcare big data analytics.
Benjelloun et al. [29]	✓		The researchers present a brief review on security challenges in terms of big data including the solutions for protecting big data.
Uchibeke et al. [30]		✓	The researchers developed a blockchain access control system for protecting access to big data.
Kashyap and Piersson [31]	✓		The researchers have discussed the big data challenges in the study including the recent status of these challenges.
Kalejahi et al. [33]	✓		The researchers have provided a brief overview of big data in healthcare and also highlight the recent trends and challenges in that regard.
Esposito et al. [34]	✓		The researchers study the potential of blockchain technology toward protecting healthcare data hosted within the cloud.
Khaloufi, et al. [35]	✓		The researchers provided an overview of big data characteristics and challenges in healthcare and present a brief discussion on security threats that target healthcare big data throughout its life cycle in this study.
Jain et al. [36]	✓		In this study, the researchers focused on the security and privacy of big data and present a brief overview of security and privacy requirements.

13.6.1 Discussion

Big data has undeniable benefits for the healthcare industry toward improving the quality of patient care and magnifying the benefits from it. Security and privacy, on the other hand, is a key issue that big data in healthcare faces as of now, according to the literature we have reviewed. Based on the above summarization (Table 13.5), it is evident that many researchers have contributed to this subject where many have conducted surveys/reviews and research toward security and privacy aspects pertaining to the medical big data. Further, medical information is vulnerable to security concerns such as inappropriate patient information disclosure, unauthorized use of patient information and unauthorized data loss as we discussed earlier. As a result, the relevant stakeholders (e.g., physicians, medical staff, device manufactures and insurance service providers) in healthcare should take appropriate actions toward the protection of this medical data where the medical device manufacturers should take care of the security and privacy protection of these devices so that the data can be protected. On the other hand, when designing/setting up the medical environment and designing and deployment of security solutions the relevant stakeholders should think that security and privacy protection should be an integral part of the big data life cycle which is data generation [51, 52], data processing and data storage where optimal protection can be guaranteed to the underlying big data. The following resolutions are made in this respect in order for the healthcare system to benefit from the numerous benefits of big data in healthcare:

1. According to healthcare providers and BDA developers, healthcare data should be adequately safeguarded and secured.
2. Tools that ensure the security, integrity and availability of protected health information should be used while analyzing big data in healthcare.
3. To secure healthcare data throughout its life cycle, physical security, data encryption, user authentication and application security should all be employed.
4. Adoption of audit trail system should be an added advantage as all the transactions can be traced.

13.7 Conclusion

As big data possess the capability toward transforming healthcare to the next level, the underlying challenges that impede the thrive of technology needed to be addressed with urge, among which the security and privacy of medical big data are becoming an utmost concern among many researchers in this area. Thus in this regard, in this study, we reviewed the security and privacy aspects, affiliated with medical big data and foresee the need for security and privacy prevention mechanisms, which we proposed in a separate secure framework that can be used in secure solution development in terms of medical big data. We hope all our contributions would pave the way for future researchers to work in this area. What we have understood through this review is secure patient data management is becoming an inevitable part of global healthcare; hence, these secure protection mechanisms should be an integral part of big data life cycle that is data generation, data processing and data storage stages in the medical big data life cycle. To contribute in this regard, many researchers have done surveys/reviews and novel preventive mechanisms with regard to each phase of the medical big data life cycle whereas in this research we have collated all this knowledge into one study, emphasizing that security and privacy preventive mechanisms should be an integral part of the medical big data lifecycle.

First, we have provided a brief overview of big data and then about the medical data. Second, we have provided a brief discussion on the security and privacy of medical big data and afterward, we have evaluated the security and privacy preventive mechanisms in this regard. Next based on the reviewed literate we have proposed a secure framework for medical big data and next we have summarized the related work followed by our conclusion that security and privacy should be an integral part of the big data life cycle. Finally, day by day the big data and associated technologies are evolving with a rapid phase where security and privacy-preserving real-time analytics will be the key toward propelling proactive healthcare and wellness in global healthcare in near future.

References

[1] Kaur, P., Sharma, M. & Mittal, M. (2018). Big data and machine learning based secure healthcare framework. Procedia Computer Science, 132, 1049–1059.

[2] Jiang, R., Shi, M. & Zhou, W. (2019). A privacy security risk analysis method for medical big data in urban computing. IEEE Access, 7, 143841–143854.

[3] Al Hamid, H. A., Rahman, S. M. M., Hossain, M. S., Almogren, A. & Alamri, A. (2017). A security model for preserving the privacy of medical big data in a healthcare cloud using a fog computing facility with pairing-based cryptography. IEEE Access, 5, 22313–22328.

[4] Rice, M. (n.d.). 17 big data examples and applications. Built In. Retrieved October 20, 2021, from https://builtin.com/big-data/big-data-examples-applications.

[5] Taylor, D. (October, 2021). What is big data? Introduction, types, characteristics and examples. Guru99. Retrieved October 20, 2021, from https://www.guru99.com/what-is-big-data.html.

[6] 27+ big data statistics – how big it actually is in 2021? TechJury. (October, 2021). Retrieved October 20, 2021, from https://techjury.net/blog/big-data-statistics/#gref.

[7] Abouelmehdi, K., Beni-Hessane, A. & Khaloufi, H. (2018). Big healthcare data: Preserving security and privacy. Journal of Big Data, 5(1), 1–18.

[8] Siddique, M., Mirza, M. A., Ahmad, M., Chaudhry, J. & Islam, R. (August, 2018). A survey of big data security solutions in healthcare. In International Conference on Security and Privacy in Communication Systems. Springer, Cham, 391–406.

[9] Youssef, A. E. (2014). A framework for secure healthcare systems based on big data analytics in mobile cloud computing environments. International Journal of Ambient Systems and applications, 2(2), 1–11.

[10] Manogaran, G., Thota, C., Lopez, D. & Sundarasekar, R. (2017). Big data security intelligence for healthcare industry 4.0. In Cybersecurity for Industry 4.0. Springer, Cham, 103–126.

[11] Manogaran, G., Thota, C., Lopez, D., Vijayakumar, V., Abbas, K. M. & Sundarsekar, R. (2017). Big data knowledge system in healthcare. In Internet of Things and Big Data Technologies for Next Generation Healthcare. Springer, Cham, 133–157.

[12] Jee, K. & Kim, G. H. (2013). Potentiality of big data in the medical sector: Focus on how to reshape the healthcare system. Healthcare Informatics Research, 19(2), 79–85.
[13] https://www.digitalauthority.me/resources/big-data-in-healthcare/.
[14] Jagadeeswari, V., Subramaniyaswamy, V., Logesh, R. & Vijayakumar, V. (2018). A study on medical Internet of Things and Big Data in personalized healthcare system. Health information science and systems, 6(1), 1–20.
[15] Kankanhalli, A., Hahn, J., Tan, S. & Gao, G. (2016). Big data and analytics in healthcare: Introduction to the special section. Information Systems Frontiers, 18(2), 233–235.
[16] Price, W. N. & Cohen, I. G. (2019). Privacy in the age of medical big data. Nature Medicine, 25(1), 37–43.
[17] Olaronke, I. & Oluwaseun, O. (December, 2016). Big data in healthcare: Prospects, challenges and resolutions. In 2016 Future technologies conference (FTC) (pp. 1152–1157). IEEE.
[18] Sarkar, B. K. (2017). Big data for secure healthcare system: A conceptual design. Complex & Intelligent Systems, 3(2), 133–151.
[19] Thilakarathne, N. N., Kagita, M. K. & Gadekallu, T. R. (2020). The role of the Internet of Things in health care: A systematic and comprehensive study. International Journal of Engineering and Management Research (IJEMR), 10(4), 145–159.
[20] Thilakarathne, N. N. (2021). Review on the use of ICT driven solutions towards managing global pandemics. Journal of ICT Research & Applications, 14(3).
[21] Thilakarathne, N. N., Kagita, M. K., Gadekallu, T. R. & Maddikunta, P. K. R. (2020). The adoption of ict powered healthcare technologies towards managing global pandemics. arXiv preprint arXiv:2009.05716.
[22] Mahendran, R. K. & Velusamy, P. (2020). A secure fuzzy extractor based biometric key authentication scheme for body sensor network in Internet of Medical Things. Computer Communications, 153, 545–552.
[23] Mustafa, M. M., Parthasarathy, V., Kumar, M. R. & Hemalatha, S. (2016). An efficient DTDM H-MAC protocol with self-calibrating algorithm in BSN for sporting application.
[24] Samarasinghe, R., Yasutake, Y. & Yoshida, T. (March, 2005). Optimizing the access performance and data freshness of distributed cache objects considering user access pattern. In 19th International Conference on Advanced Information Networking and Applications (AINA'05) Volume 1 (AINA papers) (Vol. 2, pp. 325–328). IEEE.
[25] Samarasinghe, N. R. (2006). A framework of adaptable access strategies for enhancing access performance and QoD in open distributed environment (Doctoral dissertation, 九州工業大学).
[26] Patil, H. K. & Seshadri, R. (June, 2014). Big data security and privacy issues in healthcare. In 2014 IEEE international congress on big data (pp. 762–765). IEEE.
[27] Rao, S., Suma, S. N. & Sunitha, M. (May, 2015). Security solutions for big data analytics in healthcare. In 2015 s international conference on advances in computing and communication engineering (pp. 510–514). IEEE.
[28] Kuo, M. H., Sahama, T., Kushniruk, A. W., Borycki, E. M. & Grunwell, D. K. (2014). Health big data analytics: Current perspectives, challenges and potential solutions. International Journal of Big Data Intelligence, 1(1–2), 114–126.
[29] Benjelloun, F. Z. & Lahcen, A. A. (2019). Big data security: Challenges, recommendations and solutions. In Web Services: Concepts, Methodologies, Tools, and Applications (pp. 25–38). IGI Global.

[30] Uchibeke, U. U., Schneider, K. A., Kassani, S. H. & Deters, R. (July, 2018). Blockchain access control Ecosystem for Big Data security. In 2018 IEEE International Conference on Internet of Things (iThings) and IEEE Green Computing and Communications (GreenCom) and IEEE Cyber, Physical and Social Computing (CPSCom) and IEEE Smart Data (SmartData) (pp. 1373–1378). IEEE.

[31] Kashyap, R. & Piersson, A. D. (2018). Big data challenges and solutions in the medical industries. In Handbook of Research on Pattern Engineering System Development for Big Data Analytics (pp. 1–24). IGI Global.

[32] Gupta, D. N. K. (2018). Addressing big data security issues and challenges. International Journal of Computer Engineering & Technology, 9(4), 229–237.

[33] Kalejahi, B. K., Meshgini, S., Yariyeva, A., Ndure, D., Maharramov, U. & Farzamnia, A. (2019). Big data security issues and challenges in healthcare. arXiv preprint arXiv:1912.03848.

[34] Esposito, C., De Santis, A., Tortora, G., Chang, H. & Choo, K. K. R. (2018). Blockchain: A panacea for healthcare cloud-based data security and privacy?. IEEE Cloud Computing, 5(1), 31–37.

[35] Khaloufi, H., Abouelmehdi, K., Beni-hssane, A. & Saadi, M. (2018). Security model for big healthcare data lifecycle. Procedia Computer Science, 141, 294–301.

[36] Jain, P., Gyanchandani, M. & Khare, N. (2016). Big data privacy: A technological perspective and review. Journal of Big Data, 3(1), 1–25.

[37] Raghupathi, W. & Raghupathi, V. (2014). Big data analytics in healthcare: Promise and potential. Health information science and systems, 2(1), 1–10.

[38] Kim, M. J. & Yu, Y. S. (2015). Development of real-time big data analysis system and a case study on the application of information in a medical institution. International Journal of Software Engineering and Its Applications, 9(7), 93–102.

[39] Patel, S. & Patel, A. (2016). A big data revolution in health care sector: Opportunities, challenges and technological advancements. International Journal of Information, 6(1/2), 155–162.

[40] Chawla, N. V. & Davis, D. A. (2013). Bringing big data to personalized healthcare: A patient-centered framework. Journal of general internal medicine, 28(3), 660–665.

[41] Kuriyan, J. & Cobb, N. (2013). Forecasts of cancer and chronic patients: Big data metrics of population health. arXiv preprint arXiv:1307.3434.

[42] Abinaya, K. (2015). Data mining with big data e-health service using map reduce. International Journal of Advanced Research in Computer and Communication Engineering, 4(2), 123–127.

[43] Wang, L. & Alexander, C. A. (2016). Big data analytics as applied to diabetes management. European Journal of Clinical and Biomedical Sciences, 2(5), 29–38.

[44] Shinde, K. V. (2016). A real time monitoring system in healthcare with Hadoop. Research Journey'International Multidisciplinary E-Research Journal, Special Issue-I, 15–19.

[45] Luo, J., Wu, M., Gopukumar, D. & Zhao, Y. (2016). Big data application in biomedical research and health care: A literature review. Biomedical informatics insights, 8, BII–S31559.

[46] Balladini, J., Rozas, C., Frati, F. E., Vicente, N. & Orlandi, C. (2015). Big data analytics in intensive care units: Challenges and applicability in an Argentinian hospital. Journal of Computer Science & Technology, 15(02), 61–67.

[47] Boukenze, B., Mousannif, H. & Haqiq, A. (2016). A conception of a predictive analytics platform in healthcare sector by using data mining techniques and Hadoop. International Journal of Advanced Research in Computer Science and Software Engineering, 6(8), 65–70.

[48] Herland, M., Khoshgoftaar, T. M. & Wald, R. (2014). A review of data mining using big data in health informatics. Journal of Big data, 1(1), 1–35.

[49] Belle, A., Thiagarajan, R., Soroushmehr, S. M., Navidi, F., Beard, D. A. & Najarian, K. (2015). Big data analytics in healthcare. BioMed Research International.

[50] Elhoseny, M., Thilakarathne, N. N., Alghamdi, M. I., Mahendran, R. K., Gardezi, A. A., Weerasinghe, H. & Welhenge, A. (2021). Security and privacy issues in medical internet of things: Overview, countermeasures, challenges and future directions. Sustainability, 13(21), 11645.
[51] Thilakarathne, N. N., Priyashan, W. M. & Premarathna, C. P. (July, 2021). Artificial intelligence-enabled IoT for health and wellbeing monitoring. In 2021 12th International Conference on Computing Communication and Networking Technologies (ICCCNT) (pp. 01–07). IEEE.
[52] Thilakarathne, N. N., Weerasinghe, H. D., Welhenge, A. & Kagita, M. K. (July, 2021). Privacy dilemma in healthcare: A review on privacy preserving medical internet of things. In 2021 12th International Conference on Computing Communication and Networking Technologies (ICCCNT) (pp. 1–10). IEEE.

Jay Gohil
14 Big data analytics in effective implementation of healthcare management

Abstract: Healthcare sector happens to be one of the most vital, fast growing, and economically significant sectors across the globe, while currently standing at $116 billion expected market in the future with lives along the line. This makes each and every aspect of it crucial to understand and thus is the advent of big data and associated big data analytics (BDA). Moreover, management of the healthcare sector or industry has always been a challenging feat to accomplish, and with the generation of humongous size of data (termed as "big data"), it's now possible to use the technological advancements such as BDA to make the management process less time-extensive, resource-hungry, and costly (and hence more feasible to execute). Thus, this chapter sheds some light on the big data by introducing it alongwith BDA, characteristics, workflow, and much more. Upon complete comprehension of the chapter, the reader will be precisely equipped with inclusive knowledge of the associated concepts mentioned in the chapter, while possessing the ability to apply and understand these topics in the future real-world cases.

Keywords: Healthcare, management, big data, implementation, big data analytics

14.1 Introduction

Big data simply denotes massive and perplexed datasets (or sets of data) which are naturally humongous that make storing, managing, and processing of the same in a time-effective and economically viable manner beyond traditional data-management methods or systems' capabilities. Usually found in the size of petabytes, it can be divided into structured, unstructured, and semi-structured types of data. Moreover, it is in itself pretty much redundant and non-useful. However, this can potentially change with the help of BDA that helps in data acquisition, storing, encoding, sharing, processing, and visualizing in a feasible manner for big data [1].

Jay Gohil, Department of Information and Communication Technology, School of Technology, Pandit Deendayal Energy University, Gandhinagar 382007, Gujarat, India, e-mail: jay.gict19@sot.pdpu.ac.in

https://doi.org/10.1515/9783110750942-014

Considering the fact that big data happens to be in its infant stage in terms of adoption and implementation while being a disruptive phenomenon, exploiting the capabilities of the big data can pose several benefits that are beyond one's comprehension. For instance, due to its catered benefits, it is already been used in finance, environmental research, genomics, healthcare, retail, and life science research despite being in its early stages of implementation! In fact, by the end of 2027, its market is predicted to rise to a whopping $116 billion [2]!

In lieu of the advances in big data and BDA (along with its catered advantages), its role pertaining to the healthcare sector will be of significant importance as it happens to be one of the world's most critical, fastest, and biggest advancing industries [3, 4]! Pertaining to healthcare, big data simply comprises patient management data such as doctoral notes, lab reports, imagery reports, historical cases, diet plan, doctors and nurses' list, surgical instruments data, medicinal metadata, and expiry date data, among various others.

This exponential growth has been made possible due to the data acquired such as e-health records, IoT devices, and/or registries which simply has resulted in a big data advancements' tsunami in the healthcare industry! The application of BDA on the same can help healthcare organizations in capturing all of this information about a patient to get more comprehensive outlook and insights into care synchronization, patient engagement, result-based compensation models, and health monitoring, among others. Moreover, it can also result into an enhanced life quality, illness diagnosis and treatment, and waste minimization resulting in viable healthcare management in general [5].

In a nutshell, a proper healthcare management system comprises and enables the following:
- Patients' engagement (along with their family members)
- Reduction of health-based inequalities
- Improvement in care-service synchronization
- Increase in transparency and patients' empowerment
- Ensuring the security and privacy of patients' medical data
- Improvement of safety, speed, effectiveness, and service quality
- Creation of rich health-systems-based research-oriented data
- Enhancement of patient and population-based medical treatment results

The chapter's organization is as per the following structure. After introduction (section X.1), it enumerates various characteristics of big data (section X.2) followed by big data platforms (section X.3), BDA workflow (section X.4), machine learning algorithms (section X.5), and healthcare management applications (section X.6); ended by challenges (section X.7), future scope (section X.8), and conclusion (section X.9).

14.2 The 6Vs of big data in healthcare

Until now, it is evident that the importance of big data is unparalleled. However, to understand the intricate aspects and how application of big data helps, we need to comprehend the several Vs associated with it that include volume, variety, velocity, value, veracity, and variability [14, 15].

- **Volume**

It is one of the simplest aspects of big data and denotes the data size or quantity at hand along with processing capacity of the same. The volume, especially in healthcare sector, has been on the rise for years now and is on the verge of exponential explosion in the decades to come due to betterments in the equipment and data generation tools (that has resulted in higher quality images, audio, X-ray scans, and check-up data, among others). For instance, EMC states that 4.4 zettabytes of healthcare data existed globally in 2013 and set out to reach 44 zettabytes by 2020 (and thus it's likely a lot more as of now).

- **Variety**

Variety, in a nutshell, refers to the diversity and multiplicity in various "types" of data formats in which big data exists. It is majorly divided into three types, namely structured, unstructured, and semi-structured data [16]. It also includes a combination of two or all in it, although it has been reported that almost 90% of all data generated is unstructured [17]. In healthcare, the variety is surplus and include genomics, metabolomics, transcriptomics, interactomics, pharmacogenomics, diseasomics, biomedical, epigenomics, proteomics, and e-health records data.

- **Velocity**

Velocity denotes the methodology for handling of data (along with its generation speed) as well as transferring of the same across devices, platforms, and/or cloud services. Its characterization includes near time, real time, batches, and streams. Moreover, it also deals with time and latency aspects of data management that is tremendously vital in the healthcare sector. Few instances of velocity characteristic of big data in healthcare include patient record transfer across service providers, medicine availability data sync across hospitals, hospital transportation system updates on the main server, patient data transfer in inter-hospital franchises, and real-time equipment handling for surgeries.

- **Value**

Value on the other hand denotes the advantages that big data's implementation in a constructive manner imparts. It also involves the understanding of potential to create revenue, uncover opportunities, and improve efficiency, among others, through big data. In a nutshell, it simply outlines the results that the proper and educated application of big data caters. Although massive, few instances of value provided by big data in healthcare include efficiency improvements, wastage reduction, real-time monitoring, reduced analysis time duration, remote treatment, and accurate AI-ML-based disease classification.

- **Variability**

Variability simply refers to the change in big data and its application methodology for feasibility and includes data management in a methodology that imparts a proper structuring of the application (in the impulsive and ever-changing data environments as well). In healthcare, variability can resonate with different sources of data (of different types) that are supposed to be analyzed together for a cohesive outcome or a cumulation of different outcomes (such as patient imagery data, health record, and real-time vitals for a cumulative analysis of patient's condition)!

- **Veracity**

It refers to big data quality being provided by the healthcare services providers; which includes the ability to use the potential provided by different data types (structured, unstructured, and semi-structured) as well as sources to best application scenario while being implemented in a feasible manner. In healthcare, it simply refers to the richness as well as accuracy of data for aspects such as patient records, medicine information, real-time vitals, check-up results, or reports. On a side note, it needs to be taken into consideration that healthcare data quality is highly important for major improvements in offered services [20] and reduction in their delivery expenditure [18].

On a side note, there are various other (less widespread) Vs related to big data as well, including Validity (that refers to the precision and accuracy of available data for future use), Viscosity (that is a subset of velocity that specifically deals with lag and latency of big data), and Visualization (referring to the visual representation of humongous data for clear and direct comprehension).

Moreover, the comprehensive information about all the big data Vs can be comprehended with the help of condensed diagram in Figure 14.1. As perceived until now, conclusion can be derived that the major aim here is to allow entities using it to process and analyze complex data within feasible amount of time and resources (that would otherwise be impossible to achieve using traditional methods).

14.3 Big data platforms

Considering all the characteristics of big data, there is a need for managing and handling it in a single place or platform to make the execution of BDA feasible, which is where big data platforms come. Although in their initial stages of development, they do help in battling a lot of difficulties in big data applications. Major big data platforms include:

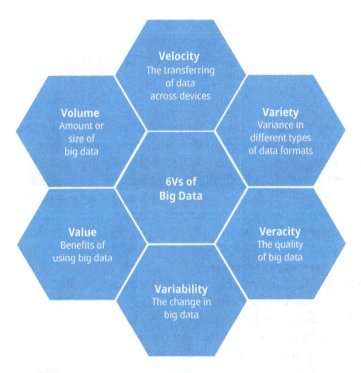

Figure 14.1: Big data's 6Vs.

– **Hadoop**

Apache Hadoop refers to an amalgamation of open-source packages that enables computer networks' usage for solving issues that involve working with humongous data sizes (or big data) along with extensive calculational resources. Simply, it facilitates the underlying Hadoop clusters' storage while dividing the information or data into tiny chunks and distributes them across different nodes or servers for feasible access and processing of the same (big data).

– **Apache Cassandra**

It's an open source NoSQL database management system (while being distributed and wide-column store) designated as a top-level project modeled for managing large chunks of data (or big data) distributed across several commodities or utility servers while ensuring great availability that has zero failure point. This ensures that the big data in usage is handled correctly and efficiently in a feasible manner.

– **Hive**

It's a runtime Hadoop support architecture and data warehouse infrastructure that uses Hadoop platform-enabled SQL (Structure Query Language) and creates interaction between user and HDFS (Hadoop Distributed File System). It allows coders to create statements of Hive Query Language (similar to standard statements of SQL). It also supports Hive HD Insight, Web UI, and CMD among others as added functionalities. In short, the aforementioned tools and services make the handling of big data through Hive on top of Hadoop with viable management of the same.

– **MapReduce**

MapReduce refers to a programming paradigm that provides capability for massive scalability across hundreds (or even thousands) of Hadoop cluster servers. As the processing component, MapReduce stands as the heart of Apache Hadoop. In a nutshell, it offers an interface for outputs and sub-tasks distribution; and once they are performed, each server or node's processing is tracked by MapReduce (easing the process of data management). Hence, MapReduce helps in proper processing and execution of big-data-based operations (on a huge scale with ease).

– **Oracle Architecture Development Process**

OADP is an Oracle platform that is specifically dedicated for big data analytics that consists of different products that cater to different data management needs. Few concepts offered by OADP architecture include Oracle Real-time Decisions, Exadata, Big Data Discovery, Endeca, NoSQL Database, and Data Integrator (ODI). Being a pioneer in cloud technology, the cloud-based architecture does provide a lot of benefits to healthcare providers on top of big data-based benefits if used wisely. Therefore, OADP simply aids in proper management and feasible analysis of big data on Oracle infrastructure.

– **IBM InfoShpere**

IBM InfoSphere is a data integration software platform that helps in mitigating a vital issue with analyzing humongous amounts of datasets, which is time and resources required for analysis. It consists of tools such as IBM InfoSphere DataStage which is an extract, transform, and load (ETL) tool. It solves a major problem of time and resources by undertaking complex computations in a comparatively less amount of time, while supporting massive amounts of data. In a nutshell, InfoSphere helps in complete big data pipeline management including data ETL, storing, processing, analyzing, and deploying.

The use of these platforms among others provides several benefits in healthcare management that include overall cost reduction, feasible data management, ease of use by non-tech professionals, superior tools availability, resource requirement reduction, aesthetic visualizations, and increased analysis performance.

14.4 Big data application workflow in healthcare management

Once comprehension of the characteristics and platforms pertaining to big data is done, it is vital to understand how exactly the application of BDA is actually undertaken by shedding light on its workflow or architecture [42] and is hereby mentioned.

– **Concept statement**
This stage simply defines the problem at hand and the requirement for BDA implementation for the situation (pertaining to healthcare management). For instance, the problem can be the accurate and efficient assignment of hospital resources to all patients in a hospitable franchise.

– **Project proposal**
This stage defines the intricacies of the project or implementation including:
  – solution to be addressed
  – importance in healthcare management
  – reason for interest in implementation
  – reason for BDA approach
  – background information on the problem

For instance, it could be about seamless assignment of hospitable resources in an automated manner for saving time of health professionals that would lead to better delivery of hospital services.

– **Data collection**
Data collection consists of the big data acquisition for the actual implementation and marks the beginning for BDA. There are various big data sources that are external, internal, multi-media, multiple sources, and implementations among others. For instance, the acquisition of big data in healthcare management can occur from a cumulation of internal patients' data, real-time customer data, partnered medical-facilities' data, and inter-franchise data.

– **Data transformation**
Also known as data cleaning and engineering, data transformation stage takes care of converting the raw data that comes in from the collection stage into something that can be sent for actual analysis process. It takes care of removing noise and unwanted junk from big data, making it workable. It also consists of data classification where the input raw healthcare data is classified for easier analysis in further stages into unstructured, structured, and semi-structured. On a side note, this also resonates with

the ETL (extract, transform, and load) process. For instance, this step can involve medical unit synchronization, data type-casting, and dataset(s) merging in healthcare management.

- **Analysis methodology**

This stage is where decisions on the actual analysis implementation occur. The selection of variables (for taking into consideration), selection of platforms pertaining to big data (including tools to be used), analytical techniques selection, and different model selection (to be discussed in next chapter) happen here. For instance, this sub-process decides whether the assignment AI algorithm based on big data should aim for super-high accuracy but with long execution time or moderate accuracy with fast execution time.

- **Data modeling**

This stage comprises implementation of BDA through several steps that include:
- big data transfer to platform and usage
- data classification and modification for feeding
- tool, technique, and model implementation
- execution of BDA
- retrieve results of analysis

In a nutshell, in healthcare management, this simply refers to the actual process of implementation of big data tools and services.

- **Performance analysis**

This stage takes of understanding whether the execution of BDA on healthcare management's several aspects is viable or not by analyzing the performance of implementation results. This is done by taking several factors into consideration such as time and resources used, accuracy of results, and value of results received among others. If the results are satisfactory, the last stage is executed. For instance, this includes testing of whether the assignment is being done accurately in a feasible amount of time.

- **Deployment**

This is the last stage in implementation workflow where the data analytics implementation is successful and deemed satisfactory. Having mentioned that, the deployment phase begins, where the analysis system (software, cloud service, etc.) resets in place and starts to be used on a daily basis. Once it is set up, scheduled reports and insights can start being generated. Moreover, the stage also keeps a check on post-production testing where feedback is taken on a consistent basis to keep improving the system in the long term. For instance, this sub-process signifies the actual deployment and starting of the automated assignment of hospitals' resources.

A successful execution of the aforementioned workflow helps in seamless and effective working of BDA; while ensuring that there are no hurdles along the way. Moreover, the workflow can be visually comprehended in Figure 14.2.

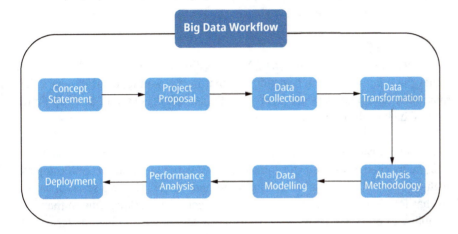

Figure 14.2: Big data workflow.

14.5 ML in BDA and different algorithms

One key part of the BDA implementation discussed earlier is the actual analysis process that uncovers hidden patterns and provides insights that would be tremendously useful in entire healthcare management process. In the recent years, considering the massive amount of data at hand, BDA has mostly revolved upon the use machine learning algorithms to provide the insights from the data. Thus, knowing that ML algorithms play such a huge role (the actual analysis) in BDA implementation, it's vital to look at major algorithms in machine learning domain (and how they operate).

– **Linear regression (LR)**
LR refers to a rectilinear methodology to create two (or more) dependent and independent variables' relationship(s). It is one of the most common, easy to use, and feasible algorithms to implement when the data at hand is not complex (and only big).

– **Support vector machine (SVM)**
SVMs are an instance-based and supervised ML model that aim to find a unique (and most effective) hyperplane that creates a form of separation between different classes of data points (or information) and is generally used for mostly classification purposes (but also for regression purposes seldomly).

- **K-Nearest Neighbour (KNN)**
K-Nearest Neighbour algorithms are meant for classification of information or data points, while taking the metadata, parameters, or value of their nearest neighbor into consideration. Its implementation usually results in decrease of error occurrence and thus is a viable option when error avoidance is vital [21].

- **Decision tree (DT)**
Decision trees are a type of supervised ML algorithm that require explanation on what does the input map to corresponding output in the training dataset) where the information or data points are continuously split (according to certain decisions) into entities that include decision nodes and leaves.

- **Artificial neural network (ANN)**
Artificial neural networks are algorithms that possess the ability to process complex and high-dimensional information or data points and simply refer to a series of calculations that focus on imitating the human brain's complex working. Due to their inherent ability to process humongous amounts of data and fetch hidden patterns and insights due to deep learning methodology (that they are based on), they are widely used in every industry.

These algorithms portray the majority of machine learning implementation upon which BDA takes place during actual analysis. However, healthcare service providers can use a combination of them (or even develop custom algorithms) for improved analysis in terms of accuracy, resources, and time constraints.

14.6 Application of BDA in healthcare management

Now, once most of healthcare management's aspects of BDA implementation are comprehended successfully including characteristics (6 Vs), platforms, workflow, and algorithms, it is now the best instance to take a look at various applications of the same for effective healthcare management.

- **Medical diagnosis**
Medical diagnosis simply refers to the process of understanding which condition and/or disease resonates with a person's symptoms and signs in healthcare. It is usually the first thing that one might think of, when thinking about healthcare industry. Considering the fact that it is seamless with the actual treatment process of patients in the industry and is portrayed as the main spotlight, big data possess various benefits such as diagnosis-based detection of nascent stage illnesses which might result in reduction of complications during the actual treatment [9, 30] and classification and detection of

cervical cancerous cells based on AI neural networks [46] that prove to be tremendously useful.

– **Prevention measure**
A major aspect of hospital and medical entities' management happens to be the preventive measure that they undertake in order to avoid major escalations in health-based issues. It's important basically because of the reason that rather than treating, it is better to prevent an illness. Thus, big data helps in ensuring effective preventive measures by predicting patients' potential health hazard which helps significantly in decision-making by health professionals for individual treatment [23] and help healthcare authorities that work hard on taking preventive steps against predicted chronic disease risks among a population [23] and contagious disease outbreaks [31]. It has been useful so far in applications such as big data-based reporting for preventive health management using wearable technologies [25, 26] and customized health assessment, disease management, and wellness plan [24].

– **Disease transmission prediction**
BDA has a great application of modeling various scenarios and disease transmission (communicable diseases' transfer from a disease-ridden person or group of contagious organisms to others) modeling in healthcare management helps in prevention and control of the transmission of the disease (especially in an epidemic like COVID outbreak). It has had several real-world implementations as well such as monitoring system based on big data for continuous control and dengue surveillance with the help of real-time environmental data acquired through a combination of sensors, BDA and AI [22].

– **Health insurance**
In a nutshell, it refers to coverage (complete or partial) of economic risk of a person's clinical or health-based expenditures due to which it lies at the center of healthcare management. Considering this and the fact that insurance is basically finance (and numbers at its core), big data does and can act in a major role in streamlining along with improving efficiency of the same. For instance, Delen et al. [27] in their 2009 study used predictive analytics for the identification of significant factors for possessing healthcare coverage.

– **Service delivery system**
Healthcare management decides healthcare service delivery's quality through health workforce, procurement, supplies, and financing. Thus, healthcare service providers must ensure that they meet a threshold standard of quality by taking aforementioned aspects into consideration. Major measurement parts of systems (pertaining to service delivery) include the principles, user experience, employee involvement, and quality of service(s). Considering this, it's rather pointless to note that BDA in healthcare man-

agement provides quality insights and quality of rendered services and improves decision making [28, 29].

– **Patient care**
Patient care is another vital aspect of healthcare management and takes a huge portion of time and resources spent in the health industry. Thus, the fact that BDA can aid in ensuring that time and resources are used in the most efficient manner is surely something that has led to its widespread usage. It has also been tested successfully. For instance, customized patient care facilitated by BDA can result in provision of rapid relief [33] and reduction of readmission rates in hospitals [34].

– **Hospital monitoring**
One of the key parts of healthcare management is the monitoring and surveillance of the very place that performs the actual healthcare tasks, which are hospitals. Considering the fact that there can be multiple avenues to monitor (at different hospitals and different time-zone among other difficulties), big data can ease the process of doing so and unburden the service providers so that they can focus on service delivery for the betterment of everyone. Big data has been useful in the real world as well, and one instance is the real-time monitoring of hospitals that can help government authorities in ensuring optimal service quality as noted by Archenaa and Anita in their 2015 study [32].

14.7 Challenges

Considering all the aspects pertaining to BDA discussed in this chapter, there are various challenges and hurdles that currently restrict the healthcare sector's usage of big data in a widespread and effective manner. First of all, the high volume, variability, veracity, and vitality of big data make its management (including data acquisition, data storage, transfer, and analysis) in real time, a difficult task to undertake. Moreover, it is also difficult for BDA to live up to the expectations of healthcare institutions, its patients, providers, employees, and several institutions (regulatory and monitory) as it is still in its infancy [6].

Moving forward, the nonuniformity of the sector's big data happens to a major issue as it leads to poor analytical performance, higher requirement of resources, and increased execution time. The presence of additional variables in the dataset is also a plus to the already complex data in the sector. As a result of this, it leads to the requirement of parallel processing and real-time data sharing which in itself leads to several other issues.

The lack of professional expertise (whether due to lack of investment or sheer absence of available talent) also happens to be a major hurdle, as the success of everything else depends on it; and without it, there's no point of investments, strategies, or workflows/plans. The lack of transparency, job security, and clear outlook of future roles also makes it a less viable career option that eventually results in less talent pool that keeps getting more expensive.

Furthermore, a need for BDA platforms is also there that possess the capability to perform necessary actions/tasks for successful implementation along with the inclusion of accessibility, feasibility, privacy, scalability, steadiness, granular manipulability, security, and quality [8–10]. And finally, considering the fact that most data pertaining to privacy is disjoined or in improper datatype and isn't standardized [9], there's a dire need for proper expertise in the sector! Moreover, Figure 14.3 summarizes all the mentioned challenges for quick and easy comprehension of all of them.

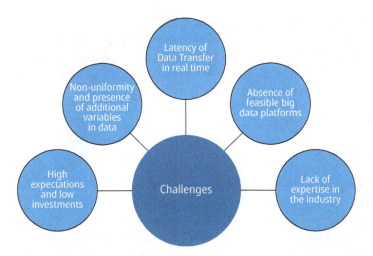

Figure 14.3: Big data challenges.

There are various strategies that might help in solving the aforementioned issues to a certain degree as well and include:

– **Introduction of big data governance**
Healthcare service providers incur huge financial losses (costs) in their IT investment due to poor governance [39], which can be tackled by creating business value through enterprise-wide data resources by using proper data governance [35, 40].

– **Development of an information sharing culture**
In a short and concise manner, sharing and aggregation information can address issues such as interoperability while enabling effective utilization of BDA and capability of prediction [35, 38].

– **Employment of security measures**
To ensure the for security and confidentiality maintenance of information, measures such as strong data encryption, source data validation, access control, and authentication [36] and deidentification [37] can be put into place for seamless BDA implementation.

– **Incorporation of cloud computing**
The major hurdle for storing of humongous amount of data may be potentially undertaken or solved by using cloud services as it enables healthcare service providers (whether it be minor, major or medium scale) to eliminate service expenditure and data storage issues [35].

– **Increase in professional expertise expenditure**
Despite the incorporation and upholding of aforementioned aspects, the success of those incorporations depends on how well the execution has been done, and that in return depends upon the professional expertise employed to undertake it. Hence, there must be an increase in expenditure on professional expertise.

14.8 Future scope

Despite the aforementioned challenges, the future potential and scope of big data is truly humongous due to hereby mentioned reasoning. In comparison to the rest of the industries, it has been discovered that there's going to be exponential growth for the availability of big data in healthcare sector in the years to come. As an example, big data is acquired, stored, and interchanged in most of the developed countries by the healthcare-associated entities comprising laboratories, hospitals, governmental institutions, doctors, dispensaries, X-ray centers, and insurance organizations among others [7].

Besides, there are various challenges that the healthcare industry in general is facing that include increasing costs of care delivery, raising patient volumes, high chronic disease pertained older population, re-admission-based punishments, lack of sufficient medical professionals, and major reimbursements' reduction. Keeping this in mind, the fact that BDA application in proper healthcare management can potentially help tremendously with all the aforementioned issues poses a positive outlook to its future scope. Coupling this with the fact that most countries have a significant portion of their economy dedicated to healthcare (US spends around 18% of its GDP on health care [13]), it is definitely a plus.

Moreover, the inherent benefits of big data are massive. As per a publication titled "The Promise of Big Data" by Harvard School of Public Health, thousands of terabytes of raw data residing in various computer systems silos [11] could help in understanding various issues including tuberculosis prevention to healthcare bills' reduction; given that this data is properly analyzed [12]! And finally, it has been observed that the majority of research work and implementation has been focused on the developed countries, and thus, future scope exists for the preferment of BDA in healthcare research of the developing countries as well [41].

14.9 Conclusion

The chapter has shed light on several aspects of big data, analytics, and its application pertaining to proper management in the healthcare sector. It can be clearly established that BDA can potentially transform the usage of technology by healthcare providers (aforementioned) to find data insights for informed decision-making. It is almost guaranteed to see a hastened widespread application and use of BDA across healthcare institutions and the industry as a whole due to its catered advantages.

On that front, several challenges or hurdles mentioned in the previous section need to be addressed for seamless application in effective healthcare management. Moreover, as BDA attains widespread attention, issues such as privacy guaranteeing, security safeguard, standards and governance establishment, and continuous improvement of tools. Products, technologies, and services will gather interest and also need to be addressed. Furthermore, it must also be taken into consideration that the availability of standardized data, level of data security and privacy, and data leaks and invasions control are considered as core success metrics of BDA in healthcare management as well [18, 19], and there has been significant amount of research in the domain as well [43–45].

Although at an early stage of usage and development, the swift tools and platforms advancements have the potential to accelerate the maturing process of BDA to a huge degree. Moreover, as the chapter has provided big data's introduction, enumerated various characteristics, platforms, analytics workflow, ML algorithms, applications, challenges, and future scope, on an ending note, this chapter attempts to equip every reader to comprehend and gain familiarity with general aspects of BDA and how its application benefits healthcare industry while providing all the relevant and necessary information pertaining to it.

References

[1] Nambiar, R., Bhardwaj, R., Sethi, A. & Vargheese, R. (2013). A look at challenges and opportunities of Big Data analytics in healthcare. 2013 IEEE International Conference on Big Data, 17–22. https://doi.org/10.1109/bigdata.2013.6691753

[2] GlobeNewswire (2021). Big Data Technology Market to Rise at 14% CAGR till 2027. https://www.globenewswire.com/en/news-release/2021/08/10/2277863/0/en/Big-Data-Technology-Market-to-Rise-at-14-CAGR-till-2027-Growing-Internet-Penetration-will-Provide-Impetus-to-Market-Growth-says-Fortune-Business-Insights.html

[3] Bernard, A. (2013). Healthcare Industry Sees Big Data As More Than a Bandage. https://www.cio.com/article/2383577/healthcare-industry-sees-big-data-as-more-than-a-bandage.html

[4] TED: The Economics Daily (2020). 5 out of 20 fastest-growing industries from 2019 to 2029 are in healthcare and social assistance. https://www.bls.gov/opub/ted/2020/5-out-of-20-fastest-growing-industries-from-2019-to-2029-are-in-healthcare-and-social-assistance.htm

[5] Austin, C. & Kusumoto, F. (2016). The application of Big Data in medicine: Current implications and future directions. Journal of Interventional Cardiac Electrophysiology, 47(1), 51–59. https://doi.org/10.1007/s10840-016-0104-y.

[6] Kumar, N. A., Hemalatha, M. & Shakeel, P. M. (2016). Healthcare data mining in biomedical imaging, signals, and systems. Journal of Medical Imaging and Health Informatics, 6(3), 759–762. https://doi.org/10.1166/jmihi.2016.1753.

[7] Srinivasan, U. & Arunasalam, B. (2013). Leveraging big data analytics to reduce healthcare costs. IT Professional, 15(6), 21–28. https://doi.org/10.1109/mitp.2013.55.

[8] Ohlhorst, F. (2021). Big Data Analytics: Turning Big Data into Big Money, John Wiley & Sons, USA. https://onlinelibrary.wiley.com/doi/book/10.1002/9781119205005.

[9] Raghupathi, W. & Raghupathi, V. (2014). Big data analytics in healthcare: Promise and potential. Health Information Science and Systems, 2(1), https://doi.org/10.1186/2047-2501-2-3.

[10] Bollier, D. & Firestone, C. M. (2010). The promise and peril of big data, 1–66. Aspen Institute, Communications and Society Program, Washington, DC, http://www.lsv.fr/~monmege/teach/learning2013/ThePromiseAndPerilOfBigData.pdf.

[11] Dishman, E. (2013). How Big Data can revolutionize health care. Politico. https://www.politico.com/story/2013/06/how-big-data-can-revolutionize-health-care-93449_Page2.html

[12] Harward School of Public Health (2012). The promise of big data. https://www.hsph.harvard.edu/news/magazine/spr12-big-data-tb-health-costs/

[13] IMS Institute (2012). The Global Use of Medicines: Outlook – IMS Health. https://www.yumpu.com/en/document/view/9196163/the-global-use-of-medicines-outlook-ims-health

[14] Schaafsma, S. (2017). Big data: The 6 Vs you need to look at for important insights. Motivaction, https://www.motivaction.nl/en/news/blog/big-data-the-6-vs-you-need-to-look-at-for-important-insights.

[15] Jain, A. (2016). The 5 V's of big data. Watson Health Perspectives, IBM, https://www.ibm.com/blogs/watson-health/the-5-vs-of-big-data/.

[16] Sumbal, M. S., Tsui, E. & See-to, E. W. (2017). Interrelationship between big data and knowledge management: An exploratory study in the oil and gas sector. Journal of Knowledge Management, 21(1), 180–196. https://doi.org/10.1108/jkm-07-2016-0262.

[17] Ishwarappa, J. & Anuradha, J. (2015). A brief introduction on Big Data 5Vs characteristics and hadoop technology. Procedia Computer Science, 48, 319–324. https://doi.org/10.1016/j.procs.2015.04.188.

[18] Sarkar, B. K. (2017). Big data for secure healthcare system: A conceptual design. Complex & Intelligent Systems, 3(2), 133–151. https://doi.org/10.1007/s40747-017-0040-1.

[19] Sarkar, B. K. & Sana, S. S. (2018). A conceptual distributed framework for improved and secured healthcare system. International Journal of Healthcare Management, 13(sup1), 74–87. https://doi.org/10.1080/20479700.2017.1422338.

[20] Kim, M. K. & Park, J. H. (2016). Identifying and prioritizing critical factors for promoting the implementation and usage of big data in healthcare. Information Development, 33(3), 257–269. https://doi.org/10.1177/0266666916652671.

[21] Murty, M. N. & Devi, V. S. (2011). Nearest neighbour based classifiers. Undergraduate Topics in Computer Science, 0, 48–85. https://doi.org/10.1007/978-0-85729-495-1_3.

[22] Manogaran, G. & Lopez, D. (2017). Disease surveillance system for big climate data processing and dengue transmission. International Journal of Ambient Computing and Intelligence, 8(2), 88–105. https://doi.org/10.4018/ijaci.2017040106.

[23] Lin, Y. K., Chen, H., Brown, R. A., Li, S. H. & Yang, H. J. (2017). Healthcare predictive analytics for risk profiling in chronic care: A bayesian multitask learning approach. MIS Quarterly, 41(2), 473–495. https://doi.org/10.25300/misq/2017/41.2.07.

[24] Chawla, N. V. & Davis, D. A. (2013). Bringing big data to personalized healthcare: A patient-centered framework. Journal of General Internal Medicine, 28(S3), 660–665. https://doi.org/10.1007/s11606-013-2455-8.

[25] Wu, J., Li, H., Liu, L. & Zheng, H. (2017). Adoption of big data and analytics in mobile healthcare market: An economic perspective. Electronic Commerce Research and Applications, 22, 24–41. https://doi.org/10.1016/j.elerap.2017.02.002.

[26] Jiang, P., Winkley, J., Zhao, C., Munnoch, R., Min, G. & Yang, L. T. (2016). An intelligent information forwarder for healthcare big data systems with distributed wearable sensors. IEEE Systems Journal, 10(3), 1147–1159. https://doi.org/10.1109/jsyst.2014.2308324.

[27] Delen, D., Fuller, C., McCann, C. & Ray, D. (2009). Analysis of healthcare coverage: A data mining approach. Expert Systems with Applications, 36(2), 995–1003. https://doi.org/10.1016/j.eswa.2007.10.041.

[28] Batarseh, F. A. & Latif, E. A. (2016). Assessing the quality of service using big data analytics. Big Data Research, 4, 13–24. https://doi.org/10.1016/j.bdr.2015.10.001.

[29] Chae, Y. M., Kim, H. S., Tark, K. C., Park, H. J. & Ho, S. H. (2003). Analysis of healthcare quality indicator using data mining and decision support system. Expert Systems with Applications, 24(2), 167–172. https://doi.org/10.1016/s0957-4174(02)00139-2.

[30] Gu, D., Li, J., Li, X. & Liang, C. (2017). Visualizing the knowledge structure and evolution of big data research in healthcare informatics. International Journal of Medical Informatics, 98, 22–32. https://doi.org/10.1016/j.ijmedinf.2016.11.006.

[31] Antoine-Moussiaux, N., Vandenberg, O., Kozlakidis, Z., Aenishaenslin, C., Peyre, M., Roche, M., Bonnet, P. & Ravel, A. (2019). Valuing health surveillance as an information system: Interdisciplinary insights. Frontiers in Public Health, 7, 1–12. https://doi.org/10.3389/fpubh.2019.00138.

[32] Archenaa, J. & Anita, E. M. (2015). A survey of big data analytics in healthcare and government. Procedia Computer Science, 50, 408–413. https://doi.org/10.1016/j.procs.2015.04.021.

[33] Salomi, M. & Appavu Alias Balamurugan, S. (2016). Need, application and characteristics of big data analytics in healthcare - a survey. Indian Journal of Science and Technology, 9(16), https://doi.org/10.17485/ijst/2016/v9i16/87960.

[34] Gowsalya, M., Krushitha, K. & Valliyammai, C. (2014). Predicting the risk of readmission of diabetic patients using MapReduce. 2014 Sixth International Conference on Advanced Computing (ICoAC), 297–301. https://doi.org/10.1109/icoac.2014.7229729

[35] Wang, Y., Kung, L. & Byrd, T. A. (2018). Big data analytics: Understanding its capabilities and potential benefits for healthcare organizations. Technological Forecasting and Social Change, 126, 3–13. https://doi.org/10.1016/j.techfore.2015.12.019.

[36] McNutt, T. R., Moore, K. L. & Quon, H. (2016). Needs and challenges for big data in radiation oncology. International Journal of Radiation Oncology*Biology*Physics, 95(3), 909–915. https://doi.org/10.1016/j.ijrobp.2015.11.032.

[37] Naydenov, R., Liveri, D., Dupre, L., Chalvatzi, E. & Skouloudi, C. (2015). Big data security: Good practices and recommendations on the security of big data systems. European Union Agency for Network and Information Security (ENISA), Greece, https://www.enisa.europa.eu/publications/big-data-security/at_download/fullReport.

[38] Dimitrov, D. V. (2016). Medical internet of things and big data in healthcare. Healthcare Informatics Research, 22(3), 156–163. https://doi.org/10.4258/hir.2016.22.3.156.

[39] Feldman, B., Martin, E. M. & Skotnes, T. (2013). Big data in healthcare – hype and hope, Dr. Bonnie 360 degree, Bus. Development Digital Health, 1, 122–125. http://www.riss.kr/link?id=A99883549.

[40] Wu, J., Li, H., Cheng, S. & Lin, Z. (2016). The promising future of healthcare services: When big data analytics meets wearable technology. Information & Management, 53(8), 1020–1033. https://doi.org/10.1016/j.im.2016.07.003.

[41] Mehta, N. & Pandit, A. (2018). Concurrence of big data analytics and healthcare: A systematic review. International Journal of Medical Informatics, 114, 57–65. https://doi.org/10.1016/j.ijmedinf.2018.03.013.

[42] Patel, A. D., Jhaveri, R., Parmar, J. & Shah, S. (2010). Security Issues and Recommendations for the Lifecycle of Data in Cloud Computing. https://www.academia.edu/35389344/Security_Issues_and_Recommendations_for_the_Lifecycle_of_Data_in_Cloud_Computing

[43] Han, B., Jhaveri, R., Wang, H., Qiao, D. & Du, J. (2021). Application of robust zero-watermarking scheme based on federated learning for securing the healthcare data. IEEE Journal of Biomedical and Health Informatics, 27, 1. https://doi.org/10.1109/jbhi.2021.3123936.

[44] Kupwade Patil, H. & Seshadri, R. (2014). Big data security and privacy issues in healthcare. 2014 IEEE International Congress on Big Data, 762–765. https://doi.org/10.1109/bigdata.congress.2014.112.

[45] Abouelmehdi, K., Beni-Hessane, A. & Khaloufi, H. (2018). Big healthcare data: Preserving security and privacy. Journal of Big Data, 5(1), 1–18. https://doi.org/10.1186/s40537-017-0110-7.

[46] Khamparia, A., Gupta, D., De albuquerque, V. H. C., Sangaiah, A. K. & Jhaveri, R. H. (2020). Internet of health things-driven deep learning system for detection and classification of cervical cells using transfer learning. The Journal of Supercomputing, 76(11), 8590–8608. https://doi.org/10.1007/s11227-020-03159-4.

Brief biographies

Dr. Akash Kumar Bhoi (BTech, MTech, PhD) is listed in the World's Top 2% Scientists for single-year impact for the year 2022 (compiled by John P. A. Ioannidis, Stanford University and published by Elsevier BV) and currently associated with Directorate of Research, Sikkim Manipal University as Adjunct Research Faculty. He is also working as a Research Associate at Wireless Networks (WN) Research Laboratory, Institute of Information Science and Technologies, National Research Council (ISTI-CRN) Pisa, Italy. He was appointed as the honorary title of "Adjunct Fellow" at Institute for Sustainable Industries and Liveable Cities (ISILC), Victoria University, Melbourne, Australia, for the period from 1 August 2021 to 31 July 2022. He was the University PhD Course Coordinator for "Research & Publication Ethics (RPE) at SMU." He is the former Assistant Professor (SG) of Sikkim Manipal Institute of Technology and served about 10 years. He is a member of IEEE, ISEIS and IAENG; an associate member of IEI and UACEE; and an editorial board member reviewer of Indian and international journals. He is also a regular reviewer of reputed journals by publishers, namely, IEEE, Springer, Elsevier, Taylor and Francis, Inderscience, etc. His research areas are biomedical technologies, the Internet of Things, computational intelligence, antenna and renewable energy. He has published several papers in national and international journals and conferences and 150+ publications registered in the Scopus database. He has also served on numerous organizing panels for international conferences and workshops. He is currently editing several books with Springer Nature, Elsevier, Routledge and CRC Press. He is also serving as Guest Editor for special issues of journals of Springer Nature, Wiley, Hindawi and Inderscience.

Dr. Ranjit Panigrahi is an accomplished academician and researcher in the field of Computer Applications, specializing in Biomedical Data Analysis and Cybersecurity. He is currently Assistant Professor in the Department of Computer Applications at Sikkim Manipal Institute of Technology, located in Majitar, Sikkim, India. Dr. Panigrahi's academic journey began with a Master of Technology in Computer Sciences and Engineering from Sikkim Manipal Institute of Technology in 2013. He further pursued his passion for research and earned a PhD degree in Computer Applications from Sikkim Manipal University in March 2020. His doctoral thesis focused on the "Design and Development of a Host-Based Intrusion Detection System with Classification of Alerts," showcasing his expertise in the field of cybersecurity. As an esteemed member of the academic community, Dr. Panigrahi has demonstrated exceptional dedication and commitment to his profession. He has been actively involved in teaching and guiding students as an Assistant Professor in the Department of Computer Applications at Sikkim Manipal Institute of Technology since July 2010. Over the years, he has held different positions and responsibilities within the department and currently serves as the Head of the IT Council at the institute. His research contributions have garnered recognition and praise, evident from the numerous publications he has authored in reputed journals and conferences. Dr. Panigrahi has an impressive track record with many articles published in SCI and Scopus-indexed journals. Additionally, he has also contributed significantly to the academic community through the publication in many conference proceedings. He is a sought-after reviewer for various technical publications and has also chaired sessions at prominent international conferences. Beyond his academic achievements, Dr. Panigrahi is also actively engaged in intellectual property research and has secured five patents. Outside of his professional life, Dr. Panigrahi is a native of India. He can be reached at his official email address ranjit.p@smit.smu.edu.in or his personal email ranjit.panigrahi@gmail.com.

Dr. Victor Hugo C. de Albuquerque (Senior Member of IEEE) is a Professor and Senior Researcher at the Department of Teleinformatics Engineering (DETI)/Graduate Program in Teleinformatics Engineering (PPGETI) at the Federal University of Ceará (UFC), Brazil. He earned a PhD in Mechanical Engineering from the Federal University of Paraíba (UFPB, 2010), an MSc in Teleinformatics Engineering from the PPGETI/UFC (UFC, 2007). He completed a BSE in Mechatronics Engineering at the Federal Center of Technological Education of Ceará (CEFETCE, 2006). He has experience in Biomedical Science and Engineering, mainly in the research fields of Applied Computing, Intelligent Systems, Visualization and Interaction, with specific interest in Pattern Recognition, Artificial Intelligence, Image Processing and Analysis, as well as Automation with respect to biological signal/image processing, biomedical circuits and human/brain-machine interaction, including augmented and virtual reality simulation modeling for animals and humans. Prof. Victor is a full Member of the Brazilian Society of Biomedical Engineering (SBEB). He is Editor-in-Chief of the *Journal of Biomedical and Biological Sciences* and also of the *Journal of Artificial Intelligence and Systems*, and *Journal of Biological Sciences*, as well as Associate Editor of the *IEEE Journal of Biomedical and Health Informatics, Computers in Biology and Medicine, Frontiers in Cardiovascular Medicine, Computational Physiology and Medicine, Applied Soft Computing, IEEE Access, Frontiers in Communications and Networks, Computational Intelligence and Neuroscience, Measurement* and *IET Quantum Communication*. He has been Lead Guest Editor of several high-reputed journals, and TPC member of many international conferences.

Dr. Rutvij H. Jhaveri (Senior Member, IEEE) is an experienced educator and researcher working in the Department of Computer Science and Engineering, Pandit Deendayal Energy University, Gandhinagar, Gujarat, India. He conducted his Postdoctoral Research at Delta-NTU Corporate Lab for Cyber-Physical Systems, Nanyang Technological University, Singapore. He completed his PhD in Computer Engineering in 2016. In 2017, he was awarded with prestigious Pedagogical Innovation Award by Gujarat Technological University. Currently, he is co-investigating a funded project from GUJCOST. He was ranked among top 2% scientists around the world in 2022 and 2021. He has 3000+ Google Scholar citations with h-index 29. He is an editorial board member in various journals of repute, including *IEEE Transactions on Industrial Informatics and Scientific Reports*. He also serves as a reviewer in several international journals and also as an advisory/TPC member in renowned international conferences. He has authored 145+ articles including the *IEEE/ACM Transactions* and flagship IEEE/ACM conferences. Moreover, he has several national and international patents and copyrights to his name. He also possesses memberships of various technical bodies such as ACM, CSI, ISTE and others. He is coordinator of SCAN – Smart Cities Air Quality Network (https://scan-network.com/index.html). Moreover, he is a member of the Advisory Board in Symbiosis Institute of Digital and Telecom Management and other reputed universities since 2022. He is an editorial board member in several Springer and Hindawi journals. He also served as a committee member in "Smart Village Project" of Government of Gujarat at the district level during the year 2017. His research interests are cyber security, IoT systems, SDN and smart healthcare.

Index

1918 influenza pandemic 125
1D convolutional and pooling layers 66
2D image 114, 116
3D image 108, 116
3-D image processing 101
3D measurement 111
3D videos of surgery 111
3-dimensional images 113

a patient-centered approach 229
abdominal surgery 186, 188
absorption 181–182, 188
access control 251–252
accuracy 85, 88–90, 95, 98
AdaBoost regression 85, 89
AdaBoost regressor 91
AdaBoost trees 91
AdaBoost's 90
adaptive deep learning 199
adaptive weight learning 199
adoption and implementation 312
AES 279, 284
ageing population 129
AI 101, 103–108, 111–113, 121, 261–262, 264–266, 268
AI application 102
AI methods 133
AI techniques 158
AIC 89
AiCure 111
algorithms 262, 267–268, 273–274, 278–280, 284
Anaconda platform 139
analysis implementation 318
analytical models 227
analytical performance 322
analytical techniques 318
analyzing the performance of implementation results 318
analyzing unorganized data 153
anatomical regions 111
anatomical variations 188
ANN 261, 264, 275
ANN model 196
anomaly detection 194
anonymity algorithm 251
anonymization 301
ansomware 299

antibodies 87
Apache Hadoop 157
Apache Spark 163
Apache Storm 154
application in health care 203
application of AI 133
archetypal's residual 137
ARIMA 88
ARIMA models 88
artificial intelligence 1–2, 3, 4, 6, 14–15, 17, 20, 22–23, 28, 56, 101, 108, 117, 119, 121, 132, 169, 189, 288–289, 293–294
artificial intelligence applications 57
artificial neural network 261, 264, 270
artificial neural network (ANN) 169
artificial neural networks 320
artificial neural networks (ANN) 88
artificial neurons 264
ASK 278
associated layers of perceptron 62
association 6
assymmetric methods 280
attacks 252, 256
attribute-based encryption 298
AU detector 120
audio detection 120
augmented intelligence 261–263, 265, 268–270
authorization 254
autism spectrum disorder 56
autoencoder 57, 63
auto-encoder 194, 199
automatic analysis 109
automatic learning 188
automatic pathology 109
automatic surgery 111
automation system 107
autonomous robot 15
autonomous vehicles (AV) 86

back propagation approaches 164
backpropagation 70
bariatric surgery 106
basal cell cancer 10
based compensation models 312
Bat Algorithm 49
Bayesian 120
Bayesian networks 166

BDA 311–312, 317, 319–323, 325
BIC 89
big data 225, 227–234, 236–238, 288, 291–294, 304, 311–314, 316–325
big data analytical methods 261
big data analytics 225–227, 246, 291, 311–312, 314, 316–320, 322, 324–325
big data analytics approaches 288
big data and analytics techniques 290
big data platforms 312, 314
big data tools 170
big data variability 232
Bio Medical Image Segmentation 192
biological domains 163
biomarker information 181
biomarkers 153
biomedical 233–234, 245
biomedical data 152
biometric 120, 238
black boxes 169
blood pressure, heart beat 120
Blowfish algorithm 284
body sensor network 132
body sensor network (BSN) 246
bone fracture 107, 115
bone X-ray 110
boosting 89, 91
boosting algorithm 90
boosting models 89
bootstrap replication 138
brain tumor 110, 197, 261, 263, 266, 270
BrainGluSchi 70, 73
breast cancer 3, 9, 15–16, 19–20, 22, 166, 182
bronchitis 12
BSN 246, 252
BSN-medical scheme 132

CAE (convolutional auto-encoder) 106
cancer 104, 108–109
cancerous and non-cancerous lesions 109
cancerous cells 2
CAPTCHA technology 7
carcinoma 2, 10–11
cardiovascular pathology 109
care-service synchronization 312
CatBoost 136
CDC 127, 144
Centers for Disease Control and Prevention (CDC) 231

cervical cancer 12
chaotic watermarking 26
cholecystectomy 186–187
cholecystectomy procedure 188
chronic disorders 56
class imbalance 276
classification 5, 179, 184, 188–190, 192, 195–197, 199, 203, 207–211, 214–215, 217–218, 221, 314, 319–320
classification model 164, 166
clinical data 133
clinical data analytics 158
clinical data warehouse 153
clinical decision support 227
clinical decision-making 16, 20
clinical evaluation 154
clinical practice 156
clinical trials 110–111
cloud computing 129–131, 136, 256
cloud environment 296
cloud infrastructures 130
cloud platform 131
cloud services 131, 233
Cloud-based database 129
Cloud-IoMT-based 125–126, 129, 144
Cloud-IoT-based diagnostic 144
Cloud-IoT-Health 131
CLUB-DRF 165
clustering 6
CNN 104–106, 108–110, 114–115, 120–121, 189, 191–192, 196–198, 203
CNN technique 121
CNN,DNN model 121
CNNs 192, 196, 202
coefficient selection 28
collective knowledge 275
colon cancer 11, 183
complete blood count (CBC) 86
complex data 229, 239
compound annual growth rate 289
computational intelligence 2, 20
computational science 89
computational time 189
computed tomography 86, 88, 101, 109, 116
computed tomography (CT) 154
computer science 102
computer vision 101–113, 116–121, 188
computer-aided detection 19
computing skills 108

confidentiality 253, 256
conglomeration 2
conventional health bioinformatics 156
convolutional 188, 192
convolutional network (DenseNet 169) 88
convolutional neural network 55, 63–64, 116
convolutional neural network (CNN) 169
convolutional neural networks 62
convolutional neural organization 57
corona disease diagnosis 86
coronary artery disease 184
coronavirus 2 98
coronaviruses 85
corporate network 250
correlation neural network (CorrNN) 164
correlations 232
cost-effective 126
COVAXIN 94
COVID 85, 87, 95–98, 321
COVID-19 85–89, 92, 94–96, 98, 112–116, 125, 127–130, 132–135, 138, 140, 143–144
COVID-19 epidemic 85
COVID-19 outbreak 86, 98
COVID-19 repositories 98
COVID-19 severity 113
COVID-19 virus 112
COVIDSHIELD 94
CRI Maestro 199
cropping 274
cryptographic algorithm 284
cryptographic algorithms 297
cryptographic protocols 250
cryptography 18, 267–268, 278–280
CT scan 88, 115–116
CT scans and blood tests 18
CT-scan 103, 105, 108, 112, 116
CT-scan image 114
CT-scan images 109, 113–114
CT-scans 102
CV 101–113, 116, 119, 121
CXR images 133
cybercrimes 268

data 245–257
data analytics 149–152, 154, 156, 158, 161–162, 167–170
data anonymization 251, 301
data augmentation 189

data classification 317–318
data cleaning 317
data collection 150, 161, 168, 229, 232
data confidentiality 296
Data controllers 254
data encryption 324
data governance in healthcare 299
data hackers 232
data integration 233
data minimization 300
data mining 151–152, 165, 167
data pre-processing 161, 164, 167
data pre-processing 152
data privacy 233
data processing 129, 134, 136
data processing and data storage 305
data processing procedures 134
data protection 144, 254
Data Protection Act (DPA) 254
data security 233, 247, 249, 325
data set 245, 251
data sets 251
data storage 149, 167
data validation 232, 324
data visualization 233
database management system 315
databases 149, 151–153, 157
data-driven models 159, 169
data-driven treatment 18
datasets 88, 98
death rate 85, 87, 93, 98
decision analytics 159
decision stumps 90
decision support systems 158
decision tree 85, 89, 95, 165
decision trees 89–91, 98, 320
decrypting 278, 281
deep bottle-neck features 120
deep feature 199
deep feature learning 199
deep learning 55–57, 63–66, 70, 76, 88, 149, 169, 171, 179, 188–190, 196–200, 202–203
deep learning algorithms 149
deep learning (DL) 179
deep learning model 58, 62, 73
deep learning networks 203
deep learning techniques 179, 190, 195, 197, 202
deep neural network 67, 191

deep neural network (DNN) 111, 169
deep neural networks 164
DenseNet-201 88
depression 55–56, 74–76
dermatologist 108–109
detect blood 110
detection 86, 94
detection techniques 196–199
DeTraC technique 133
developing countries 325
devices 265, 279
devices and sensors 126, 130, 132, 134, 136
diabetes data set 166
diabetes prediction system 163
diabetic foot ulceration 185
diagnose patient 103
diagnosis 101, 103–105, 108–109, 112, 115–117, 119, 121, 238, 270
diagnostic and treatment gadgets 126
diagnostic errors 101, 262
diagnostic information 181, 198
diagnostic medical equipment 127
diagnostic technique 164
diagnostic techniques 155, 184
diagnostic tests 226
digital data analysis 203
digital images 102
digital imaging 179
digital signal processing 188
discriminative network 110
disease 86, 94–95, 98, 101, 103, 109, 111–112
disease diagnosis result 101
disease transmission 321
diseases 101, 103–110, 112–113, 115–117, 119–121
distributed denial of service 301
distributed denial of service (DDoS) 252
Distributed Machine Learning Tools 136
diverse information systems 131
DL 88
DL-HSI integration 203
DNA 163
DNN 191, 199
domain of logical artificial intelligence systems 69
domain-specific restrictions 159
double-layer security 25
drug datasets 160
drug sickness 160

ECC 261, 263, 267, 272–273, 279–283
ECG 207–218, 220–221
econometrics 89
edge-to-edge technology 3
e-health records 312–313
EHR 157, 226, 228–229, 232
electroencephalogram 64
electromagnetic (EM) 179
electromagnetic spectrum 179
electronic health record 25, 226, 296
electronic health record (EHR) 102
electronic health records 19, 289
electronic health records (EHRs) 246
electronic medical records 299
electronic patient records 2
electronic record 106
elliptical curve cryptography (ECC) algorithm 261
EMC 313
emerging technologies 126
empirical procedures 227
EMR 226
EMRs 226
EMS 179, 181
encoding 273
encryption 297–298
encryption algorithm 250–251
encryption method 272
endocrine pancreatic cancer 11
endoscopic probe 197
ensemble eXtreme gradient boosting (XGBoost) 88
ensemble learning 91
entire population 159
environmental data 321
environmental research 312
epidemic 125–126, 128–129, 134, 140
epidemiological models 98
equalization attacks 50
equivocal information 61
estrogen 14
etymological highlights 60
Euclidean distance 96
evaluation 88, 97
event management (SIEM) 268
exocrine pancreatic cancer 10
explainable artificial intelligence 207–208, 210, 217, 221
extra tree regression 85, 89

extracted features 134
extreme learning machine (ELM) 88
extremely random trees 89
eye movement 119

face appearance 117
face detection technique 111
face reorganization 106
facial authentication 106
facial detection 120
facial expression 117
FCN 192, 197–198
feasible algorithms 319
feature engineering 161
feature extraction 70, 88, 138
feature in medical treatment 102
feature selection 158, 161, 163–164
feature selection technique 164
feedforward neural organization 57
five Vs to ten Vs 291
fluorescence 181–182, 184, 199
forecast therapy 134
forecasting 227, 229, 234
fragmented data environment 21
frame ratio 274
fraud detection 230
fundus camera 184
fuzzy logic 2, 4, 15, 20

gall bladder 187
gene-drug response 160
General Data Protection Regulation 300
generalized data 256
generative adversarial networks 110
generative adversial network (GAN) 88
genome-scale data 155
genome-scale datasets 155
genomics 312–313
genomics research 157
genotype-phenotype 160
glaucoma 20
Google's Inception v3 CNN engineering 70
GPS-enabled monitor 231
gradient boost trees 91
gradient boosting 85, 89, 91, 95
gradient boosting algorithm (GBA) 91
gradient boosting regression 85, 95
gradient boosting regression models 95, 97
gradient boosting strategy 91

gradients strategies 164
greedy method 89

Hadoop 315–316
Hadoop distributed file system (HDFS) 156
Hadoop framework 156–157
Hadoop system 131
Hadoop/Map 158
Hadoop-based architecture 153
head and neck cancer 183
health care assistants (HCA) 233
health care businesses 150
health care system 129
health challenges 171
health condition in real time 112
health data 157–160, 232, 235
health databases 150
health informatics 152, 158, 227, 236
health infrastructure 129
Health Insurance Portability and Accountability
    Act 300
health monitoring 312
health monitoring system 132
health outcome prediction 262
health problems 94
health record 107, 314
health risk 262
health service 247
health status 127, 144
health support 265
health techniques 225
health variables 227
health workforce 321
health-based expenditures 321
health-based issues 321
healthcare 85–86, 101–113, 116–121, 150–151, 160,
    203, 225–230, 232–234, 236–239, 245–253,
    256–257, 261–263, 265–266, 268, 311–314,
    316–325
healthcare analytics 151
healthcare assisting disease diagnosis 293
healthcare cost 245
healthcare costs 130
healthcare coverage 321
healthcare data 150, 154, 157, 170, 266,
    313–314, 317
healthcare data analytics 171
healthcare delivery 155–156
healthcare devices 128, 130

healthcare diagnosing equipment 127
healthcare domain 247, 253, 257
healthcare expenditures 245
healthcare experts 126
healthcare industry 126–127, 131, 245–248, 250–252, 256–257, 312, 320, 324–325
healthcare informatics 227, 233
healthcare information analytics 169
healthcare information system 296
healthcare institutions 322, 325
healthcare interventions 21
healthcare management 246, 312, 316–322, 324–325
Healthcare organization 249
healthcare organizations 150, 155, 167–168
healthcare providers 316, 325
healthcare research 149
healthcare sector 101, 107, 119, 152, 311–312
healthcare service 320–321, 324
healthcare services 131
healthcare signals 155
healthcare system 3, 20–21, 22, 23, 85, 101, 104, 106, 112–113, 121, 129–132, 150, 158, 160, 170, 225, 228, 237–238, 261–262, 265–266, 268
healthcare systems 156, 163, 169
healthcare transformation costs 130
healthcare workers 105–107, 111, 158, 168
health-systems-based research-oriented data 312
heart diseases 208, 212, 221
heart surgery 106
heath care centers 265
hemoglobin 183, 185
hemoglobin spectral 184
heterogeneous data 160
heterogeneous data sources 301
heterogeneous data streams 227
heterogeneous results 152
hidden patterns 150
high chronic disease 324
high dimensionality 89
high-dimensional data sets 165
high-dimensionality 77
HIPAA 130, 232–233
HIPAA certification 249
Hive 156, 158
(HNSCC) patients 165
home-based analytic test 126
hospitable franchise 317
hospital resources 317

hospital transportation system 313
hospitals systems 158
hospitals' resources 318
HS 179–181, 184, 186, 188, 198–199
HS cameras 179
HSI 179–189, 196, 198–199, 203
human brain 189–190
human emotions 119
human interference 107
human vision 102
hyper spectral camera 181, 187
hyper spectral imaging (HSI) 179
hyper-parameters 137
hyperspectral imaging 187, 203
hypoxia 182

IBM InfoSphere 316
IBM Watson 107, 109
ID3 technique 90
identification of patient 102, 106
illness detection 151
illness diagnosis 312
image acquiring 115
image analysis 107, 112
image classification 191
image of blood 108
image pixel 181
image processing 101, 108, 112, 120–121, 154
image recognition neurons 62
image scanner 112
ImageNet and DeTraC 133
images 263–264, 272–274, 276, 279, 282–283
imaging limitations 179
imaging technique 109
imbalanced datasets 61
imperceptibility 27, 34, 41, 44, 52
Improvement Act (PSQIA) 253
infection 192
informatics 233, 238
information system (MIS) 107
infrared and light emitting diodes 120
insurance 245–247
integrative personal omics profile (iPOP) 156
Intelligent transport systems 292
inter-connected components 190
inter-hospital franchises 313
Internet medical knowledge 130
Internet of things 149–150, 163, 168, 289
Internet of Things (IoT) 126, 132

Index — **337**

intra-operative 111
intrusion detection systems 299
IoMT 125–126, 128–129, 134, 136, 140, 144
IoT 126–132, 135, 144, 288–289, 293–294, 297–298, 301, 303
IoT data 132
IoT devices 128, 130–131, 168, 262, 312
IoT medical equipment 130
IoT sensors 233
IoT-based systems 168
isolation 126, 134
IT Act and IT (Amendment) Act 253

Kafka 154
Kaggle 263, 273–274
k-anonymity 251, 255
kernel fusion 196
key 289, 294, 297–298, 304, 306
Khaled algorithm 49
K-means 108
K-means clustering 198
K-Nearest Neighbour 320
knowledge-driven 158, 160, 169

lab automation 108
laboratory tests 226
laparoscopic procedure 187
large volume of complex data 288
l-diversity 255
Lempel–Ziv–Welch (LZW) compression 25
less time extensive 311
leukemia 2, 12–13
LGBM 89
life science research 312
LifeImage 157
lightweight gradient boosting machine (LGBM) 136
linear and logistic regression 88
linear regression 86–89, 96, 98
linear regression technique 86
lip movement 120
logic-based decision rules 159
logic-based knowledge modeling 169
long/short-term memory (LSTM) 88
long-short term memory (LSTM) 164
long-term exposure to ultraviolet 10
long-term prediction 98
lumber spine MRI 110
lung cancer 12, 109

lungs, lesions 115
lymph tissue 13
lymphatic system 13

machine learning 86–89, 91, 95, 101–102, 104, 108, 110, 112, 116–117, 121, 132, 136–137, 139–140, 189, 226–228, 261, 263–264, 272–275
machine learning algorithm 108, 112
machine learning algorithms 86–88, 95, 101, 160, 164, 312, 319
machine learning domain 319
machine learning (ML) 86
machine learning models 57, 59, 70
machine learning techniques 2, 151, 237
MAE (mean absolute error) 165
magnetic resonance imagery (MRI) 154
magnetic resonance imaging (MRI) 226
malignancy detection 197
mammograms 3, 16, 19
mammography clinics 19
MapReduce 153, 156–158, 316
mastectomy 186
mathematical operation 275
mDiabetes 248
mean absolute error (MAE) 85, 93, 95, 98
mean absolute percentage error (MAPE) 85
mean square error 85, 89, 93–95
mean square error (MSE) 85, 93–95
median filter 49
medical big analytics 158
medical big data 287–291, 293–297, 301–306
medical care 126, 128, 136
medical claims 152
medical classification tasks 61
medical cure 127
medical data 149–151, 153, 156–159, 161–162, 164, 167–169, 171, 227, 234, 236–237, 312
medical devices 130, 132, 144
medical diagnosis 181, 197, 225, 320
medical difficulties 158
medical disorders 157
medical field 101, 121
medical gadgets 134
medical hyper spectral imaging 179
medical image analysis 179, 197, 202
medical image data 154, 158
medical image diagnosis 197
medical image watermarking 26, 47
medical imaging 20–22, 86, 88, 104, 113, 116

medical industry 126–127, 130
medical information 169, 253, 296, 300, 303, 305
medical instruments 126
medical or hospital management 102
medical professionals 94, 154, 158
medical records 229, 245
Medical Things (IoMT) 126
medical treatment 103, 105
medical workers 125–126, 129
medicine information 314
melancholy 77
melanoma 14, 183
membership function 3
membrane potential 58
men-in-the-middle (MITM) attacks 250
MERS 85
metabolomics 313
metastatic brain tumor 270
MHSI 179, 182–183, 185–186, 188, 195–198, 202–203
microscopic images 106
Microsoft Azure Public Datasets 263, 273
ML 86, 88–89, 101, 104–109, 111–112, 116, 121, 261–262, 265–266, 270, 274–276, 283
ML algorithms 319, 325
ML models 139, 266, 275
ML prototypes 134
ML techniques 190
ML-based application 112
MLP 191
modern cryptography 272
modern healthcare systems 126
modern techniques 268
modified ECC algorithm 263
Mohs surgery 10
monitoring 321–322
monitoring devices 128
monitoring tumor 107
Monte Carlo simulation 237
morphological segmentation 7
mortality prognosis 98
mortality rate 94–98
MRI scan 263, 270, 273
MRI scanned images 264
MRI-scanned images 273
multicollinearity 89
multi-dimensional application 111
multidimensional data 275
multi-label 207–211, 214–215, 217, 220–221

multi-layer perceptron 62
multilayer perceptron 88, 190
multi-level security 26
multimedia medical big data 289
multi-modal fusion 119
multiple hyper-parameters 137
multi-step data transfers 157
musculoskeletal radiology 109–110
musculoskeletal radiology abnormality 109

Naïve Bayes 5, 164
naive Bayesian classifier 166
named entity recognition 7
natural language generation 7
natural language processing 6, 17, 105, 110, 192, 229, 248
natural language processing (NLP) 86
nearest neighbor 5
nervous system 111
NetSim simulators method 131
network defensive perimeter 299
network-based 248
network-level threats 299
neural network 86, 163–164, 189–190, 195, 261, 264, 275
neural network model 109, 261
neural networks 163, 264, 272, 302
neurodegenerative 71
neuroimage information 62
neurons and dropout layer 66
neutrosophic algorithms 14–22
neutrosophic dynamic fusion 15
neutrosophic logic 2, 15, 17, 20, 22
neutrosophic-based systems 16
NIR HIS 186
NIR imaging system 183
NLP 104, 110, 192
non-communicable diseases 248
non-invasive diagnosis 181
non-invasive imaging 109
non-linear 90–91
non-subsampled contourlet transform 25
normalizing 94
NoSQL Cassandra 154
NS2 131
NSCT-RDWT-SVD 26
Nuance mPower 158
nuclear medicine 105–106, 121
nuclear medicine imaging 106

numerical information 90
NUSDAST 72
NVIDIA 109

OADP 316
Omicron situation 94
one pad algorithm 250
one time password 296
online health evaluations 127
ontology quality assurance (OQA) 157
open sources 272–273
optic disc segmentation 198
optical imaging 182, 184
optimal coordinates 274
optimal embedding efficacy 41
optimal parameters 190
optimizing 91
Oracle platform 316
oral cancer 196
ovarian cancer 11
ownership attack 25

PACS framework 71
pancreatic cancer 10
pandemic 94–95, 98, 112
pandemic eruption 129
Parkinson's data sets 166
pathogens 14
pathological images 195
pathological information 289
pathologist 106
patient care 127, 322
patient data 247
patient health condition 116
patient identification information (PII) 107
patient imagery data 314
patient information disclosure 305
patient management data 312
patient outcomes 231
patient physiological data 134
patient privacy 253–254
patient records 245, 247, 249, 314
patient-owned gadgets 232
patients' empowerment 312
patients' health 126–127
patient's characteristics 159
patient's health in real-time 105
pattern recognition algorithms 169
PCA 196

Pentium Windows machine 139
performance metrics 139
peripheral artery disease (PAD) 183
personal health information 299
personal health records (PHRs) 152
personal identification information 289
Personal Information Protection and Electronic Documents Act ("PIPEDA") 254
PET 106, 109
petabytes 311
pharmaceutical research 229–230
pharmacist assistance 152
physical activity recognition and monitoring 131
physiological manifestations 154
PIL method 282
pixels 282
platforms advancements 325
polymerase chain reaction (PCR) 86
polynomial regression 87–88
polynomial ridge regression 88
Ponemon Institute report 268
poor governance 323
population health management 293
positron emission tomography-computed tomography (PET-CT) 154
posterior regressors 91
post-processing 199
post-production testing 318
PR 88
precise diagnosis 103
precision 89–90, 95, 98
predict patterns 264
predicted values 96
predicting 101
prediction 85–86, 88–89, 91–92, 94–98, 225–227, 230, 236, 238
prediction models 95, 98
predictions 86, 89–91, 96
predictive 235–236
predictive analysis 110, 112
predictive analytics 107, 112, 159, 167
predictive modeling 152
predictive models 165, 167–168, 189
predictive techniques 155
pre-processing 88, 152, 164, 199
preprocessing techniques 263
prescriptive analytics 159
preventive measure 321
principal component analysis 196

privacy 21, 245–247, 253–257, 312, 323, 325
privacy protection mechanisms 296, 301
privacy-preserving real-time analytics 306
private donors 127
private key 267, 281
probability-oriented 195
profound conviction organization 63
proper management 316, 325
prostate cancer 10
protein sequences 163
PSO algorithm 27–31, 50
PTB class 140
public cloud 256
public health concern 125
public key 267, 279–280
pulse oximetry 232
python 282
Python script 133

Q-learning 5
quantitative data 228
quantitative results 88
quarantine 126–127, 134

radiation 2, 10, 12, 14, 19–20, 22
radiation therapy 12
radio frequency identification (RFID) 233
radiologist 107, 113
radiology 202
radio-nuclide pharmaceuticals 105
random forest 198
random forest regression 85, 89, 95
random forest (RF) 164
random forests 164–165
random tree regression 89
RCNN 110
RDWT 26–28
re-admission 324
real time 101, 322
real-time 313–314, 317, 321–322
real-time activity 106
real-time analytics 246
real-time application 101
real-time base 135
real-time holistic model 246
real-time inferences 262
real-time monitoring 131, 314, 322

real-time patient health condition 107
real-time security intelligence 252
real-world cases 311
real-world implementations 321
records 132, 134
recurrent neural networks 62–63
redundant wavelet transformed PSO 29
registries 312
regression 5
regression algorithms 89, 94–95
regression analysis 86, 89
regression approaches 89
regression methodology on health records 165
regression model 85, 88–89, 91, 94–96, 98, 190
regression models 85–88, 94–98
regulated R-square 89
rehabilitation centers 248
reinforcement learning 5
remote-operative machine 119
renal surgery 186
repetitive neural organization 57
residual learning 275
residual neural network (ResNet-18) 88
ResNetV2 261, 272, 275–276
resNetV2 model 277
respiratory infection 112
retinal diseases 184
retinal imaging analysis 198
retinal ischemia 184
reverberation imaging 62
reverse-transcription polymerase chain reaction (RTPCR) 86
RGB 179–180
RGB-D device 119
ribonucleic acid (RNA) 86
RIDGE 88
ridge regression 87–88
Ridgelet transform (RT) 26
risk management 252
risk model 20–21
RNN 192, 194
robotic process automation 15
robotics 111, 120
robotics machine 111
ROC curves 140
ROI (region of interest) 115
ROI-based multiple watermarking 25

Index — 341

root mean square error (RMSE) 85, 93, 95
root mean squared logarithmic error (RMSLE) 85, 93
root mean-squared logarithmic error (RMSLE) 95, 98
R-square 89
Russian Federal Law on Personal Data 254

SARS 85, 98, 127, 133, 143
SARS-CoV2 85
SARS-COV-2 112
scalable classifier 137
schizophrenia 55–56, 59, 63, 66–73, 76–77
secure algorithm 283
secure sockets layer (SSL) 250
security 245–247, 249–253, 255–257, 261–262, 267–268, 279–280, 283–284
security and privacy 304
security information 268
security threats 270
segmentation 88, 192, 197, 203
semantic segmentation 198
semantics 7
semi-automated CAD 110
semi-structured data 313
sensitive information 247, 249, 252–257
sensor technologies 126
sensor-based technology 103
service delivery's 321
service providers 313, 320–324
shutdown tactics 126
simulations, and intelligent systems 126
single-photon emission computed tomography 105
singular value decomposition 26
SK algorithms 278
skin cancer 109, 183, 197
smart health monitoring hospital 131
smart healthcare 130–131
smart healthcare monitoring 130
soft biometric 121
SPECT 106, 109
spectral signature 181
speech reorganization 120
Sputnik V 94
stand-alone business intelligence technology 227
standard deviation 90
STARE data set 110
stationary wavelet transform 26

statistical analysis 89
stereo endoscope 111
stochastic global optimization 28
strategic planning 246–247
supervised learning 5, 166, 169
supervised learning algorithms 91
supervised learning models 60
support vector machine 120
support vector machine and dynamic time warping 158
support vector machine (SVM) 88
surgery 101, 103, 105–106, 110–111, 121
surgical excision 10
surgical system 111
surgical video 111
surveillance systems techniques 130
SVD 26–31, 41, 45–52
SVM 108, 110, 158, 162–163, 165, 196, 198
SVR 88
symmetric key algorithm 273
synthetic neurons 163
systemic repository 127

technological advancement 107–108, 121
technologies 149–150, 168, 170
technology advancement 121
telemedicine 126, 129, 293
temporal difference learning 5
TensorFlow 275
therapeutic goal 129
therapeutic pictures 235
therapy plan 127
threshold 90
tissue fingerprinting 19
tracking diseases 101
traditional data-management methods 311
traditional healthcare systems 126
train:test ratio 139
trainable parameters 58
trained data 89
training dataset 320
transport layer 250
transport layer security (TLS) 250
trapdoor function 279–280
treat diseases 227
treatment monitoring 102
treatment optimization 245
tree topology 90
tumor angiogenesis 182–183

tumor metabolism 182–183
type casting 282

UDA-IoT 132
UN-corrected image 106
U-net 192–193, 198
univariate feature selection 165
unlabeled data 190
unstructured clinical record 7
unsupervised learning 5, 166, 169, 190

VANET district 131
Verizon's data 247
vessel segmentation 110
virus 85, 87, 94–95, 98
Viscosity 314
visual data 103, 105
Visualization 314
visualize 275

waste minimization 312
watermarking 25, 27–29, 31, 41, 45, 47–52
watermarking algorithms 26
wavelengths 179–181

wearable devices 288, 293–294, 301
wearable sensors 127
weblog records 256
WEKA 163
wireless sensor networks (WSN) 233
wireless sensors 126
word segmentation 7
Word sense disambiguation 7
World Health Organization 125
Wuhan 85

XGBoost 125, 136–137, 139–140, 143–144
XGboosting 89
X-ray 88, 105–109, 112–116, 121, 324
X-ray image 112, 116
X-ray images 88
X-ray, medical diagnostics 154
x-ray scans 313
X-rays 86, 101–103, 105

YARN 156

ZooKeeper 156

Intelligent Biomedical Data Analysis (IBDA)

Already published in the series

Volume 9: Computer Intelligence Against Pandemics
Tools and Methods to Face New Strains of COVID-19
Siddhartha Bhattacharyya, Jyoti Sekhar Banerjee, Sergey Gorbachev, Khan Muhammad
and Mario Koeppen (Eds.)
ISBN 978-3-11-076766-7, e-ISBN (PDF) 978-3-11-076768-1,
e-ISBN (EPUB) 978-3-11-076775-9

Volume 8: Artificial Intelligence and Computational Dynamics for Biomedical Research
Ankur Saxena and Nicolas Brault (Eds.)
ISBN 978-3-11-076199-3, e-ISBN (PDF) 978-3-11-076204-4,
e-ISBN (EPUB) 978-3-11-076208-2

Volume 7: Deep Learning for Personalized Healthcare Services
Vishal Jain, Jyotir Moy Chatterjee, Hadi Hedayati, Salahddine Krit, Omer Deperlioglu (Eds.)
ISBN 978-3-11-070800-4, e-ISBN (PDF) 978-3-11-070812-7,
e-ISBN (EPUB) 978-3-11-070817-2

Volume 6: Computational Intelligence and Predictive Analysis for Medical Science
Poonam Tanwar, Praveen Kumar, Seema Rawat et al. (Eds.)
ISBN 978-3-11-071498-2, e-ISBN (PDF) 978-3-11-071527-9,
e-ISBN (EPUB) 978-3-11-071534-7

Volume 5: Computational Intelligence for Managing Pandemics
Aditya Khamparia, Rubaiyat Hossain Mondal, Prajoy Podder et al. (Eds.)
ISBN 978-3-11-070020-6, e-ISBN (PDF) 978-3-11-071225-4,
e-ISBN (EPUB) 978-3-11-071227-8

Volume 4: Nature Inspired Optimization Algorithms
Deepak Gupta, Nhu Gia Nguyen, Ashish Khanna, Siddhartha Bhattacharyya (Eds.)
ISBN 978-3-11-067606-8, e-ISBN (PDF) 978-3-11-067611-2,
e-ISBN (EPUB) 978-3-11-067615-0

Volume 3: Artificial Intelligence for Data-Driven Medical Diagnosis
Deepak Gupta, Utku Kose, Bao Le Nguyen, Siddhartha Bhattacharyya (Eds.)
ISBN 978-3-11-066781-3, e-ISBN (PDF) 978-3-11-066832-2,
e-ISBN (EPUB) 978-3-11-066838-4

Volume 2: Predictive Intelligence in Biomedical and Health Informatics
Rajshree Srivastava, Nhu Gia Nguyen, Ashish Khanna, Siddhartha Bhattacharyya
(Eds.)ISBN 978-3-11-067608-2, e-ISBN (PDF) 978-3-11-067612-9, e-ISBN (EPUB) 978-3-11-066838-4

Volume 1: Computational Intelligence for Machine Learning and Healthcare Informatics
R. Srivastava, P. Kumar Mallick, S. Swarup Rautaray, M. Pandey (Eds.)
ISBN 978-3-11-064782-2, e-ISBN (PDF) 978-3-11-064819-5, e-ISBN (EPUB) 978-3-11-067614-3

www.degruyter.com

Printed in the USA
CPSIA information can be obtained
at www.ICGtesting.com
JSHW051738070324
58801JS00005B/190